SUCH A
DIFFERENCE, THOUGH WE ARE THE SAME AGE...
MY APPEARANCE IS MID-TEENS TO MID-TWENTIES, SO...
WHY ARE YOU IN TRAVELING GEAR?

和月伸宏

NOBUHIRO WATSUKI

ST BARELY

TO TELL THE TRUTH, THE ORIGINAL IDEA WAS FOR KENSHIN TO BE IN HIS MID-THIRTIES, BUT MY EDITOR SAID "THE MAIN CHARACTER OF A SHONEN MANGA IN HIS MID-THIRTIES?" SO HIS AGE WAS SHIFTED TO JUST BARELY IN HIS TWENTIES, IN ORDER TO MAKE IT WORK WITH THE TIME FRAME.

I RECENTLY REALIZED THAT WATSUKI AND KENSHIN ARE THE SAME AGE.

"JUST BARELY IN THE TWENTIES" SEEMS YOUNG, BUT IS NOT YOUNG. AND VICE VERSA. GOING INTO DEFENSIVE MODE PROBABLY LEADS TO FASTER AGING...

SO I'LL GO SEEK OUT A "CHALLENGE" INSTEAD.

Rurouni Kenshin, which has found fans not only in Japan but around the world, first made its appearance in 1992, as an original short story in ***Weekly Shonen Jump Special***. Later rewritten and published as a regular, continuing ***Jump*** series in 1994, ***Rurouni Kenshin*** ended serialization in 1999 but continued in popularity, as evidenced by the 2000 publication of ***Yahiko no Sakabatô*** ("Yahiko's Reversed-Edge Sword") in ***Weekly Shonen Jump***. His most current work, ***Buso Renkin*** ("Armored Alchemist"), began publication in June 2003, also in ***Jump***.

RUROUNI KENSHIN
VOL. 27: THE ANSWER
The SHONEN JUMP Manga Edition

STORY AND ART BY
NOBUHIRO WATSUKI

English Adaptation/Pancha Diaz
Translation/Kenichiro Yagi
Touch-Up Art & Lettering/Steve Dutro
Design/Matt Hinrichs
Editor/Kit Fox

Managing Editor/Frances E. Wall
Editorial Director/Elizabeth Kawasaki
VP & Editor in Chief/Yumi Hoashi
Sr. Director of Acquisitions/Rika Inouye
Sr. VP of Marketing/Liza Coppola
Exec. VP of Sales & Marketing/John Easum
Publisher/Hyoe Narita

Printed in the U.S.A.

Published by VIZ Media, LLC
P.O. Box 77010
San Francisco, CA 94107

SHONEN JUMP Manga Edition
10 9 8 7 6 5 4 3 2
First printing, June 2006
Second printing, June 2006

T 251693

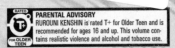

PARENTAL ADVISORY
RUROUNI KENSHIN is rated T+ for Older Teen and is
recommended for ages 16 and up. This volume con-
tains realistic violence and alcohol and tobacco use.

www.viz.com

THE WORLD'S
MOST POPULAR MANGA

www.shonenjump.com

Rurouni Kenshin™

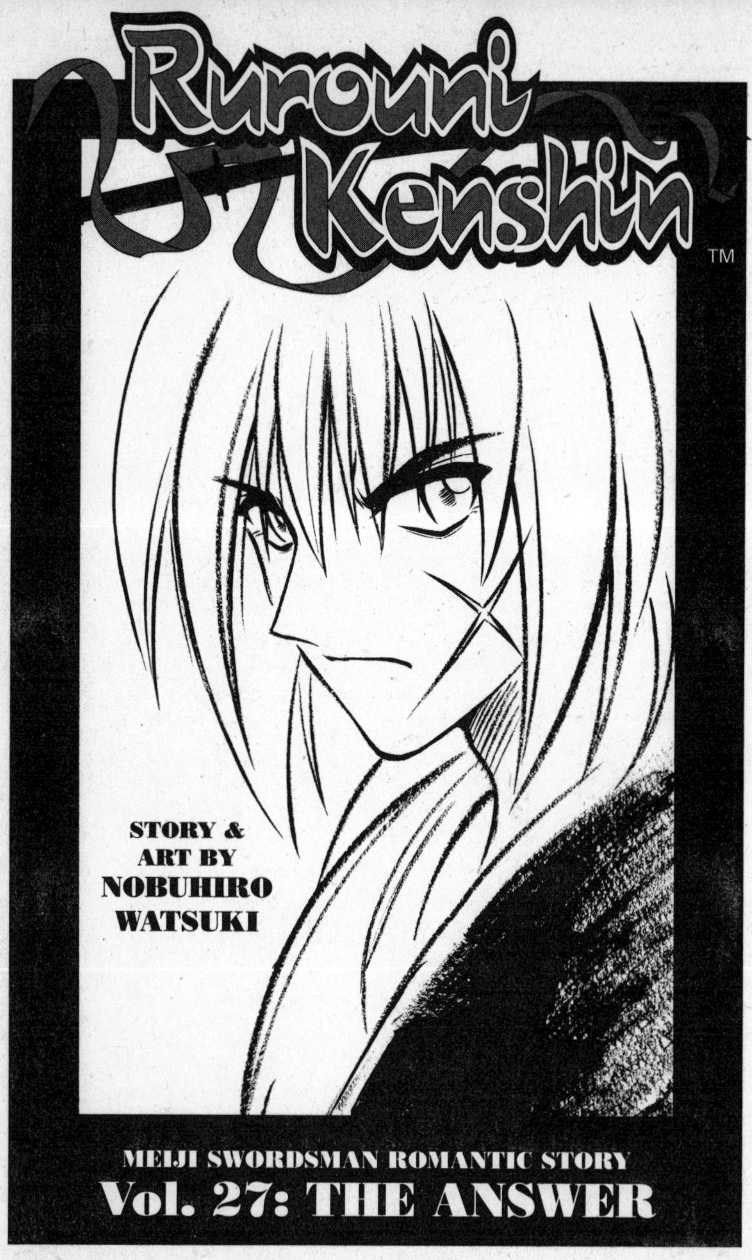

STORY & ART BY NOBUHIRO WATSUKI

MEIJI SWORDSMAN ROMANTIC STORY

Vol. 27: THE ANSWER

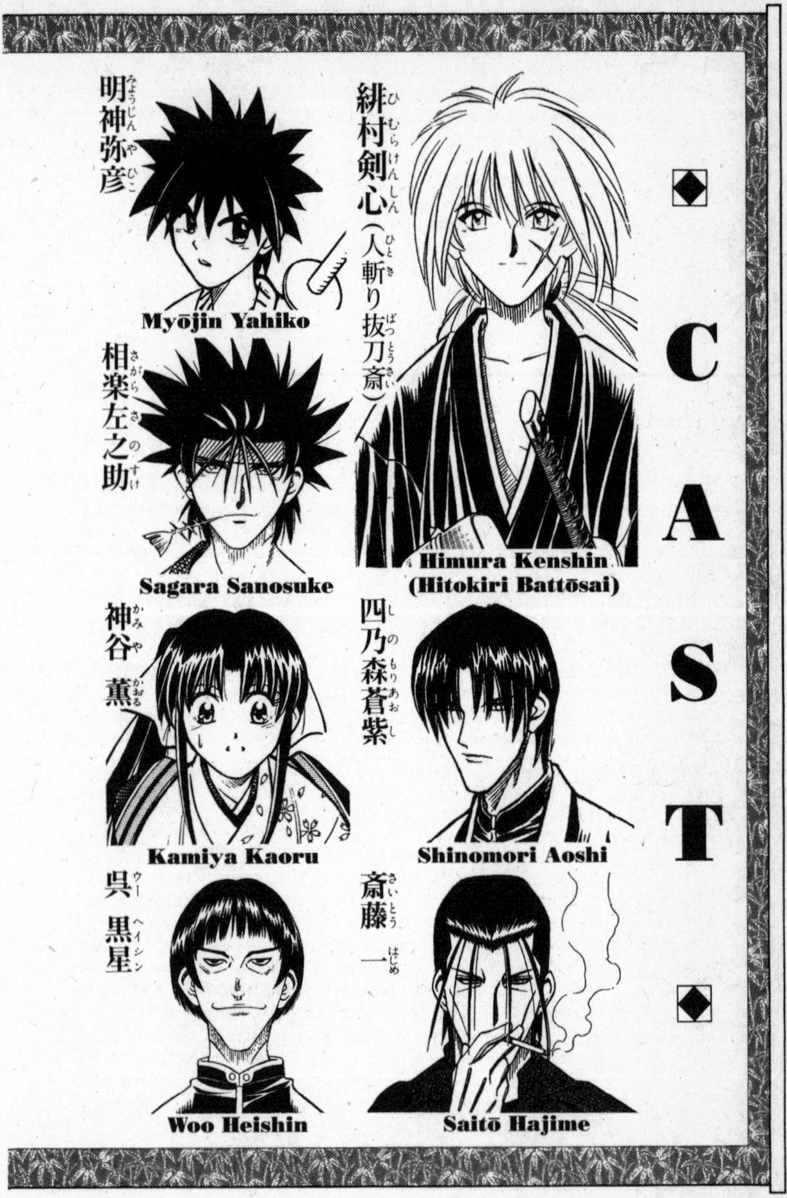

CAST
緋村剣心（人斬り抜刀斎）
Himura Kenshin
(Hitokiri Battōsai)
明神弥彦
Myōjin Yahiko
相楽左之助
Sagara Sanosuke
四乃森蒼紫
Shinomori Aoshi
神谷薫
Kamiya Kaoru
斎藤一
Saitō Hajime
呉黒星
Woo Heishin

るろうに剣心

和月伸宏

Once he was *hitokiri*, an assassin, called Battōsai. His name was legend among the pro-Imperialist or "patriot" warriors who launched the Meiji Era. Now, Himura Kenshin is *rurouni*, a wanderer, and carries a reversed-edge *sakabatō* blade, vowing to never kill another soul.

Those with grudges against Battōsai have gathered to take their revenge. To make matters worse, Kenshin finds out that the mastermind of this new attack is Enishi, the brother of Kenshin's deceased wife Tomoe—who died at Kenshin's own hand. And yet Kenshin decides to fight in order to protect the present, and begins by telling his friends of his past.

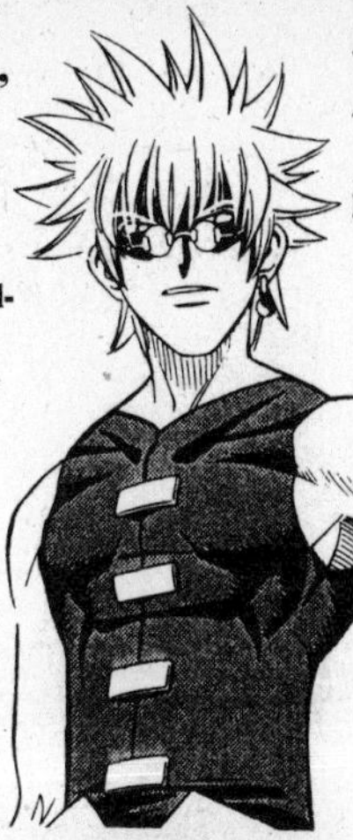

雪代(ゆきしろ) 縁(えにし)

Yukishiro Enishi

THUS FAR

Enishi and his crew appear midair above the Kamiya dojo in hot air balloons. In the midst of the battle that follows, Enishi murders Kaoru. Overwhelmed by the guilt of not saving Kaoru, Kenshin exiles himself to the "Fallen Village." However, the others discover that Kaoru's body is actually one of the "corpse dolls" created by Gein. Kaoru has actually been spirited away to the island in Tokyo bay that Enishi's organization uses as a relay point. When a little girl must beg Kenshin for help, he is finally able to realize the truth he holds within himself—a truth he cannot abandon. Meanwhile, Sanosuke has returned to his hometown for an uneasy reunion with his family. He also manages to get into a fight with the local yakuza who have ties to a revolutionary government official. Fight finished, Sanosuke returns to Tokyo in time to join Kenshin and the others on the journey to the island. Kenshin wants to end the conflict with a one-on-one duel with Enishi. But Woo Heishin, Enishi's second-in-command, and his *Sū-shin* bodyguards are waiting to greet Kenshin...

CONTENTS

RUROUNI KENSHIN
Meiji Swordsman Romantic Story
BOOK TWENTY-SEVEN: THE ANSWER

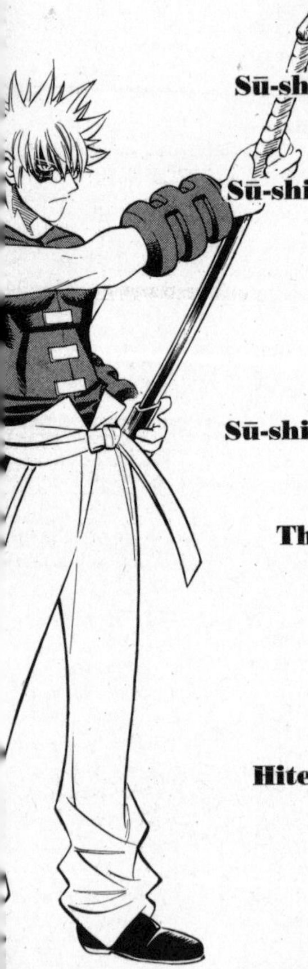

Act 238
Sū-shin Transformation

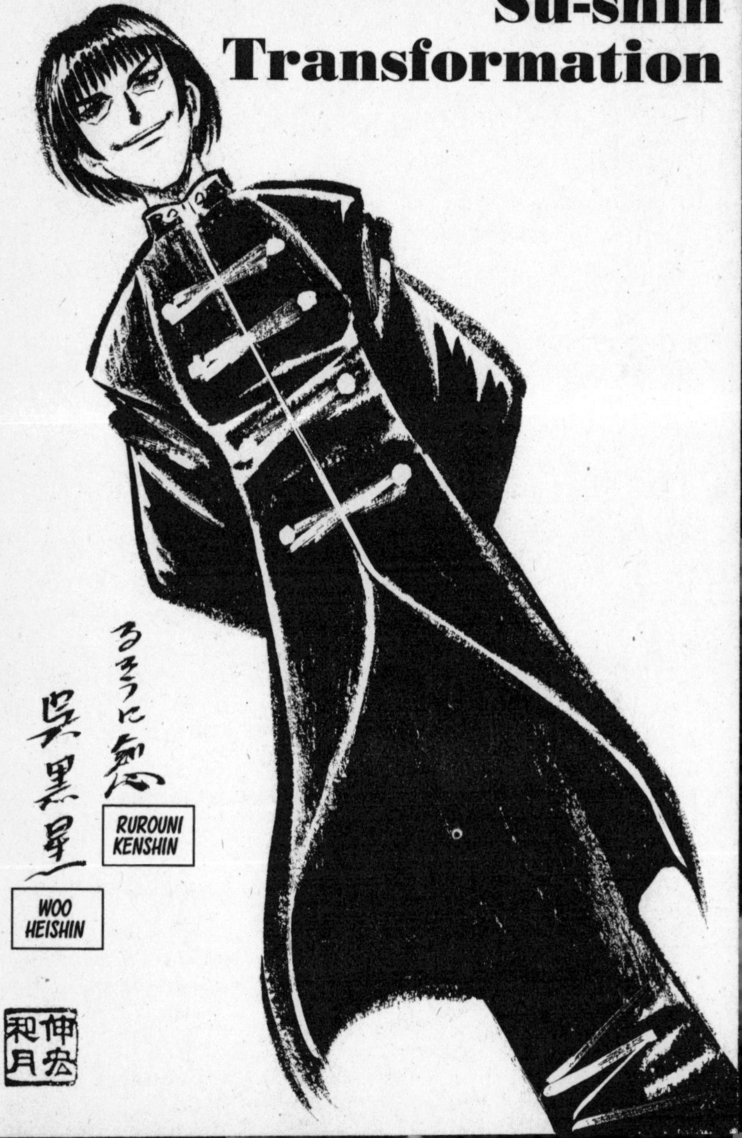

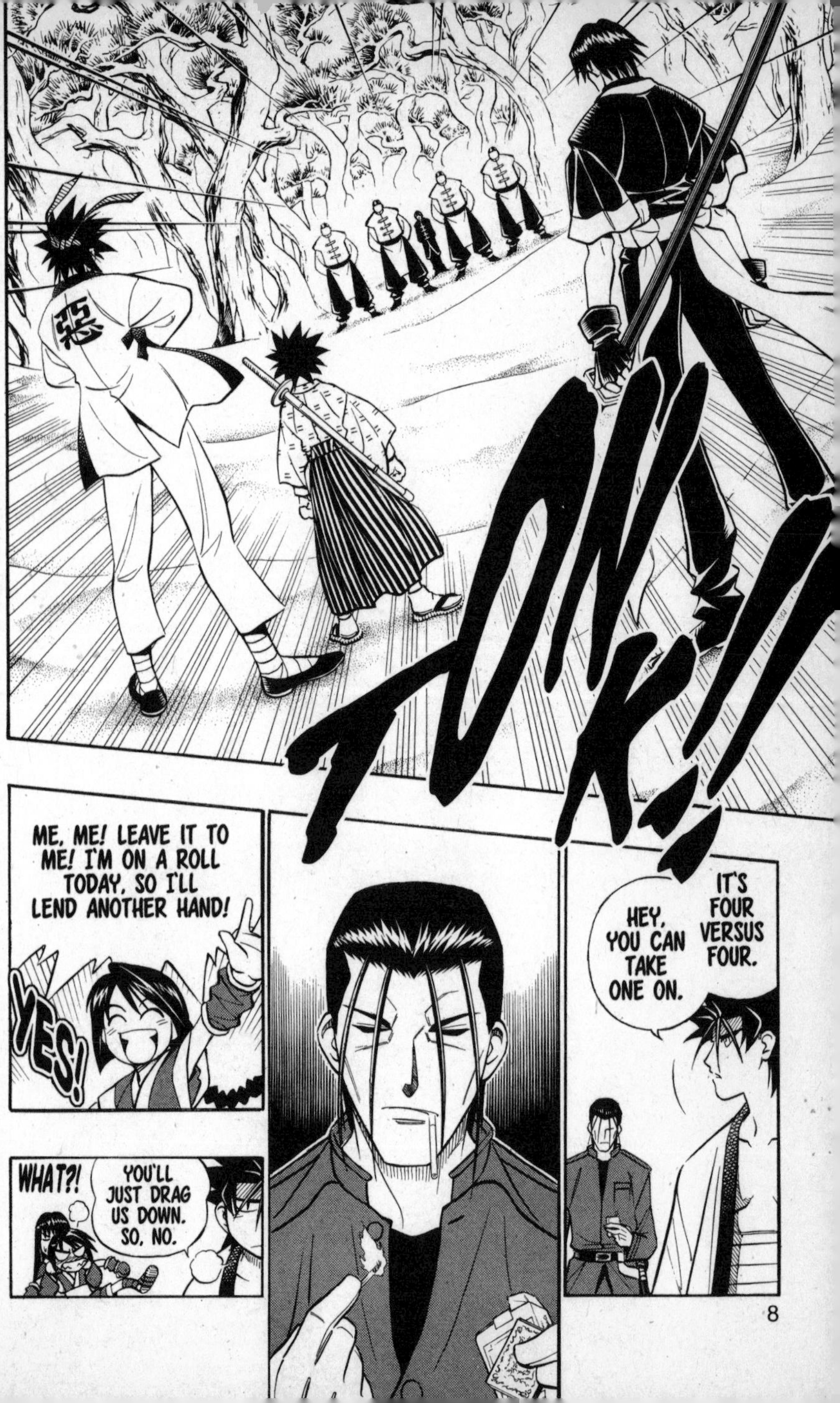
IT'S FOUR VERSUS FOUR.
HEY, YOU CAN TAKE ONE ON.
ME, ME! LEAVE IT TO ME! I'M ON A ROLL TODAY, SO I'LL LEND ANOTHER HAND!
YES!
YOU'LL JUST DRAG US DOWN. SO, NO.
WHAT?!

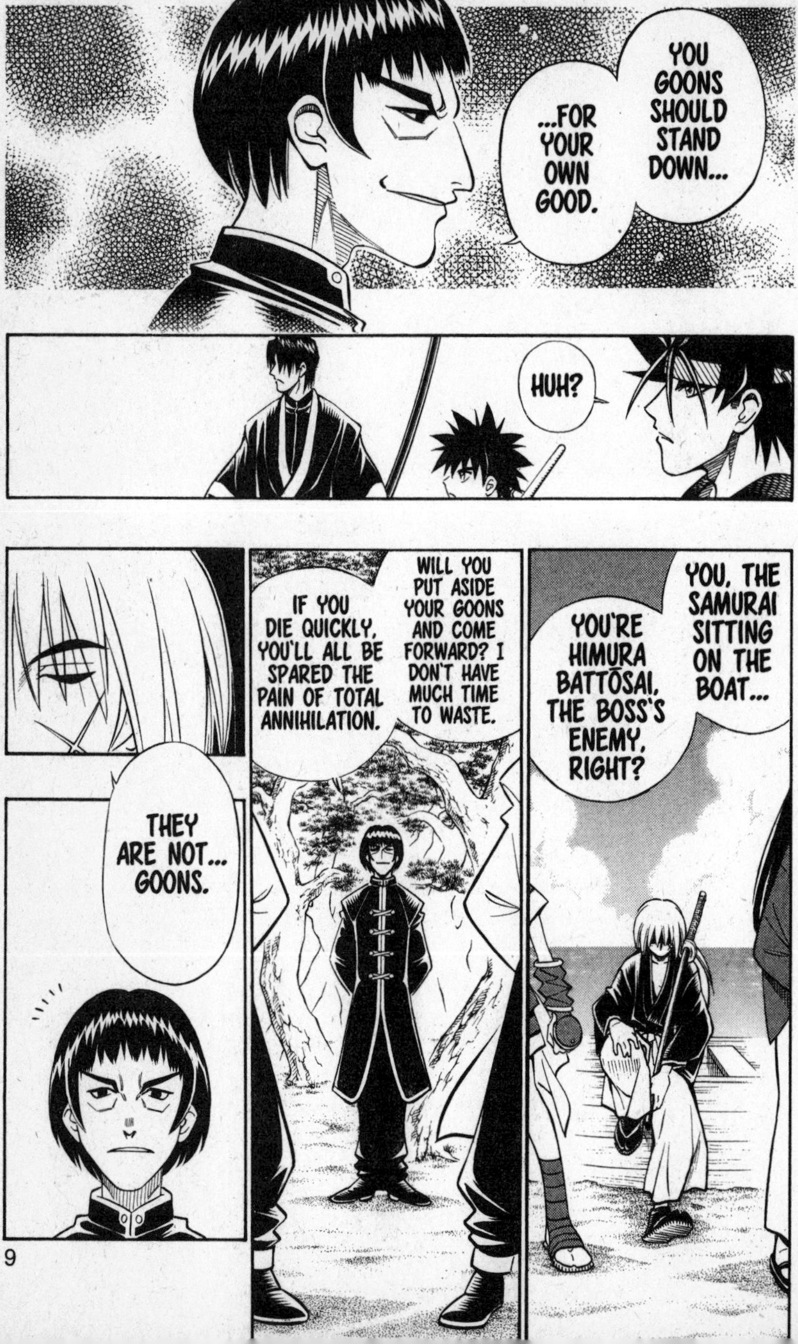
YOU GOONS SHOULD STAND DOWN...
...FOR YOUR OWN GOOD.
HUH?
YOU, THE SAMURAI SITTING ON THE BOAT...
YOU'RE HIMURA BATTŌSAI, THE BOSS'S ENEMY, RIGHT?
WILL YOU PUT ASIDE YOUR GOONS AND COME FORWARD? I DON'T HAVE MUCH TIME TO WASTE.
IF YOU DIE QUICKLY, YOU'LL ALL BE SPARED THE PAIN OF TOTAL ANNIHILATION.
THEY ARE NOT... GOONS.

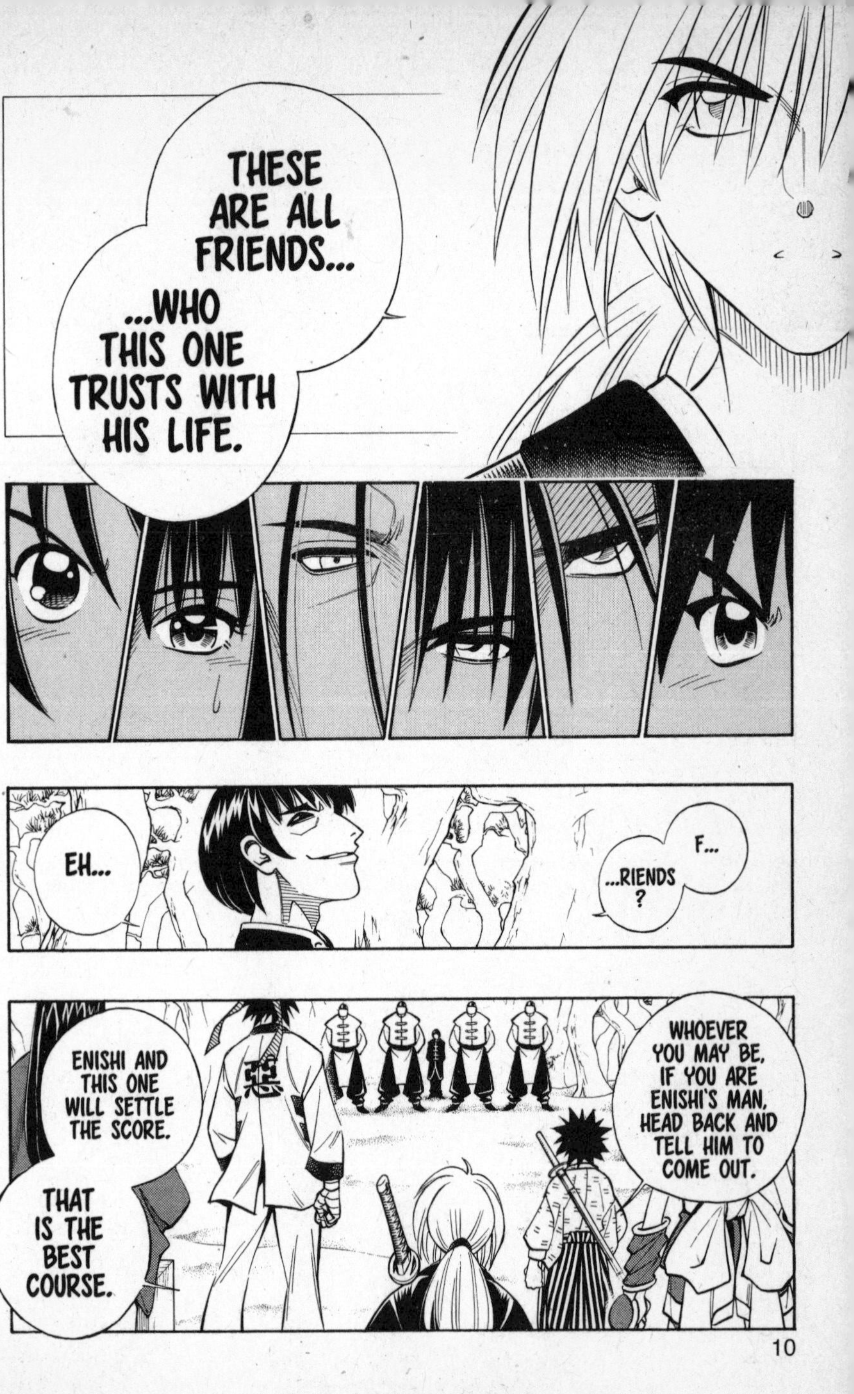
THESE ARE ALL FRIENDS...
...WHO THIS ONE TRUSTS WITH HIS LIFE.
F...
...RIENDS?
EH...
WHOEVER YOU MAY BE, IF YOU ARE ENISHI'S MAN, HEAD BACK AND TELL HIM TO COME OUT.
ENISHI AND THIS ONE WILL SETTLE THE SCORE.
THAT IS THE BEST COURSE.

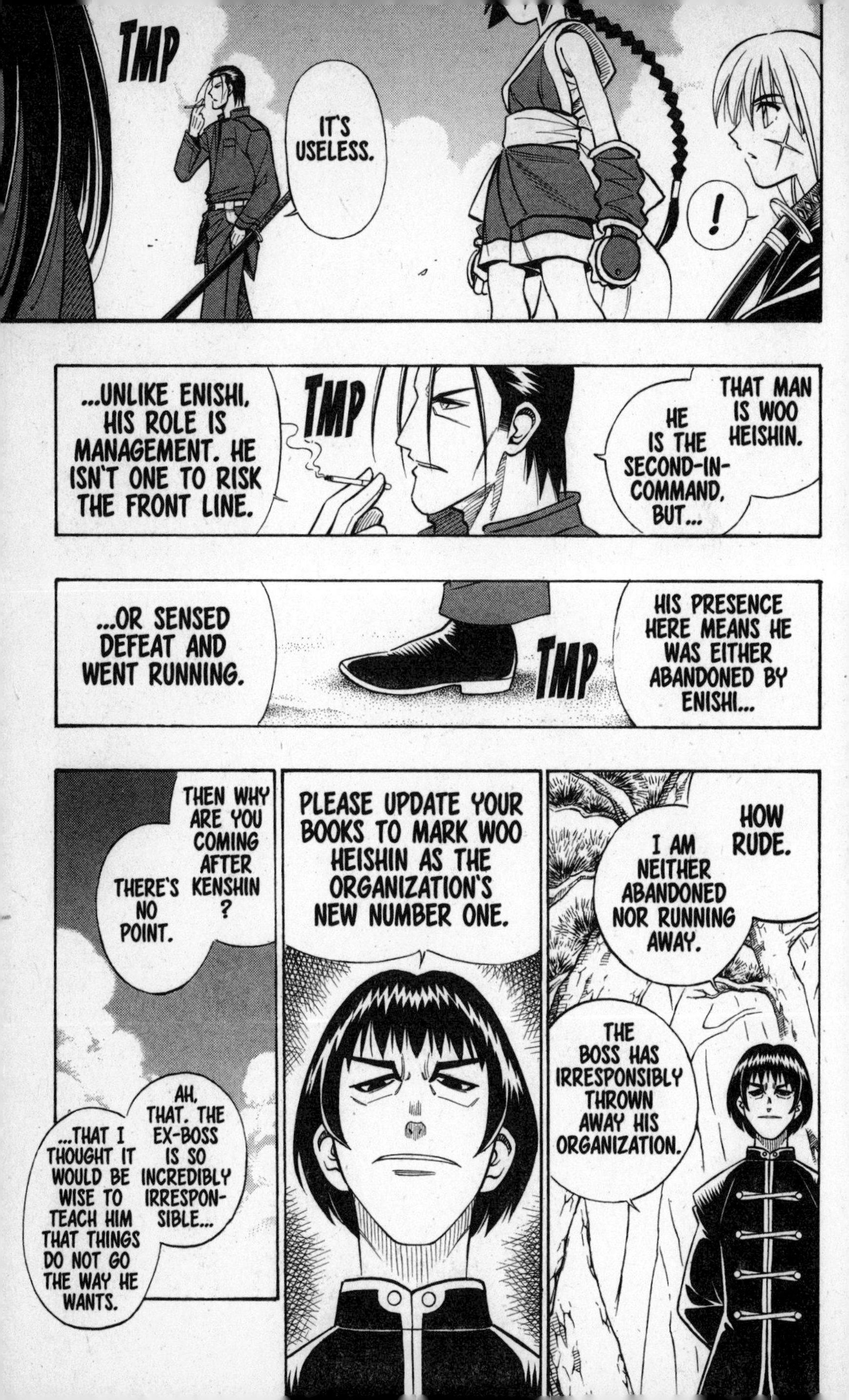
!
IT'S USELESS.
TMP
THAT MAN IS WOO HEISHIN.
HE IS THE SECOND-IN-COMMAND, BUT...
TMP
...UNLIKE ENISHI, HIS ROLE IS MANAGEMENT. HE ISN'T ONE TO RISK THE FRONT LINE.
HIS PRESENCE HERE MEANS HE WAS EITHER ABANDONED BY ENISHI...
TMP
...OR SENSED DEFEAT AND WENT RUNNING.
HOW RUDE.
I AM NEITHER ABANDONED NOR RUNNING AWAY.
THE BOSS HAS IRRESPONSIBLY THROWN AWAY HIS ORGANIZATION.
PLEASE UPDATE YOUR BOOKS TO MARK WOO HEISHIN AS THE ORGANIZATION'S NEW NUMBER ONE.
THEN WHY ARE YOU COMING AFTER KENSHIN?
THERE'S NO POINT.
AH, THAT. THE EX-BOSS IS SO INCREDIBLY IRRESPON-SIBLE...
...THAT I THOUGHT IT WOULD BE WISE TO TEACH HIM THAT THINGS DO NOT GO THE WAY HE WANTS.

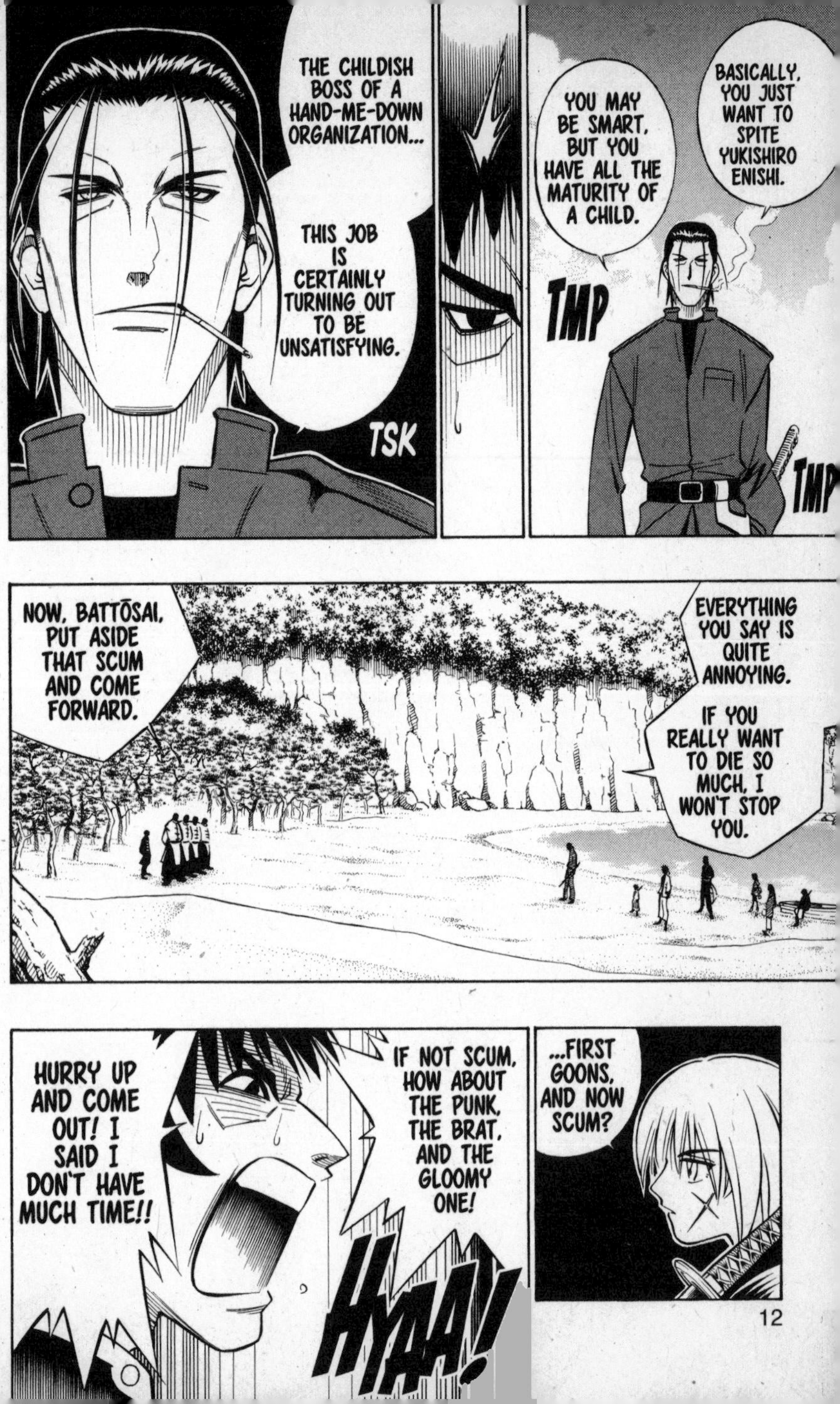
BASICALLY, YOU JUST WANT TO SPITE YUKISHIRO ENISHI.
YOU MAY BE SMART, BUT YOU HAVE ALL THE MATURITY OF A CHILD.
TMP
TMP
THE CHILDISH BOSS OF A HAND-ME-DOWN ORGANIZATION...
THIS JOB IS CERTAINLY TURNING OUT TO BE UNSATISFYING.
TSK
EVERYTHING YOU SAY IS QUITE ANNOYING.
IF YOU REALLY WANT TO DIE SO MUCH, I WON'T STOP YOU.
NOW, BATTŌSAI, PUT ASIDE THAT SCUM AND COME FORWARD.
...FIRST GOONS, AND NOW SCUM?
IF NOT SCUM, HOW ABOUT THE PUNK, THE BRAT, AND THE GLOOMY ONE!
HURRY UP AND COME OUT! I SAID I DON'T HAVE MUCH TIME!!
HYAA!

READ THIS WAY

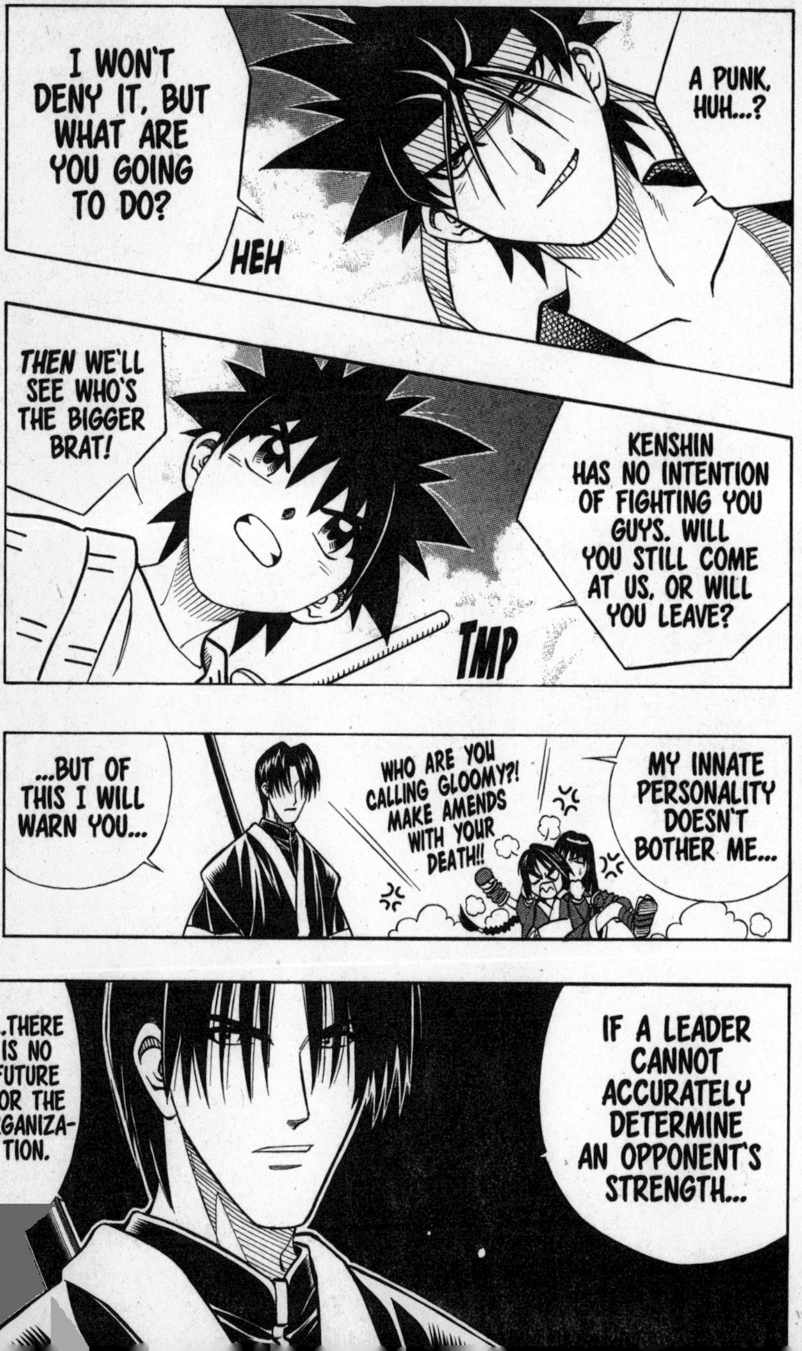
A PUNK, HUH...?
I WON'T DENY IT, BUT WHAT ARE YOU GOING TO DO?
HEH
THEN WE'LL SEE WHO'S THE BIGGER BRAT!
KENSHIN HAS NO INTENTION OF FIGHTING YOU GUYS. WILL YOU STILL COME AT US, OR WILL YOU LEAVE?
TMP
MY INNATE PERSONALITY DOESN'T BOTHER ME...
WHO ARE YOU CALLING GLOOMY?! MAKE AMENDS WITH YOUR DEATH!!
...BUT OF THIS I WILL WARN YOU...
IF A LEADER CANNOT ACCURATELY DETERMINE AN OPPONENT'S STRENGTH...
...THERE IS NO FUTURE FOR THE ORGANIZA-TION.

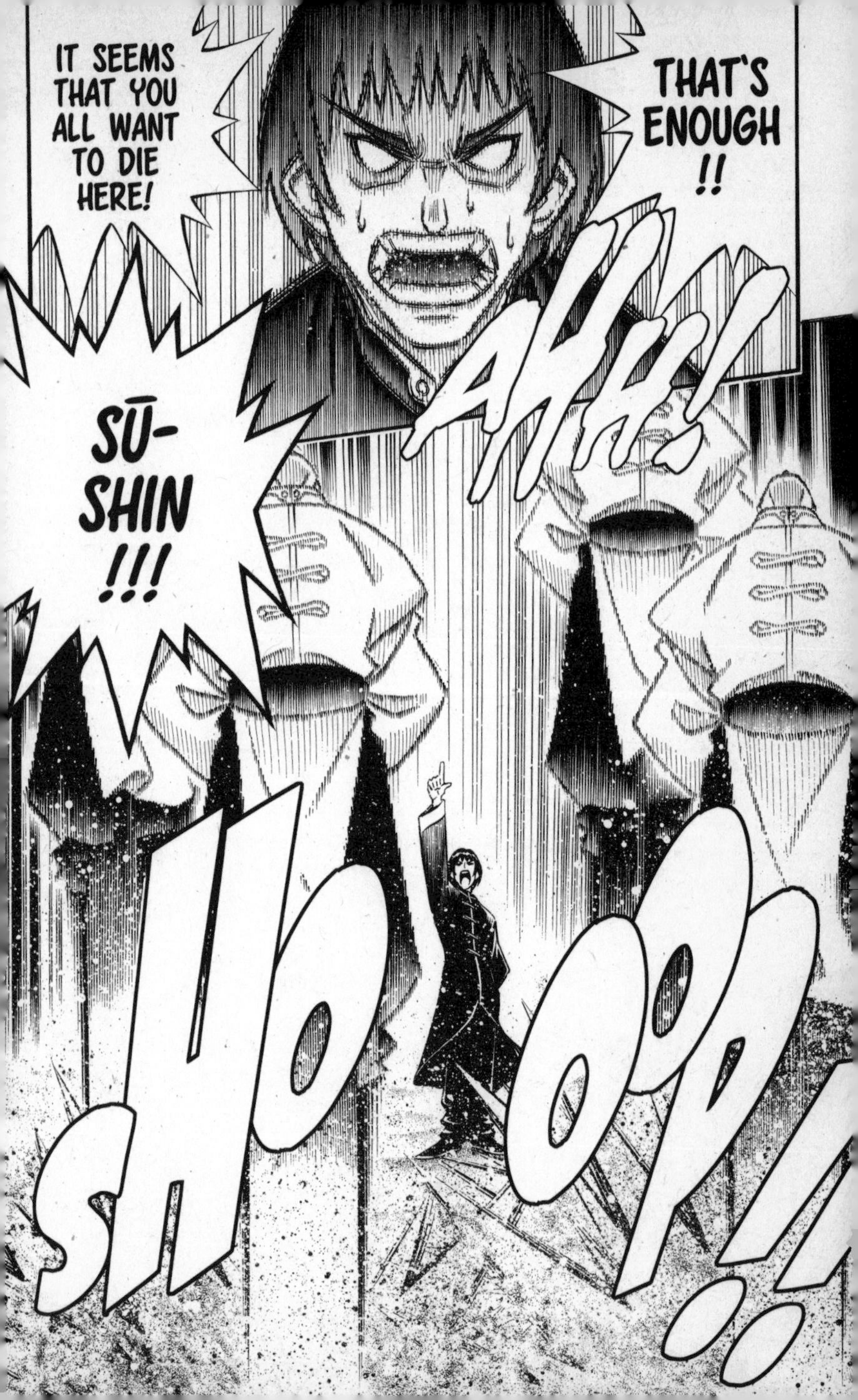
THAT'S ENOUGH !!
IT SEEMS THAT YOU ALL WANT TO DIE HERE!
AHH!
SŪ-SHIN !!!
SHOOP!!

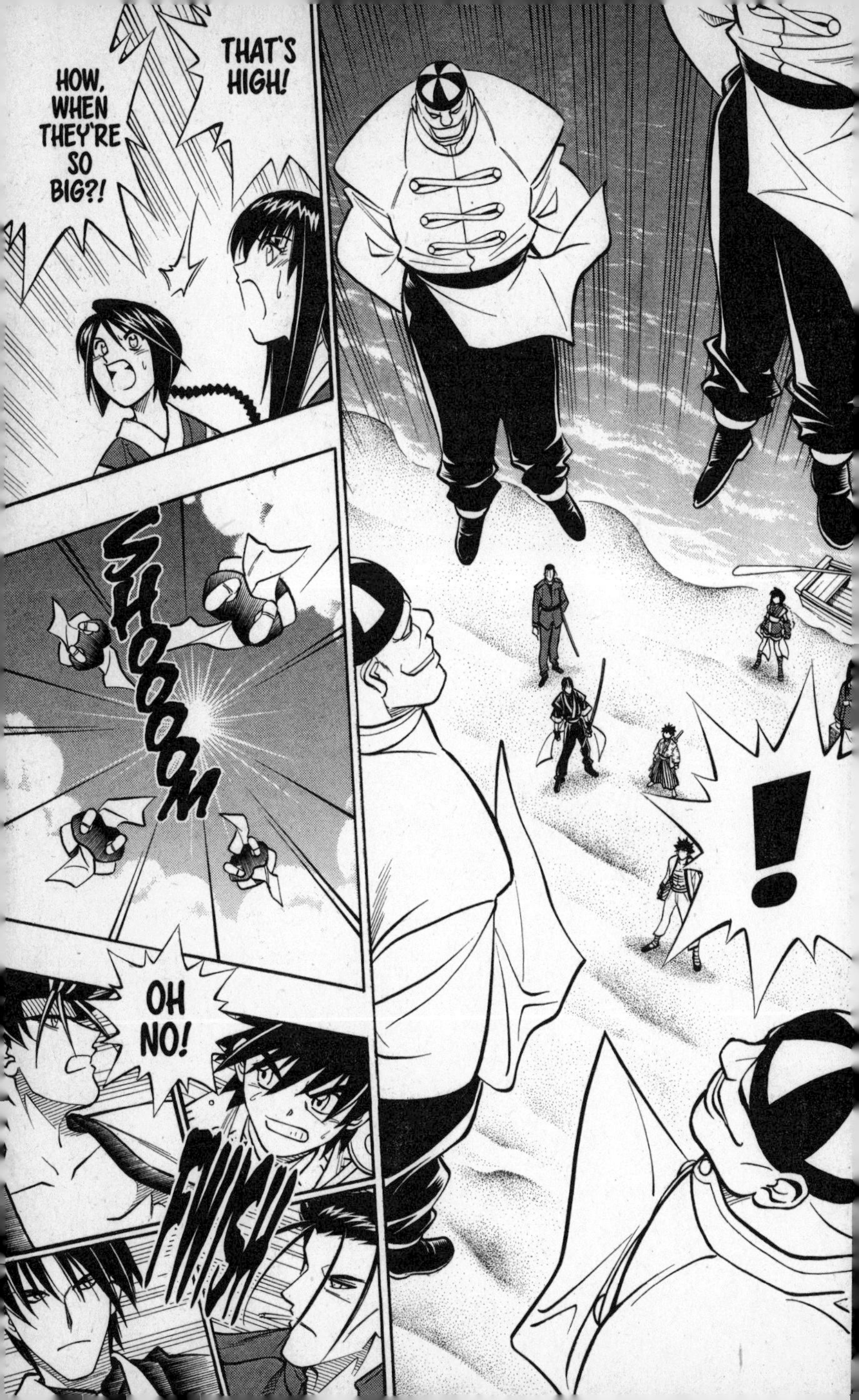
!
THAT'S HIGH!
HOW, WHEN THEY'RE SO BIG?!
SHOOOOM
OH NO!

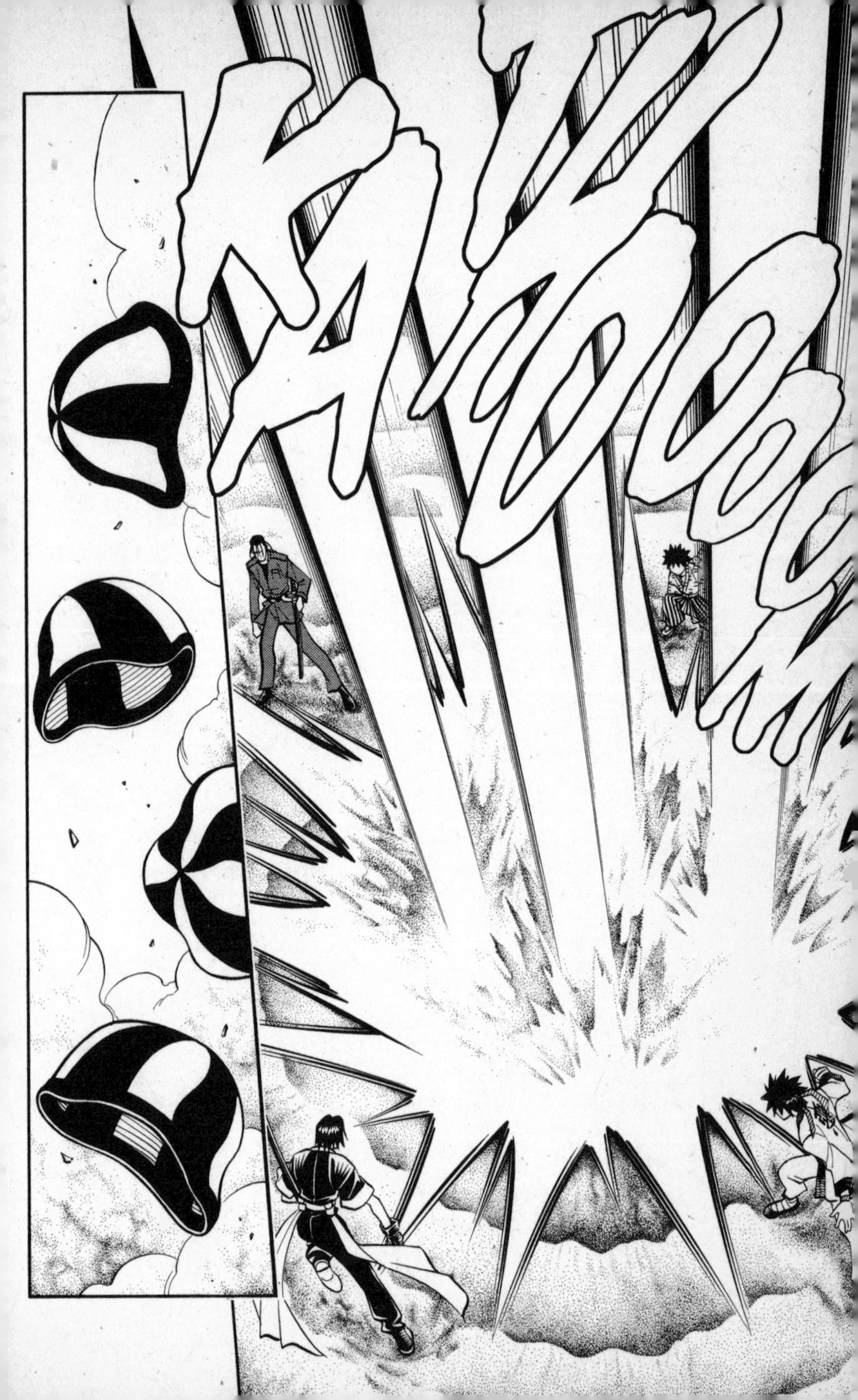
KABOOOM

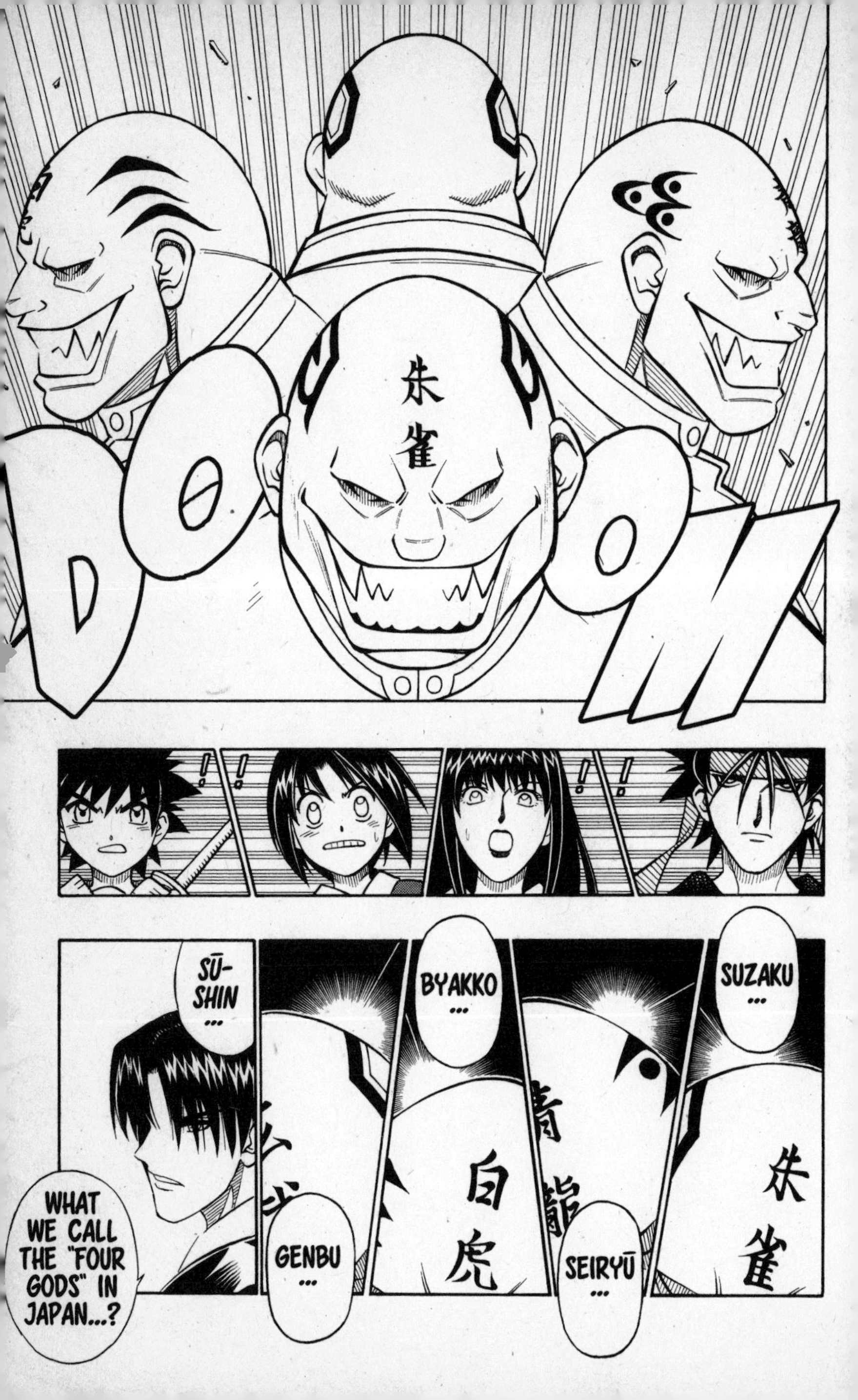
朱雀
DOOM
SUZAKU...
朱雀
SEIRYŪ...
青龍
BYAKKO...
白虎
GENBU...
SŪ-SHIN...
WHAT WE CALL THE "FOUR GODS" IN JAPAN...?

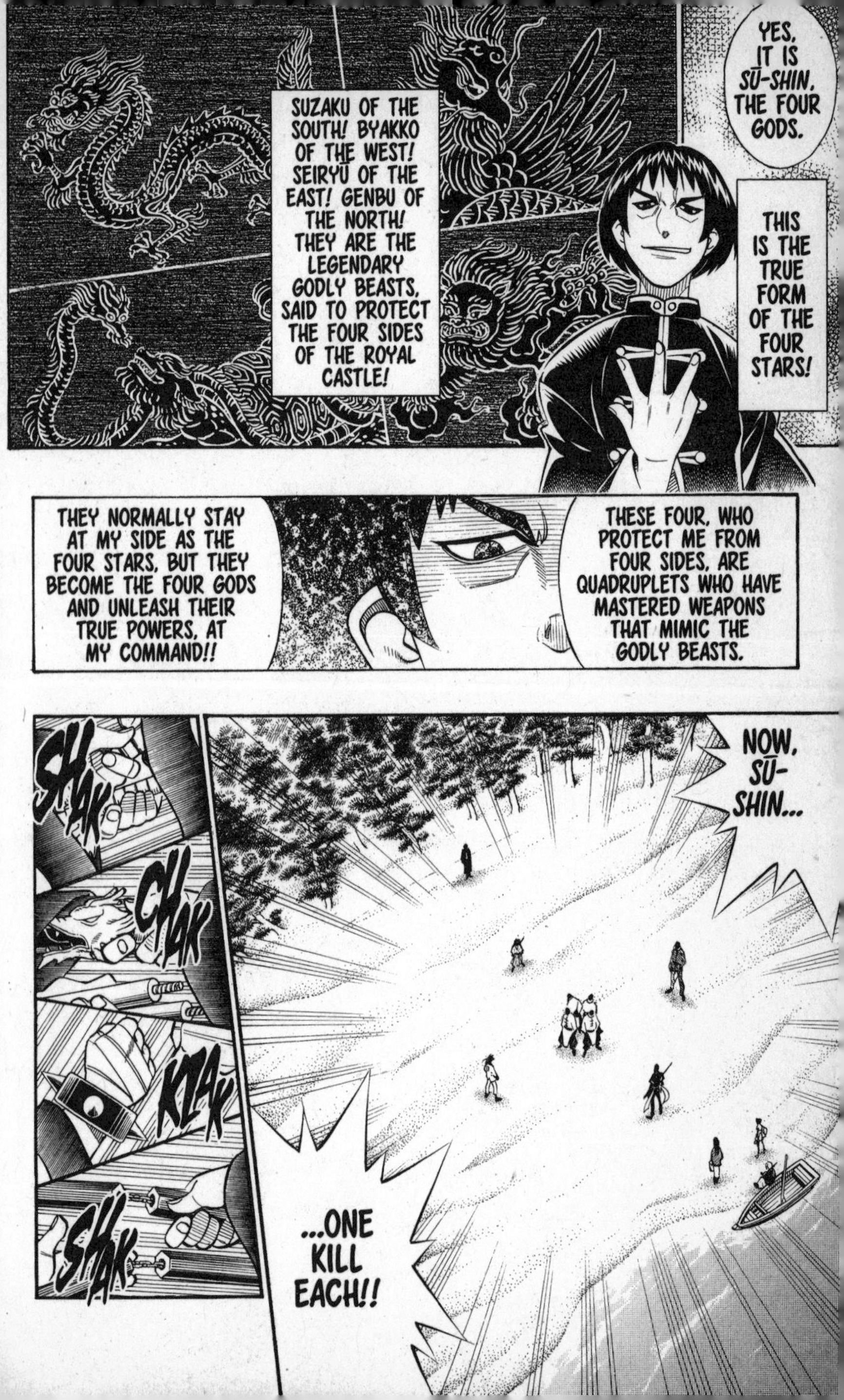
YES, IT IS SŪ-SHIN, THE FOUR GODS.
THIS IS THE TRUE FORM OF THE FOUR STARS!
SUZAKU OF THE SOUTH! BYAKKO OF THE WEST! SEIRYŪ OF THE EAST! GENBU OF THE NORTH! THEY ARE THE LEGENDARY GODLY BEASTS, SAID TO PROTECT THE FOUR SIDES OF THE ROYAL CASTLE!
THESE FOUR, WHO PROTECT ME FROM FOUR SIDES, ARE QUADRUPLETS WHO HAVE MASTERED WEAPONS THAT MIMIC THE GODLY BEASTS.
THEY NORMALLY STAY AT MY SIDE AS THE FOUR STARS, BUT THEY BECOME THE FOUR GODS AND UNLEASH THEIR TRUE POWERS, AT MY COMMAND!!
NOW, SŪ-SHIN...
...ONE KILL EACH!!
SHAK
CHAK
KLAK
SHAK

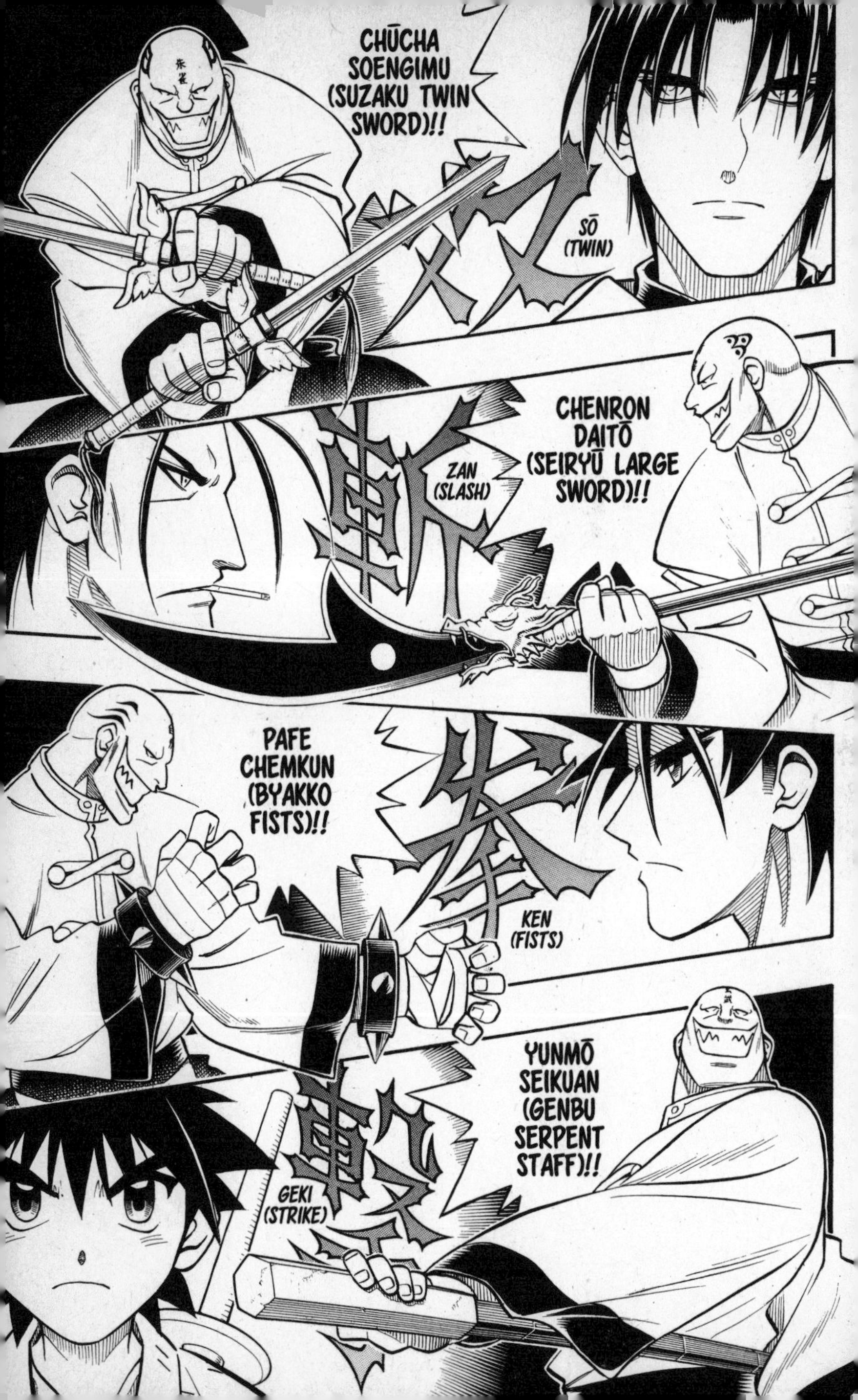
CHŪCHA SOENGIMU (SUZAKU TWIN SWORD)!!
SŌ (TWIN)
CHENRON DAITŌ (SEIRYŪ LARGE SWORD)!!
ZAN (SLASH)
PAFE CHEMKUN (BYAKKO FISTS)!!
KEN (FISTS)
YUNMŌ SEIKUAN (GENBU SERPENT STAFF)!!
GEKI (STRIKE)

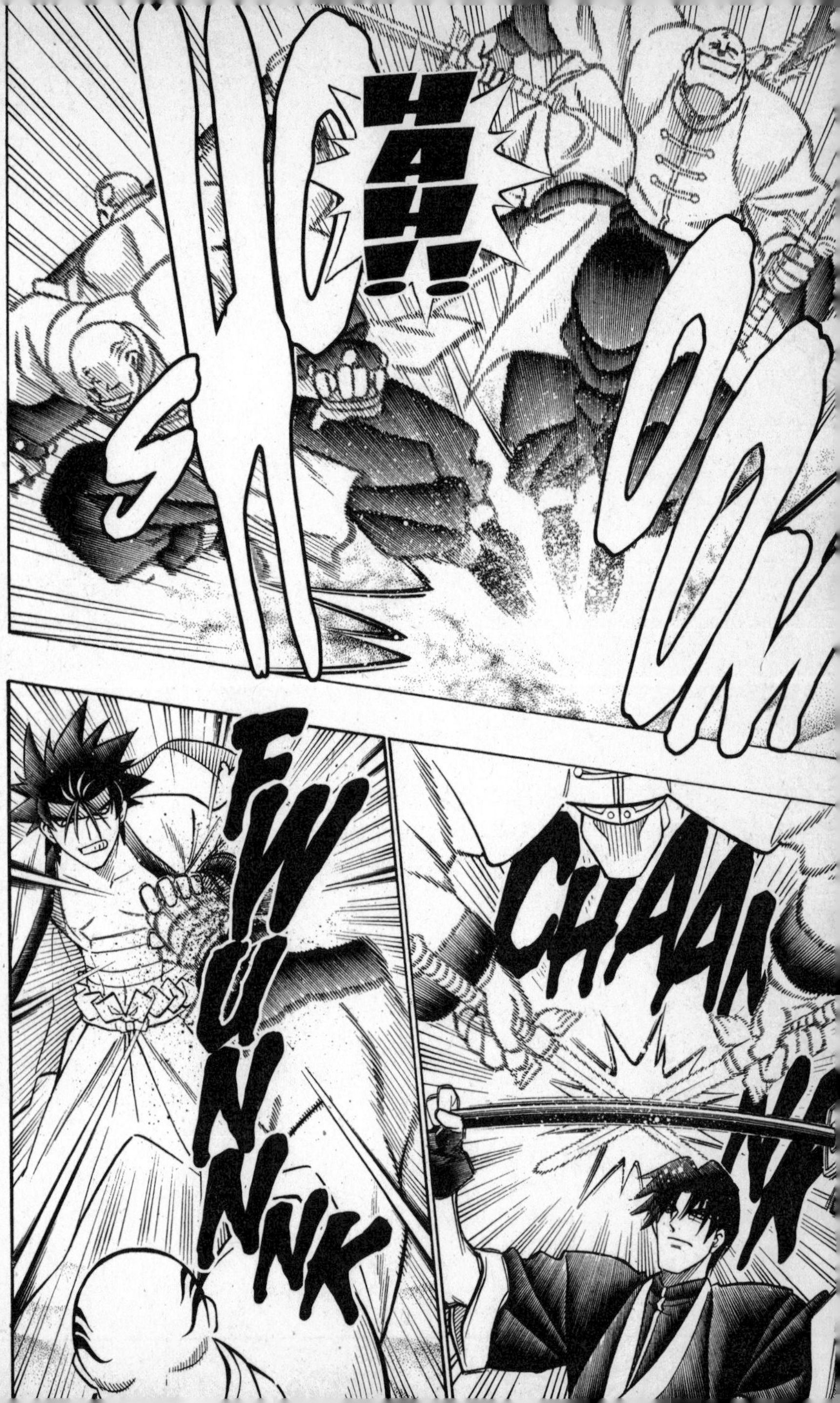
HAH!!
CHAAANK
FWUNNNK

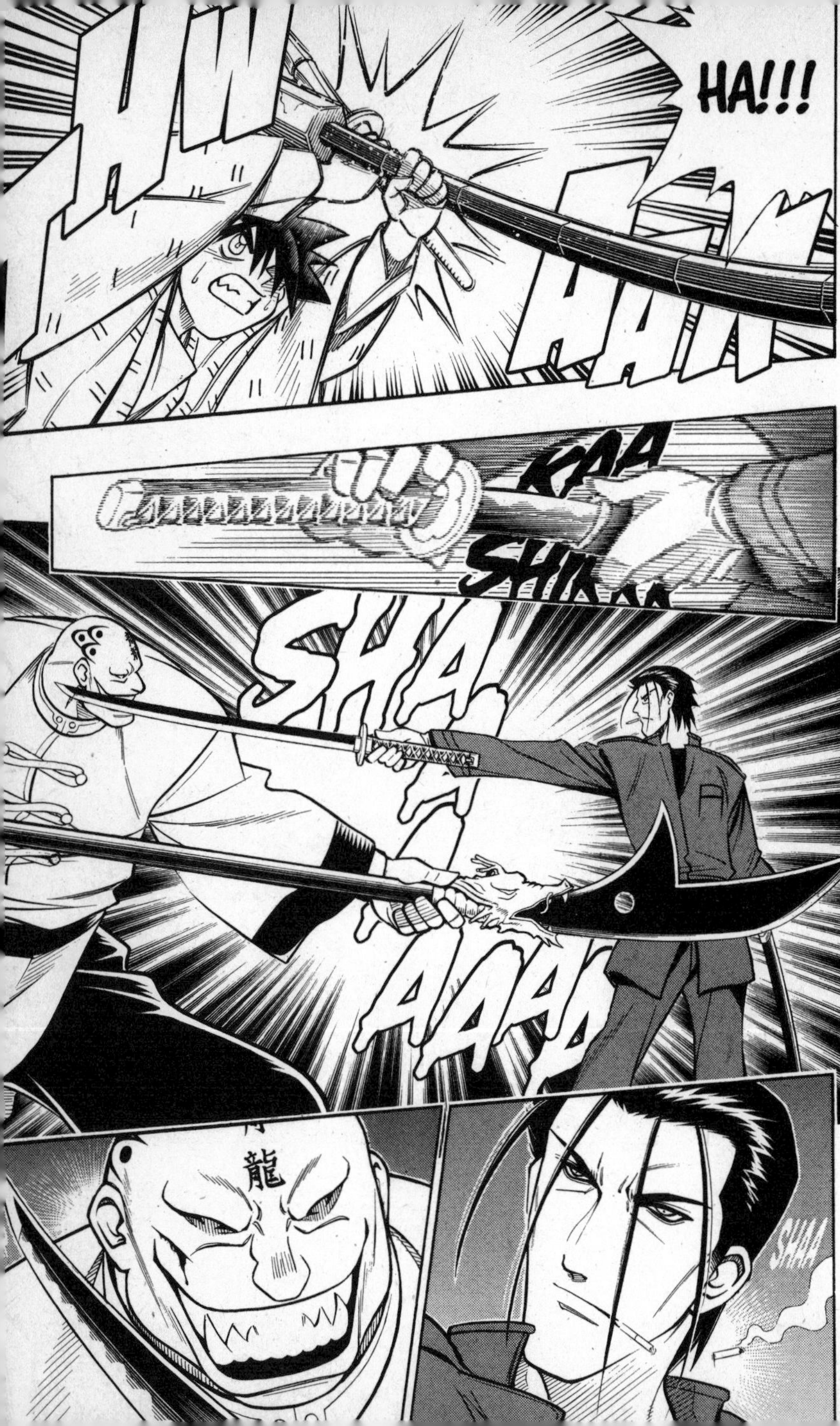
HA!!!
KAA
SHA
SHAA
龍

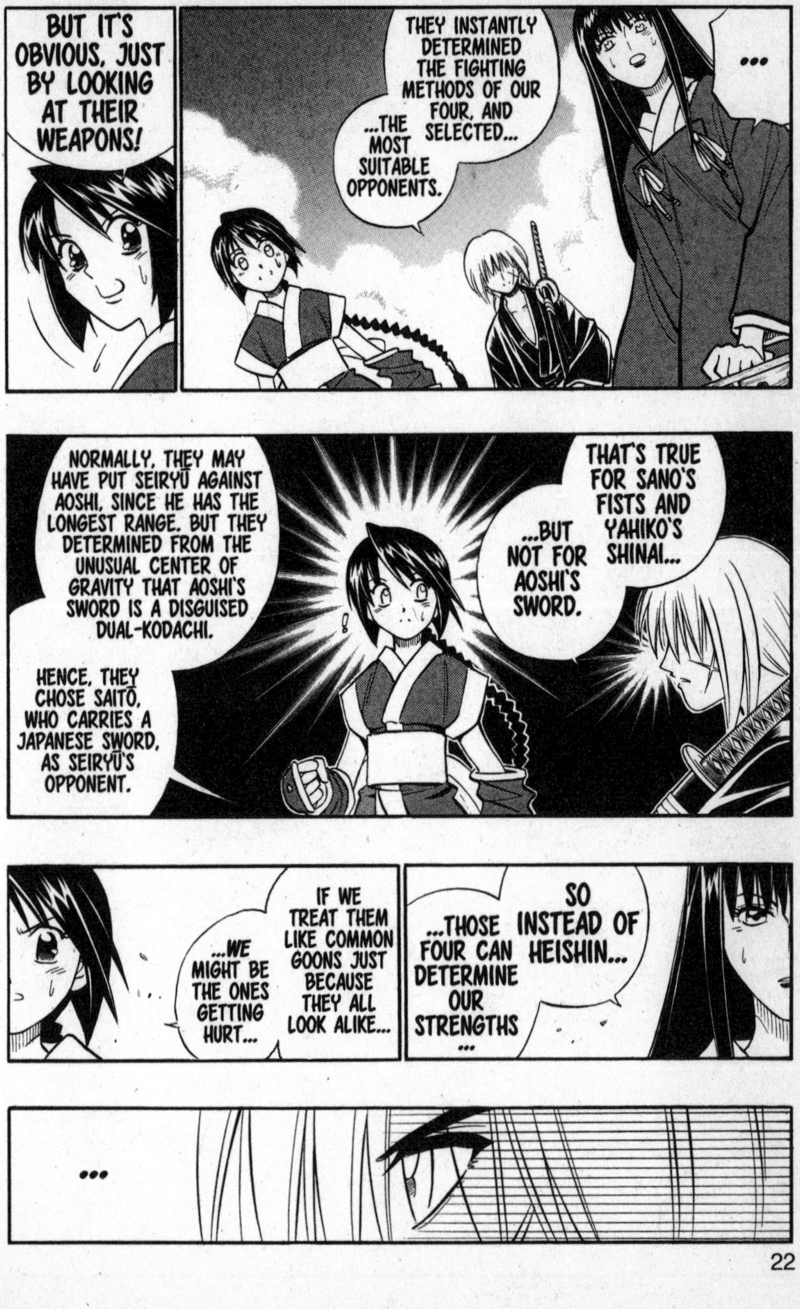
...
THEY INSTANTLY DETERMINED THE FIGHTING METHODS OF OUR FOUR, AND SELECTED...
...THE MOST SUITABLE OPPONENTS.
BUT IT'S OBVIOUS, JUST BY LOOKING AT THEIR WEAPONS!
THAT'S TRUE FOR SANO'S FISTS AND YAHIKO'S SHINAI...
...BUT NOT FOR AOSHI'S SWORD.
!
NORMALLY, THEY MAY HAVE PUT SEIRYŪ AGAINST AOSHI, SINCE HE HAS THE LONGEST RANGE. BUT THEY DETERMINED FROM THE UNUSUAL CENTER OF GRAVITY THAT AOSHI'S SWORD IS A DISGUISED DUAL-KODACHI.
HENCE, THEY CHOSE SAITŌ, WHO CARRIES A JAPANESE SWORD, AS SEIRYŪ'S OPPONENT.
SO INSTEAD OF HEISHIN...
...THOSE FOUR CAN DETERMINE OUR STRENGTHS ...
IF WE TREAT THEM LIKE COMMON GOONS JUST BECAUSE THEY ALL LOOK ALIKE...
...WE MIGHT BE THE ONES GETTING HURT...
...

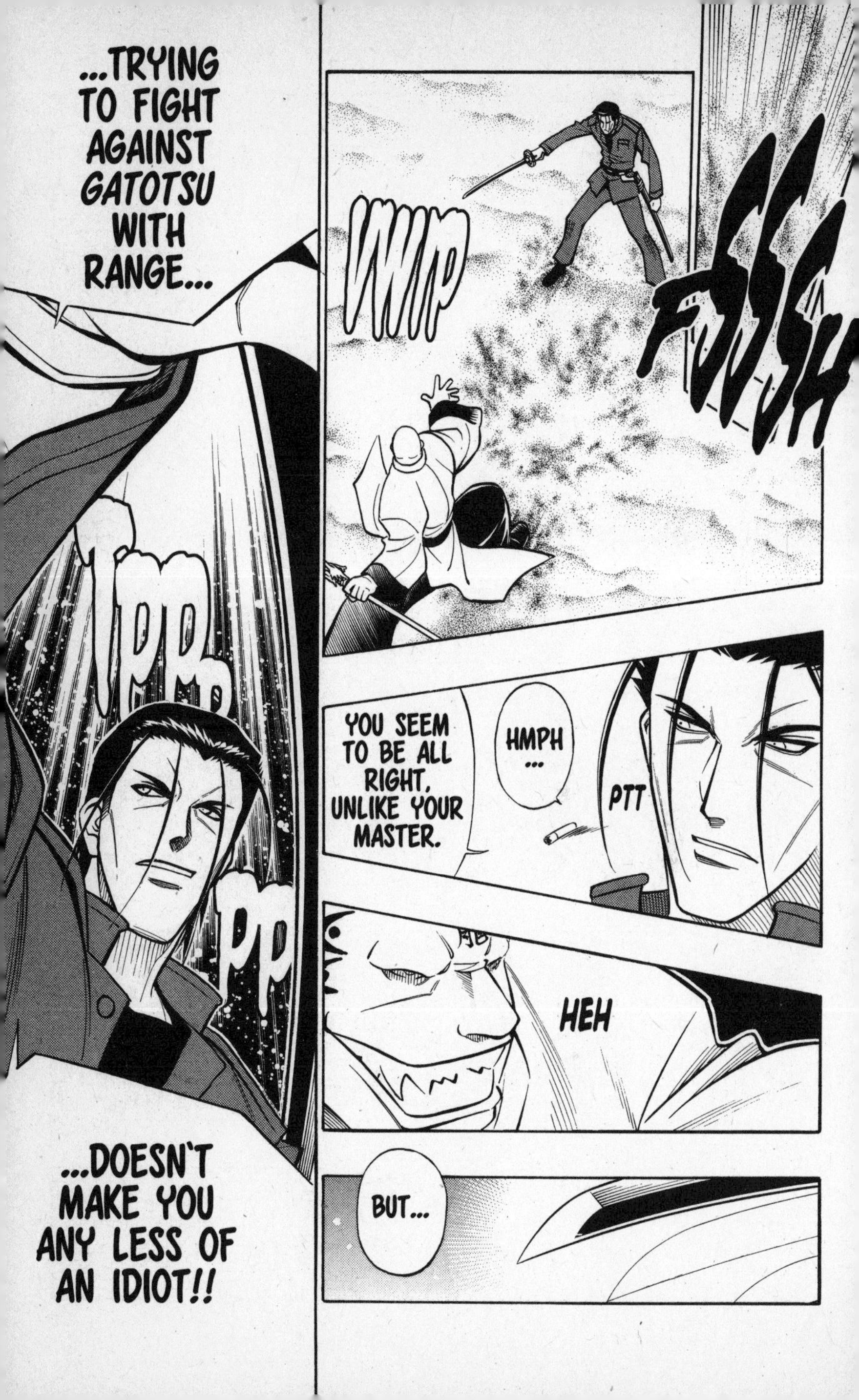
FSSSH
WHIP
PTT
HMPH...
YOU SEEM TO BE ALL RIGHT, UNLIKE YOUR MASTER.
HEH
BUT...
...TRYING TO FIGHT AGAINST GATOTSU WITH RANGE...
TPPP
PP
...DOESN'T MAKE YOU ANY LESS OF AN IDIOT!!

Rurouni Kenshin

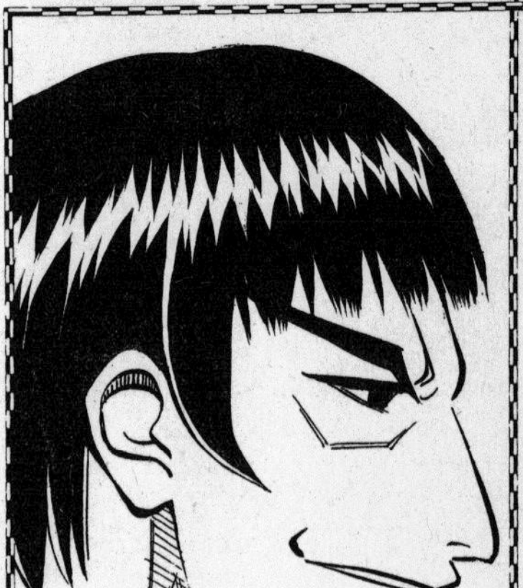

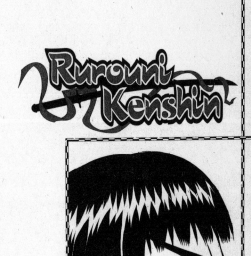

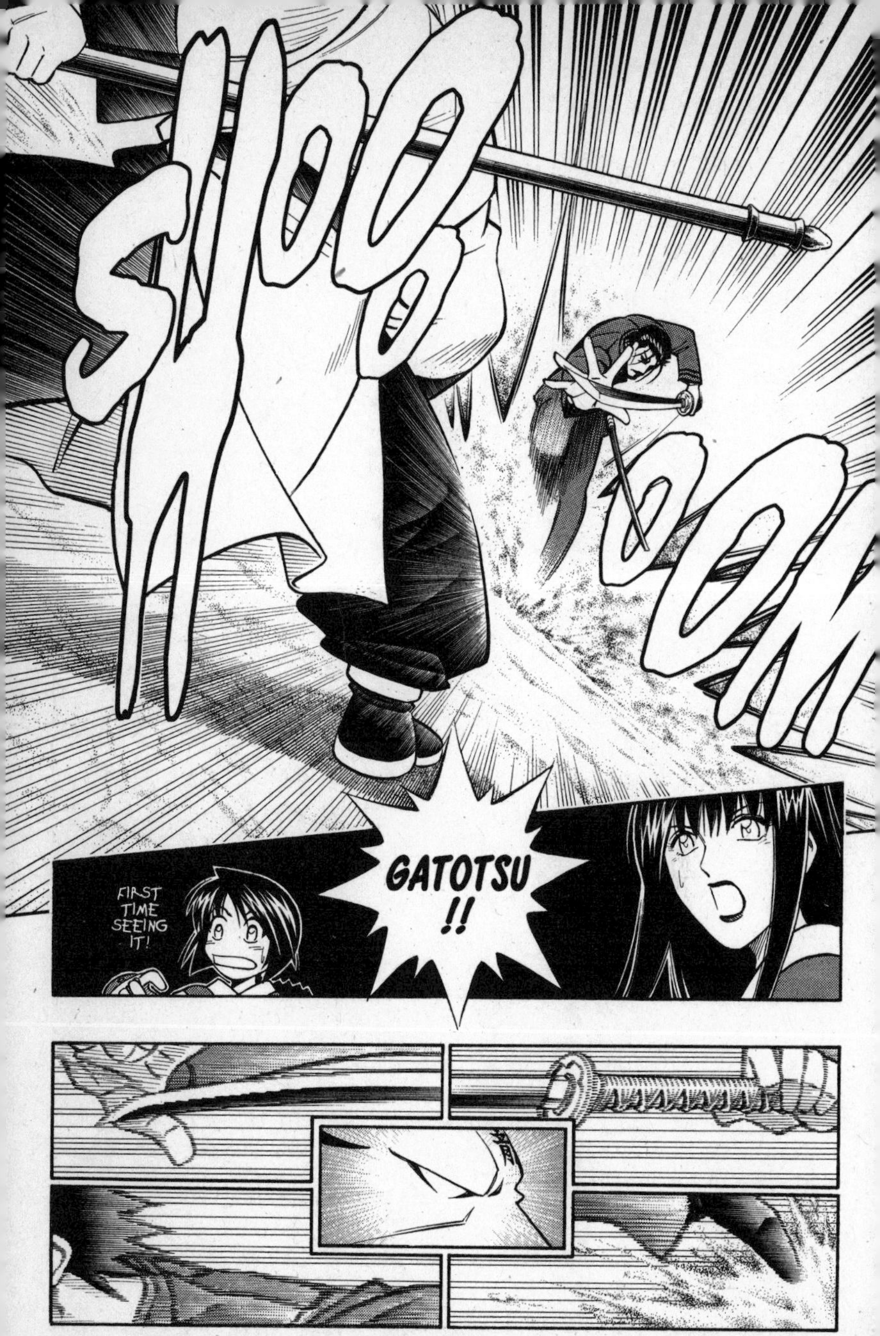
SHOOOOOM
GATOTSU!!
FIRST TIME SEEING IT!

Act 239—Sū-shin Battle—Saitō vs. Seiryū

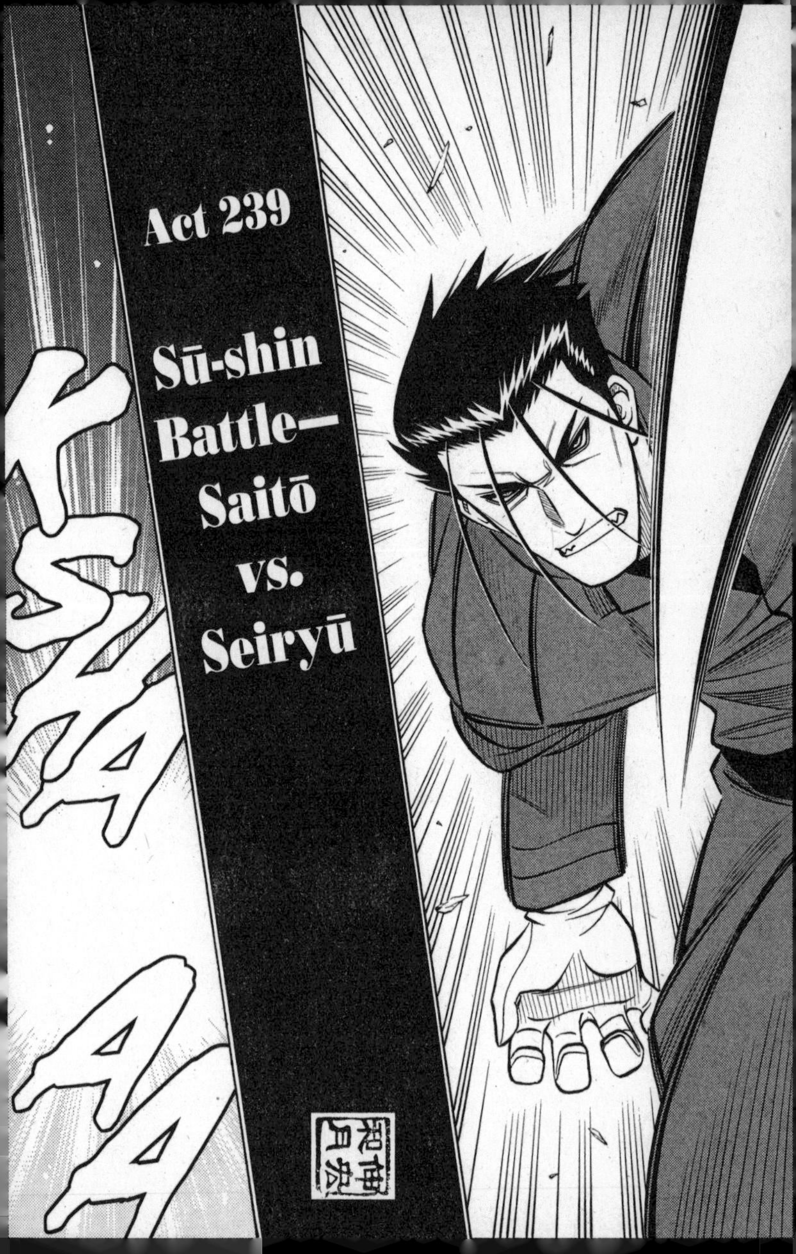
Act 239
Sū-shin Battle—Saitō vs. Seiryū

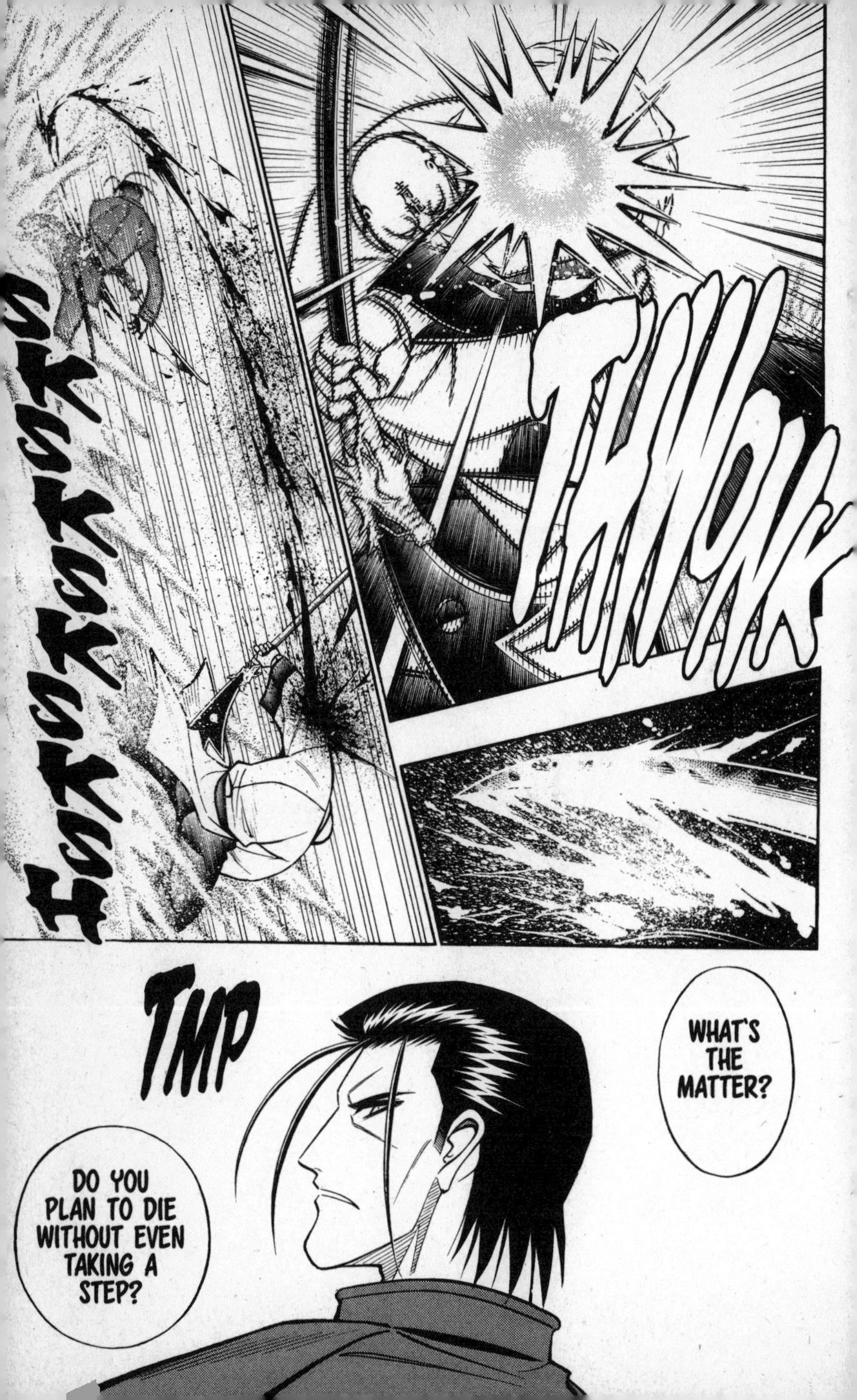

THWOK
TMP
WHAT'S THE MATTER?
DO YOU PLAN TO DIE WITHOUT EVEN TAKING A STEP?

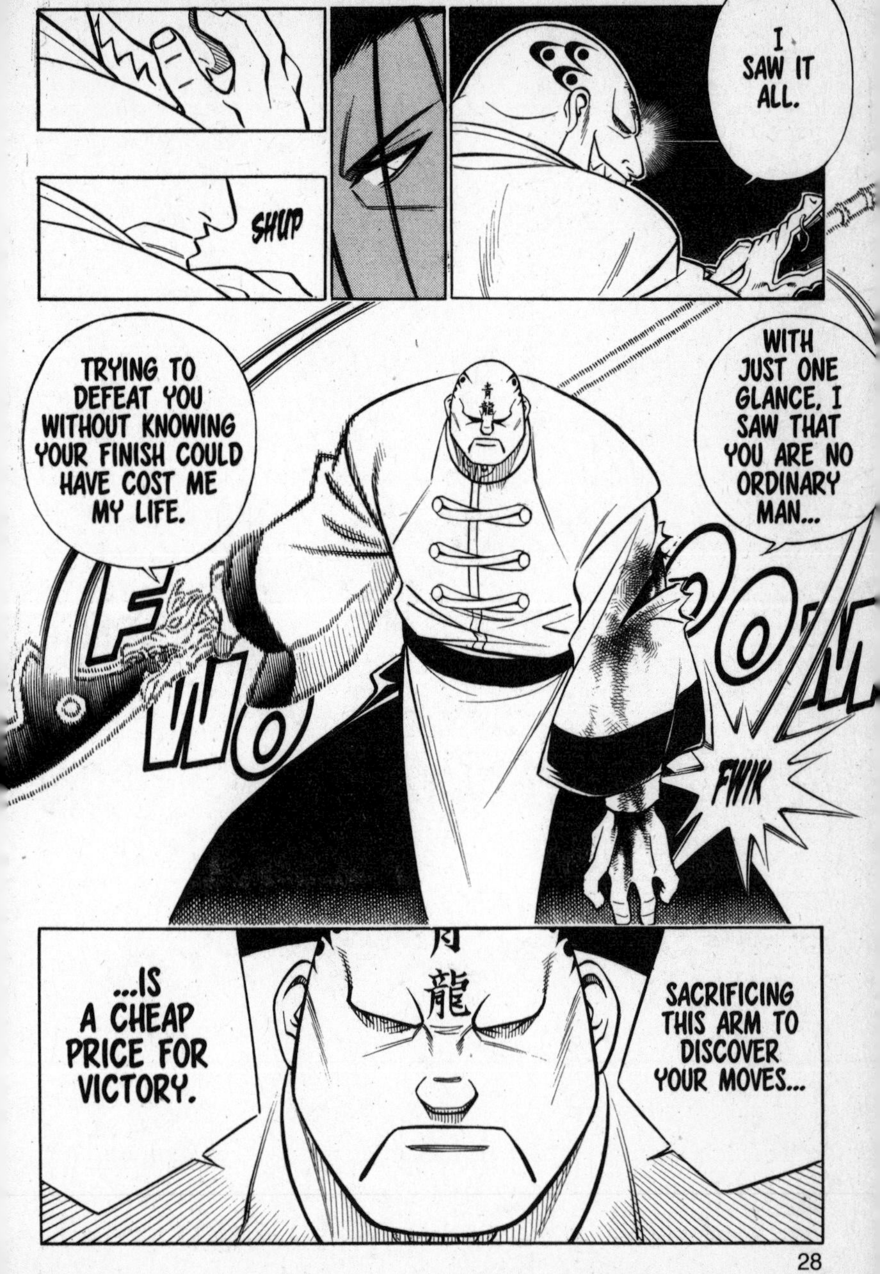
I SAW IT ALL.
SHUP
WITH JUST ONE GLANCE, I SAW THAT YOU ARE NO ORDINARY MAN...
TRYING TO DEFEAT YOU WITHOUT KNOWING YOUR FINISH COULD HAVE COST ME MY LIFE.
FWIK
SACRIFICING THIS ARM TO DISCOVER YOUR MOVES...
...IS A CHEAP PRICE FOR VICTORY.

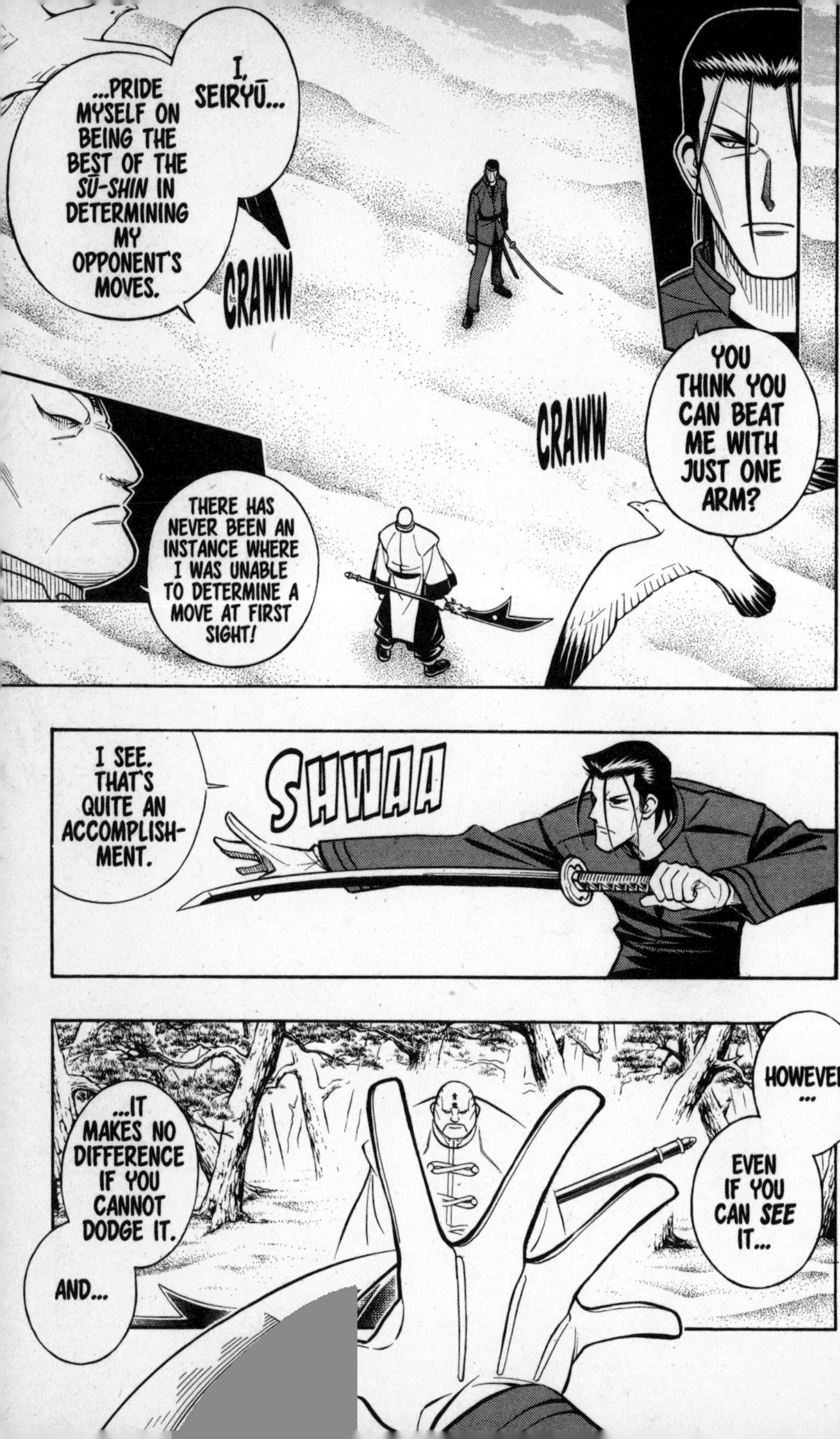
YOU THINK YOU CAN BEAT ME WITH JUST ONE ARM?
I, SEIRYŪ...
...PRIDE MYSELF ON BEING THE BEST OF THE *SŪ-SHIN* IN DETERMINING MY OPPONENT'S MOVES.
CRAWW
CRAWW
THERE HAS NEVER BEEN AN INSTANCE WHERE I WAS UNABLE TO DETERMINE A MOVE AT FIRST SIGHT!
SHWAA
I SEE. THAT'S QUITE AN ACCOMPLISHMENT.
HOWEVER...
EVEN IF YOU CAN *SEE* IT...
...IT MAKES NO DIFFERENCE IF YOU CANNOT DODGE IT.
AND...

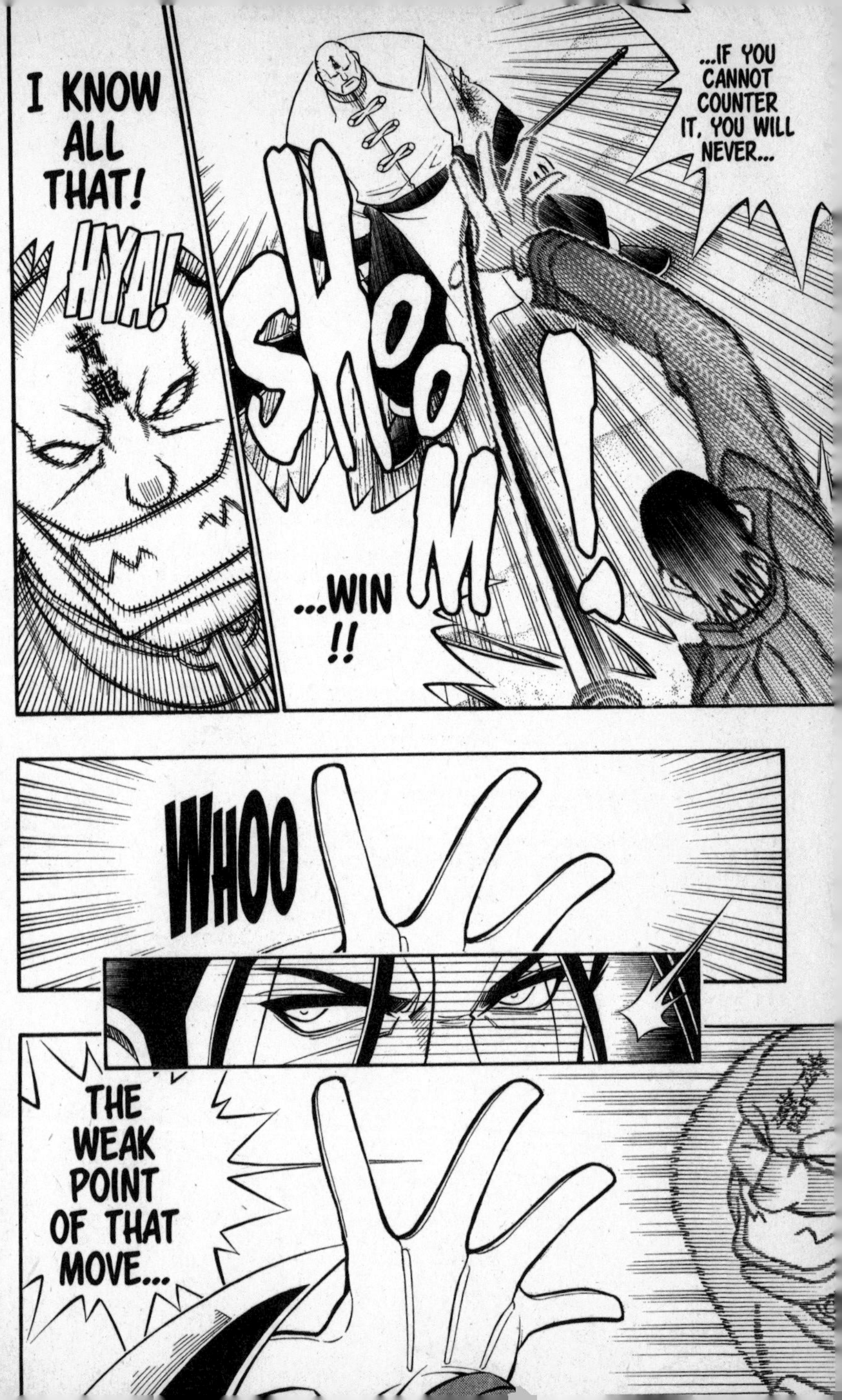
...IF YOU CANNOT COUNTER IT, YOU WILL NEVER...
SHOOM!
...WIN !!
I KNOW ALL THAT!
HYA!
WHOO
THE WEAK POINT OF THAT MOVE...

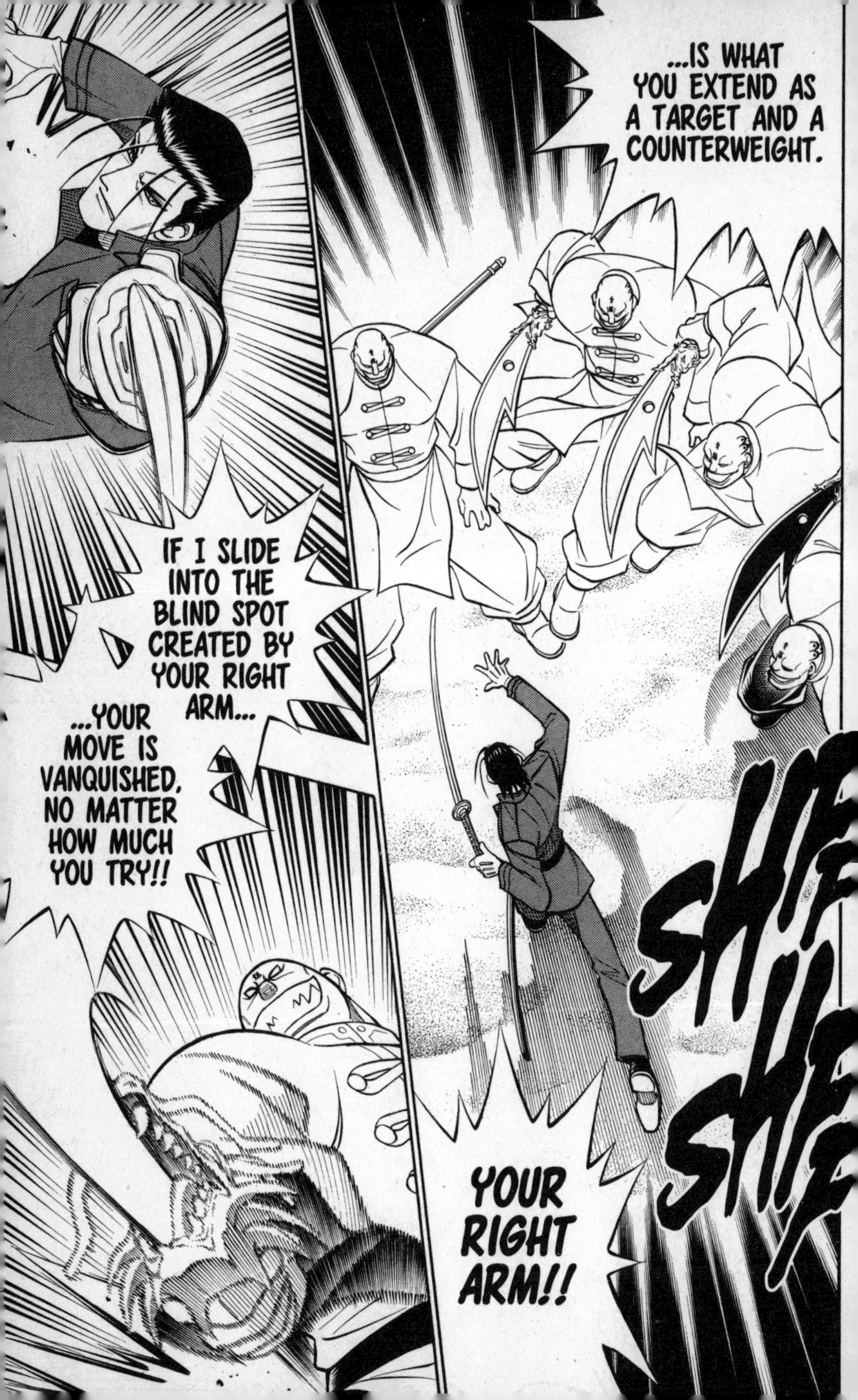
...IS WHAT YOU EXTEND AS A TARGET AND A COUNTERWEIGHT.
YOUR RIGHT ARM!!
IF I SLIDE INTO THE BLIND SPOT CREATED BY YOUR RIGHT ARM...
...YOUR MOVE IS VANQUISHED, NO MATTER HOW MUCH YOU TRY!!

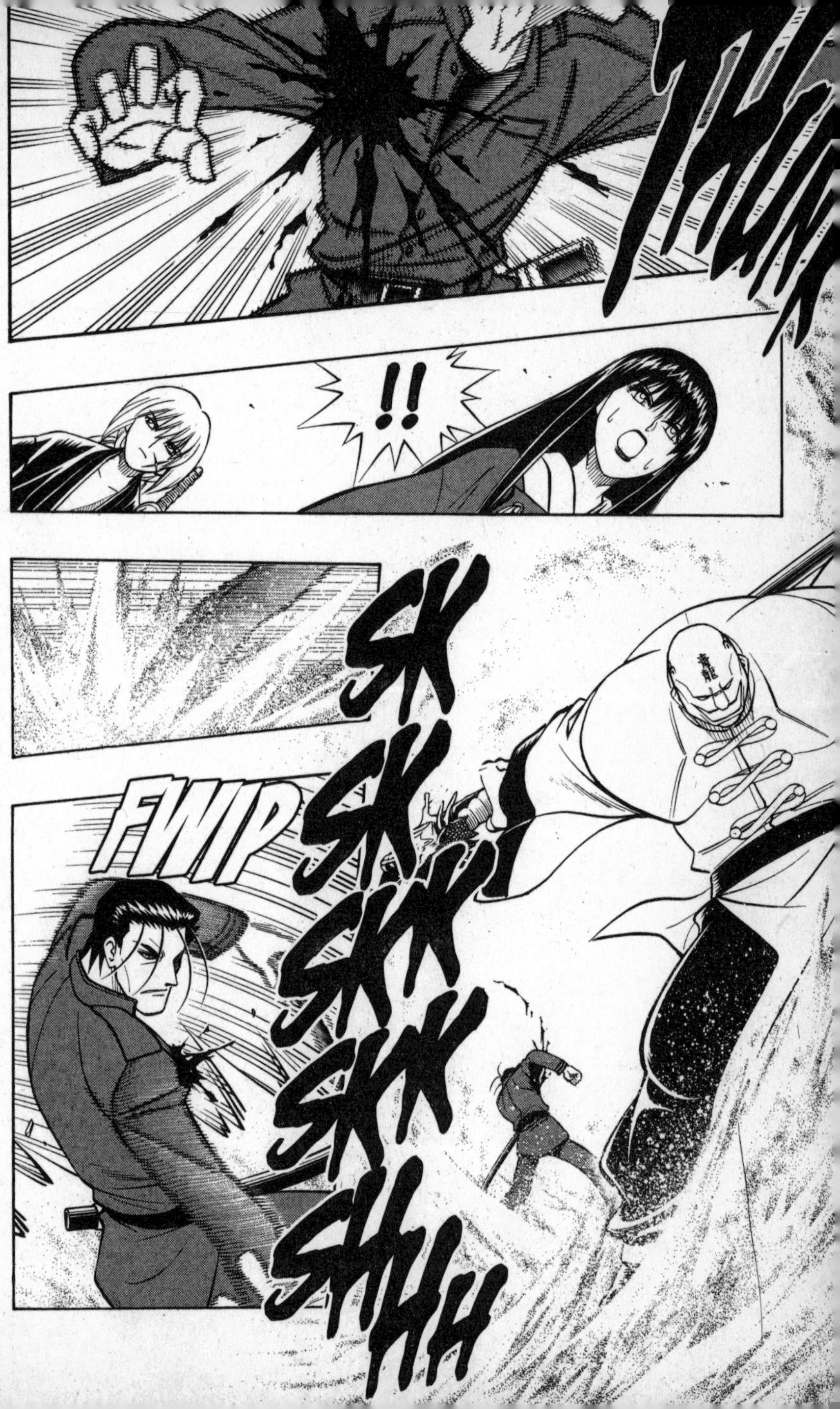
THUNK
!!
SK SK SKK SKK SKK SHHH
FWIP

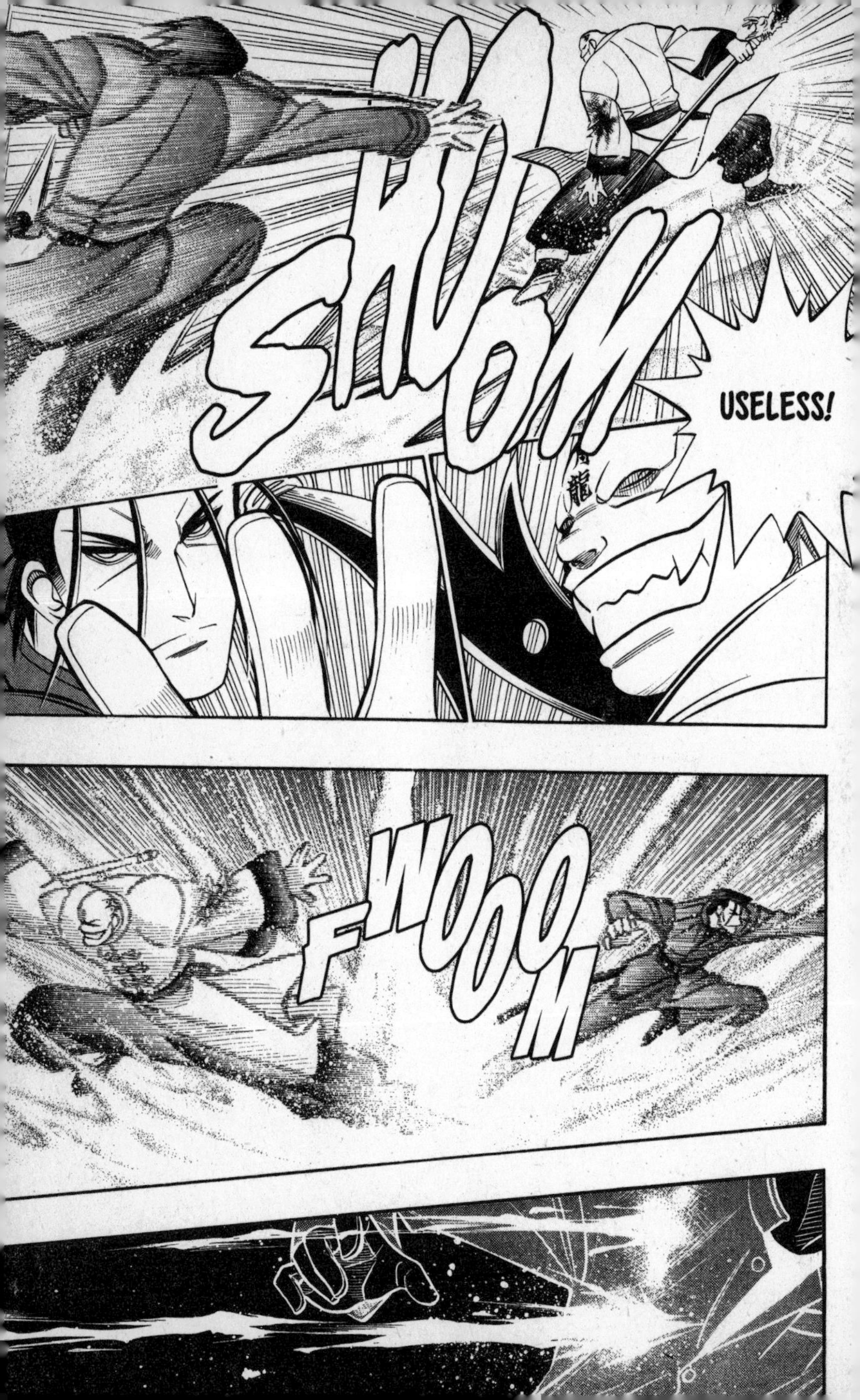
SHUOM
USELESS!
FWOOOOM

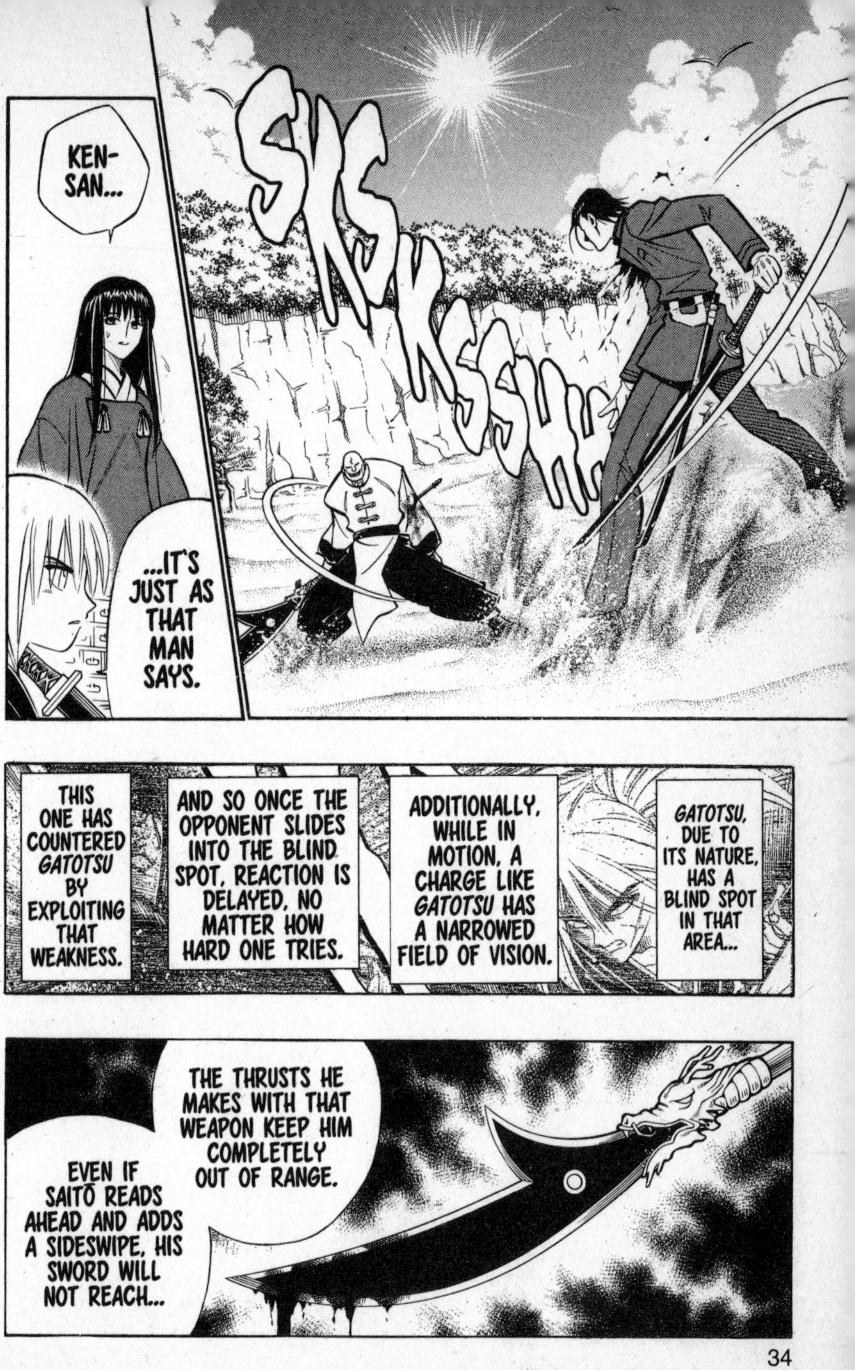
SKSKSSHH
KEN-SAN...
...IT'S JUST AS THAT MAN SAYS.
GATOTSU, DUE TO ITS NATURE, HAS A BLIND SPOT IN THAT AREA...
ADDITIONALLY, WHILE IN MOTION, A CHARGE LIKE *GATOTSU* HAS A NARROWED FIELD OF VISION.
AND SO ONCE THE OPPONENT SLIDES INTO THE BLIND SPOT, REACTION IS DELAYED, NO MATTER HOW HARD ONE TRIES.
THIS ONE HAS COUNTERED *GATOTSU* BY EXPLOITING THAT WEAKNESS.
THE THRUSTS HE MAKES WITH THAT WEAPON KEEP HIM COMPLETELY OUT OF RANGE.
EVEN IF SAITŌ READS AHEAD AND ADDS A SIDESWIPE, HIS SWORD WILL NOT REACH...

READ THIS WAY

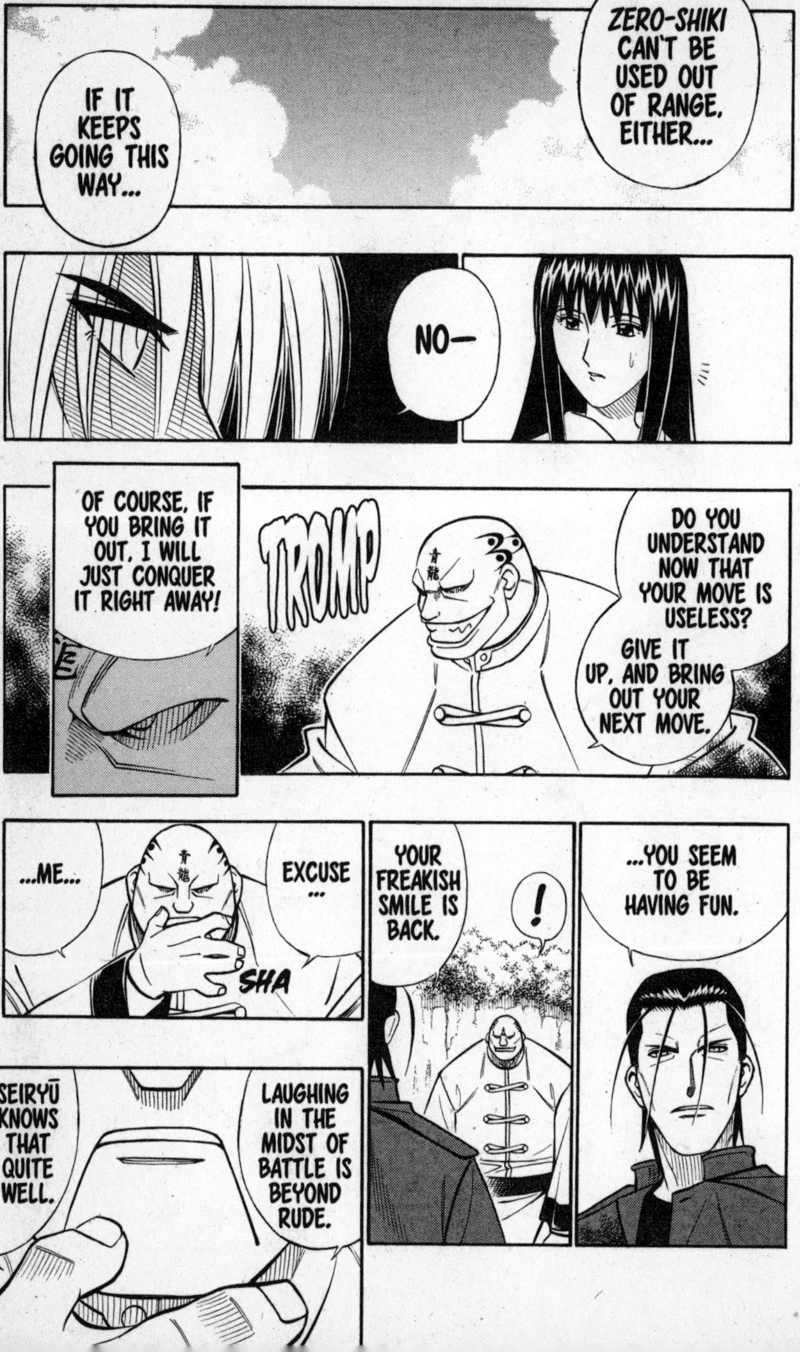

ZERO-SHIKI CAN'T BE USED OUT OF RANGE, EITHER...
IF IT KEEPS GOING THIS WAY...
NO—
DO YOU UNDERSTAND NOW THAT YOUR MOVE IS USELESS?
GIVE IT UP, AND BRING OUT YOUR NEXT MOVE.
TROMP
OF COURSE, IF YOU BRING IT OUT, I WILL JUST CONQUER IT RIGHT AWAY!
...YOU SEEM TO BE HAVING FUN.
!
YOUR FREAKISH SMILE IS BACK.
EXCUSE ...
...ME...
SHA
LAUGHING IN THE MIDST OF BATTLE IS BEYOND RUDE.
SEIRYŪ KNOWS THAT QUITE WELL.

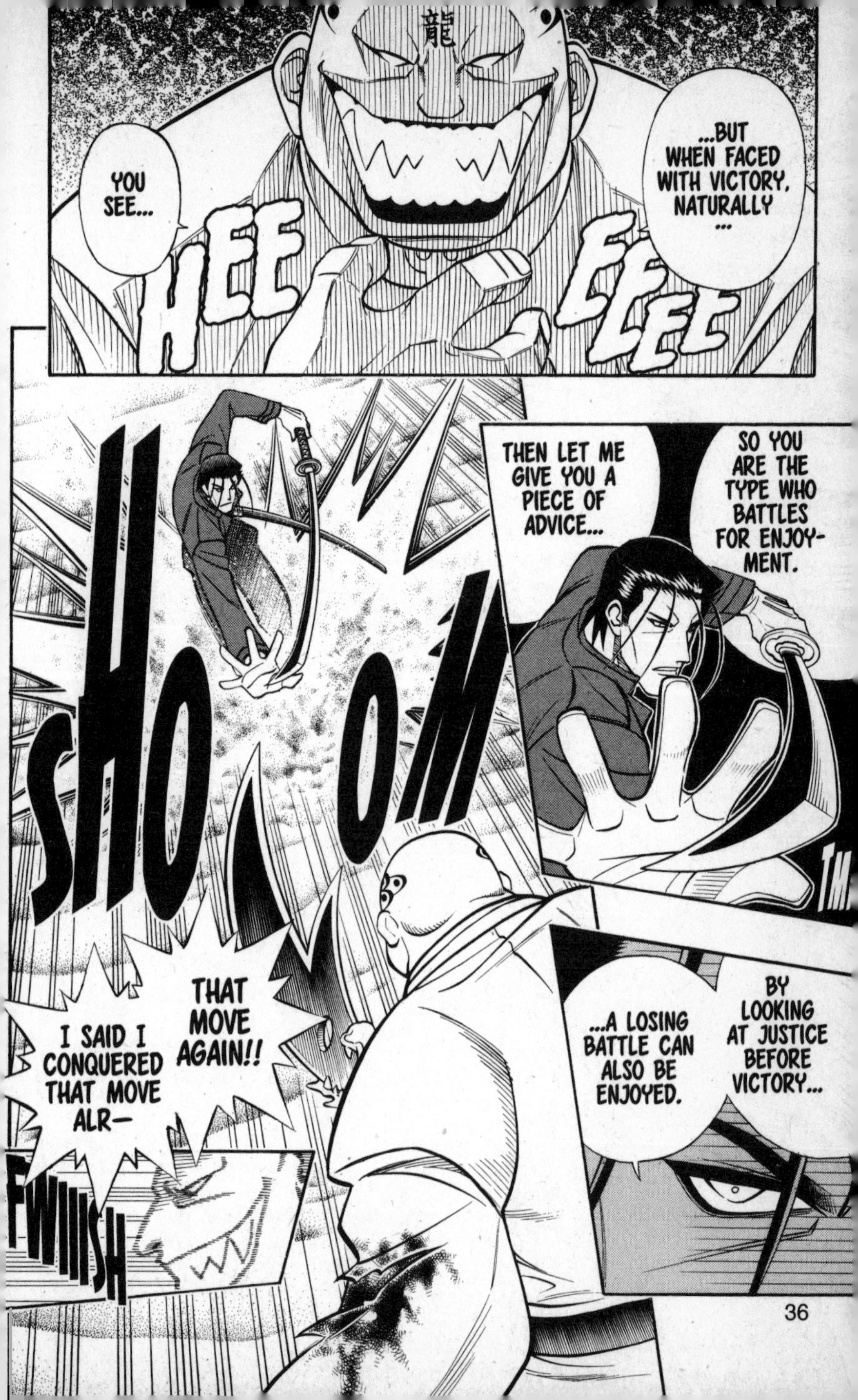
...BUT WHEN FACED WITH VICTORY, NATURALLY ...
YOU SEE...
HEE EEEE
SO YOU ARE THE TYPE WHO BATTLES FOR ENJOY-MENT.
THEN LET ME GIVE YOU A PIECE OF ADVICE...
SHOOM
BY LOOKING AT JUSTICE BEFORE VICTORY...
...A LOSING BATTLE CAN ALSO BE ENJOYED.
THAT MOVE AGAIN!!
I SAID I CONQUERED THAT MOVE ALR—
FWIIISH

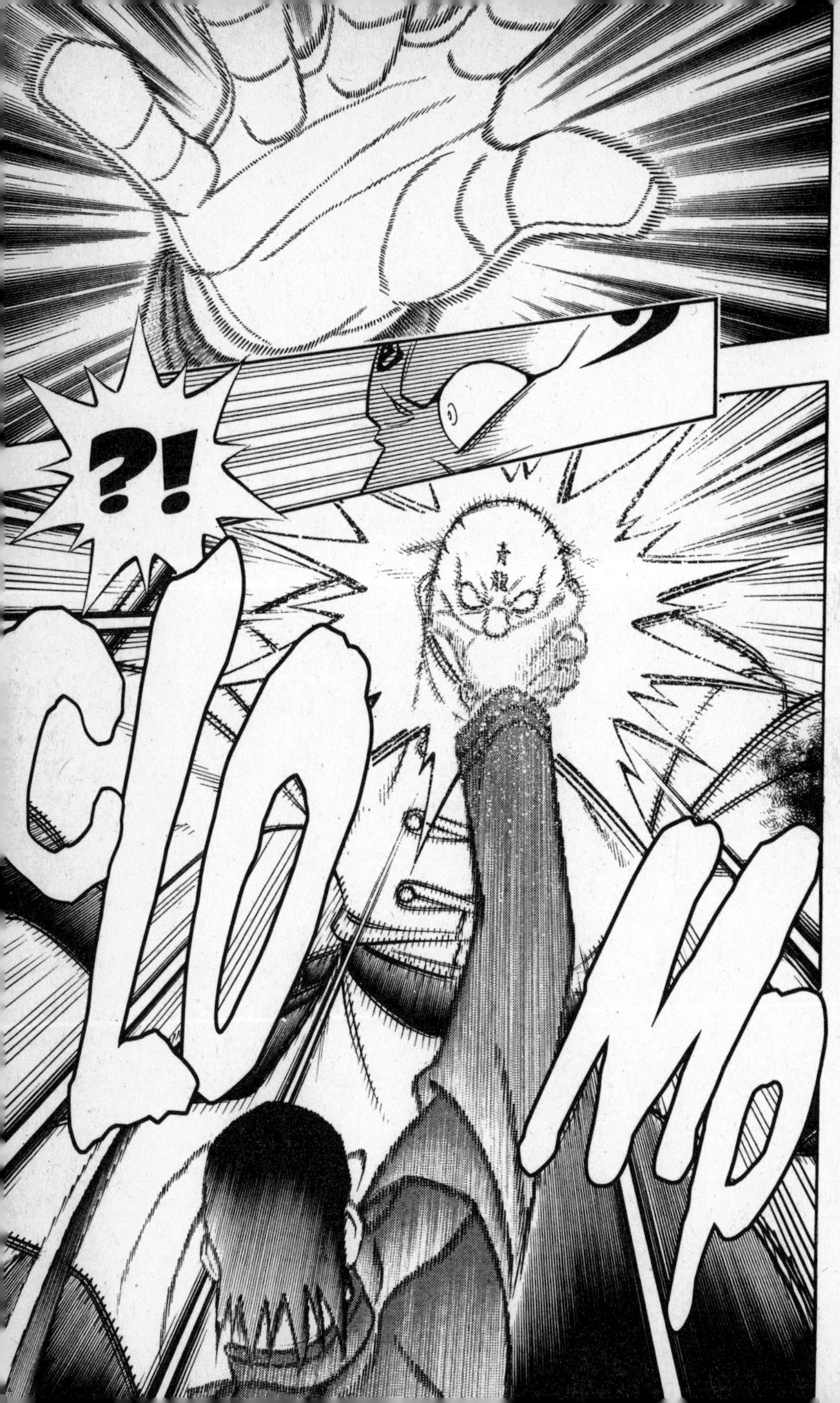
?!
青龍
CLOMP

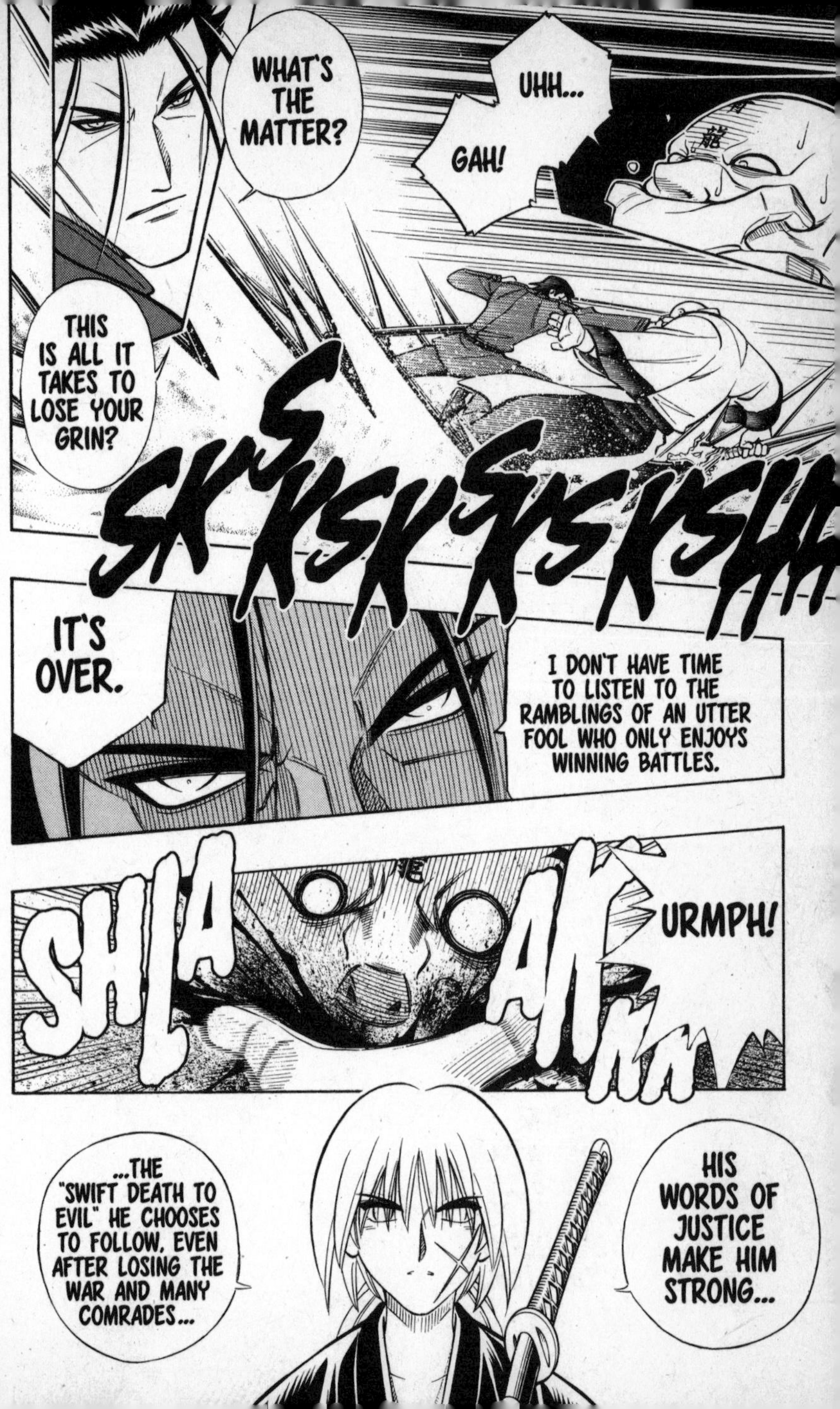
UHH...
GAH!
WHAT'S THE MATTER?
THIS IS ALL IT TAKES TO LOSE YOUR GRIN?
I DON'T HAVE TIME TO LISTEN TO THE RAMBLINGS OF AN UTTER FOOL WHO ONLY ENJOYS WINNING BATTLES.
IT'S OVER.
URMPH!
HIS WORDS OF JUSTICE MAKE HIM STRONG...
...THE "SWIFT DEATH TO EVIL" HE CHOOSES TO FOLLOW, EVEN AFTER LOSING THE WAR AND MANY COMRADES...

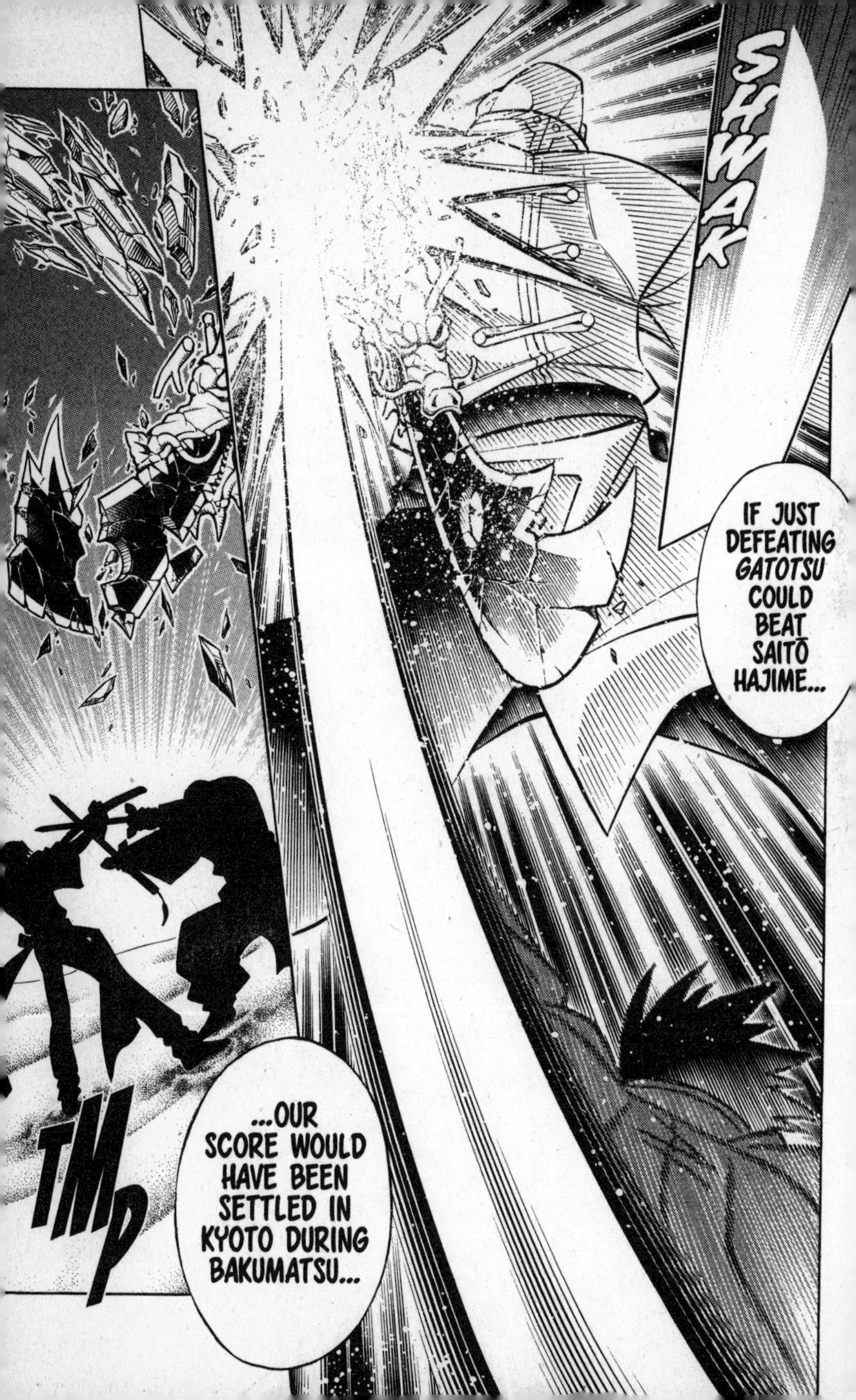
SHWAK
IF JUST DEFEATING GATOTSU COULD BEAT SAITŌ HAJIME...
TMP
...OUR SCORE WOULD HAVE BEEN SETTLED IN KYOTO DURING BAKUMATSU...

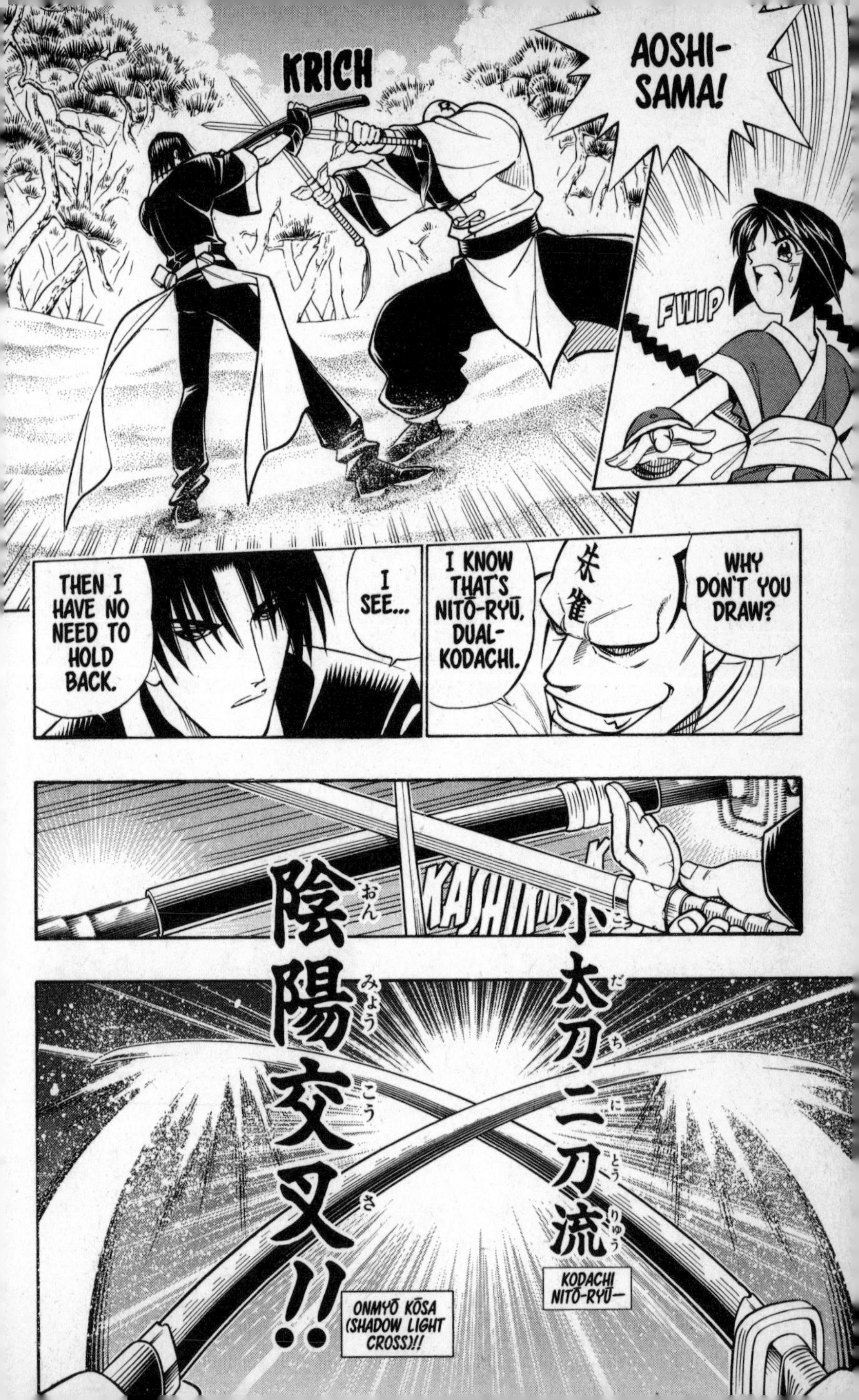
AOSHI-SAMA!
FWIP
KRICH
WHY DON'T YOU DRAW?
I KNOW THAT'S NITŌ-RYŪ, DUAL-KODACHI.
I SEE...
THEN I HAVE NO NEED TO HOLD BACK.
KASHIN
小太刀二刀流
KODACHI NITŌ-RYŪ—
陰陽交叉!!
ONMYŌ KŌSA (SHADOW LIGHT CROSS)!!

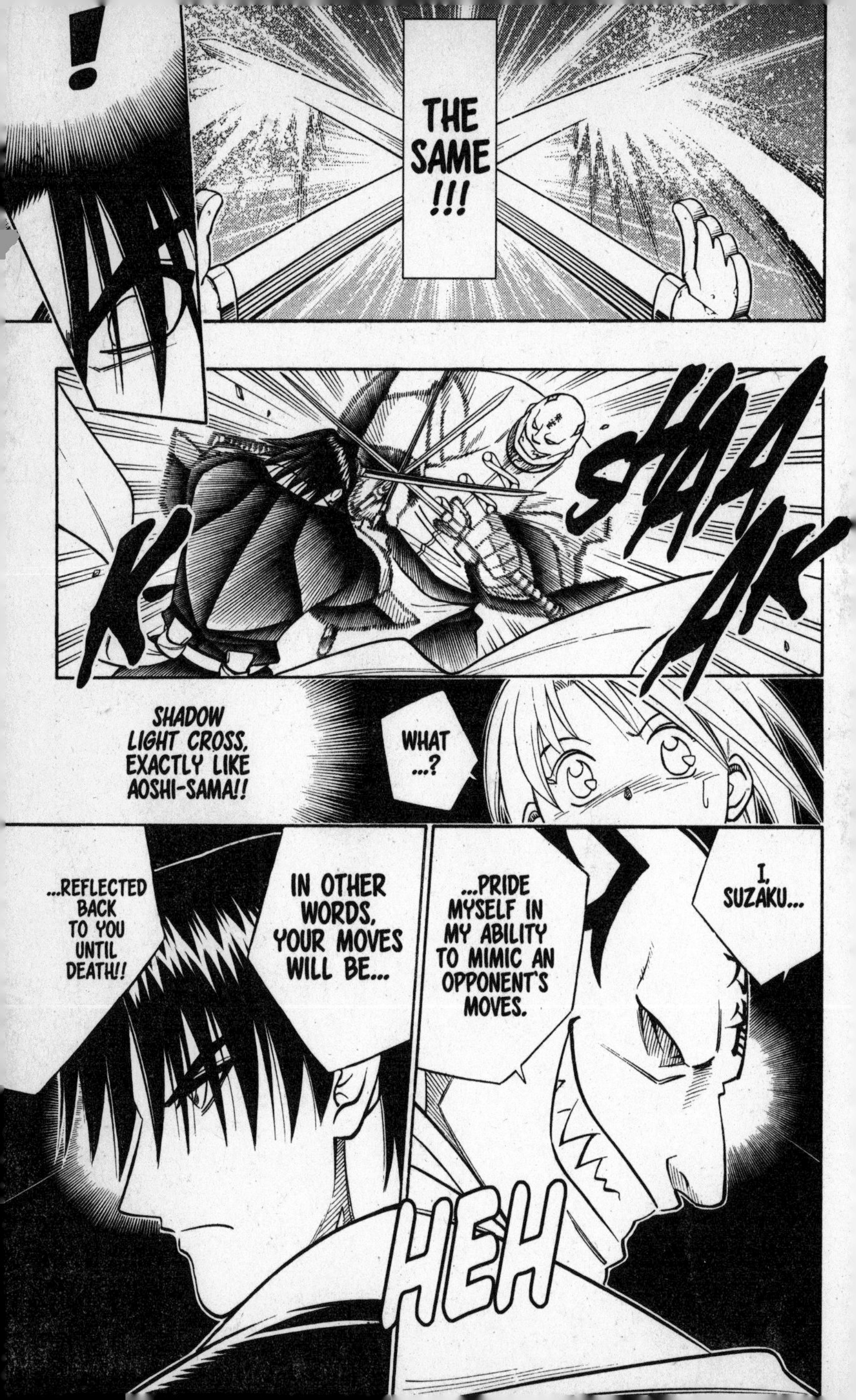
THE SAME!!!
!
SHAAAK
WHAT ...?
SHADOW LIGHT CROSS, EXACTLY LIKE AOSHI-SAMA!!
I, SUZAKU...
...PRIDE MYSELF IN MY ABILITY TO MIMIC AN OPPONENT'S MOVES.
IN OTHER WORDS, YOUR MOVES WILL BE...
...REFLECTED BACK TO YOU UNTIL DEATH!!
HEH

Rurouni Kenshin

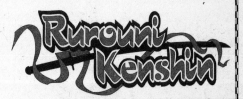

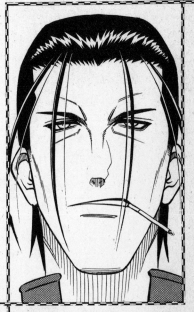

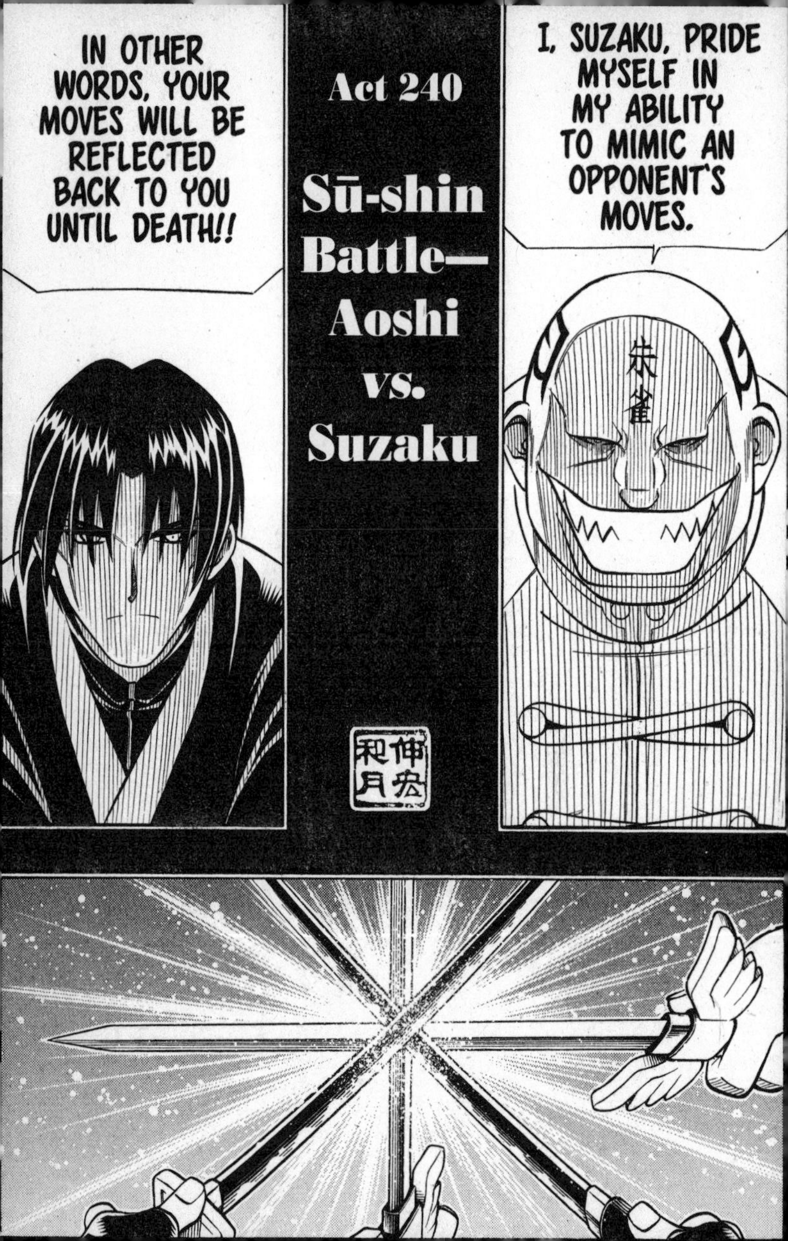
I, SUZAKU, PRIDE MYSELF IN MY ABILITY TO MIMIC AN OPPONENT'S MOVES.
Act 240
Sū-shin Battle—Aoshi vs. Suzaku
IN OTHER WORDS, YOUR MOVES WILL BE REFLECTED BACK TO YOU UNTIL DEATH!!

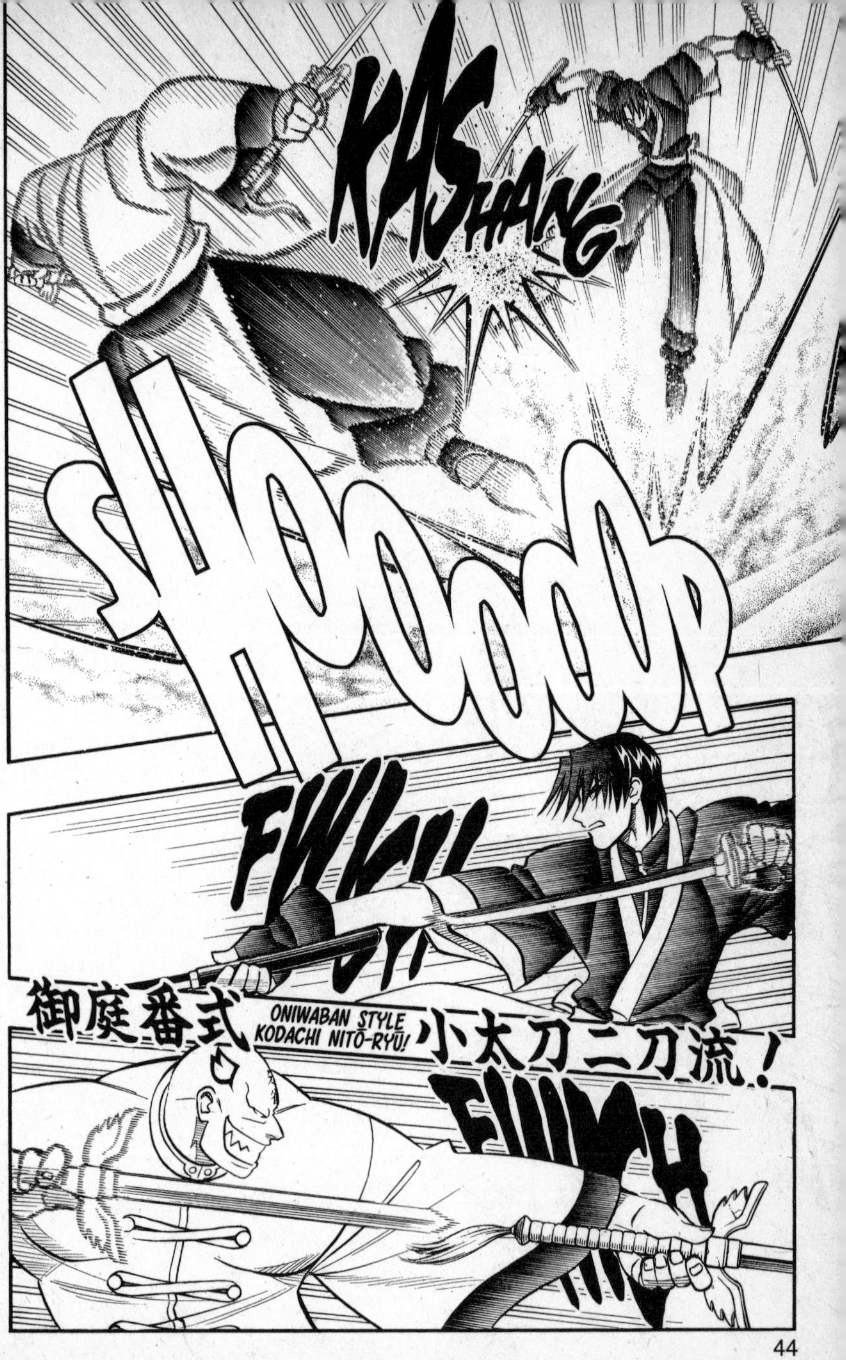
KASHANG
SHOOOOP
御庭番式
ONIWABAN STYLE KODACHI NITŌ-RYŪ!
小太刀二刀流！

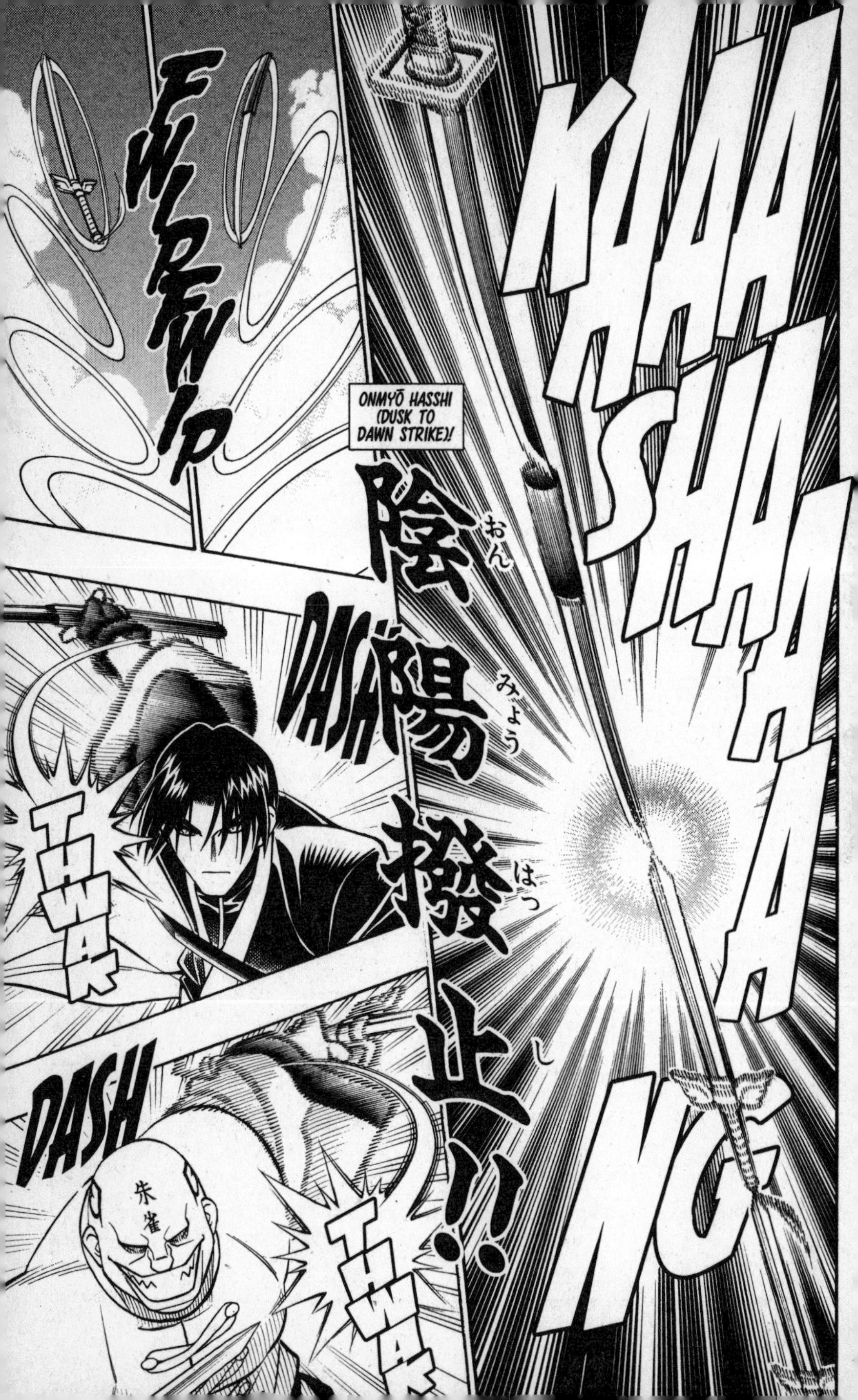
KAASHAAAANG
ONMYŌ HASSHI (DUSK TO DAWN STRIKE)!
陰陽撥止!!
FWIPEWIP
DASH
THWAK
DASH
THWAK
朱雀

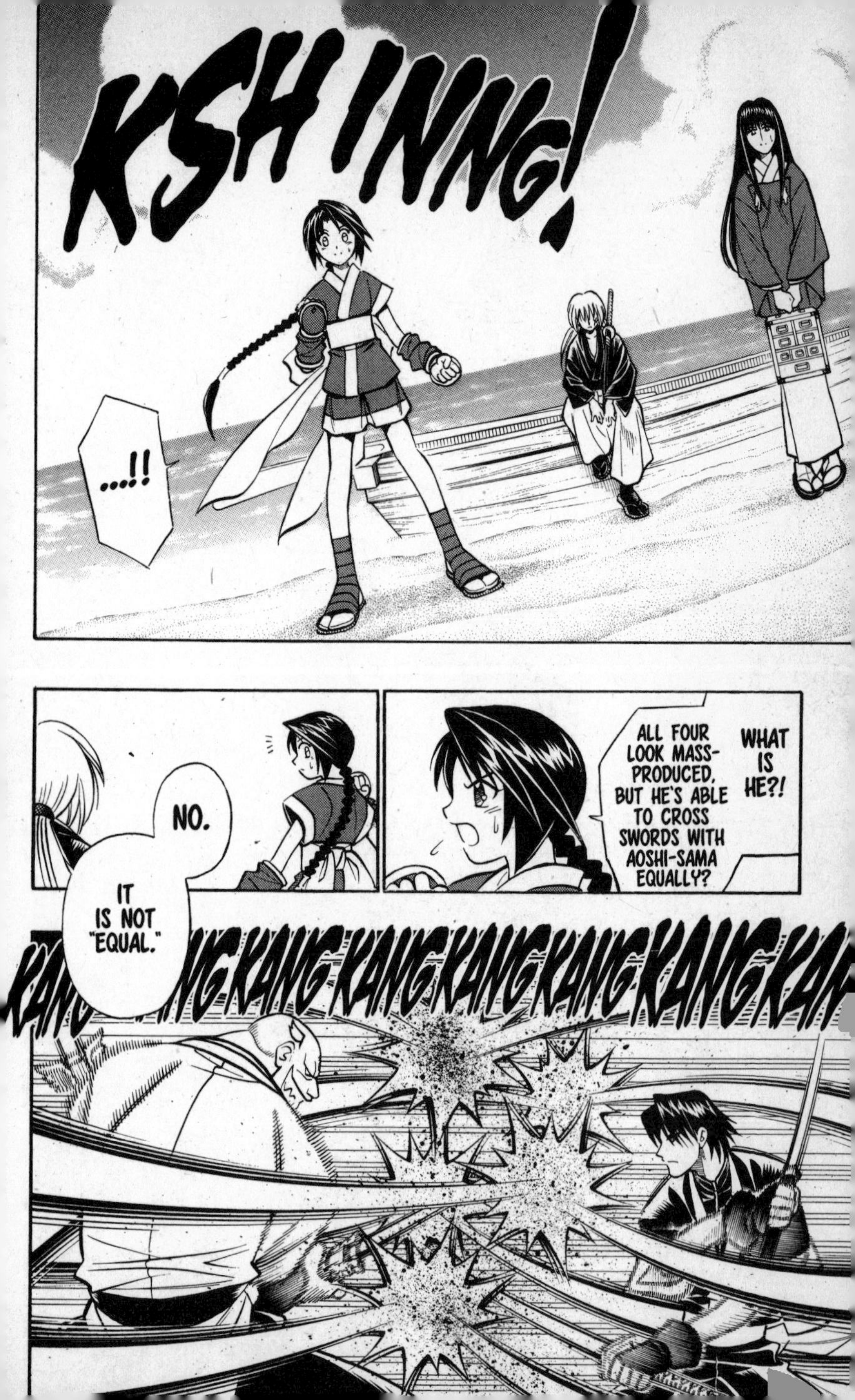
KSH INNG!
...!!
WHAT IS HE?!
ALL FOUR LOOK MASS-PRODUCED, BUT HE'S ABLE TO CROSS SWORDS WITH AOSHI-SAMA EQUALLY?
NO.
IT IS NOT "EQUAL."
KANG KANG KANG KANG KANG KANG KANG

READ THIS WAY

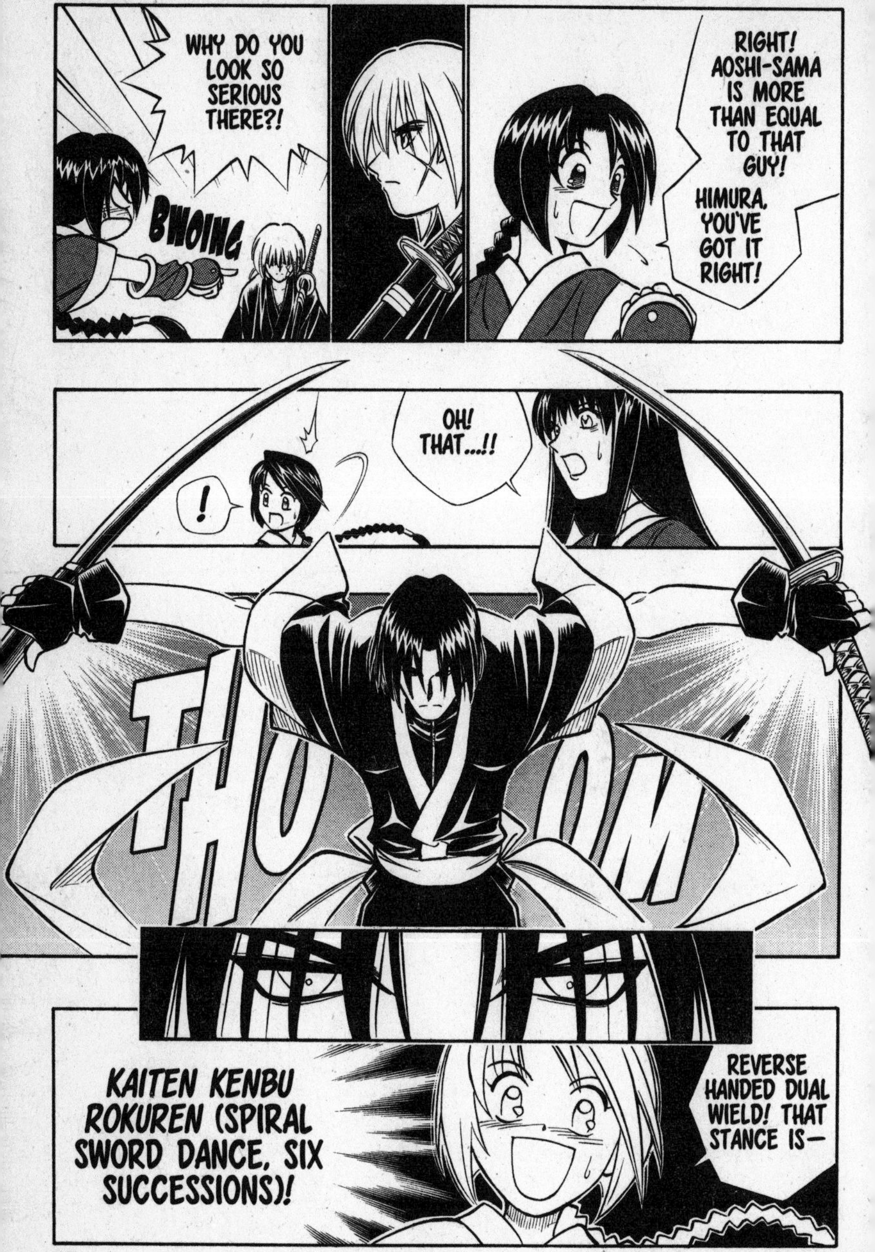
RIGHT! AOSHI-SAMA IS MORE THAN EQUAL TO THAT GUY!
HIMURA, YOU'VE GOT IT RIGHT!
WHY DO YOU LOOK SO SERIOUS THERE?!
BWOING
OH! THAT...!!
!
THOOM
REVERSE HANDED DUAL WIELD! THAT STANCE IS—
KAITEN KENBU ROKUREN (SPIRAL SWORD DANCE, SIX SUCCESSIONS)!

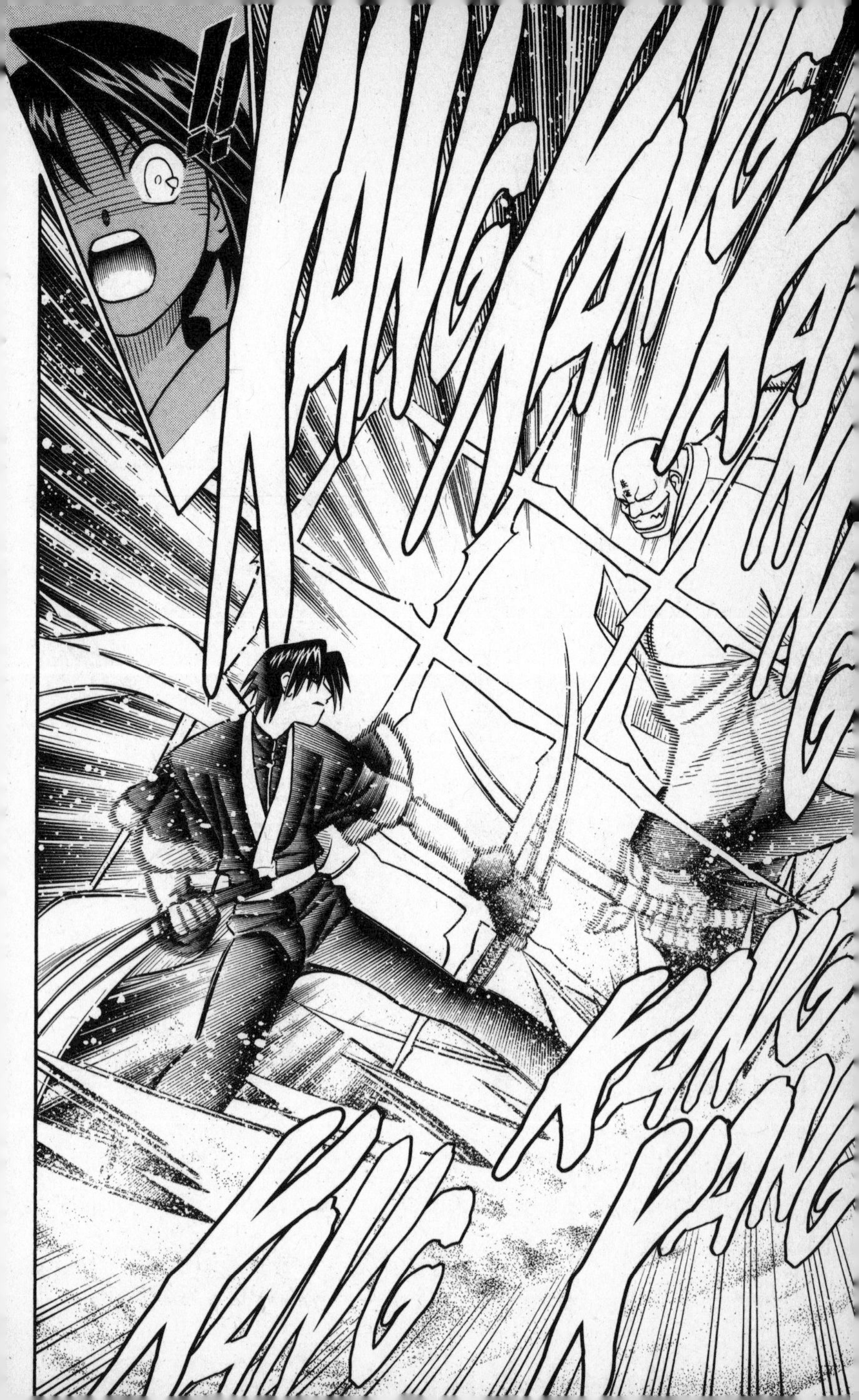

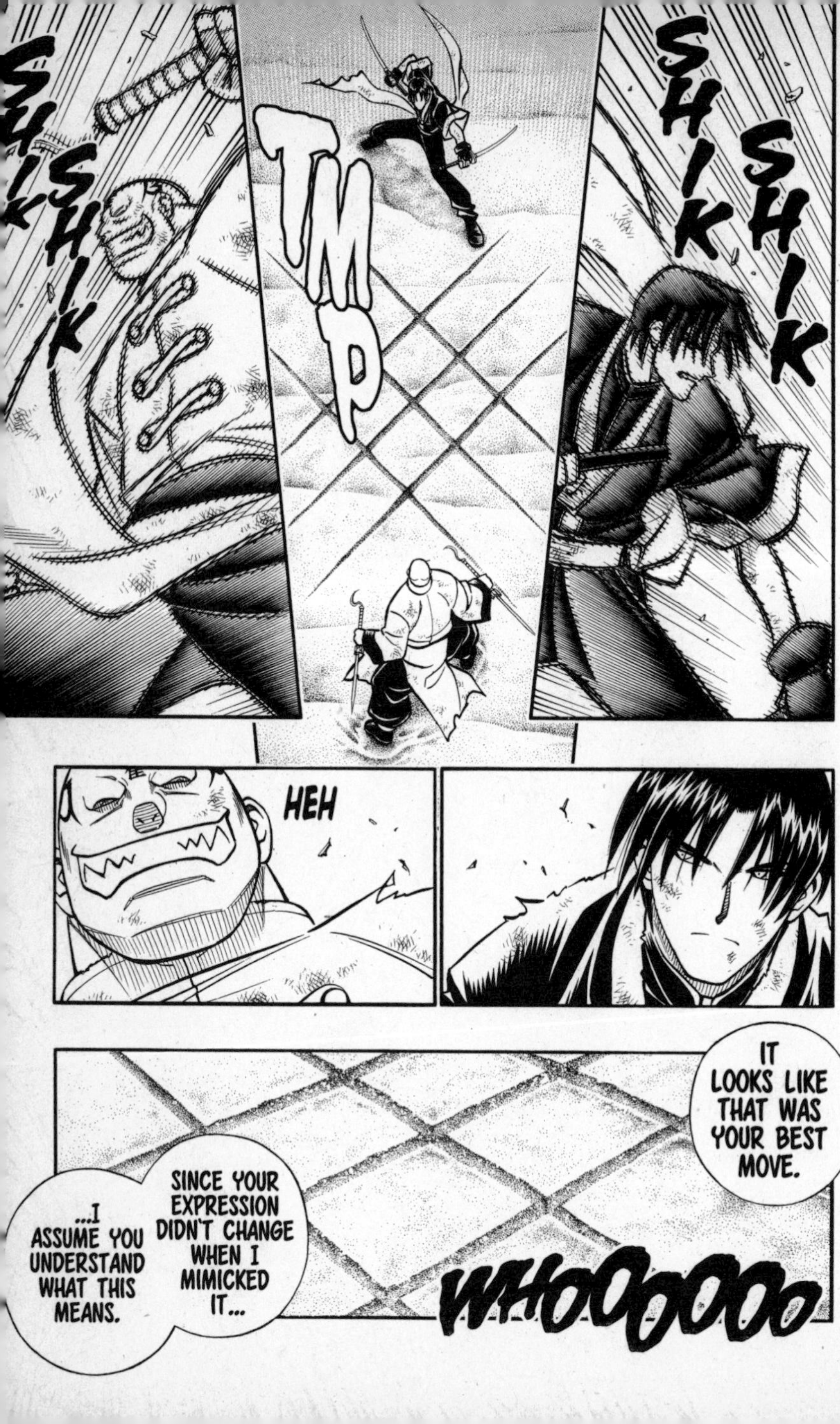
SHIK SHIK
TMP
SHIK SHIK
HEH
IT LOOKS LIKE THAT WAS YOUR BEST MOVE.
SINCE YOUR EXPRESSION DIDN'T CHANGE WHEN I MIMICKED IT...
...I ASSUME YOU UNDERSTAND WHAT THIS MEANS.
WHOOOOOO

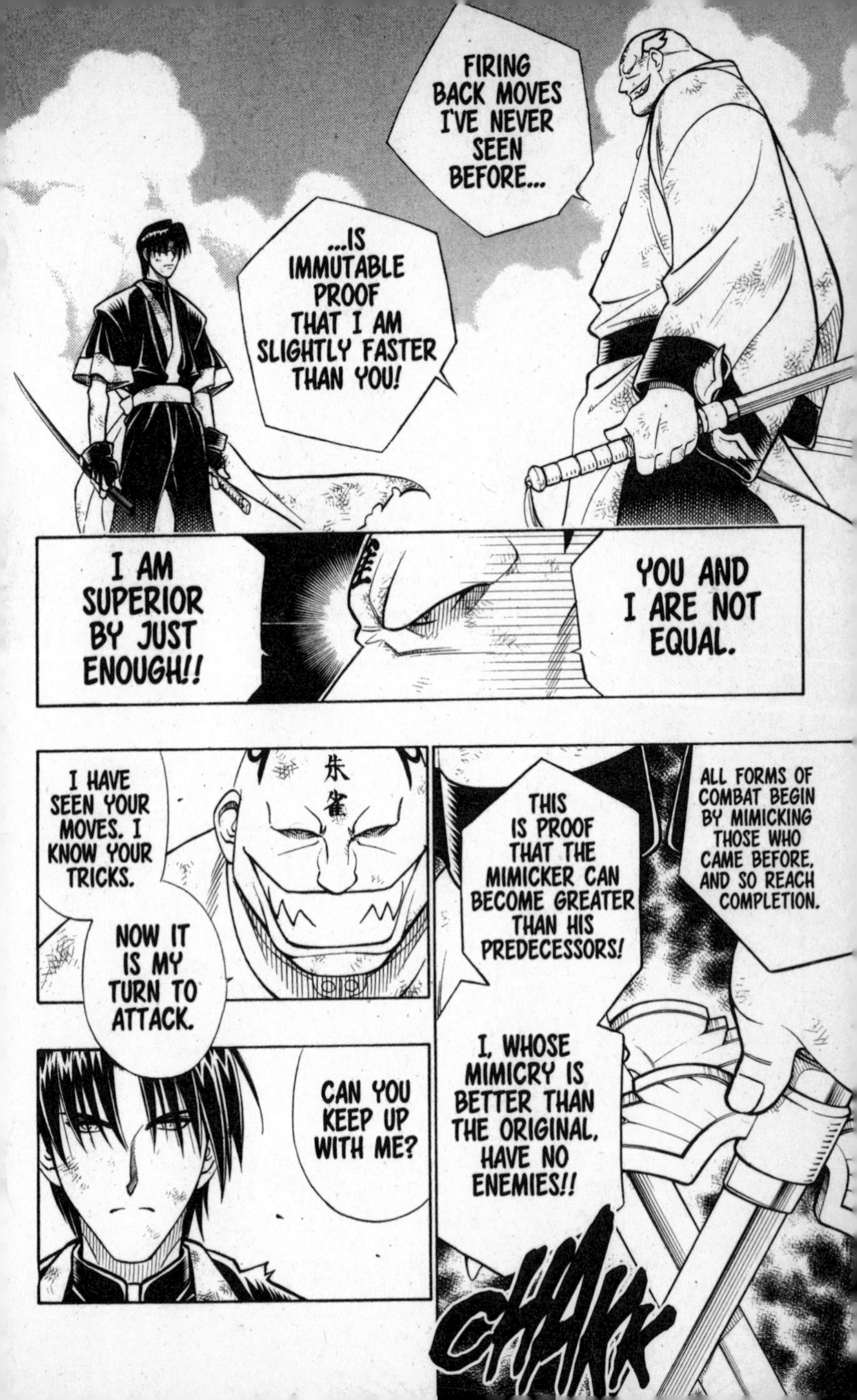
FIRING BACK MOVES I'VE NEVER SEEN BEFORE...
...IS IMMUTABLE PROOF THAT I AM SLIGHTLY FASTER THAN YOU!
YOU AND I ARE NOT EQUAL.
I AM SUPERIOR BY JUST ENOUGH!!
ALL FORMS OF COMBAT BEGIN BY MIMICKING THOSE WHO CAME BEFORE, AND SO REACH COMPLETION.
THIS IS PROOF THAT THE MIMICKER CAN BECOME GREATER THAN HIS PREDECESSORS!
I, WHOSE MIMICRY IS BETTER THAN THE ORIGINAL, HAVE NO ENEMIES!!
CHAK
I HAVE SEEN YOUR MOVES. I KNOW YOUR TRICKS.
NOW IT IS MY TURN TO ATTACK.
CAN YOU KEEP UP WITH ME?

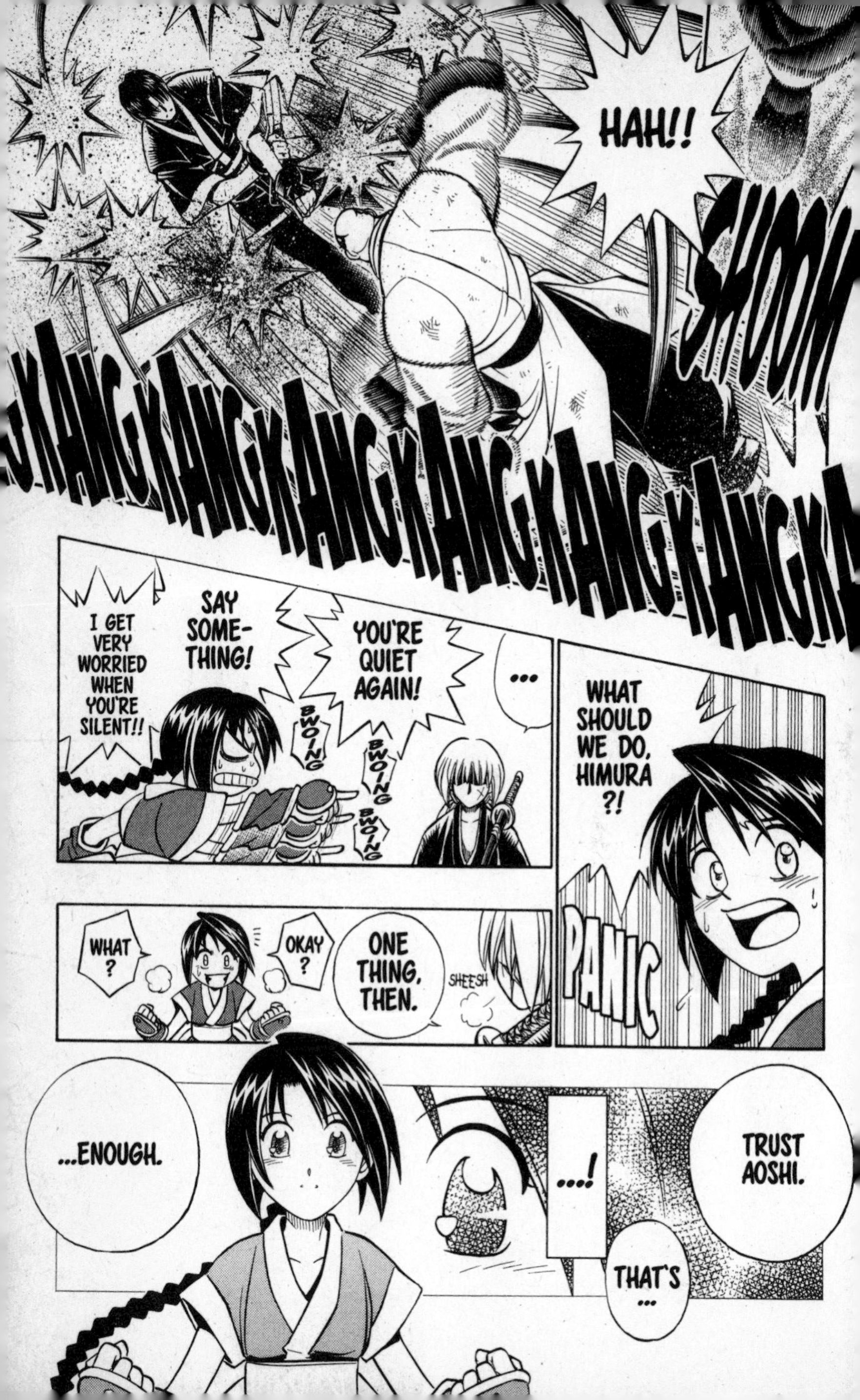
HAH!!
SHOOM
KANG KANG KANG KANG KANG KANG KANG
WHAT SHOULD WE DO, HIMURA?!
PANIC
...
YOU'RE QUIET AGAIN!
SAY SOME-THING!
I GET VERY WORRIED WHEN YOU'RE SILENT!!
BWOING BWOING BWOING
SHEESH
ONE THING, THEN.
OKAY?
WHAT?
TRUST AOSHI.
THAT'S...
...!
...ENOUGH.

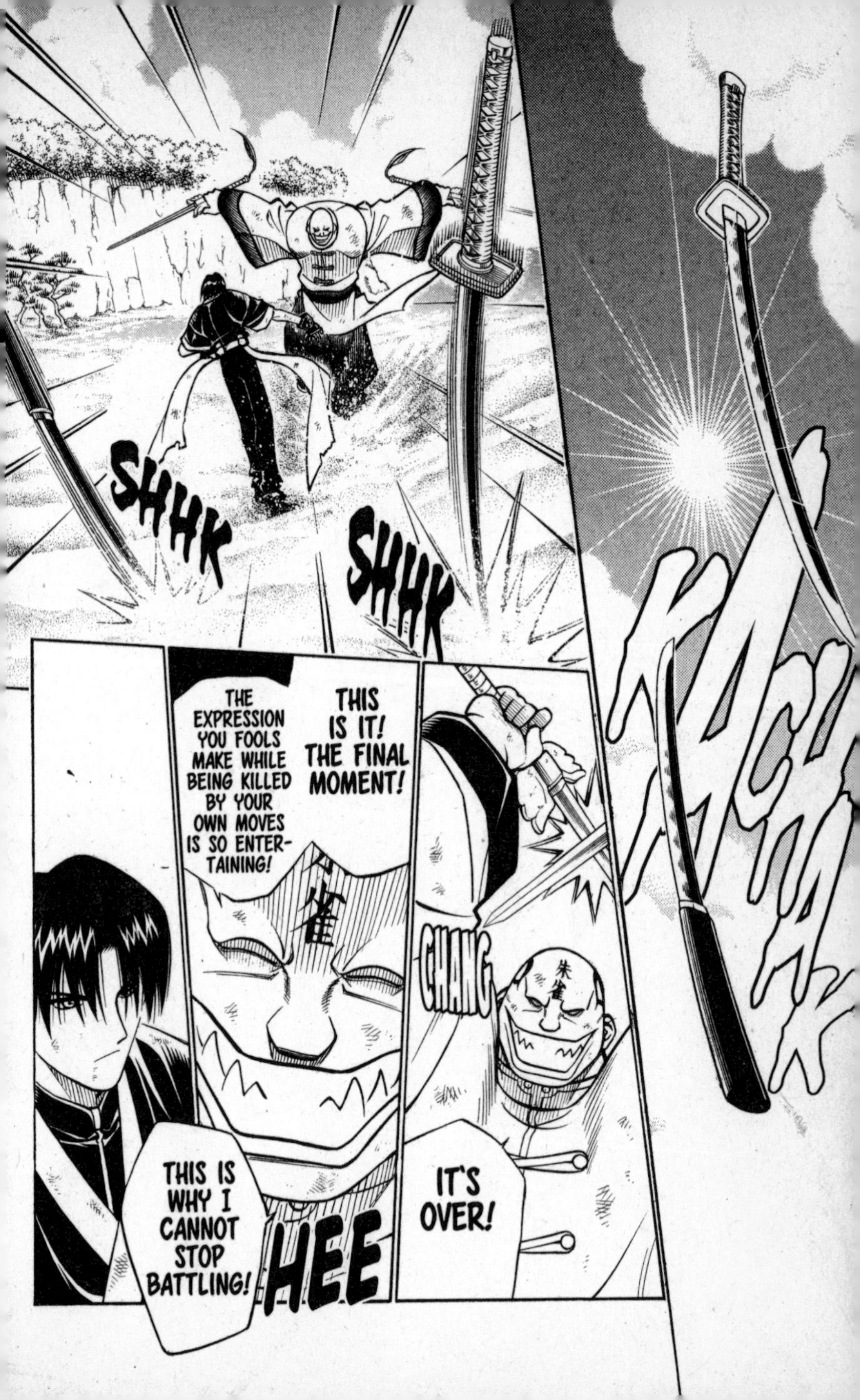
SHHK
SHHK
CHANG
IT'S OVER!
THIS IS IT! THE FINAL MOMENT!
THE EXPRESSION YOU FOOLS MAKE WHILE BEING KILLED BY YOUR OWN MOVES IS SO ENTERTAINING!
HEE
THIS IS WHY I CANNOT STOP BATTLING!

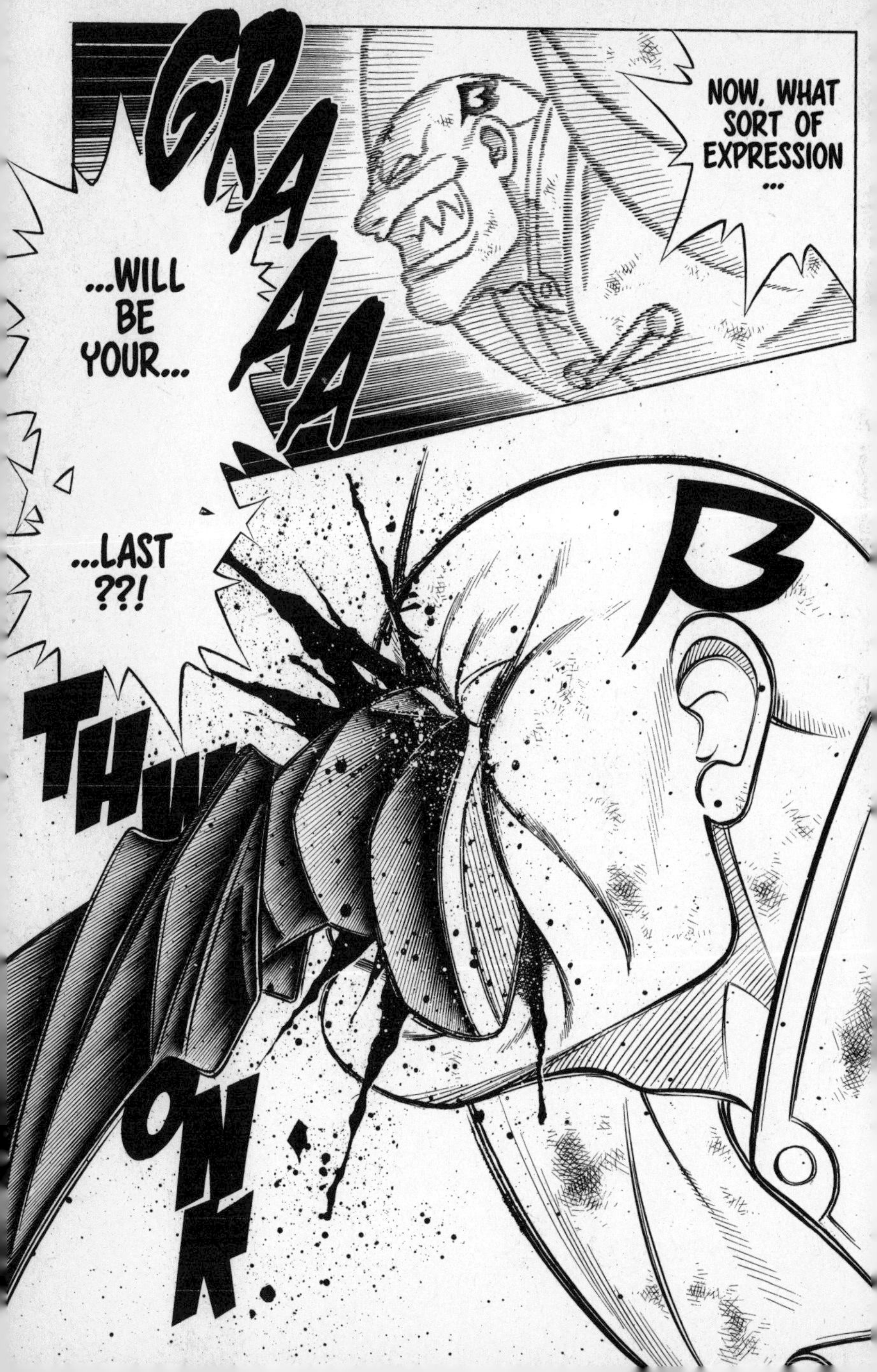
NOW, WHAT SORT OF EXPRESSION ...
GRAAAA
...WILL BE YOUR...
...LAST ??!
THWONK.

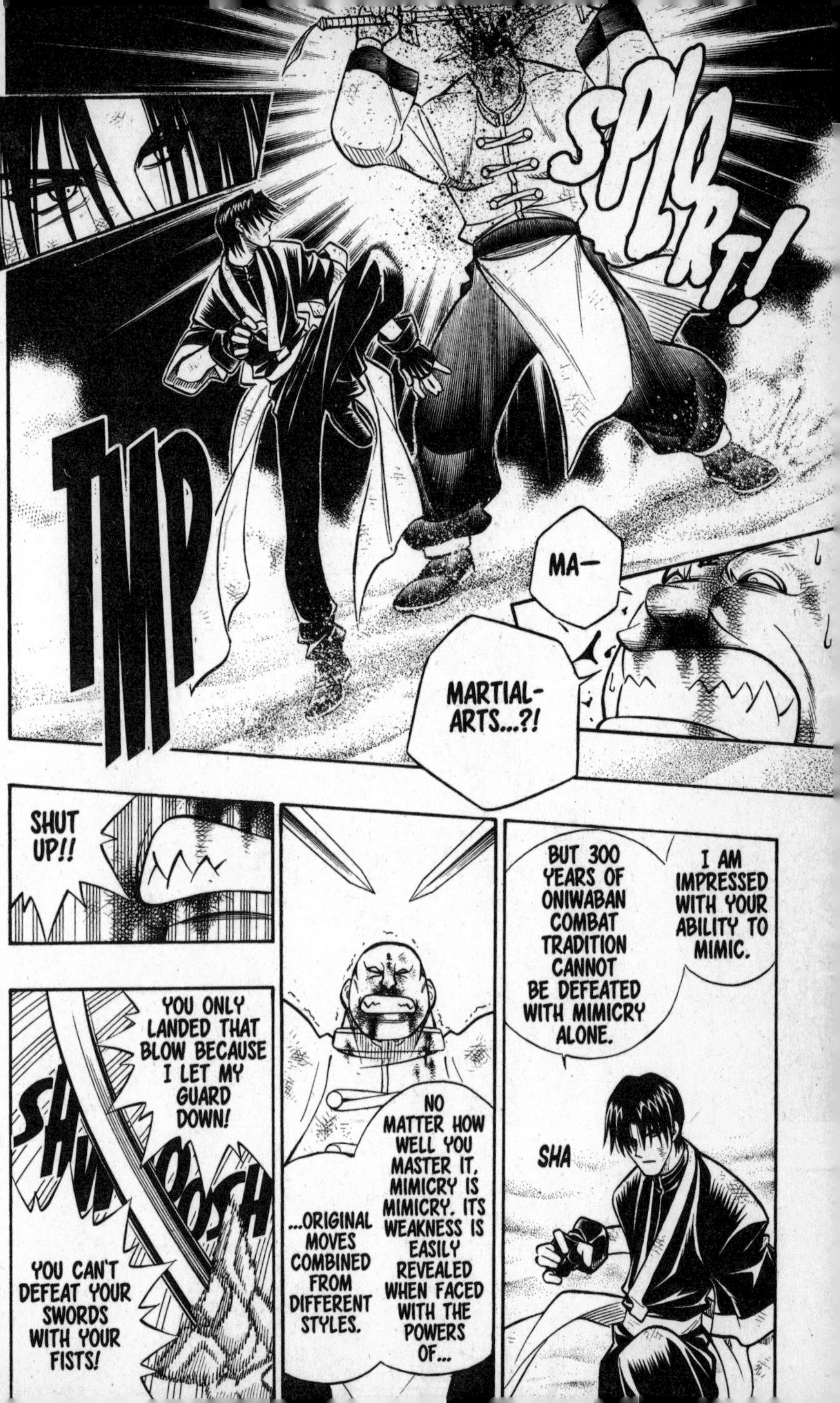
SPLORT!
TMP
MA—
MARTIAL-ARTS...?!
I AM IMPRESSED WITH YOUR ABILITY TO MIMIC.
BUT 300 YEARS OF ONIWABAN COMBAT TRADITION CANNOT BE DEFEATED WITH MIMICRY ALONE.
SHA
NO MATTER HOW WELL YOU MASTER IT, MIMICRY IS MIMICRY. ITS WEAKNESS IS EASILY REVEALED WHEN FACED WITH THE POWERS OF...
...ORIGINAL MOVES COMBINED FROM DIFFERENT STYLES.
SHUT UP!!
YOU ONLY LANDED THAT BLOW BECAUSE I LET MY GUARD DOWN!
SHWOOSH
YOU CAN'T DEFEAT YOUR SWORDS WITH YOUR FISTS!

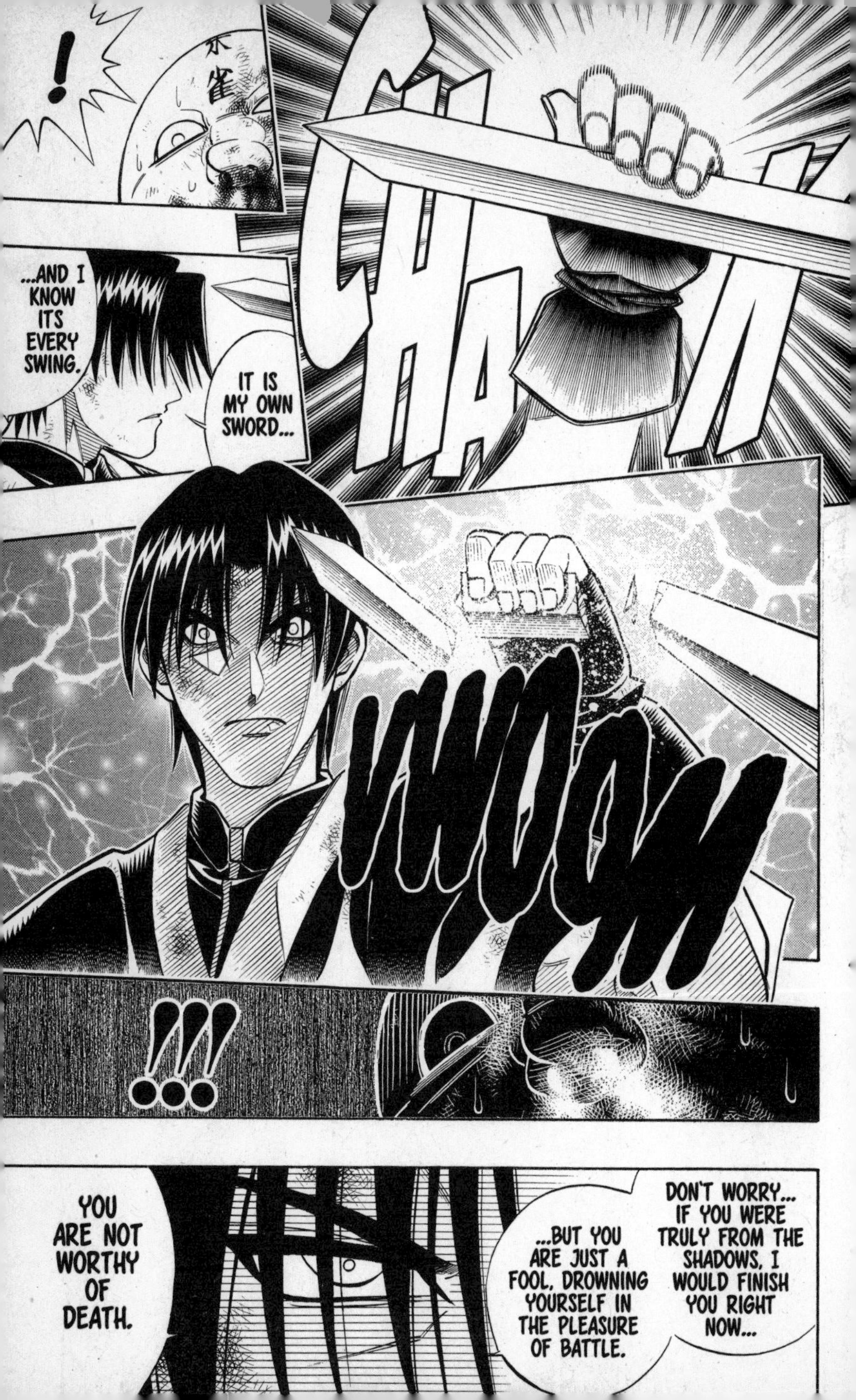

CHAN
!
IT IS MY OWN SWORD...
...AND I KNOW ITS EVERY SWING.
VWOOM
!!!
DON'T WORRY... IF YOU WERE TRULY FROM THE SHADOWS, I WOULD FINISH YOU RIGHT NOW...
...BUT YOU ARE JUST A FOOL, DROWNING YOURSELF IN THE PLEASURE OF BATTLE.
YOU ARE NOT WORTHY OF DEATH.

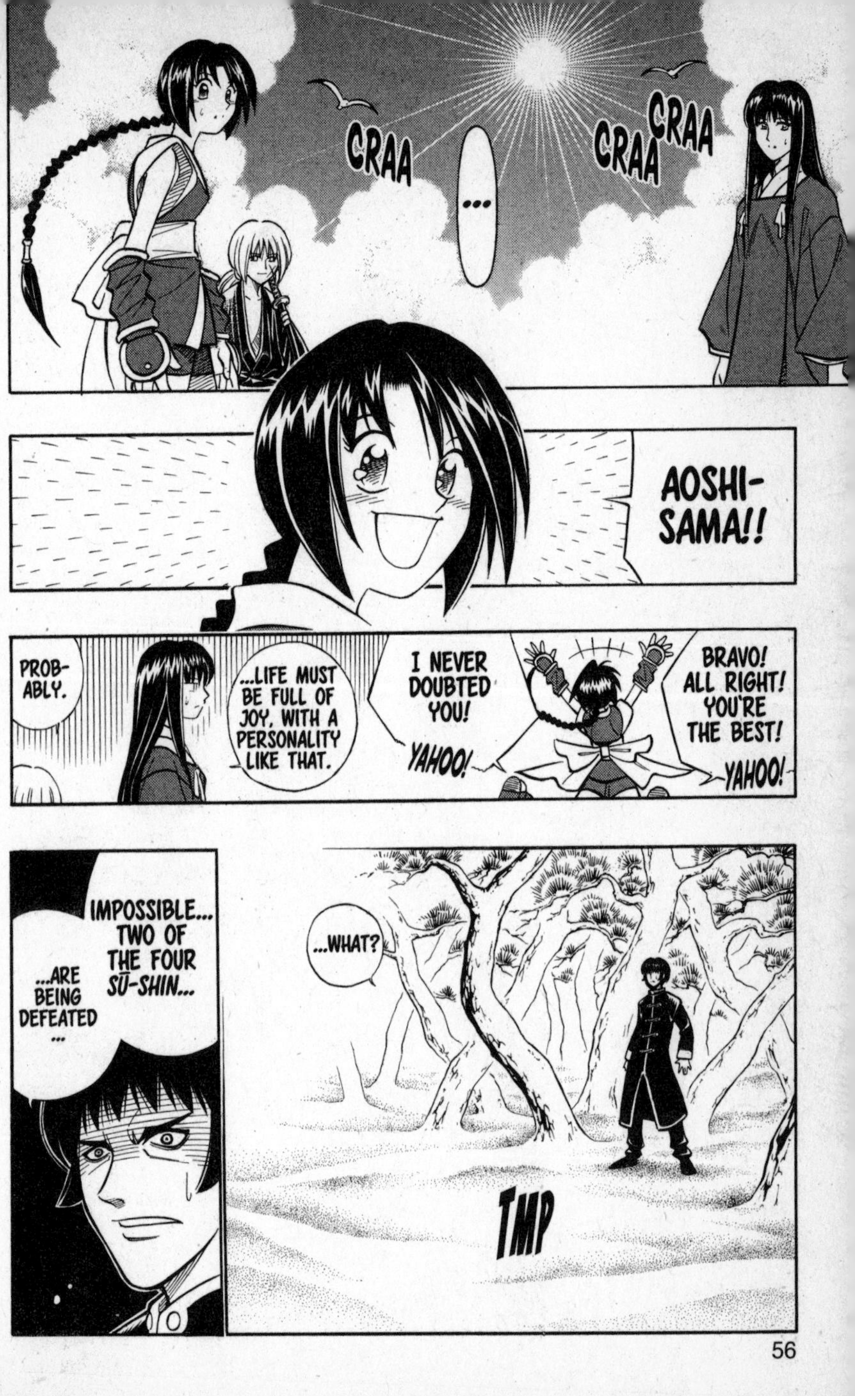
CRAA
CRAA
...
CRAA
AOSHI-SAMA!!
BRAVO! ALL RIGHT! YOU'RE THE BEST!
YAHOO!
I NEVER DOUBTED YOU!
YAHOO!
...LIFE MUST BE FULL OF JOY, WITH A PERSONALITY LIKE THAT.
PROB-ABLY.
...WHAT?
TMP
IMPOSSIBLE... TWO OF THE FOUR SŪ-SHIN...
...ARE BEING DEFEATED...

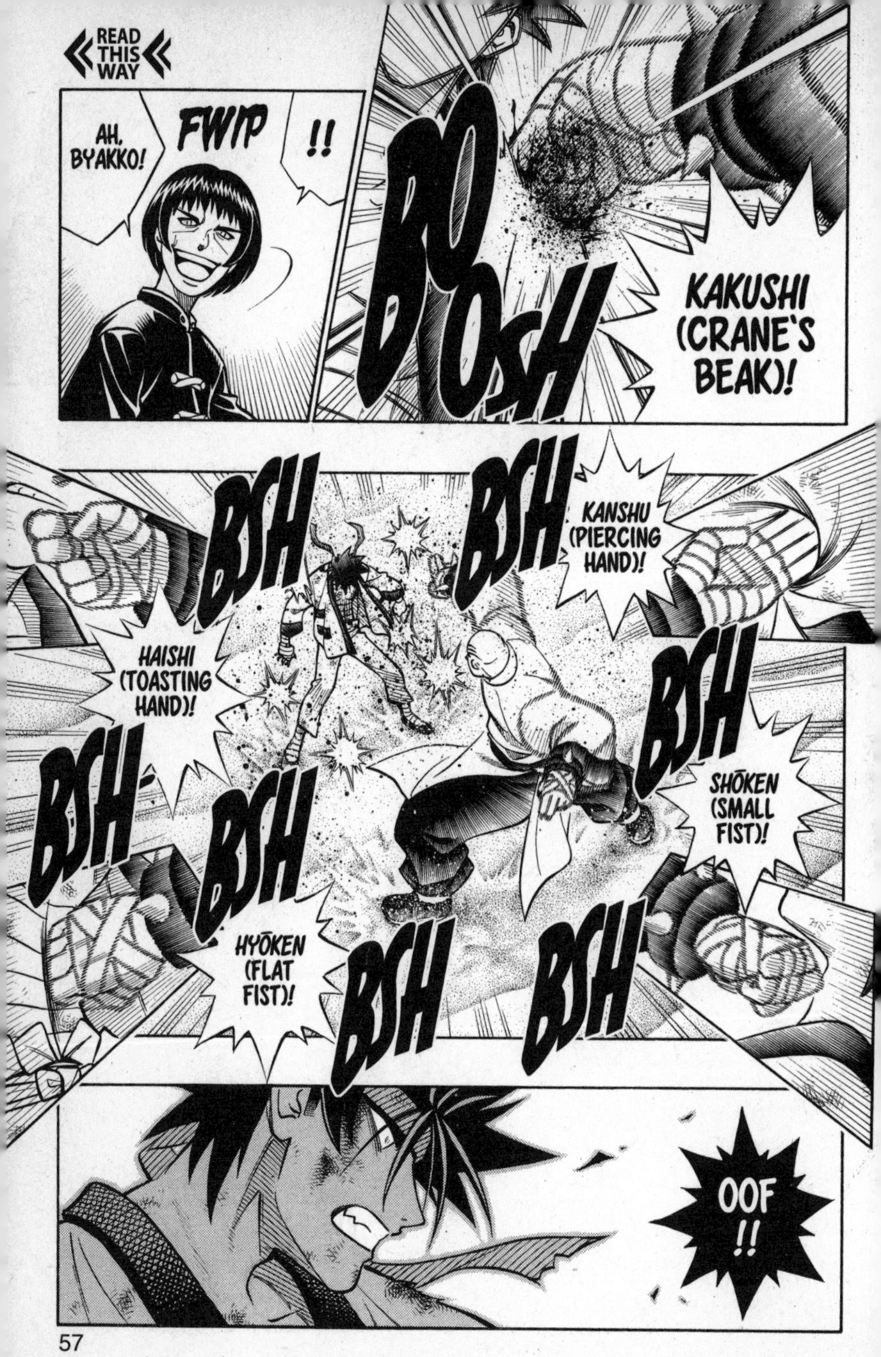
READ THIS WAY
BDOOSH
KAKUSHI (CRANE'S BEAK)!
!!
FWIP
AH, BYAKKO!
KANSHU (PIERCING HAND)!
BSH
BSH
HAISHI (TOASTING HAND)!
BSH
SHŌKEN (SMALL FIST)!
BSH
BSH
BSH
HYŌKEN (FLAT FIST)!
BSH
OOF !!

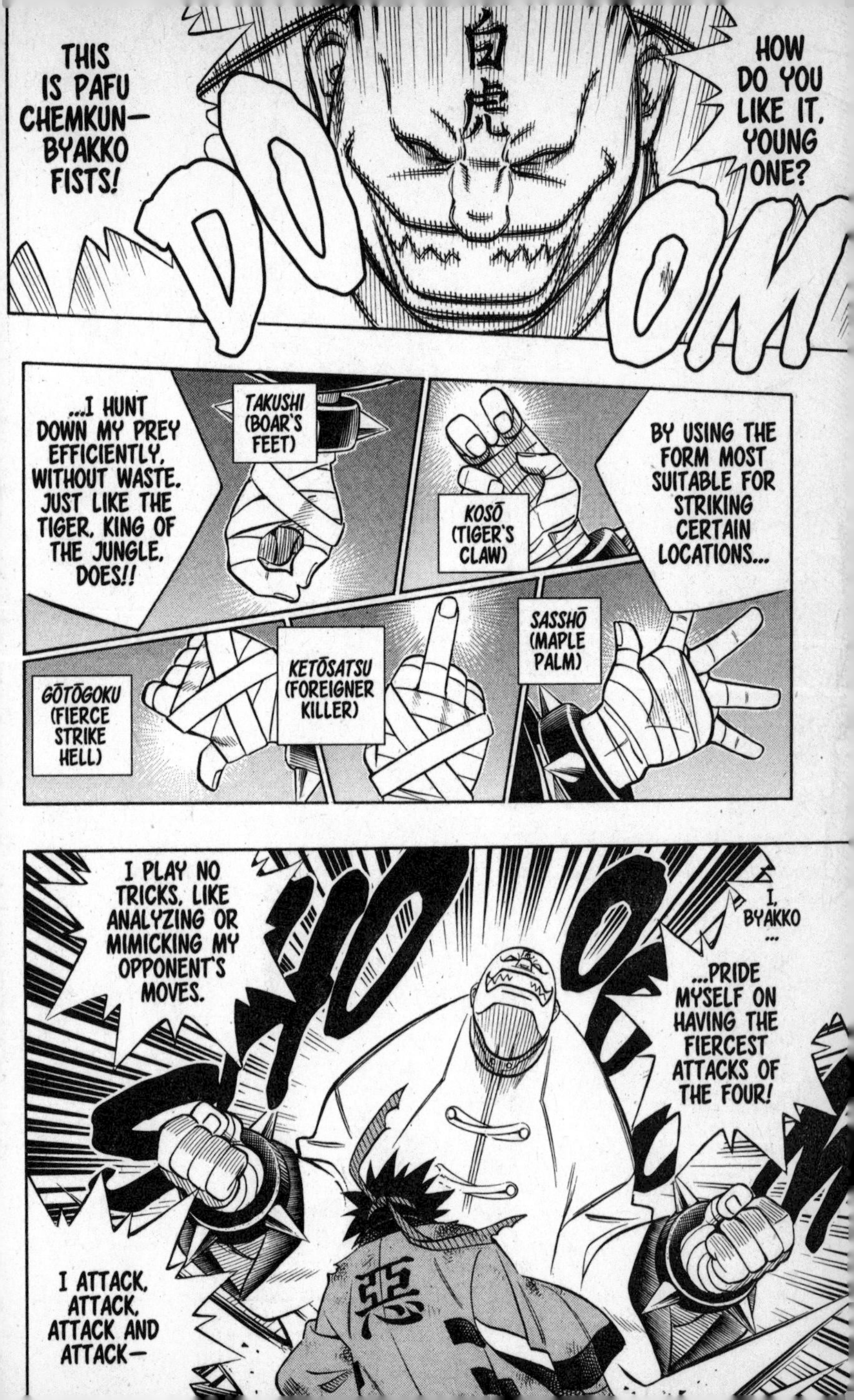
HOW DO YOU LIKE IT, YOUNG ONE?
白虎
THIS IS PAFU CHEMKUN—BYAKKO FISTS!
DOOOM
BY USING THE FORM MOST SUITABLE FOR STRIKING CERTAIN LOCATIONS...
KOSŌ (TIGER'S CLAW)
TAKUSHI (BOAR'S FEET)
...I HUNT DOWN MY PREY EFFICIENTLY, WITHOUT WASTE. JUST LIKE THE TIGER, KING OF THE JUNGLE, DOES!!
SASSHŌ (MAPLE PALM)
KETŌSATSU (FOREIGNER KILLER)
GŌTŌGOKU (FIERCE STRIKE HELL)
I, BYAKKO...
...PRIDE MYSELF ON HAVING THE FIERCEST ATTACKS OF THE FOUR!
I PLAY NO TRICKS, LIKE ANALYZING OR MIMICKING MY OPPONENT'S MOVES.
DOOOM
悪
I ATTACK, ATTACK, ATTACK AND ATTACK—

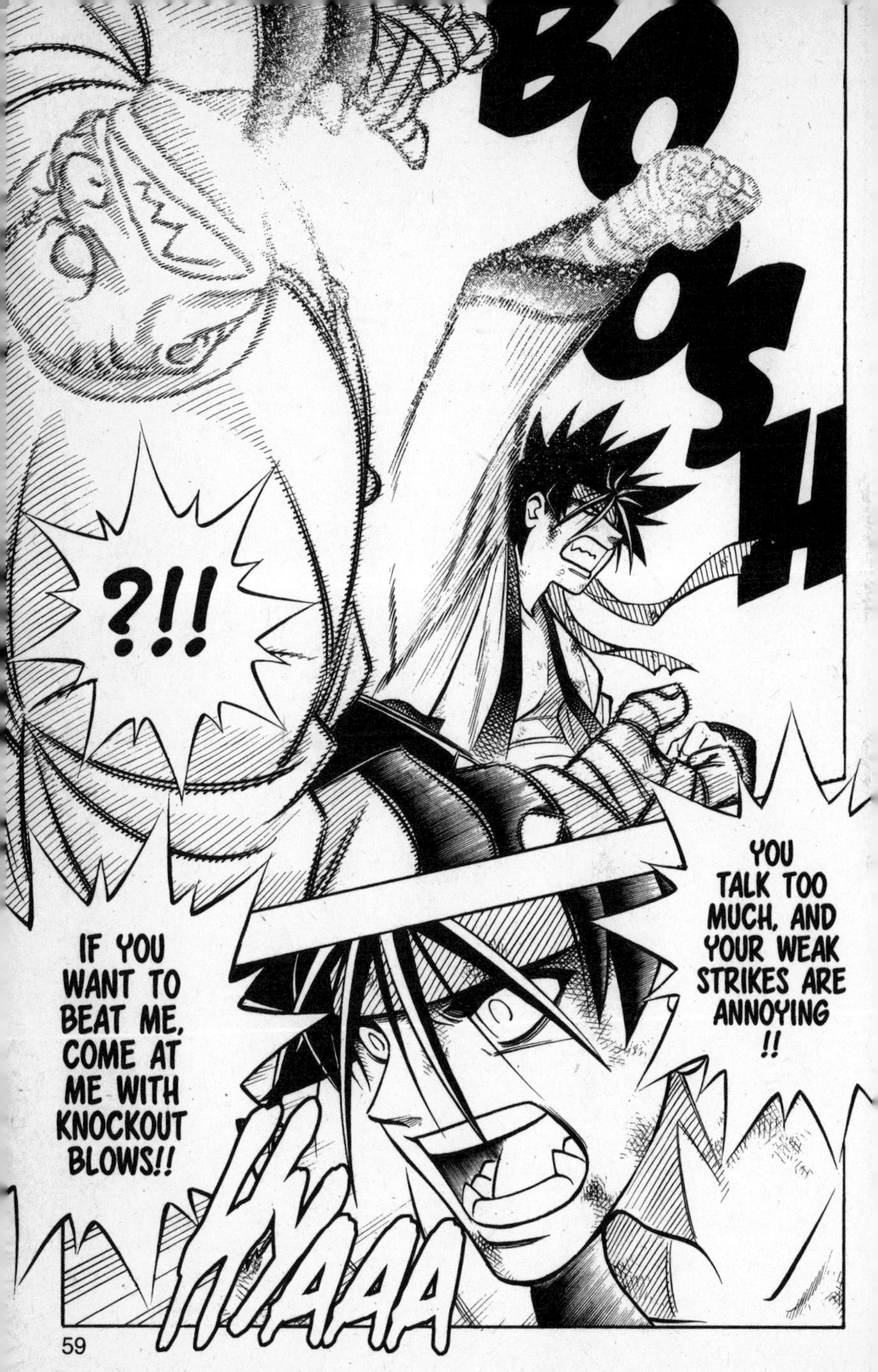

BOOSH
?!!
YOU TALK TOO MUCH, AND YOUR WEAK STRIKES ARE ANNOYING !!
IF YOU WANT TO BEAT ME, COME AT ME WITH KNOCKOUT BLOWS!!
HAAA

Rurouni Kenshin

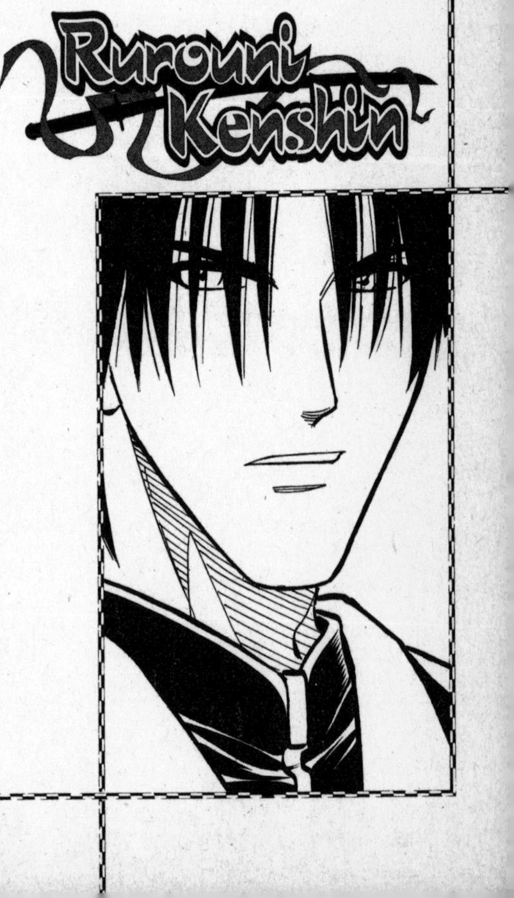

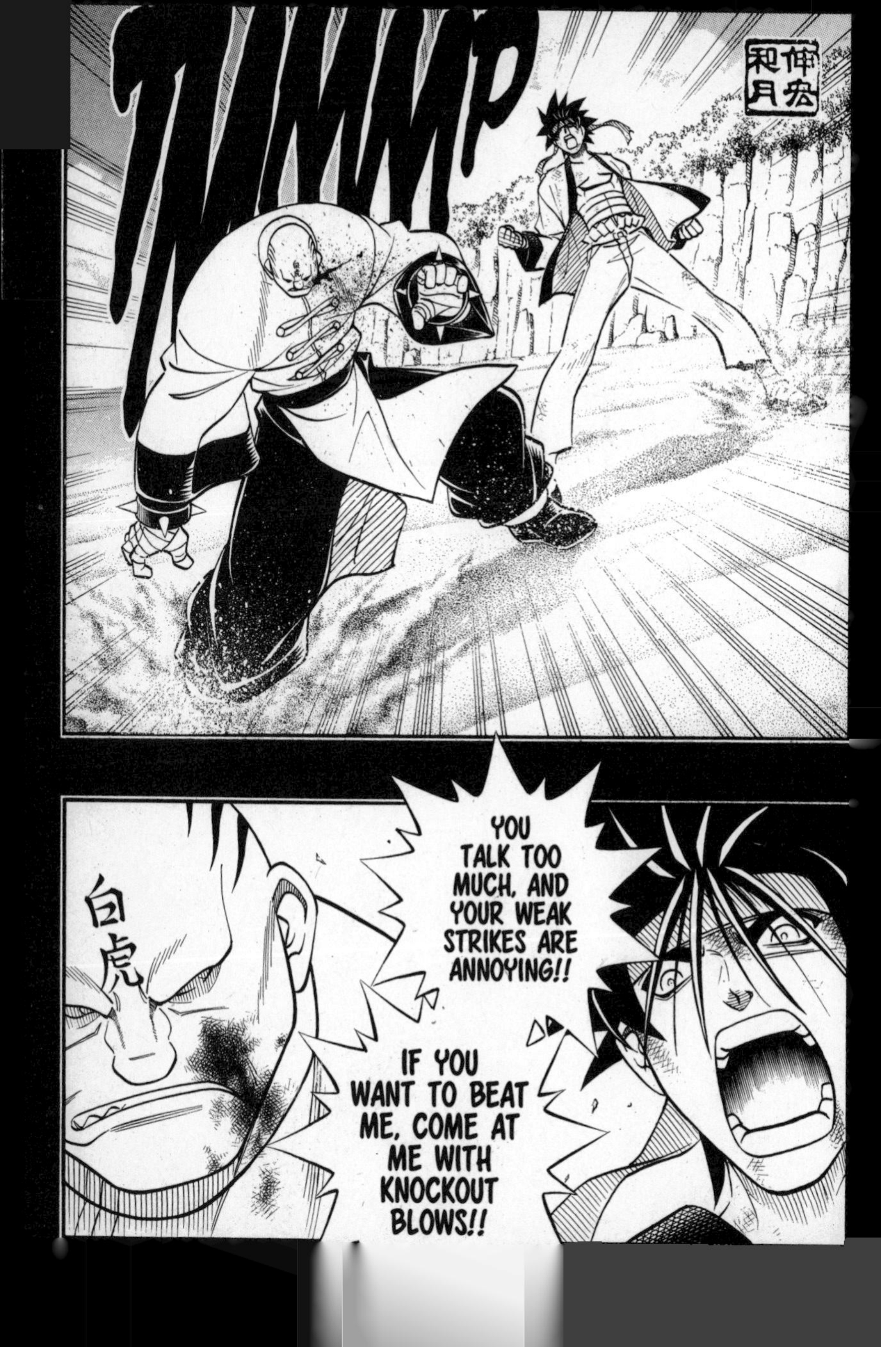
THUMP
YOU TALK TOO MUCH, AND YOUR WEAK STRIKES ARE ANNOYING!!
IF YOU WANT TO BEAT ME, COME AT ME WITH KNOCKOUT BLOWS!!
白虎

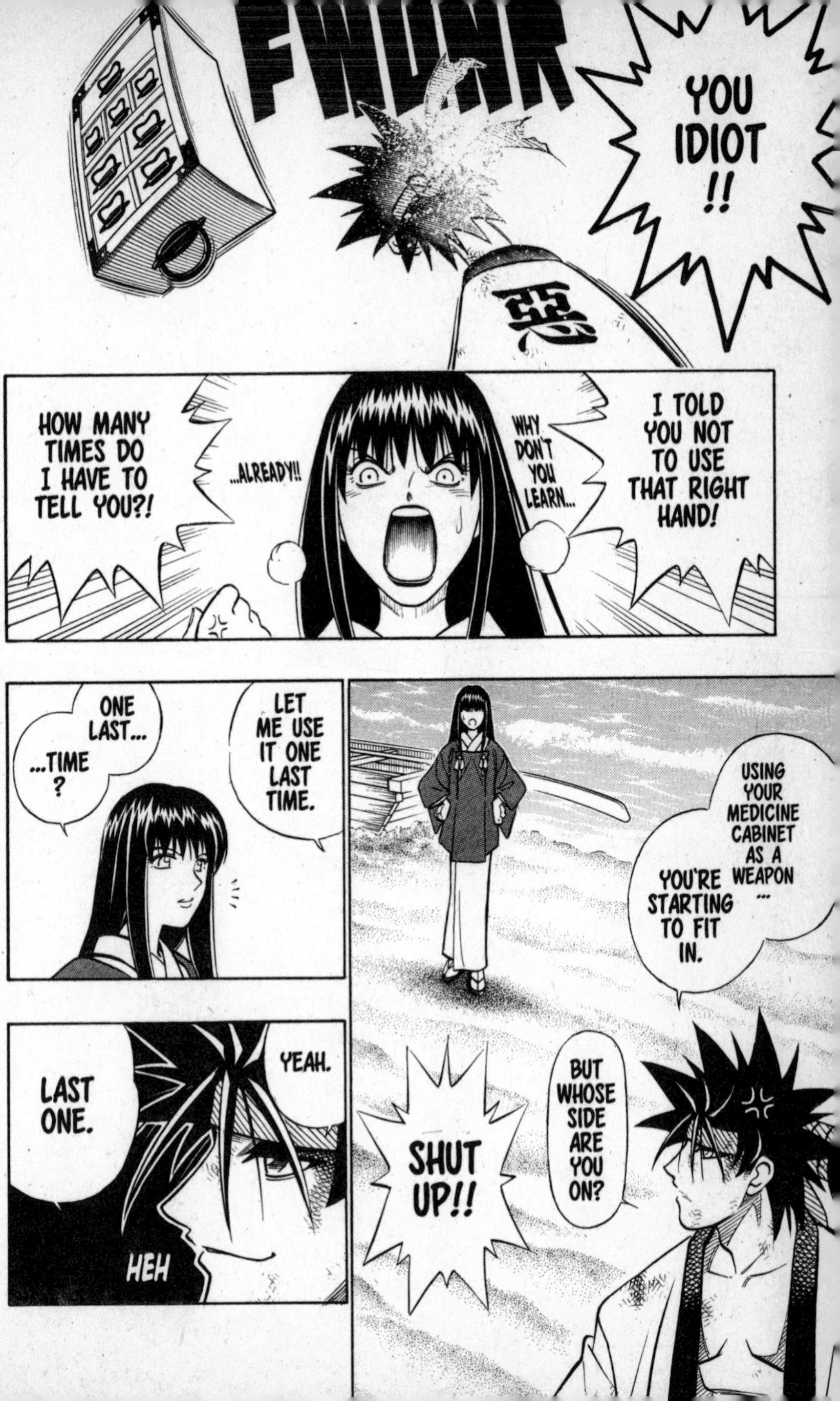
FWUNK
YOU IDIOT!!
I TOLD YOU NOT TO USE THAT RIGHT HAND!
WHY DON'T YOU LEARN...
...ALREADY!!
HOW MANY TIMES DO I HAVE TO TELL YOU?!
USING YOUR MEDICINE CABINET AS A WEAPON...
YOU'RE STARTING TO FIT IN.
BUT WHOSE SIDE ARE YOU ON?
SHUT UP!!
LET ME USE IT ONE LAST TIME.
ONE LAST...
...TIME?
YEAH.
LAST ONE.
HEH

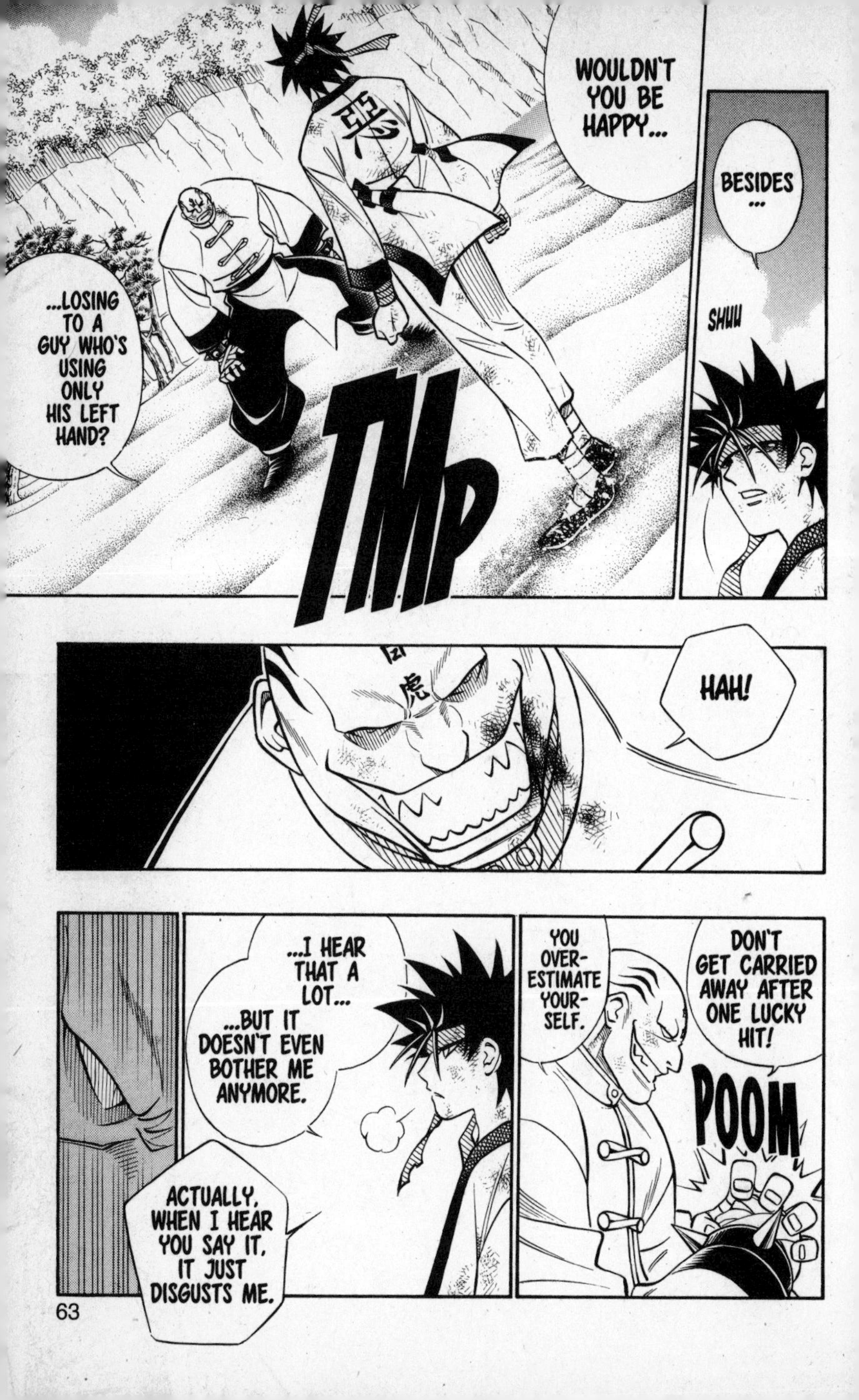
BESIDES...
SHUU
WOULDN'T YOU BE HAPPY...
...LOSING TO A GUY WHO'S USING ONLY HIS LEFT HAND?
TMP
HAH!
DON'T GET CARRIED AWAY AFTER ONE LUCKY HIT!
YOU OVER-ESTIMATE YOUR-SELF.
POOM
...I HEAR THAT A LOT... ...BUT IT DOESN'T EVEN BOTHER ME ANYMORE.
ACTUALLY, WHEN I HEAR YOU SAY IT, IT JUST DISGUSTS ME.

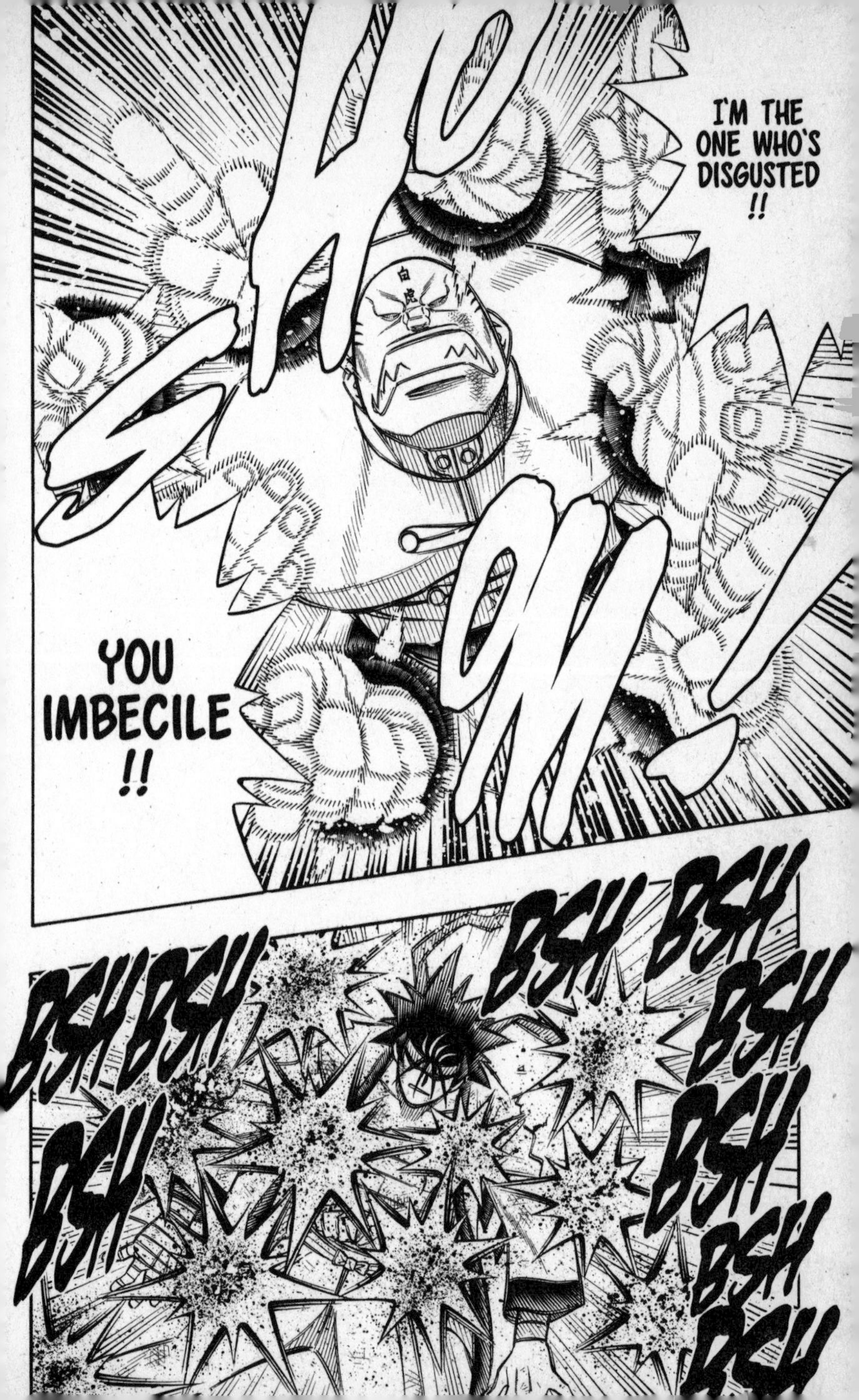
I'M THE ONE WHO'S DISGUSTED !!
YOU IMBECILE !!
BSH BSH BSH BSH BSH BSH BSH BSH
BSH BSH BSH BSH

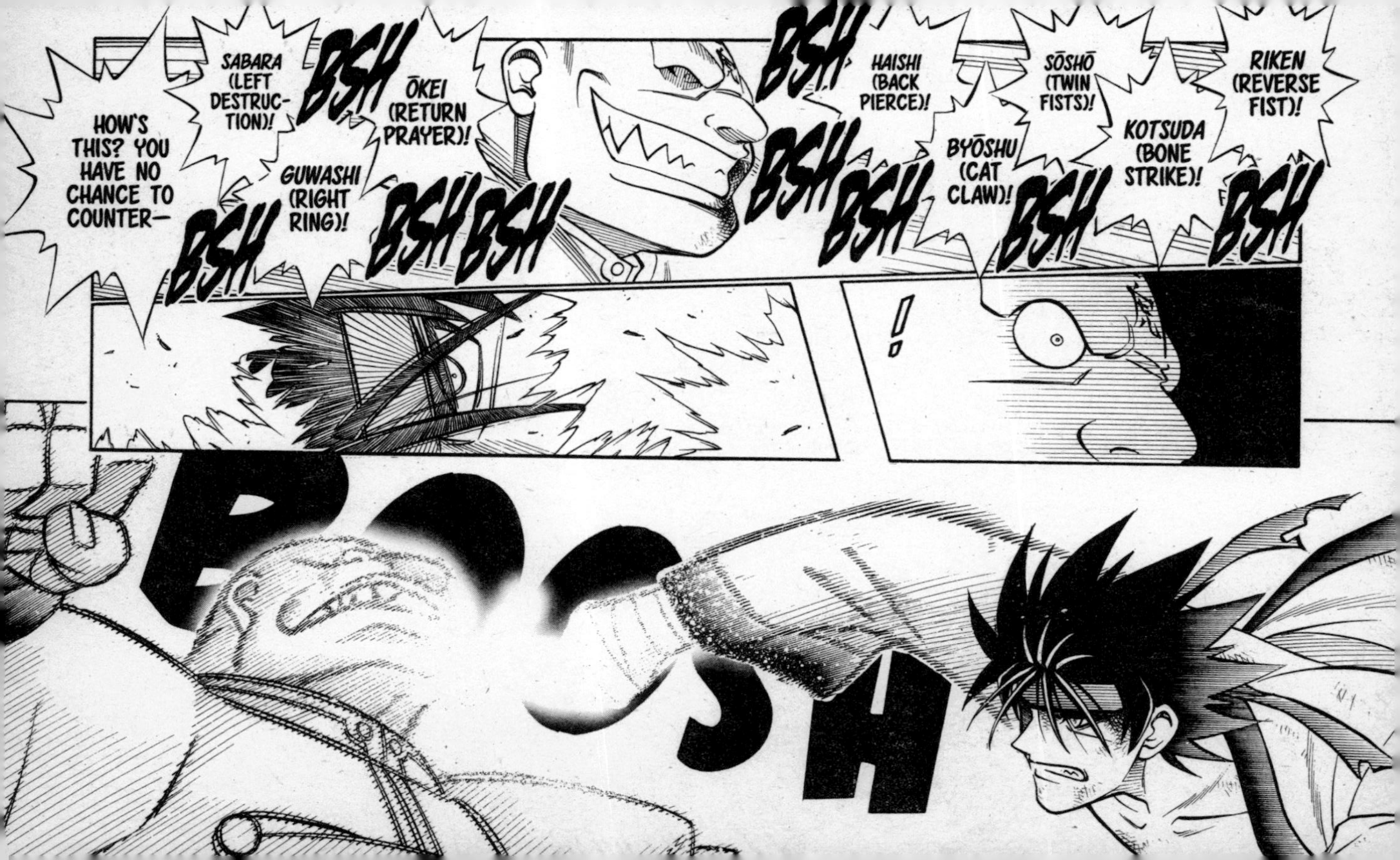
RIKEN (REVERSE FIST)!
BSH
KOTSUDA (BONE STRIKE)!
SŌSHŌ (TWIN FISTS)!
BSH
BYŌSHU (CAT CLAW)!
BSH
HAISHI (BACK PIERCE)!
BSH
BSH
BSH BSH
ŌKEI (RETURN PRAYER)!
BSH
GUWASHI (RIGHT RING)!
SABARA (LEFT DESTRUCTION)!
BSH
HOW'S THIS? YOU HAVE NO CHANCE TO COUNTER—
!
BOOSH

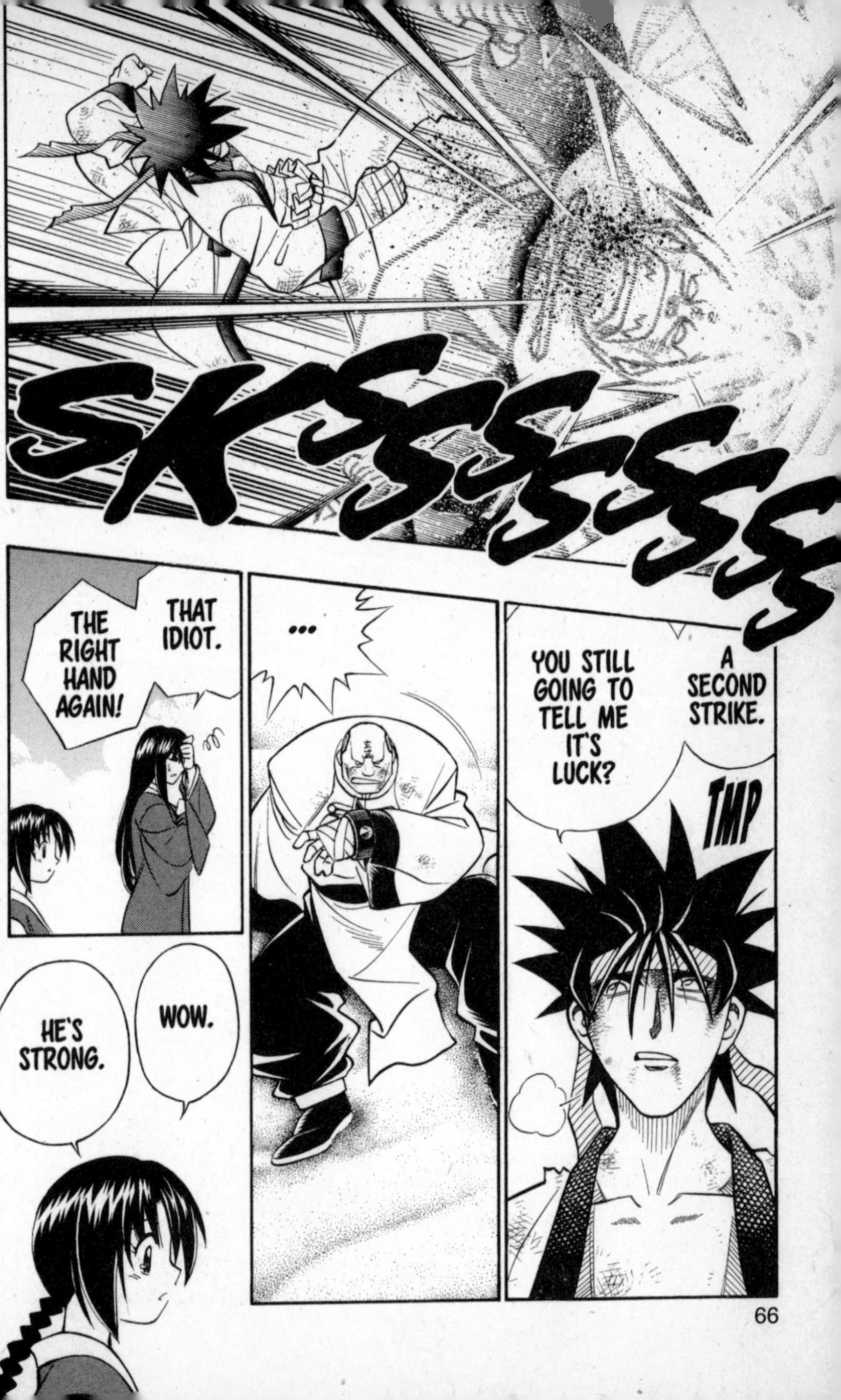
SKSSSSSS
A SECOND STRIKE.
YOU STILL GOING TO TELL ME IT'S LUCK?
TMP
...
THAT IDIOT.
THE RIGHT HAND AGAIN!
WOW.
HE'S STRONG.

READ THIS WAY

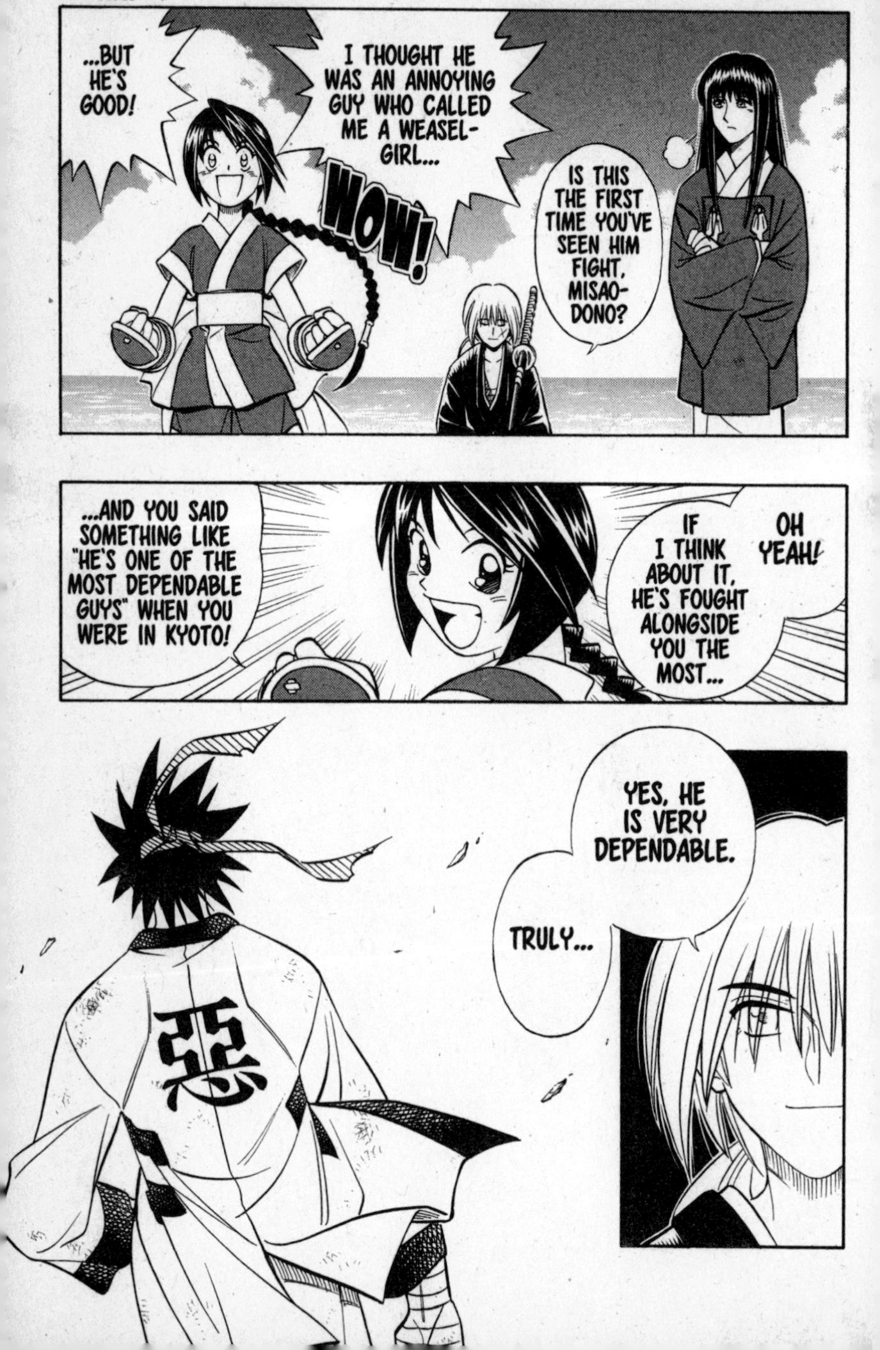
IS THIS THE FIRST TIME YOU'VE SEEN HIM FIGHT, MISAO-DONO?
I THOUGHT HE WAS AN ANNOYING GUY WHO CALLED ME A WEASEL-GIRL...
WOW!
...BUT HE'S GOOD!
OH YEAH!
IF I THINK ABOUT IT, HE'S FOUGHT ALONGSIDE YOU THE MOST...
...AND YOU SAID SOMETHING LIKE "HE'S ONE OF THE MOST DEPENDABLE GUYS" WHEN YOU WERE IN KYOTO!
YES, HE IS VERY DEPENDABLE.
TRULY...

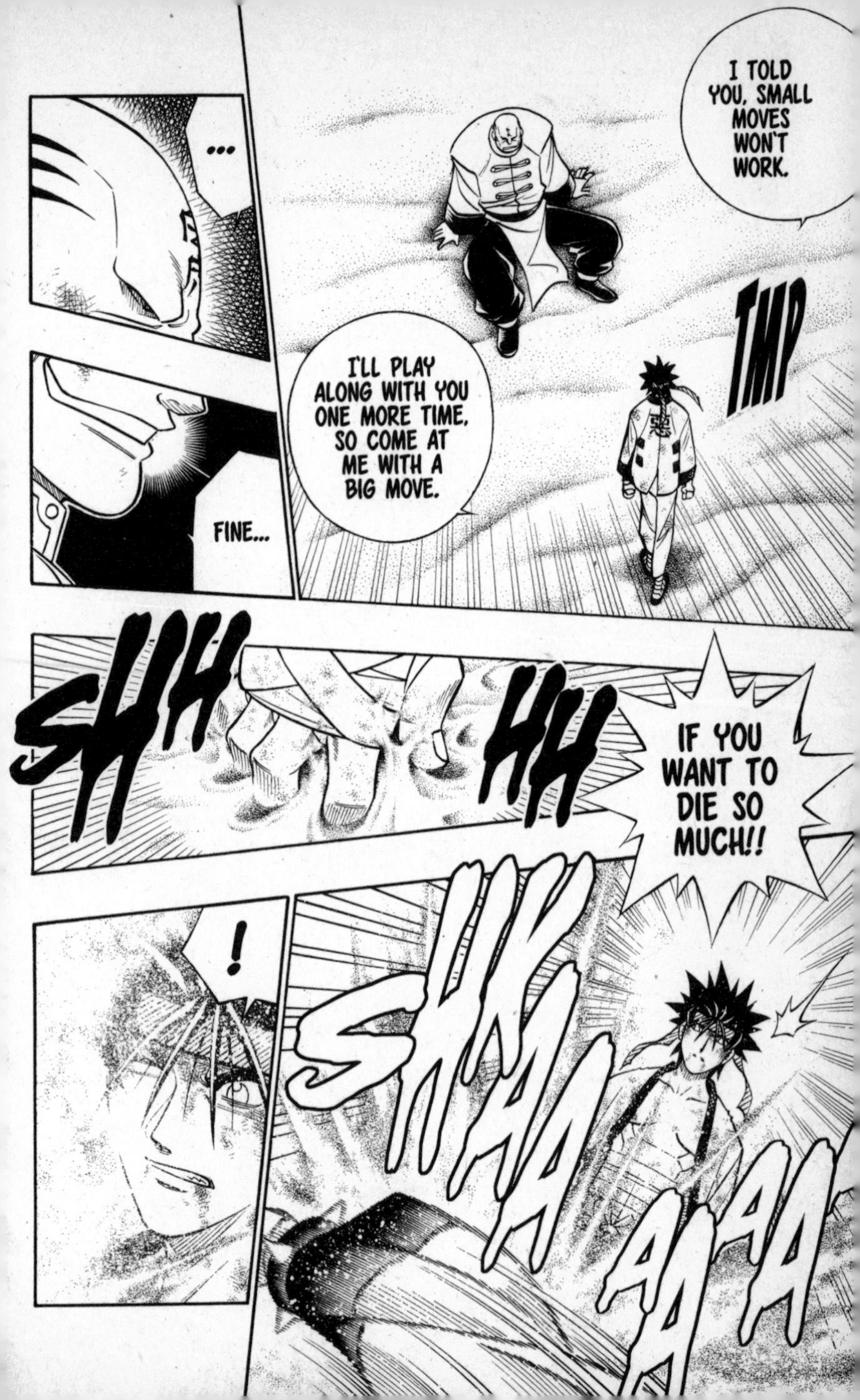
I TOLD YOU, SMALL MOVES WON'T WORK.
TMP
I'LL PLAY ALONG WITH YOU ONE MORE TIME, SO COME AT ME WITH A BIG MOVE.
...
FINE...
IF YOU WANT TO DIE SO MUCH!!
SHH HH
SHHAAAAA
!

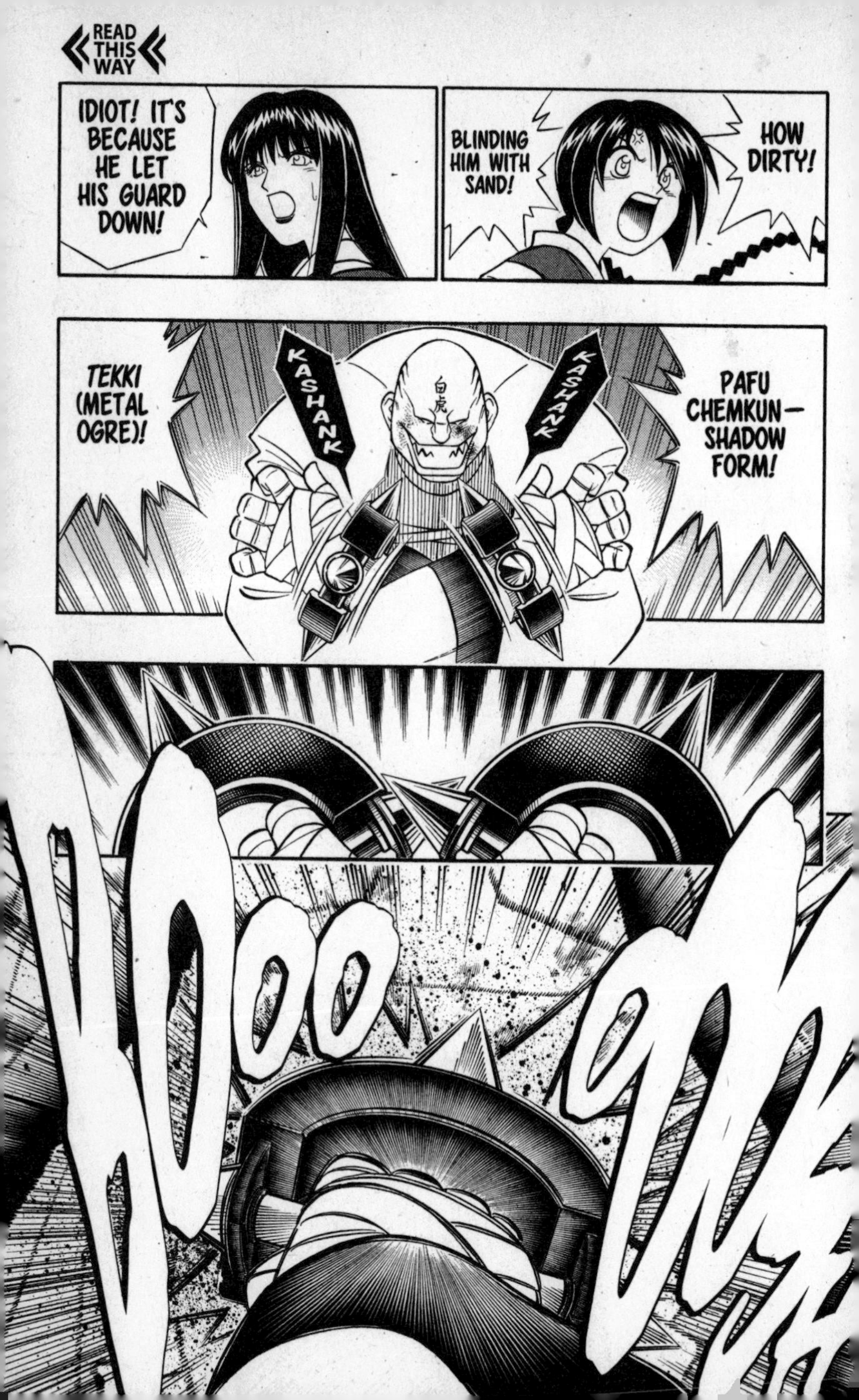
READ THIS WAY
HOW DIRTY!
BLINDING HIM WITH SAND!
IDIOT! IT'S BECAUSE HE LET HIS GUARD DOWN!
PAFU CHEMKUN-SHADOW FORM!
KASHANK
KASHANK
TEKKI (METAL OGRE)!

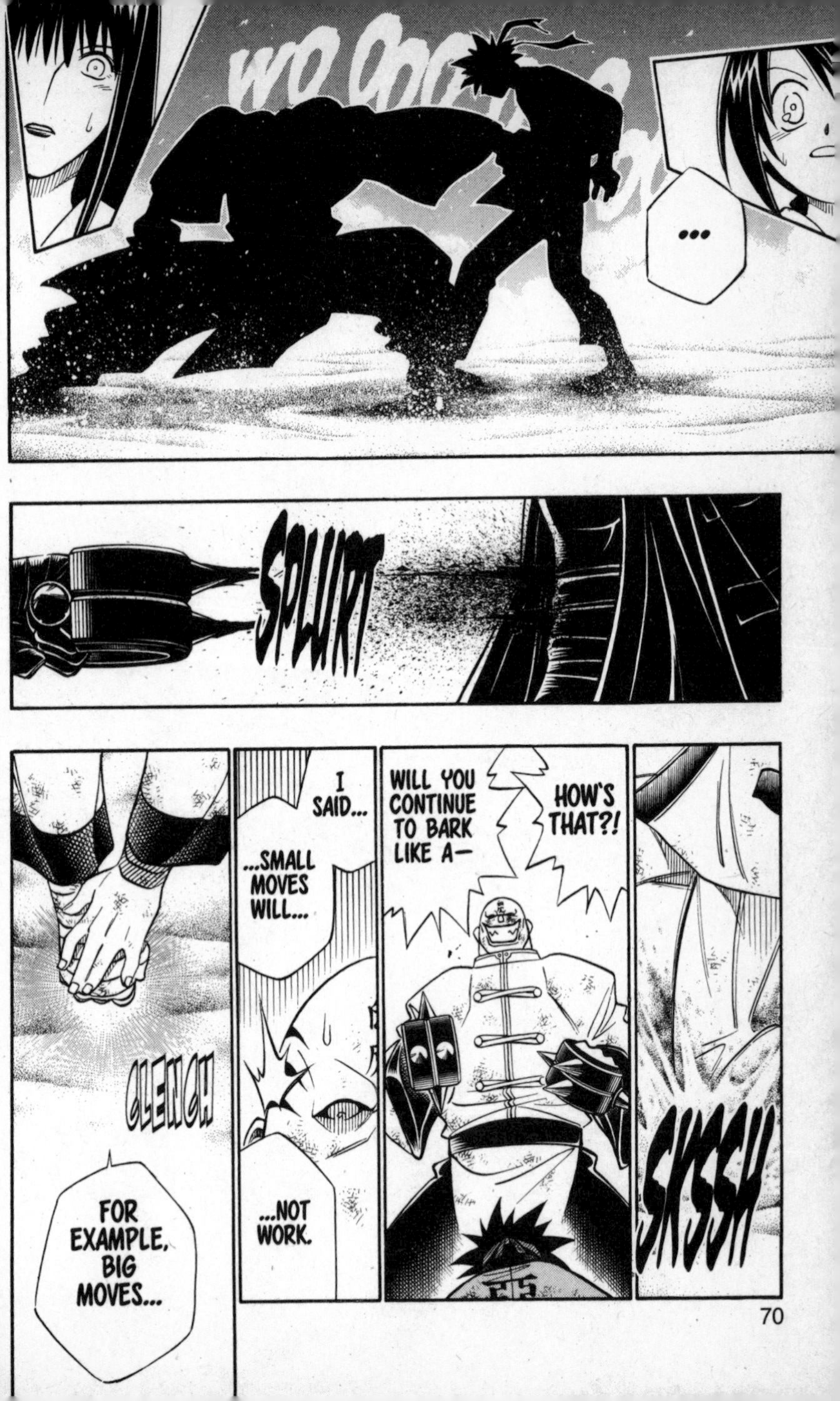
...
SPLURT
SKSSH
HOW'S THAT?!
WILL YOU CONTINUE TO BARK LIKE A—
I SAID...
...SMALL MOVES WILL...
...NOT WORK.
CLENCH
FOR EXAMPLE, BIG MOVES...

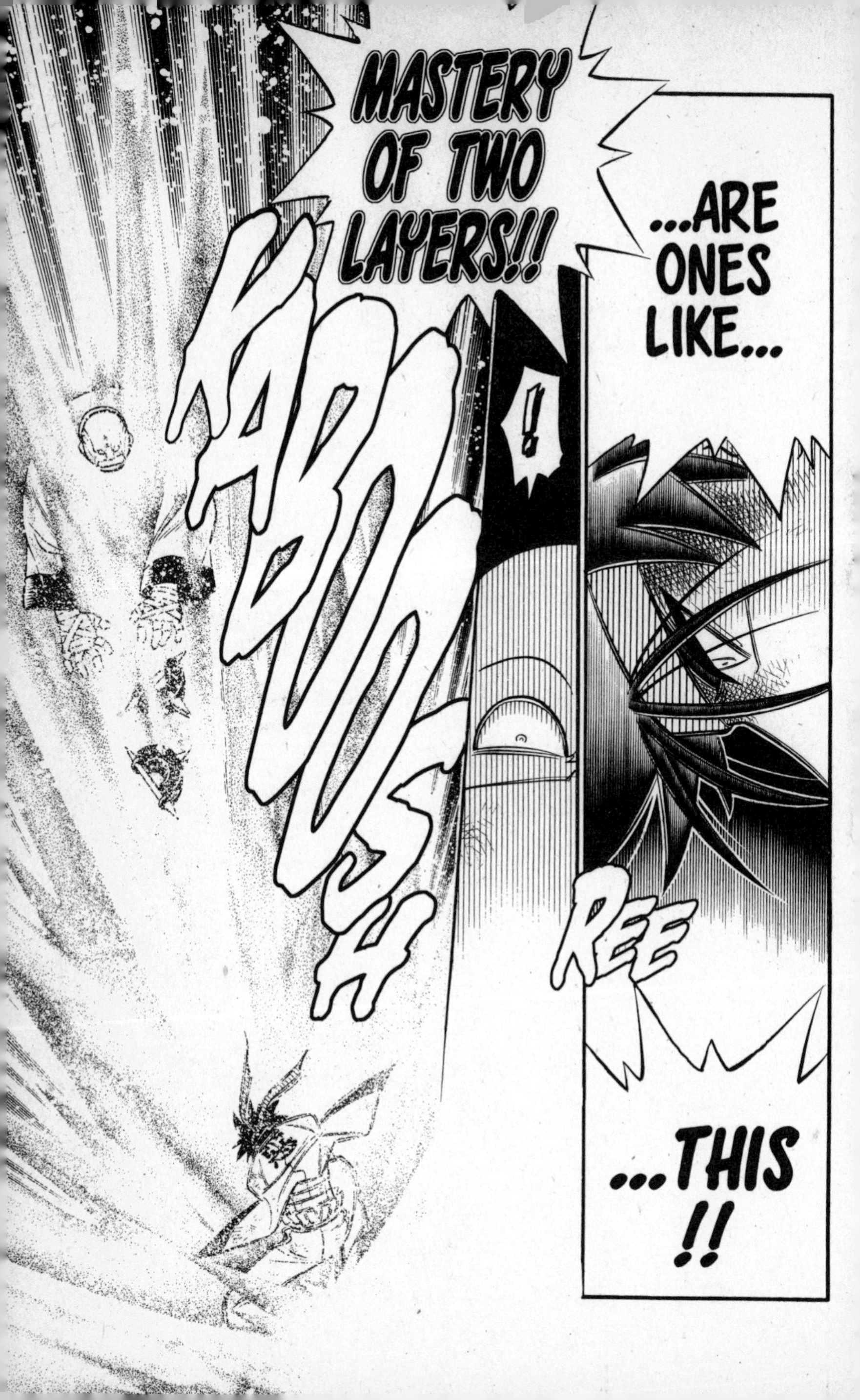
MASTERY OF TWO LAYERS!!
...ARE ONES LIKE...
REE
...THIS!!
!
KABOOSH

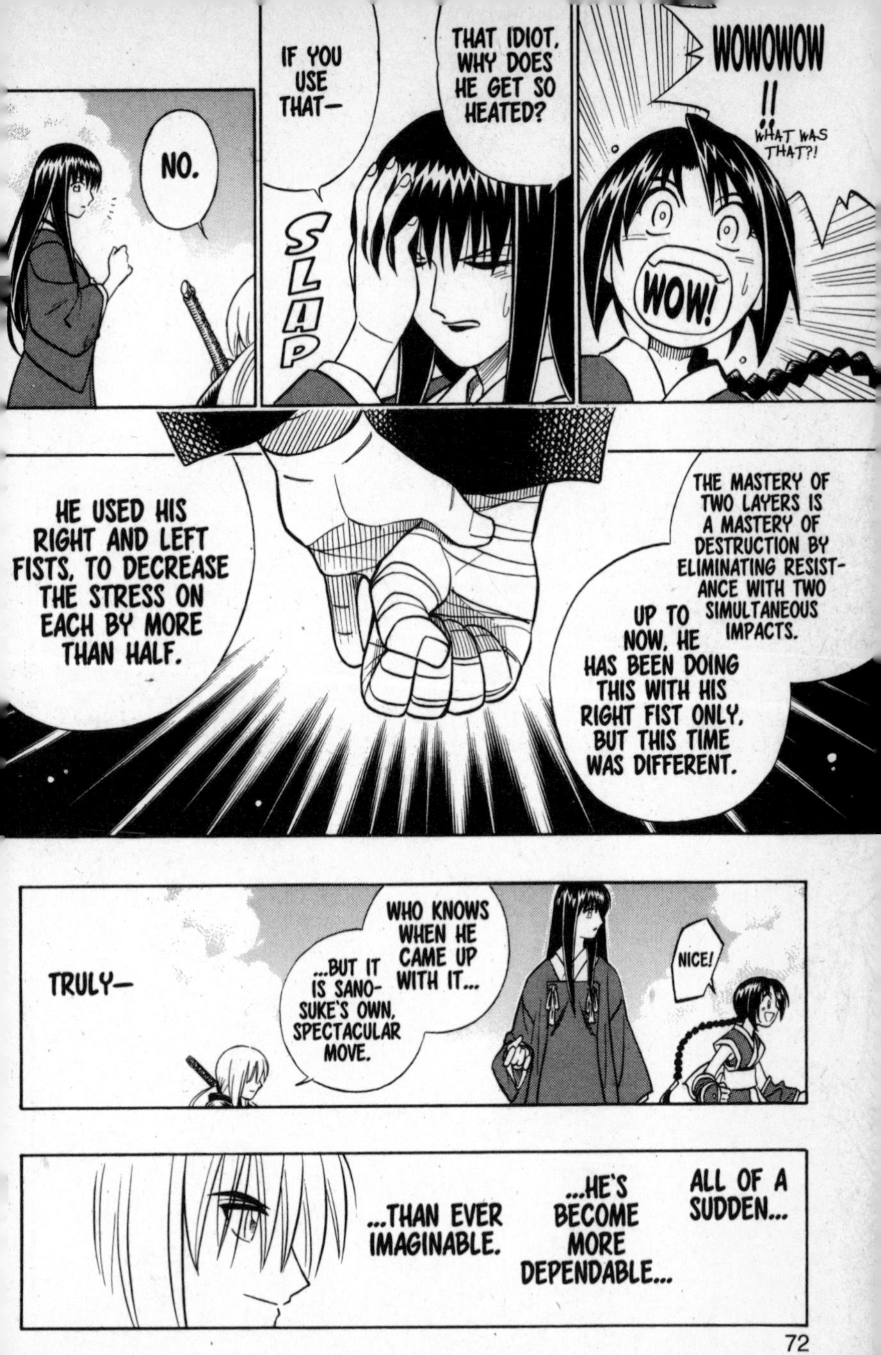
WOWOWOW!!
WHAT WAS THAT?!
WOW!
THAT IDIOT, WHY DOES HE GET SO HEATED?
IF YOU USE THAT—
SLAP
NO.
THE MASTERY OF TWO LAYERS IS A MASTERY OF DESTRUCTION BY ELIMINATING RESIST-ANCE WITH TWO SIMULTANEOUS IMPACTS.
UP TO NOW, HE HAS BEEN DOING THIS WITH HIS RIGHT FIST ONLY, BUT THIS TIME WAS DIFFERENT.
HE USED HIS RIGHT AND LEFT FISTS, TO DECREASE THE STRESS ON EACH BY MORE THAN HALF.
NICE!
WHO KNOWS WHEN HE CAME UP WITH IT...
...BUT IT IS SANO-SUKE'S OWN, SPECTACULAR MOVE.
TRULY—
ALL OF A SUDDEN...
...HE'S BECOME MORE DEPENDABLE...
...THAN EVER IMAGINABLE.

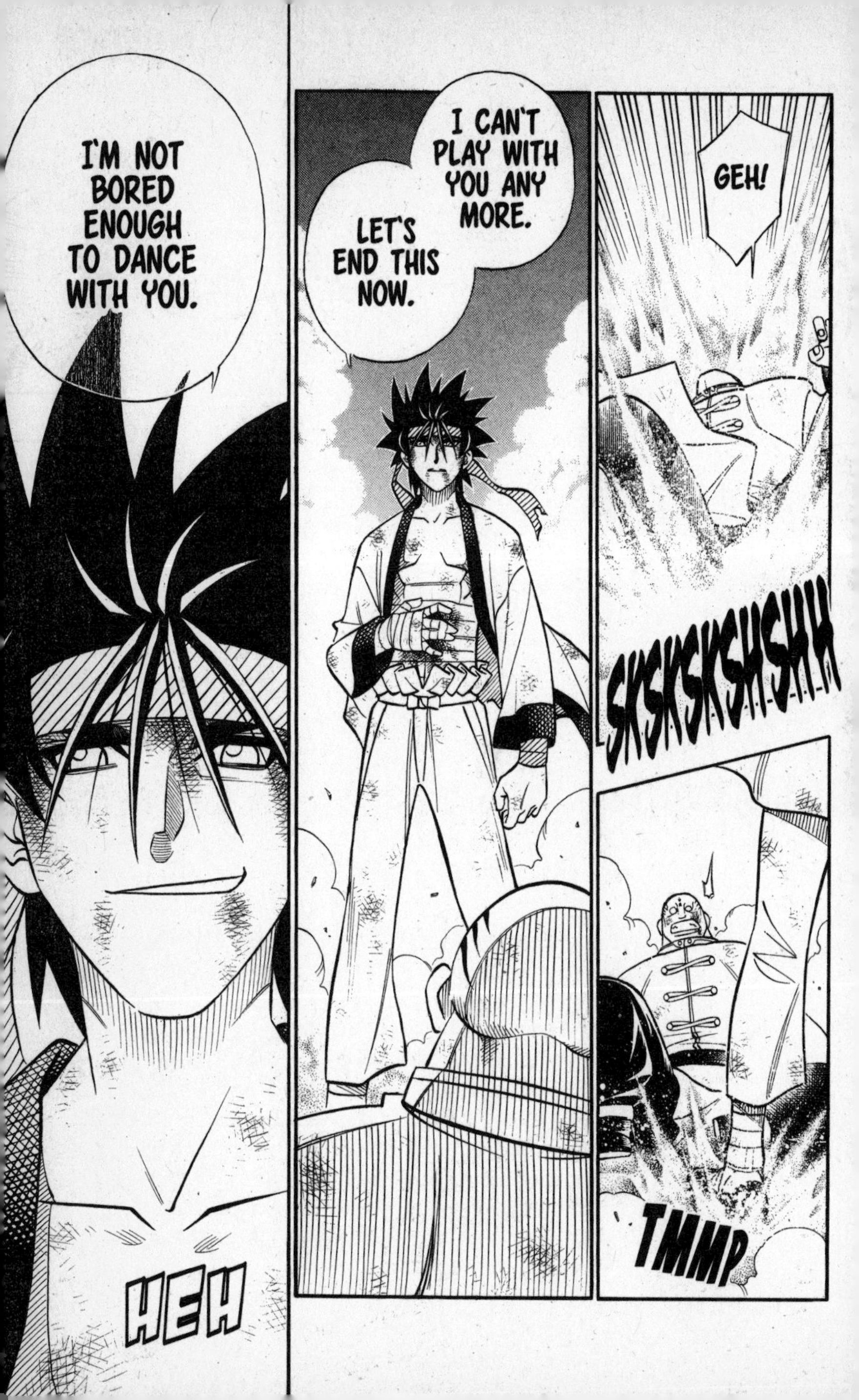
GEH!
SKSKSKSHSHH
TMMP
I CAN'T PLAY WITH YOU ANY MORE.
LET'S END THIS NOW.
I'M NOT BORED ENOUGH TO DANCE WITH YOU.
HEH

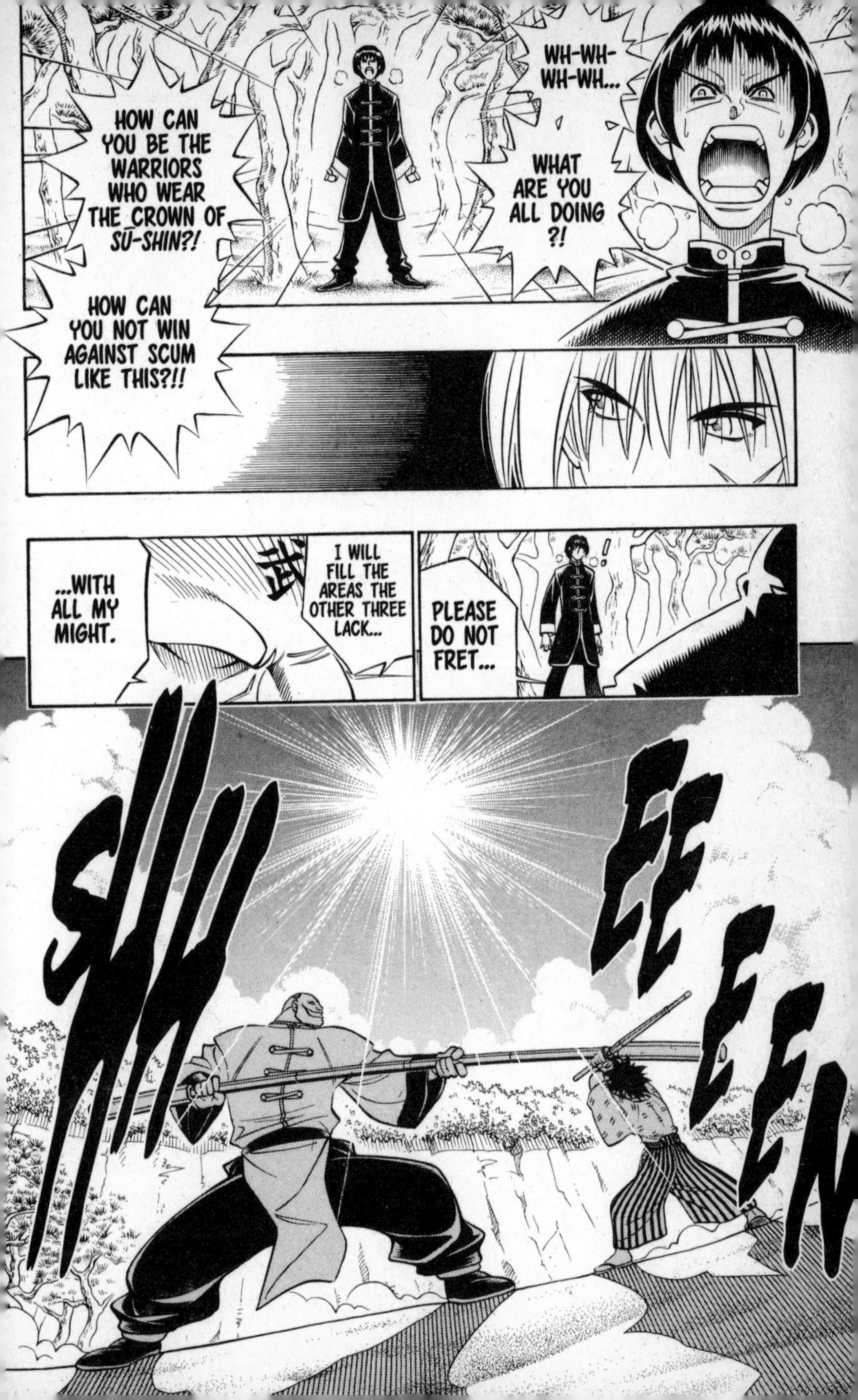
WH-WH-WH-WH...
WHAT ARE YOU ALL DOING?!
HOW CAN YOU BE THE WARRIORS WHO WEAR THE CROWN OF SŪ-SHIN?!
HOW CAN YOU NOT WIN AGAINST SCUM LIKE THIS?!!
PLEASE DO NOT FRET...
!
I WILL FILL THE AREAS THE OTHER THREE LACK...
武
...WITH ALL MY MIGHT.
SHH
EEEEEN

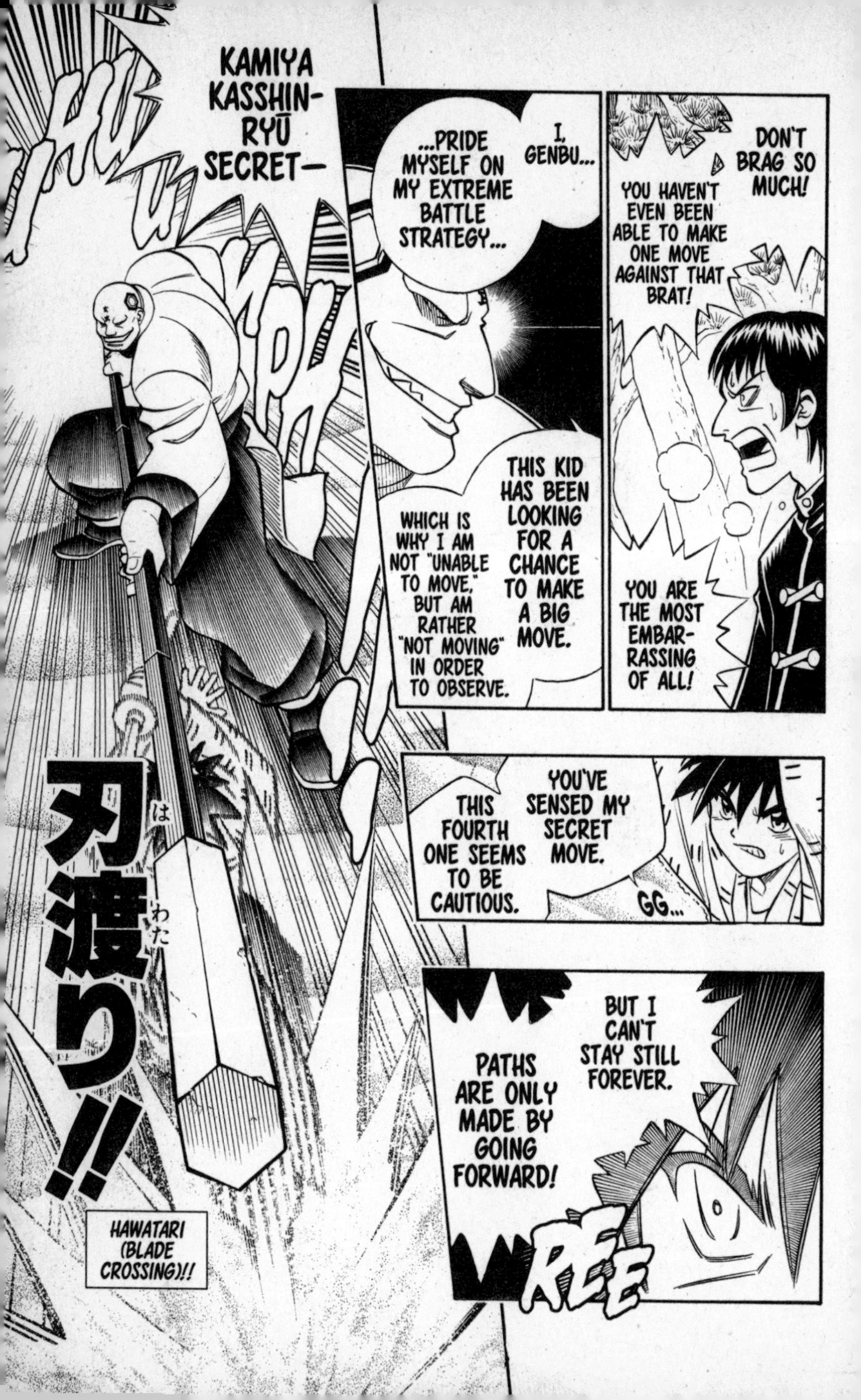
DON'T BRAG SO MUCH!
YOU HAVEN'T EVEN BEEN ABLE TO MAKE ONE MOVE AGAINST THAT BRAT!
YOU ARE THE MOST EMBARRASSING OF ALL!
I, GENBU...
...PRIDE MYSELF ON MY EXTREME BATTLE STRATEGY...
THIS KID HAS BEEN LOOKING FOR A CHANCE TO MAKE A BIG MOVE.
WHICH IS WHY I AM NOT "UNABLE TO MOVE," BUT AM RATHER "NOT MOVING" IN ORDER TO OBSERVE.
YOU'VE SENSED MY SECRET MOVE.
THIS FOURTH ONE SEEMS TO BE CAUTIOUS.
GG...
BUT I CAN'T STAY STILL FOREVER.
PATHS ARE ONLY MADE BY GOING FORWARD!
REE
KAMIYA KASSHIN-RYŪ SECRET—
刃渡り!!
HAWATARI (BLADE CROSSING)!!

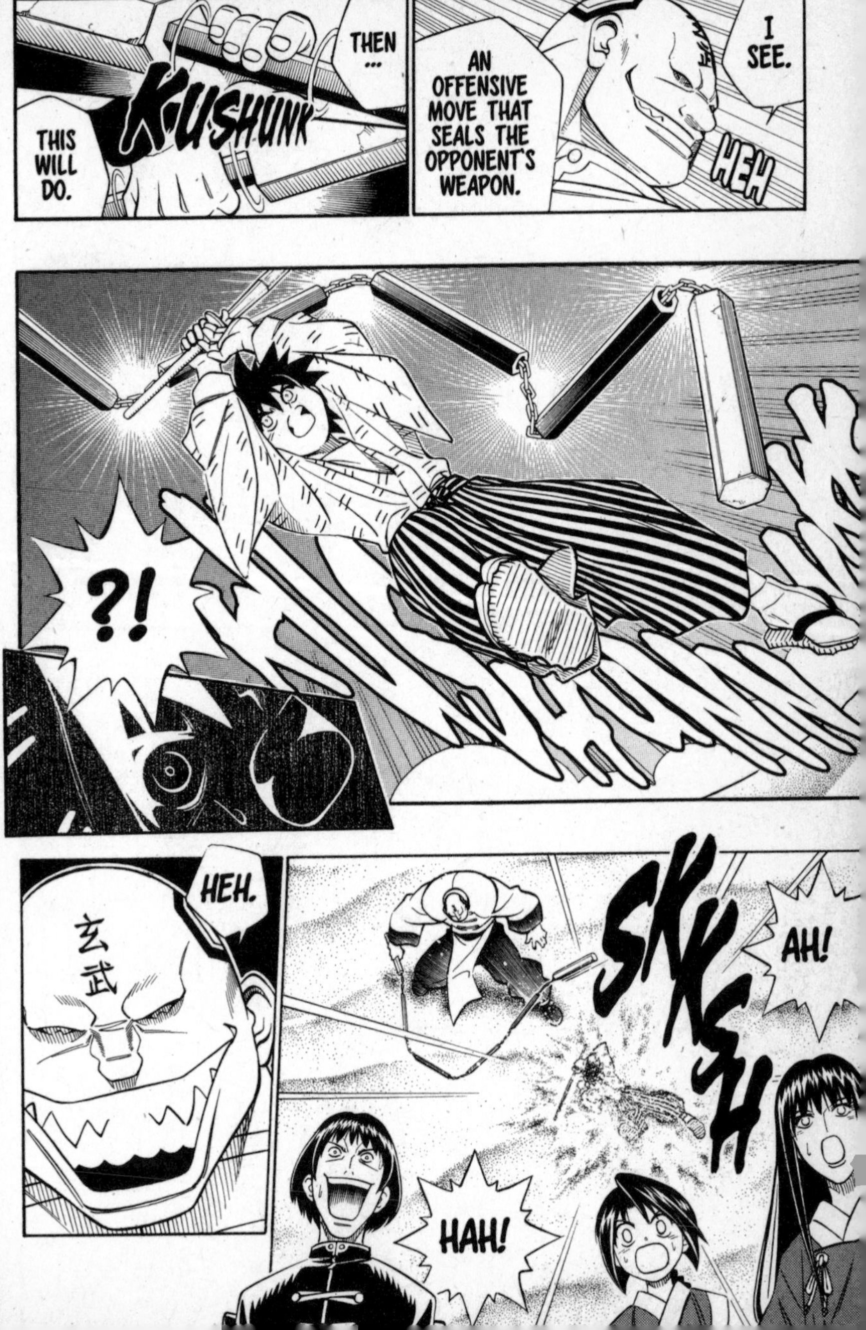
I SEE.
HEH
AN OFFENSIVE MOVE THAT SEALS THE OPPONENT'S WEAPON.
THEN...
KUSHUNK
THIS WILL DO.
?!
AH!
SKKSH
HAH!
HEH.
玄武

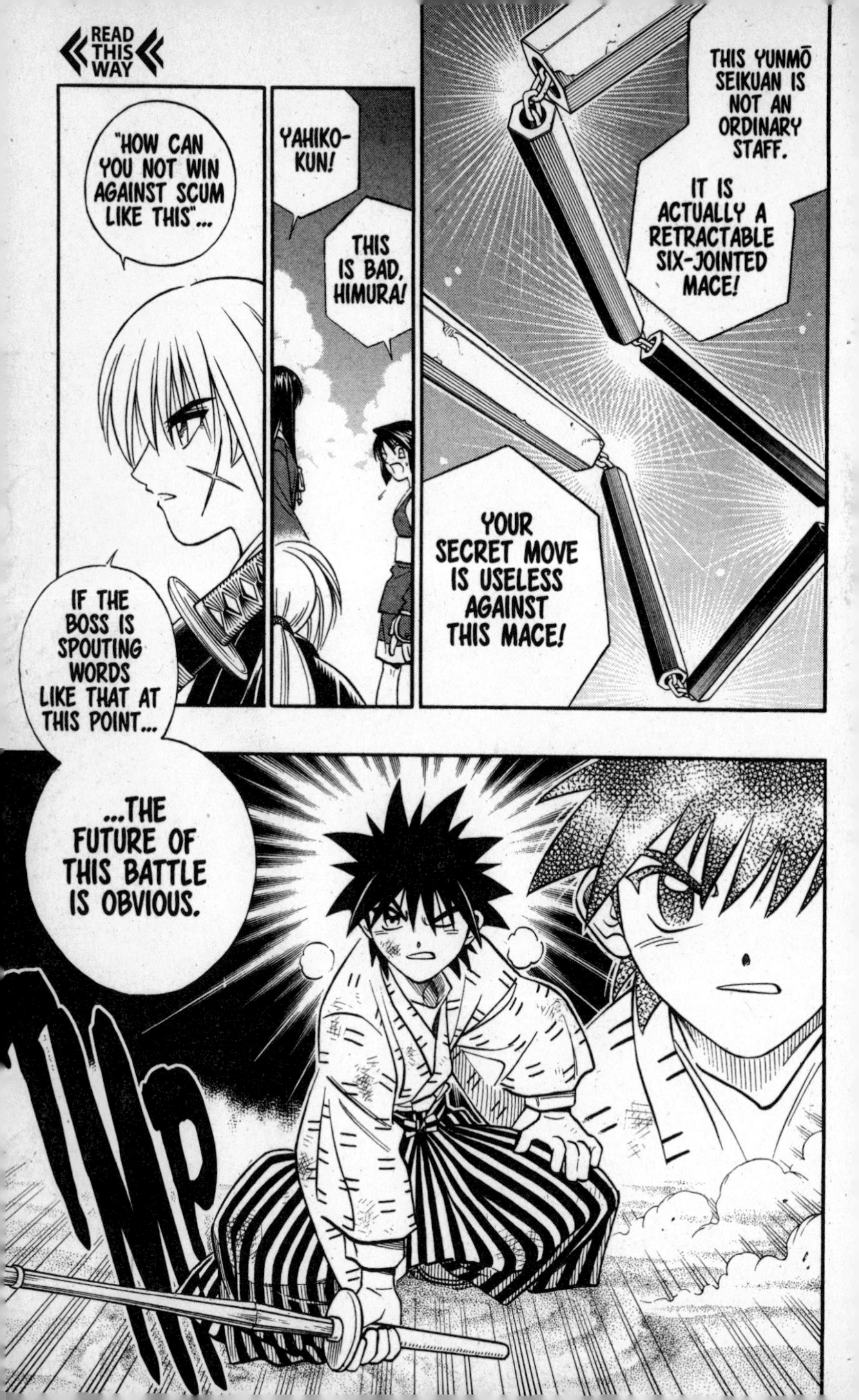
READ THIS WAY
THIS YUNMŌ SEIKUAN IS NOT AN ORDINARY STAFF.
IT IS ACTUALLY A RETRACTABLE SIX-JOINTED MACE!
YOUR SECRET MOVE IS USELESS AGAINST THIS MACE!
YAHIKO-KUN!
THIS IS BAD, HIMURA!
"HOW CAN YOU NOT WIN AGAINST SCUM LIKE THIS"...
IF THE BOSS IS SPOUTING WORDS LIKE THAT AT THIS POINT...
...THE FUTURE OF THIS BATTLE IS OBVIOUS.
THMP

Rurouni Kenshin

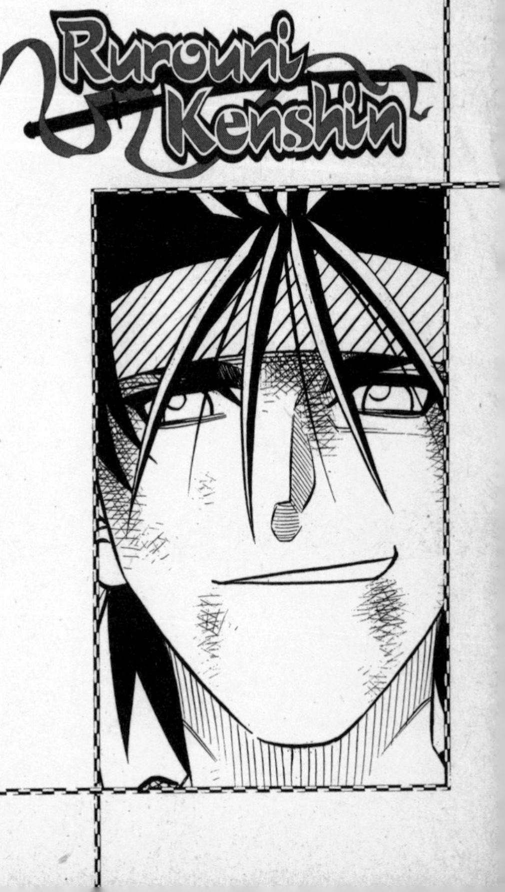

Act 242—Sū-shin Battle—Yahiko *vs.* Genbu

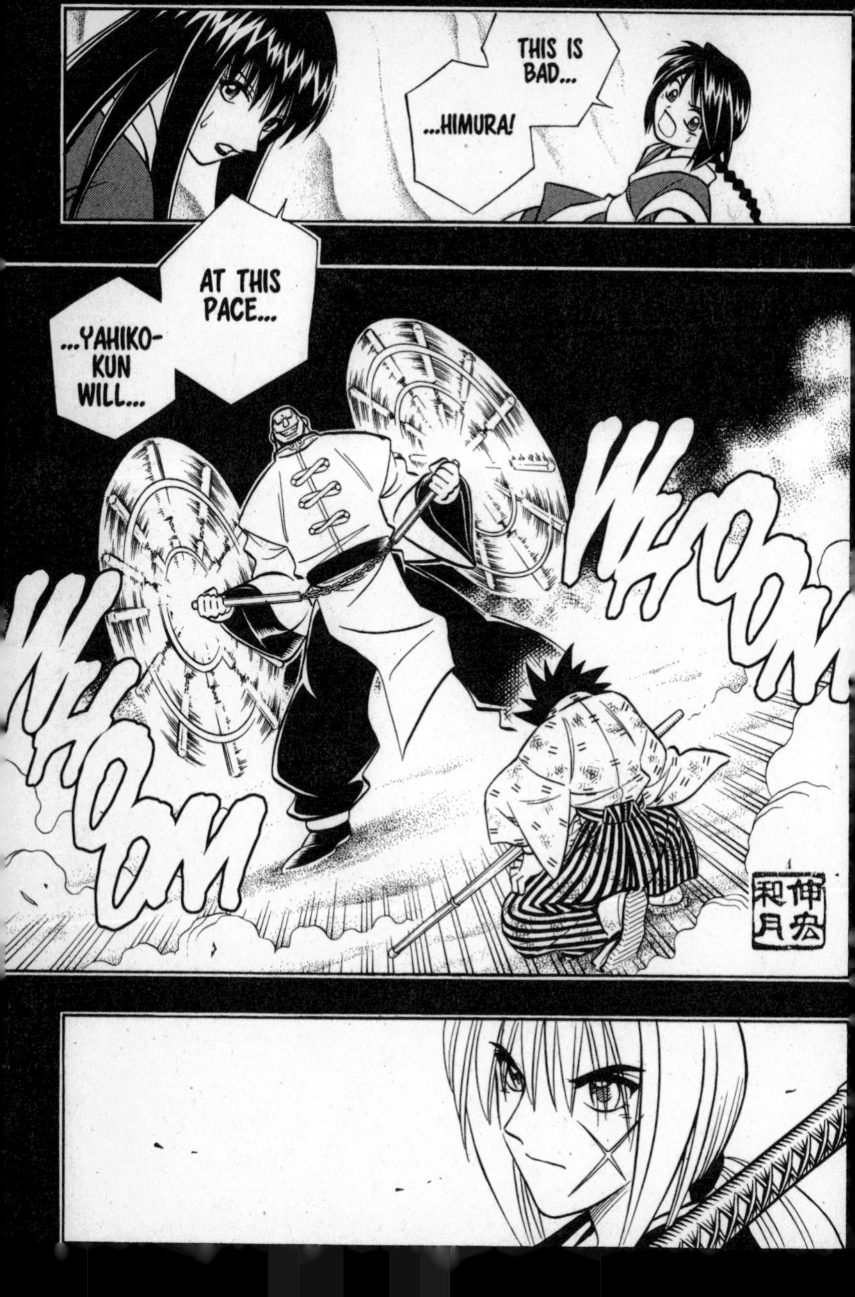
THIS IS BAD...
...HIMURA!
AT THIS PACE...
...YAHIKO-KUN WILL...

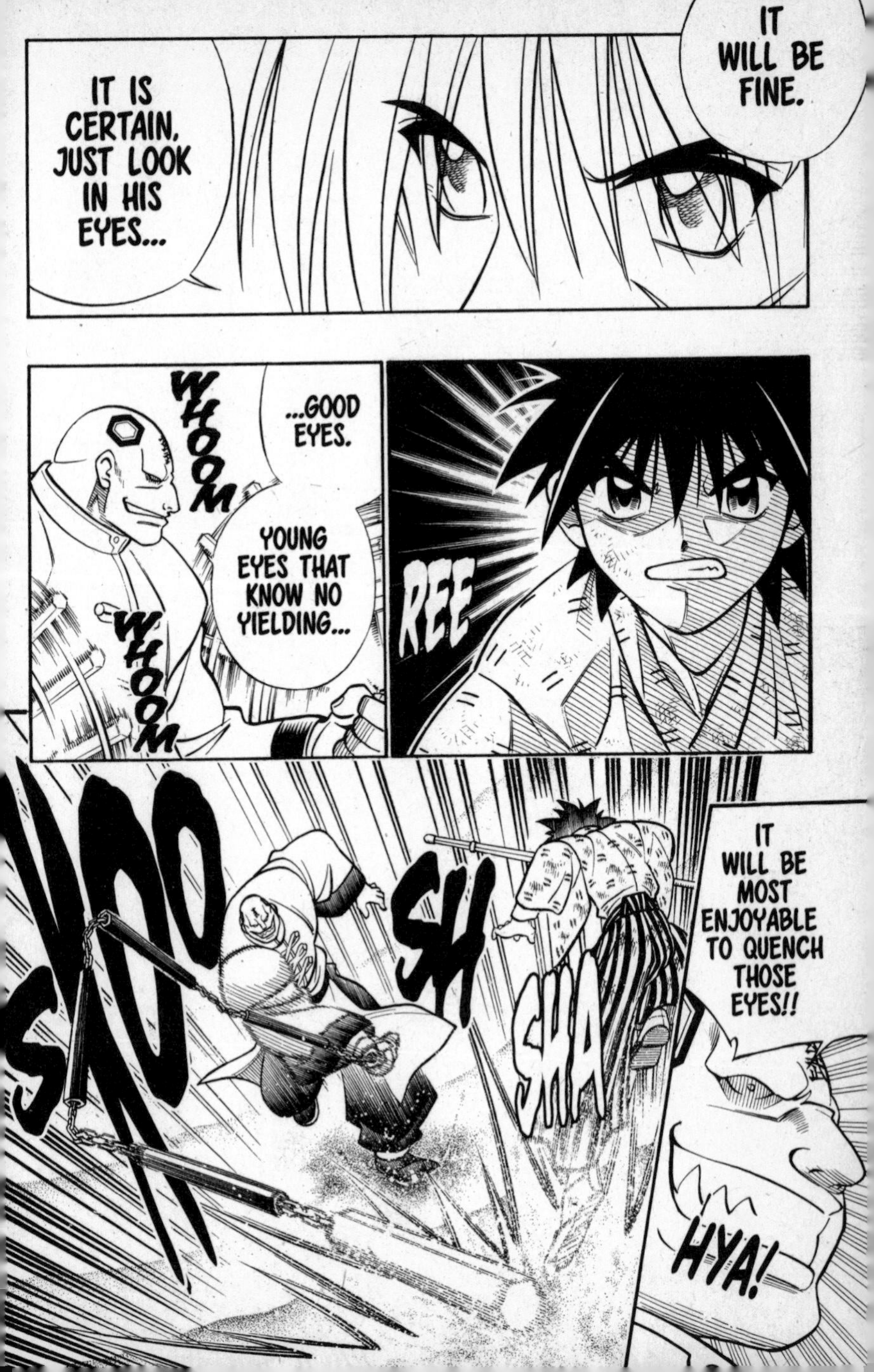
IT WILL BE FINE.
IT IS CERTAIN, JUST LOOK IN HIS EYES...
REE
WHOOM
WHOOM
...GOOD EYES.
YOUNG EYES THAT KNOW NO YIELDING...
IT WILL BE MOST ENJOYABLE TO QUENCH THOSE EYES!!
HYA!
SHA
SH
SHOO

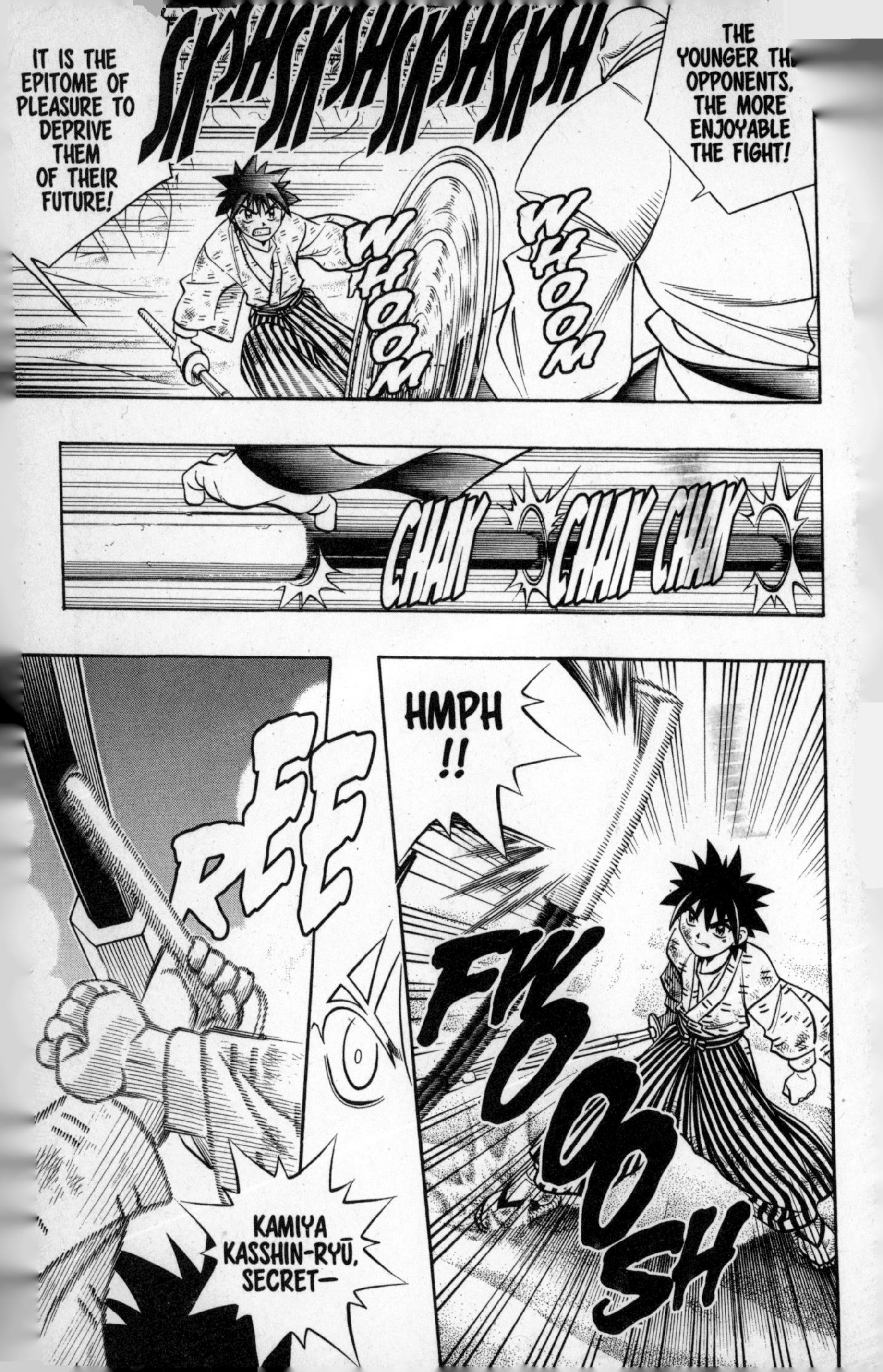
THE YOUNGER TH
OPPONENTS, THE MORE ENJOYABLE THE FIGHT!
IT IS THE EPITOME OF PLEASURE TO DEPRIVE THEM OF THEIR FUTURE!
WHOOM
WHOOM
CHAK
CHAK CHAK
HMPH !!
FWOOOSH
KAMIYA KASSHIN-RYŪ, SECRET—

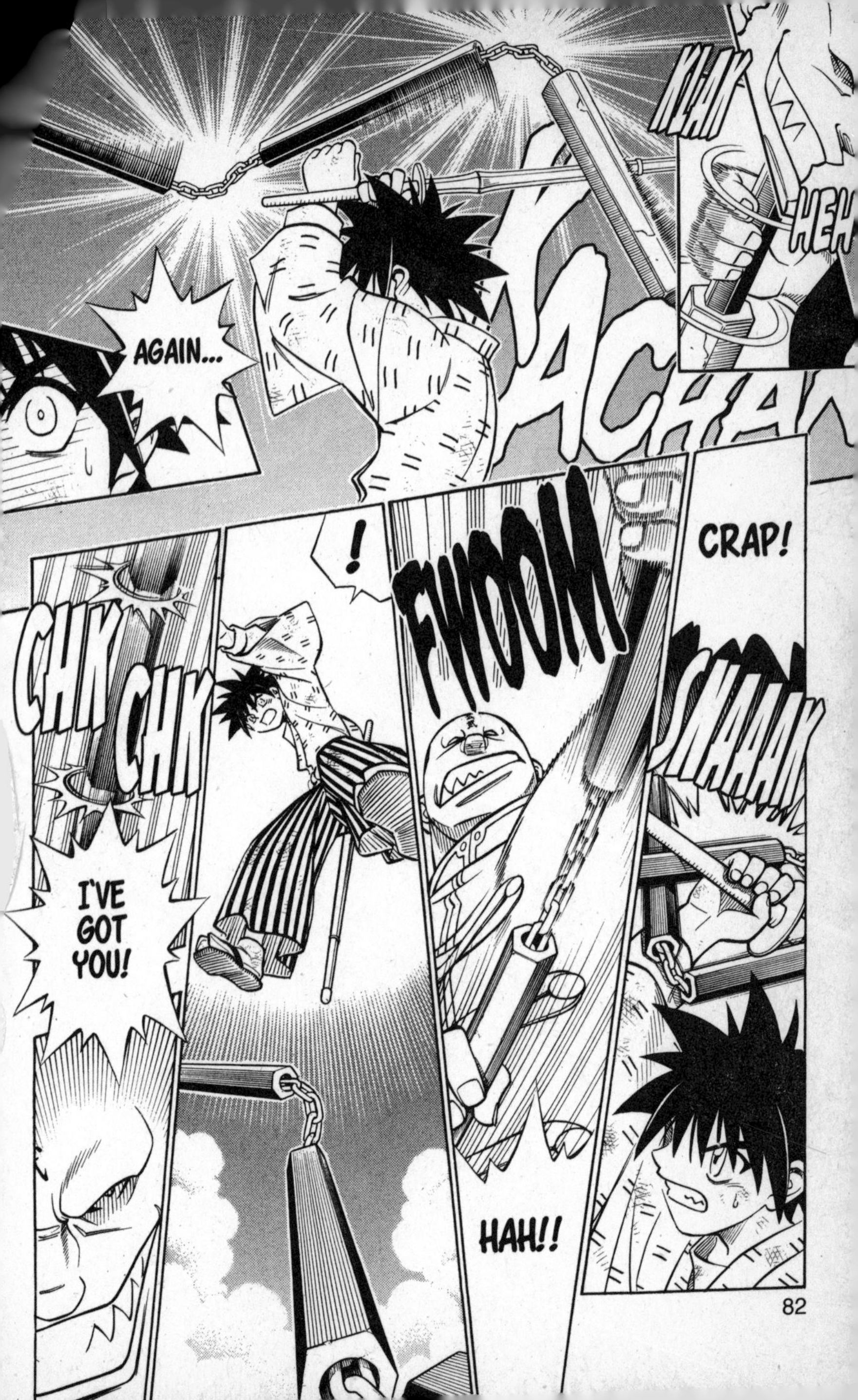
KLAK
HEH
ACHAK
AGAIN...
CRAP!
SHAAK
FWOOM
HAH!!
!
CHK CHK
I'VE GOT YOU!

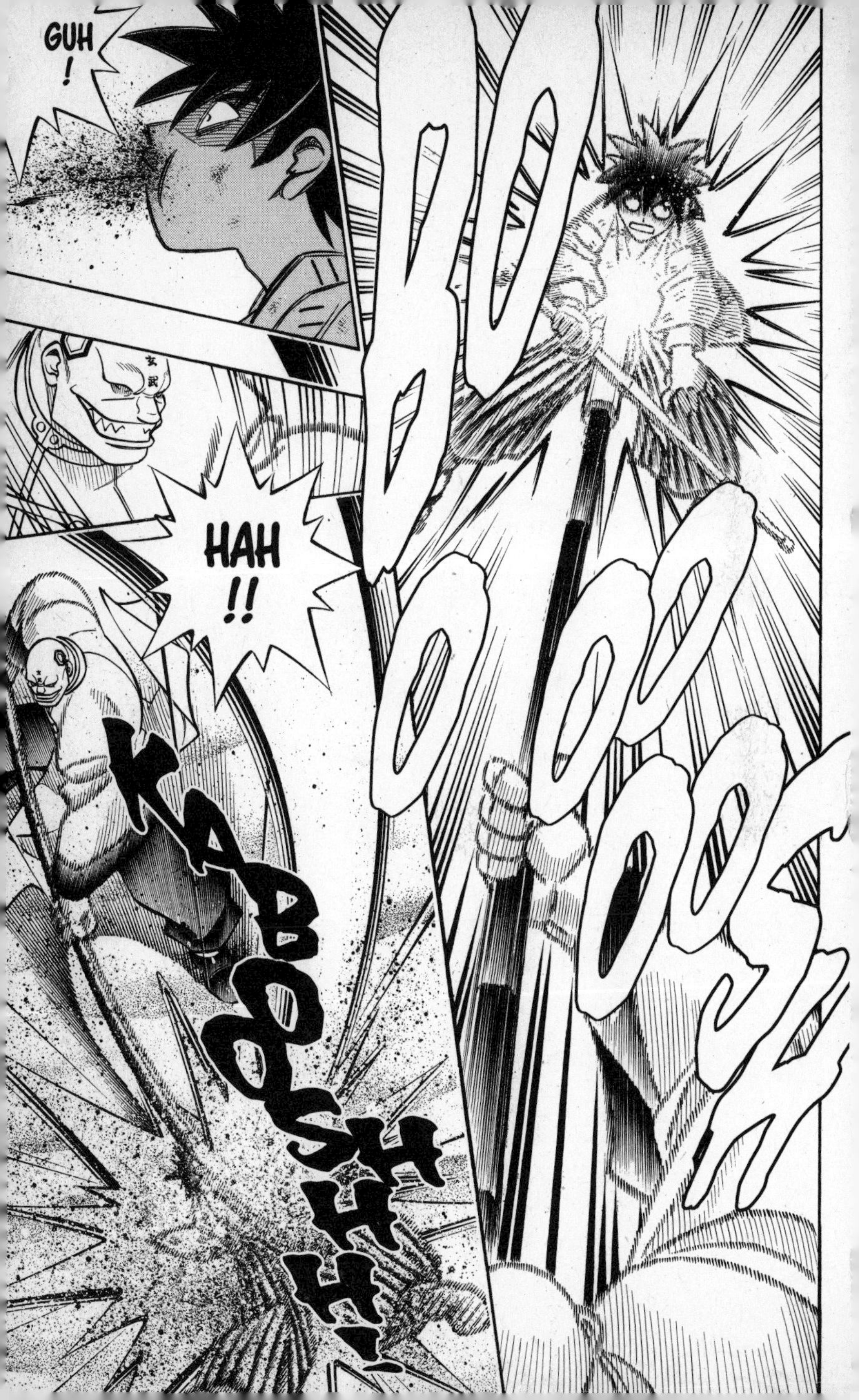
BOOOOOSH
GUH!
玄武
HAH!!
KABOOSHHH!

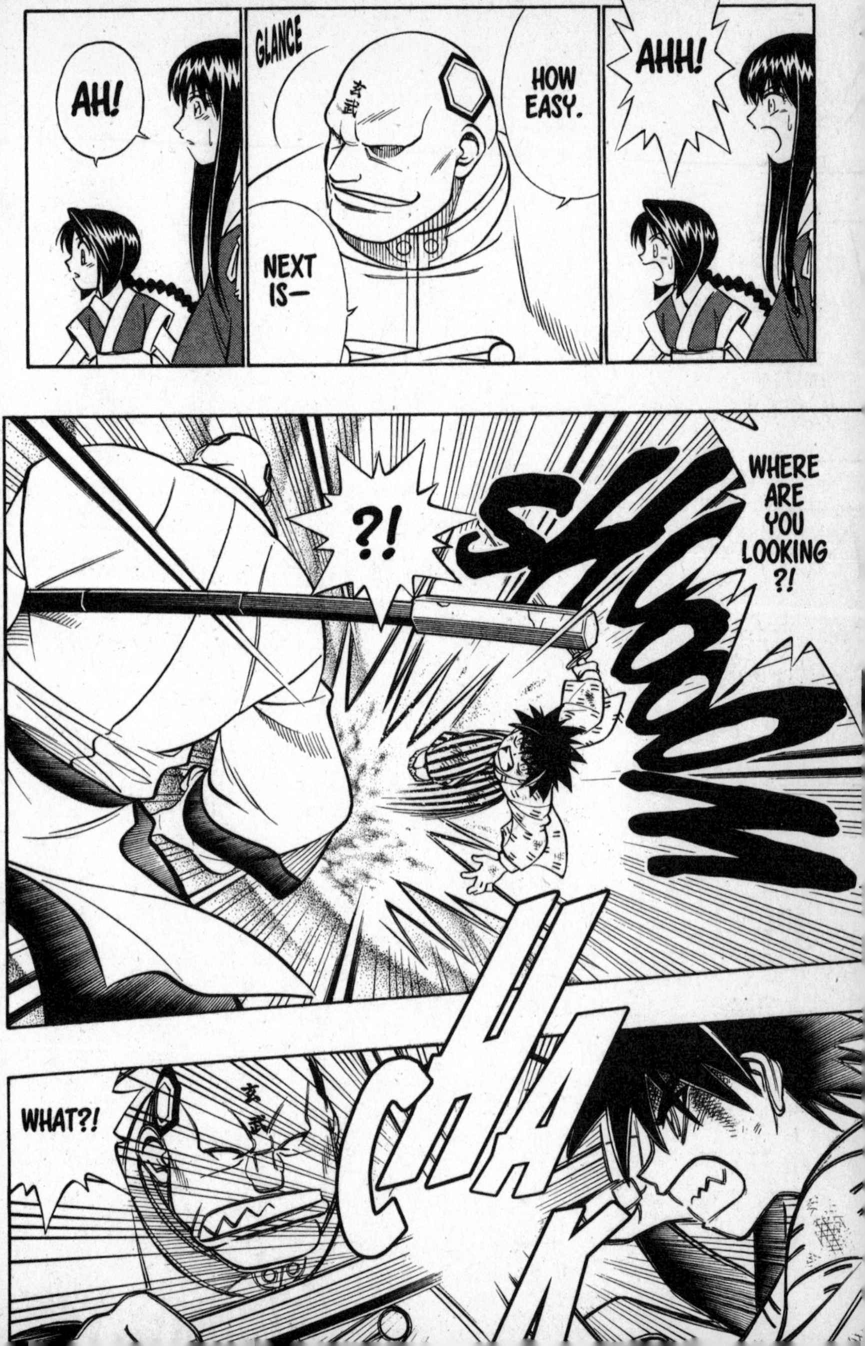
AHH!
HOW EASY.
GLANCE
玄武
NEXT IS—
AH!
WHERE ARE YOU LOOKING?!
SHOOM
?!
CHA
WHAT?!

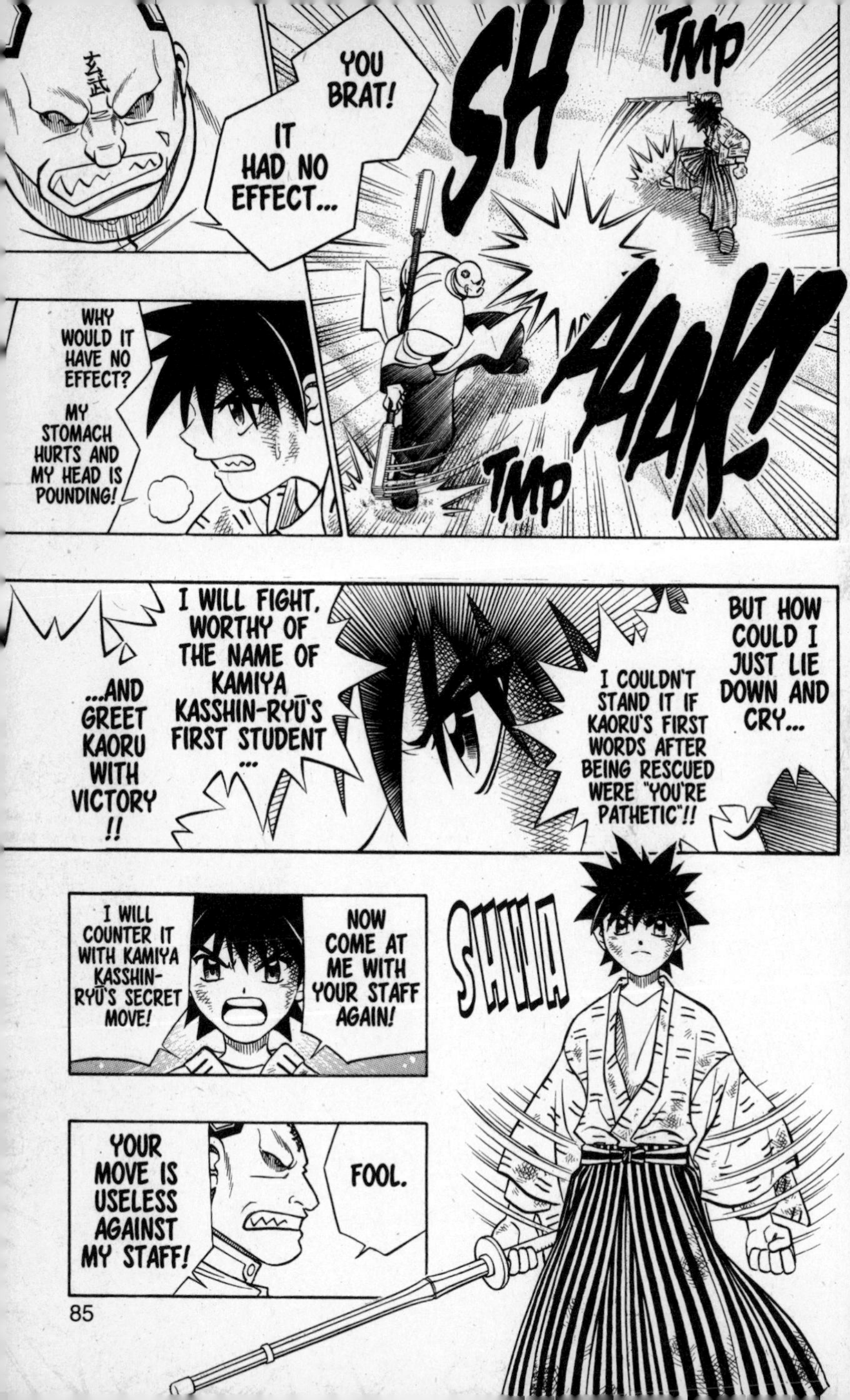

TMP
SHAAAN!
TMP
YOU BRAT!
IT HAD NO EFFECT...
WHY WOULD IT HAVE NO EFFECT?
MY STOMACH HURTS AND MY HEAD IS POUNDING!
BUT HOW COULD I JUST LIE DOWN AND CRY...
I COULDN'T STAND IT IF KAORU'S FIRST WORDS AFTER BEING RESCUED WERE "YOU'RE PATHETIC"!!
I WILL FIGHT, WORTHY OF THE NAME OF KAMIYA KASSHIN-RYŪ'S FIRST STUDENT...
...AND GREET KAORU WITH VICTORY!!
SHWA
NOW COME AT ME WITH YOUR STAFF AGAIN!
I WILL COUNTER IT WITH KAMIYA KASSHIN-RYŪ'S SECRET MOVE!
FOOL.
YOUR MOVE IS USELESS AGAINST MY STAFF!

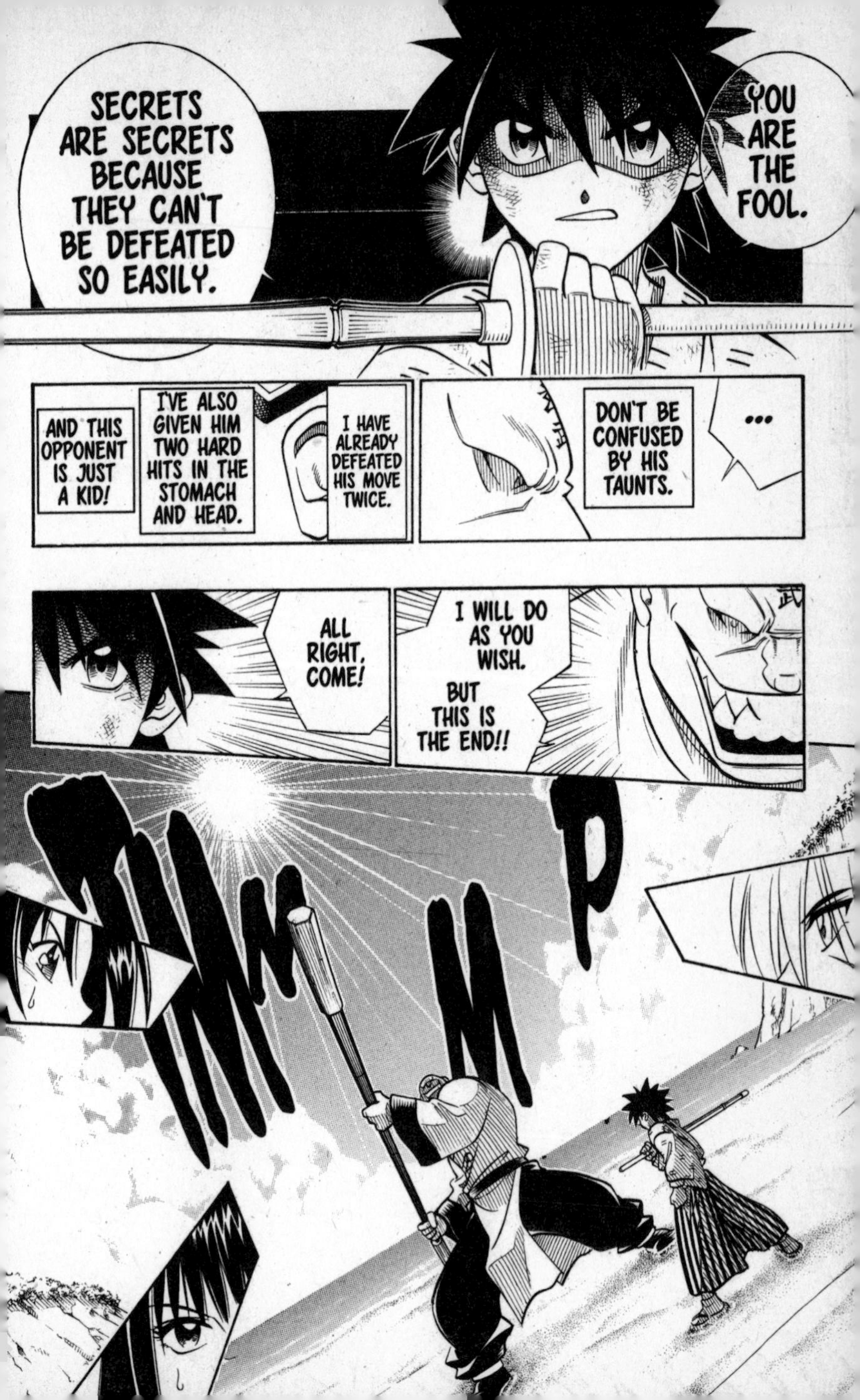
YOU ARE THE FOOL.
SECRETS ARE SECRETS BECAUSE THEY CAN'T BE DEFEATED SO EASILY.
...
DON'T BE CONFUSED BY HIS TAUNTS.
I HAVE ALREADY DEFEATED HIS MOVE TWICE.
I'VE ALSO GIVEN HIM TWO HARD HITS IN THE STOMACH AND HEAD.
AND THIS OPPONENT IS JUST A KID!
I WILL DO AS YOU WISH.
BUT THIS IS THE END!!
ALL RIGHT, COME!

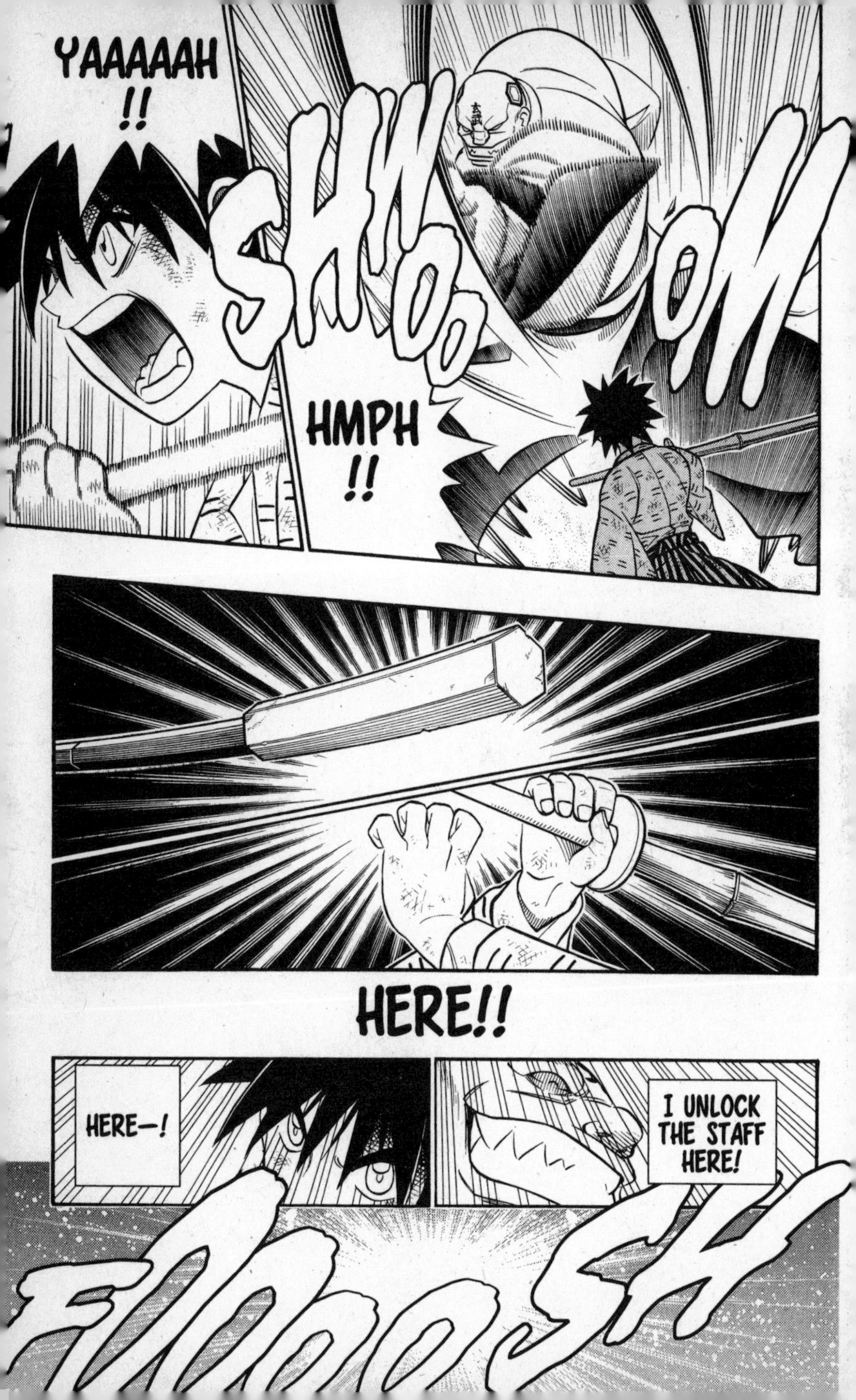
SHWOOOM
HMPH!!
YAAAAAH!!
HERE!!
I UNLOCK THE STAFF HERE!
HERE—!
FWOOOSH

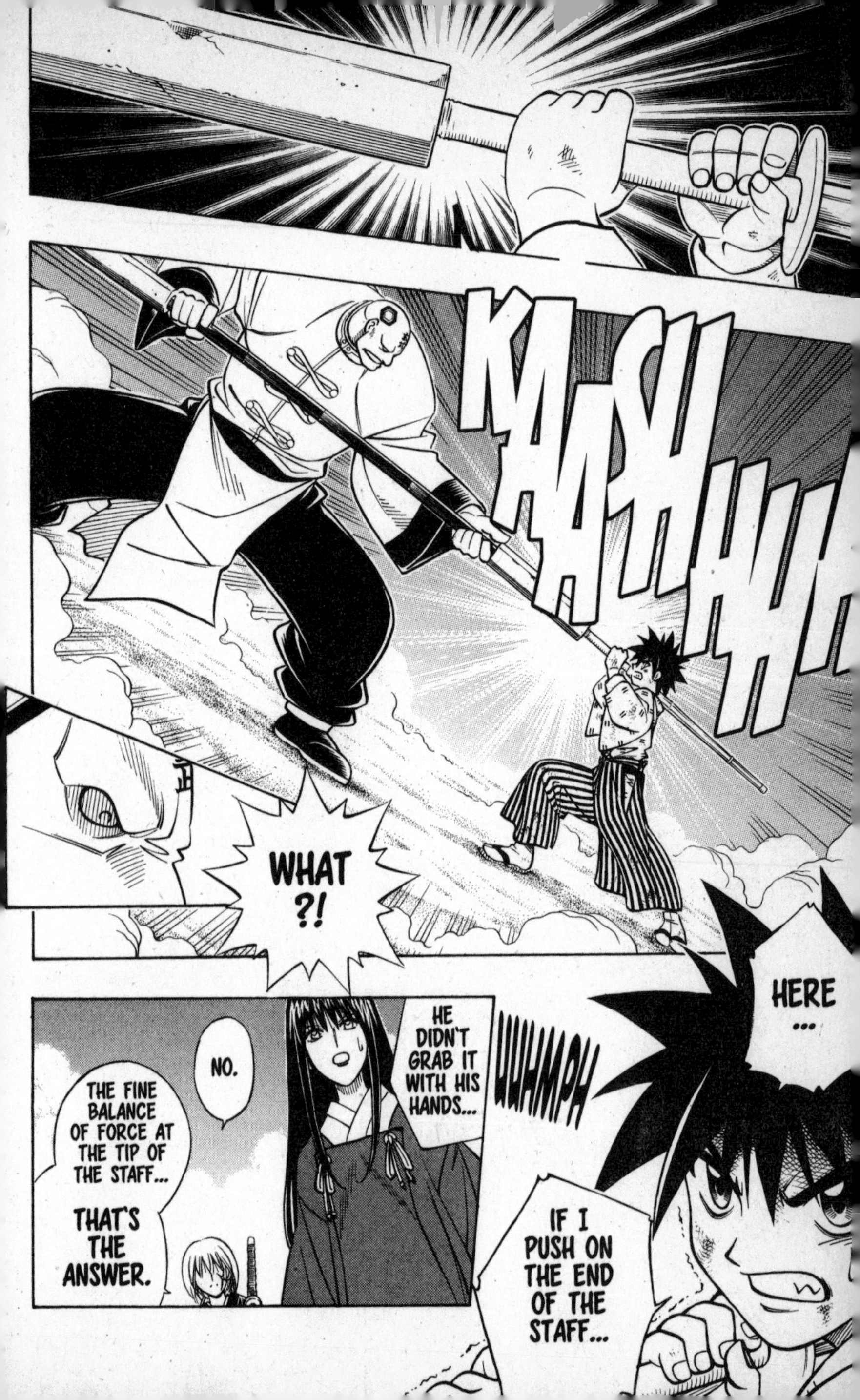
KAASHHHH
WHAT ?!
HERE...
UUHMPH
IF I PUSH ON THE END OF THE STAFF...
HE DIDN'T GRAB IT WITH HIS HANDS...
NO.
THE FINE BALANCE OF FORCE AT THE TIP OF THE STAFF...
THAT'S THE ANSWER.

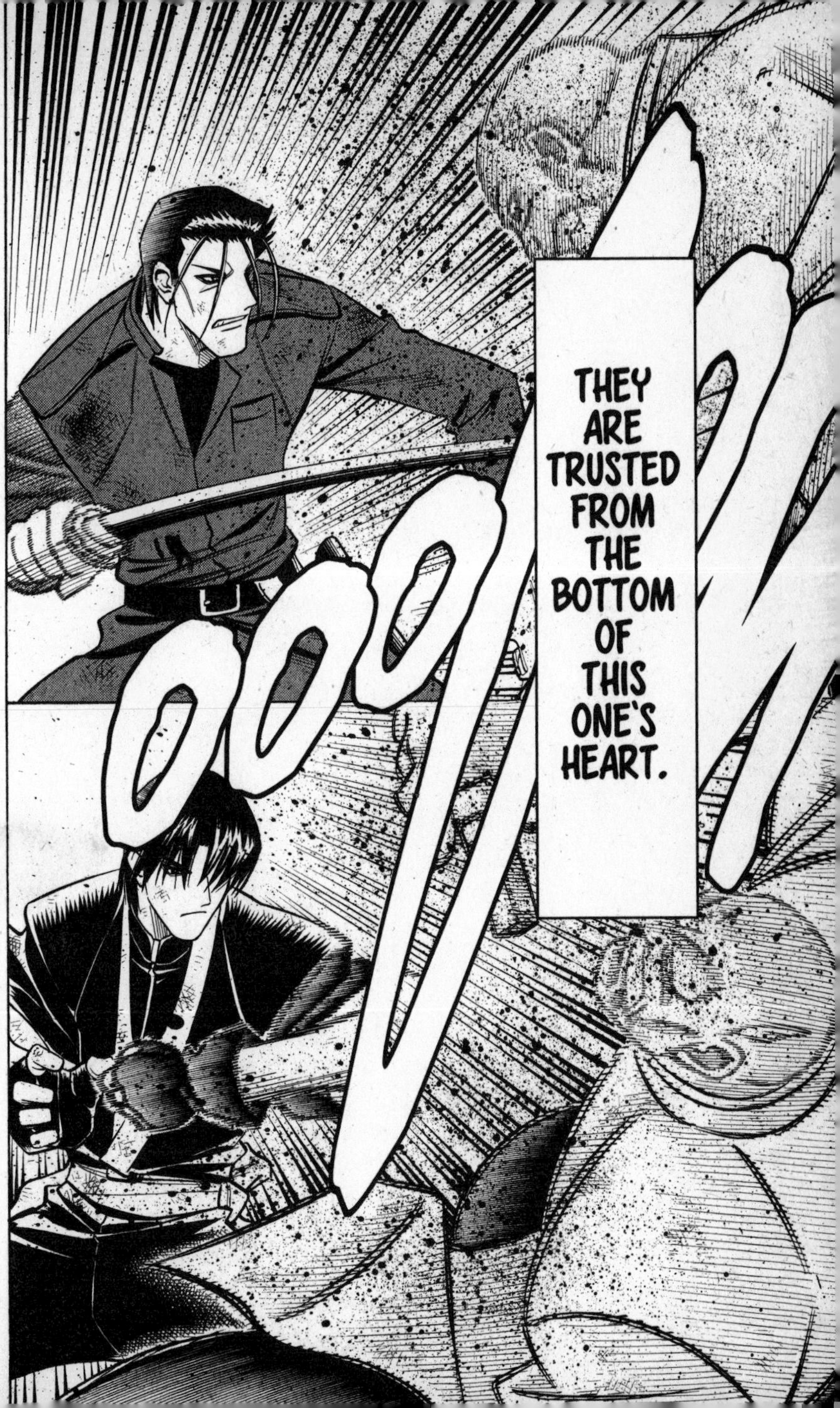
THEY ARE TRUSTED FROM THE BOTTOM OF THIS ONE'S HEART.

READ THIS WAY

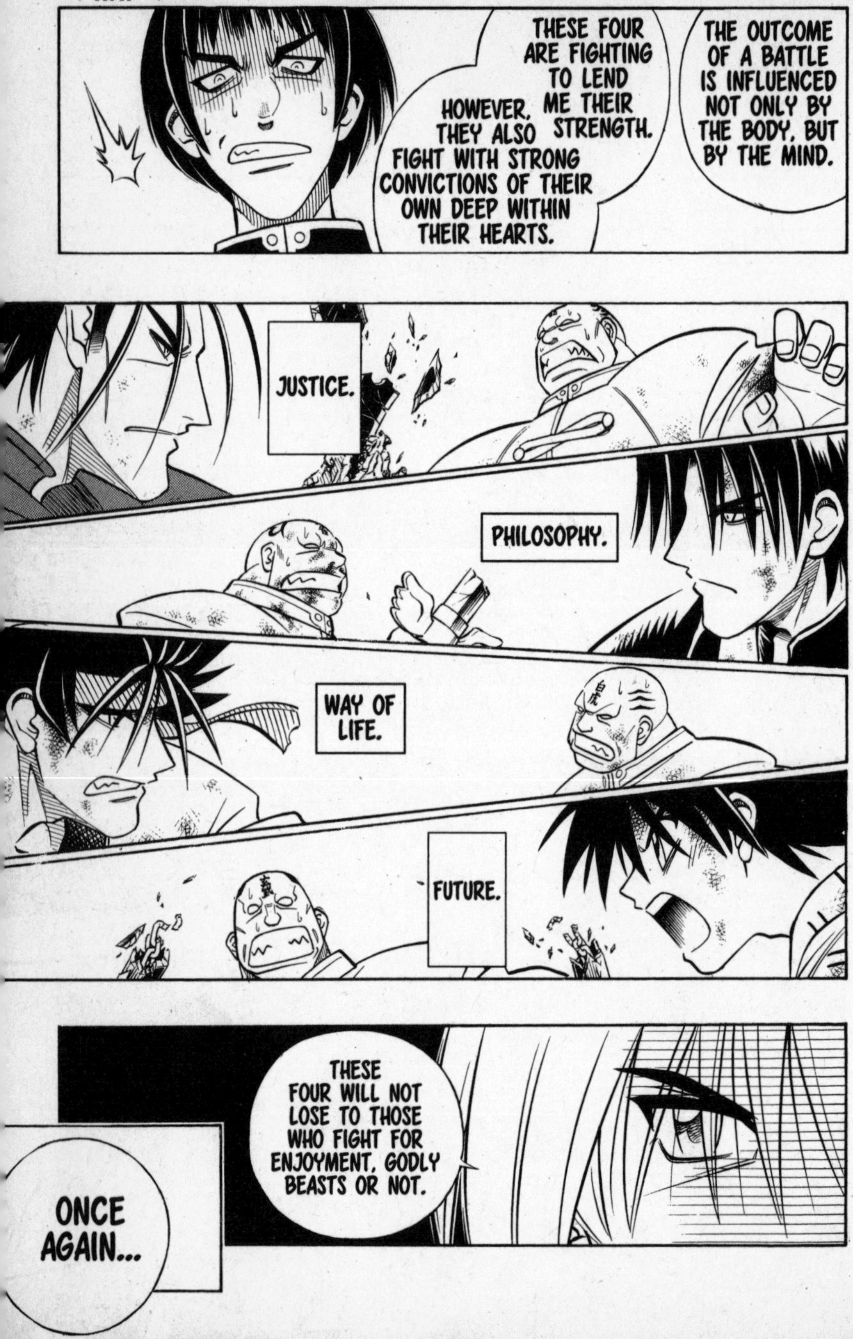

THE OUTCOME OF A BATTLE IS INFLUENCED NOT ONLY BY THE BODY, BUT BY THE MIND.
THESE FOUR ARE FIGHTING TO LEND ME THEIR STRENGTH.
HOWEVER, THEY ALSO FIGHT WITH STRONG CONVICTIONS OF THEIR OWN DEEP WITHIN THEIR HEARTS.
JUSTICE.
PHILOSOPHY.
WAY OF LIFE.
FUTURE.
THESE FOUR WILL NOT LOSE TO THOSE WHO FIGHT FOR ENJOYMENT, GODLY BEASTS OR NOT.
ONCE AGAIN...

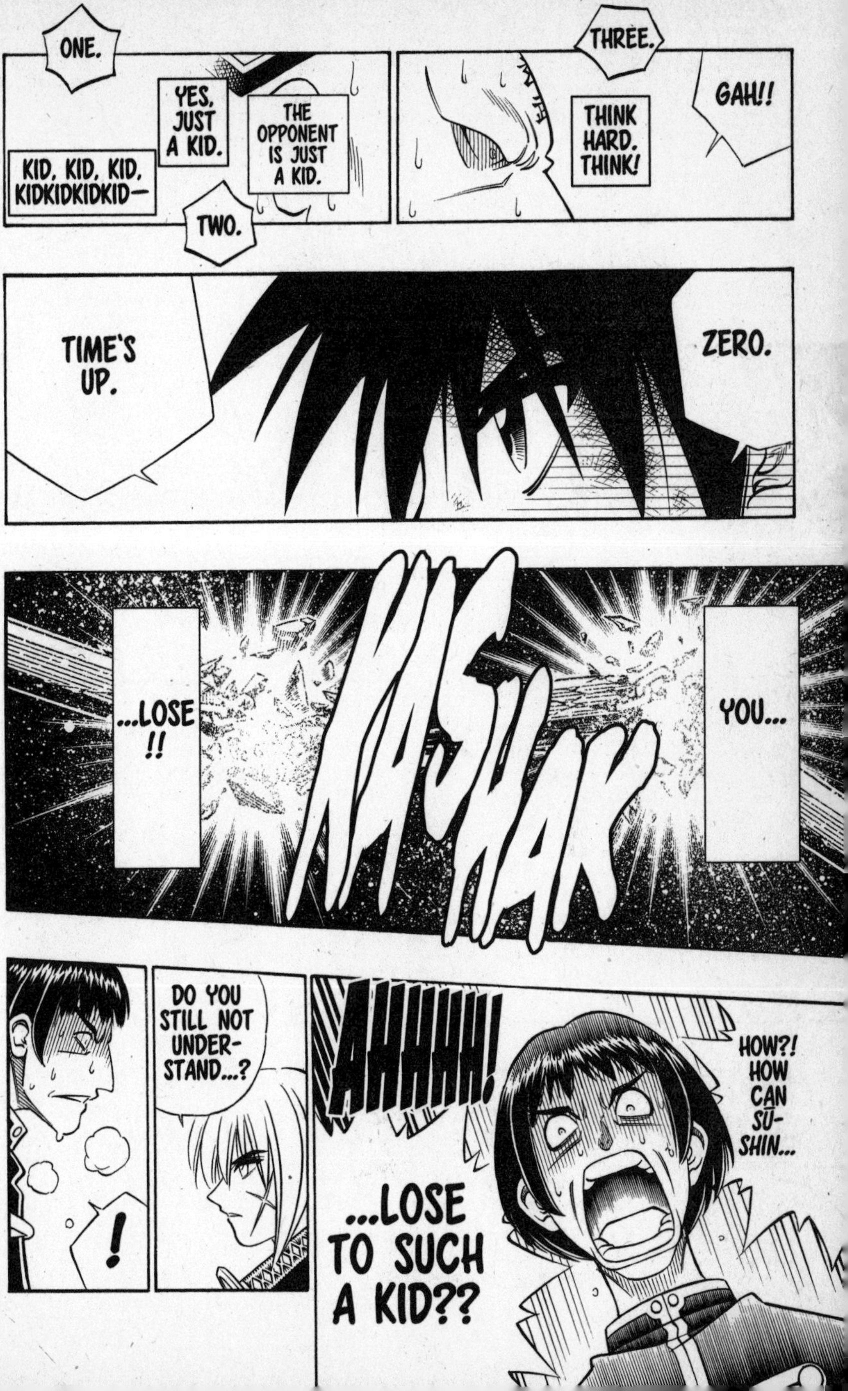
THREE.
GAH!!
THINK HARD. THINK!
THE OPPONENT IS JUST A KID.
YES, JUST A KID.
TWO.
ONE.
KID, KID, KID, KIDKIDKIDKID—
ZERO.
TIME'S UP.
YOU...
KASHAK
...LOSE !!
AHHHH!
HOW?! HOW CAN SŪSHIN...
...LOSE TO SUCH A KID??
DO YOU STILL NOT UNDERSTAND...?
!

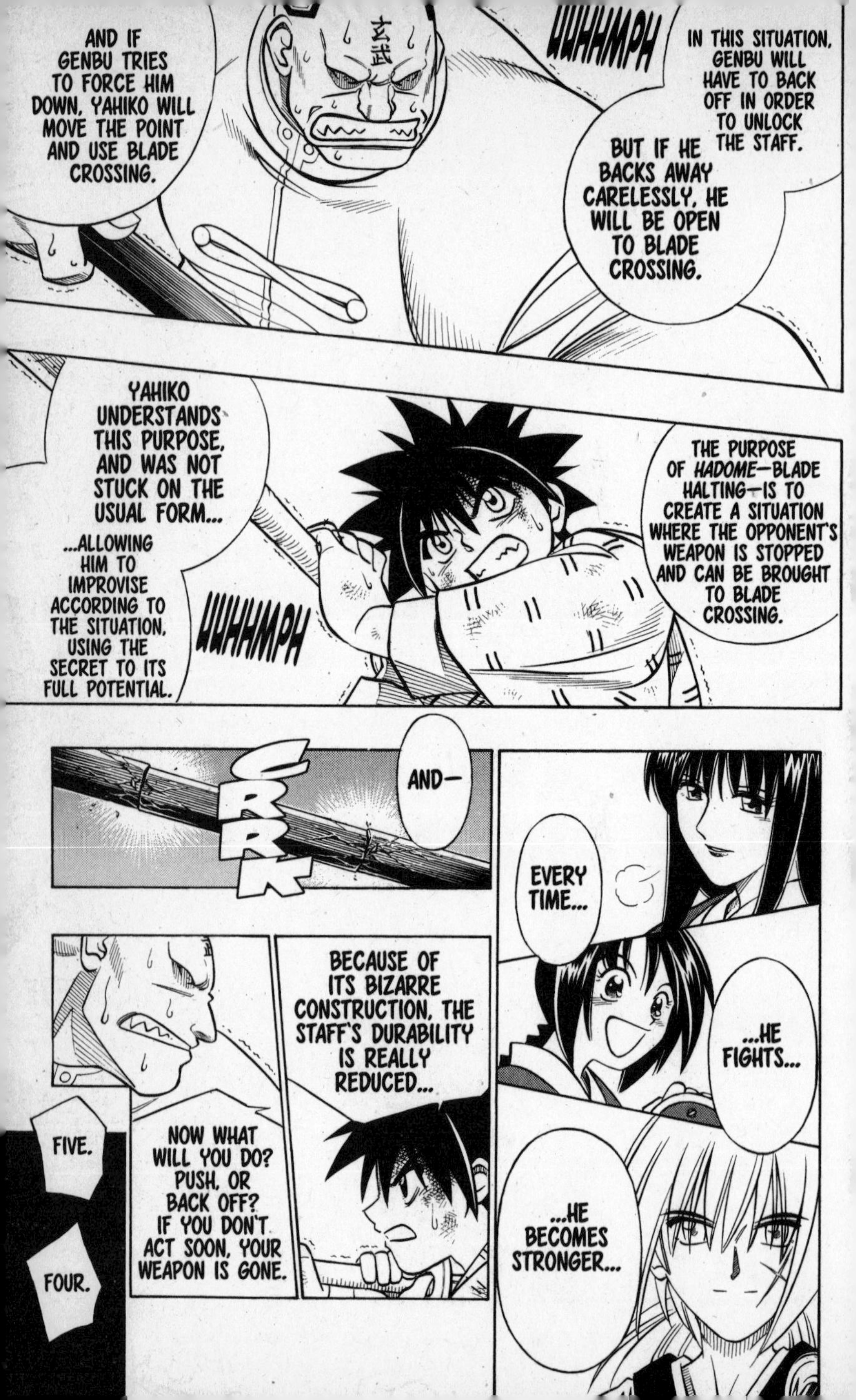

UUHHMPH
IN THIS SITUATION, GENBU WILL HAVE TO BACK OFF IN ORDER TO UNLOCK THE STAFF.
BUT IF HE BACKS AWAY CARELESSLY, HE WILL BE OPEN TO BLADE CROSSING.
玄武
AND IF GENBU TRIES TO FORCE HIM DOWN, YAHIKO WILL MOVE THE POINT AND USE BLADE CROSSING.
THE PURPOSE OF *HADOME*—BLADE HALTING—IS TO CREATE A SITUATION WHERE THE OPPONENT'S WEAPON IS STOPPED AND CAN BE BROUGHT TO BLADE CROSSING.
YAHIKO UNDERSTANDS THIS PURPOSE, AND WAS NOT STUCK ON THE USUAL FORM...
...ALLOWING HIM TO IMPROVISE ACCORDING TO THE SITUATION, USING THE SECRET TO ITS FULL POTENTIAL.
UUHHMPH
AND—
EVERY TIME...
...HE FIGHTS...
...HE BECOMES STRONGER...
CRRK
BECAUSE OF ITS BIZARRE CONSTRUCTION, THE STAFF'S DURABILITY IS REALLY REDUCED...
NOW WHAT WILL YOU DO? PUSH, OR BACK OFF? IF YOU DON'T ACT SOON, YOUR WEAPON IS GONE.
FIVE.
FOUR.

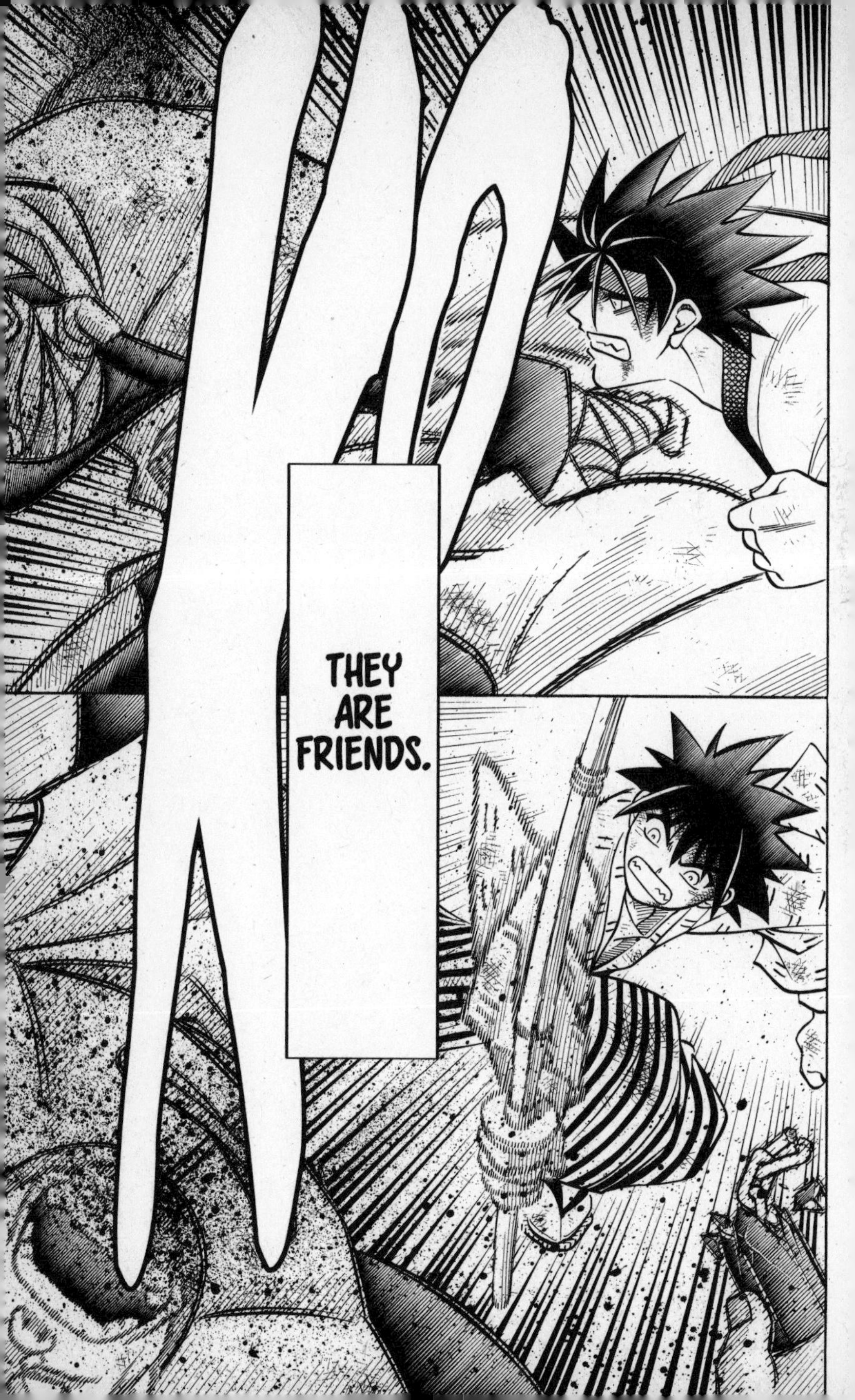
THEY ARE FRIENDS.

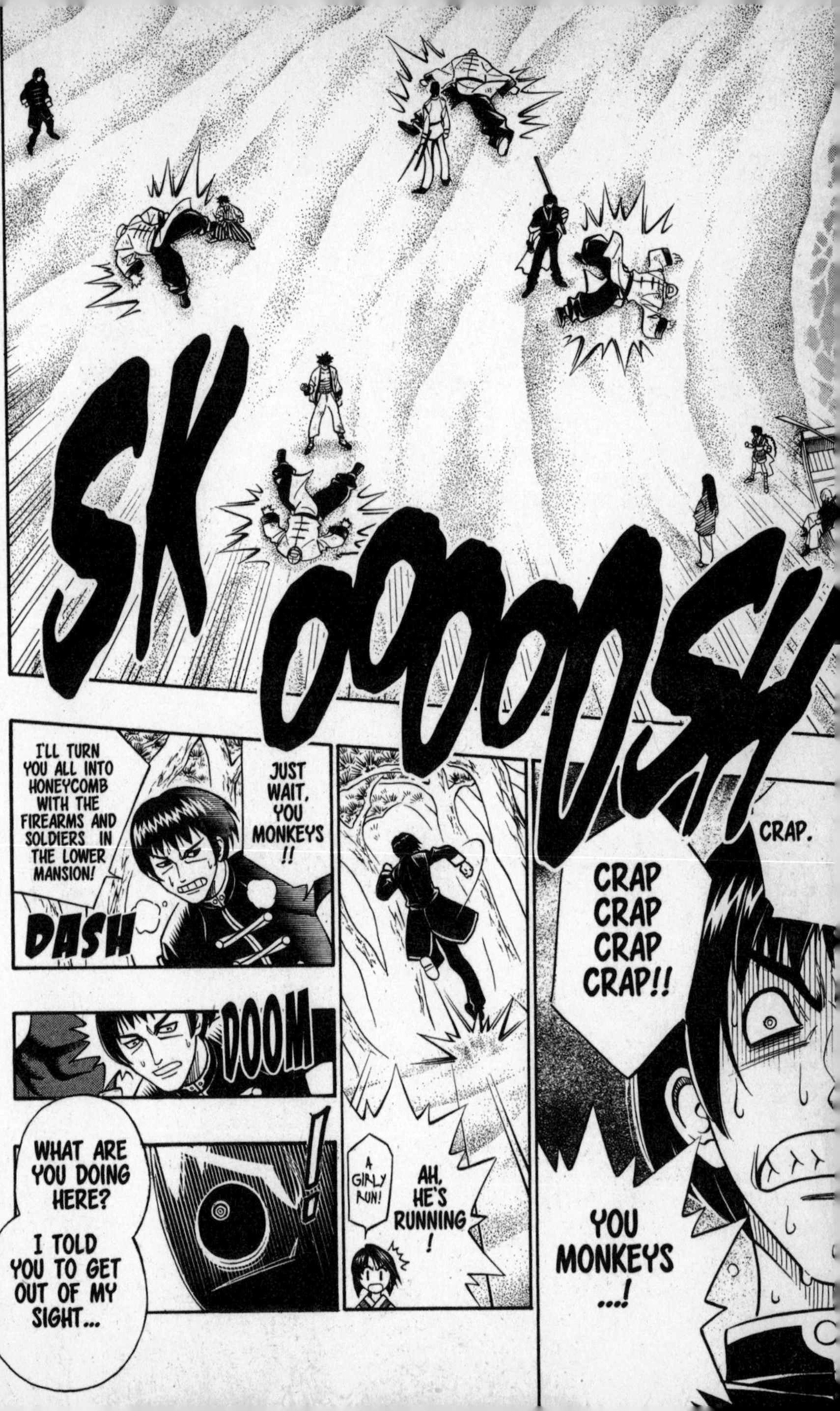
SKOOOOOSH
CRAP.
CRAP CRAP CRAP CRAP!!
YOU MONKEYS ...!
AH, HE'S RUNNING!
A GIRLY RUN!
JUST WAIT, YOU MONKEYS!!
I'LL TURN YOU ALL INTO HONEYCOMB WITH THE FIREARMS AND SOLDIERS IN THE LOWER MANSION!
DASH
DOOM
!
WHAT ARE YOU DOING HERE?
I TOLD YOU TO GET OUT OF MY SIGHT...

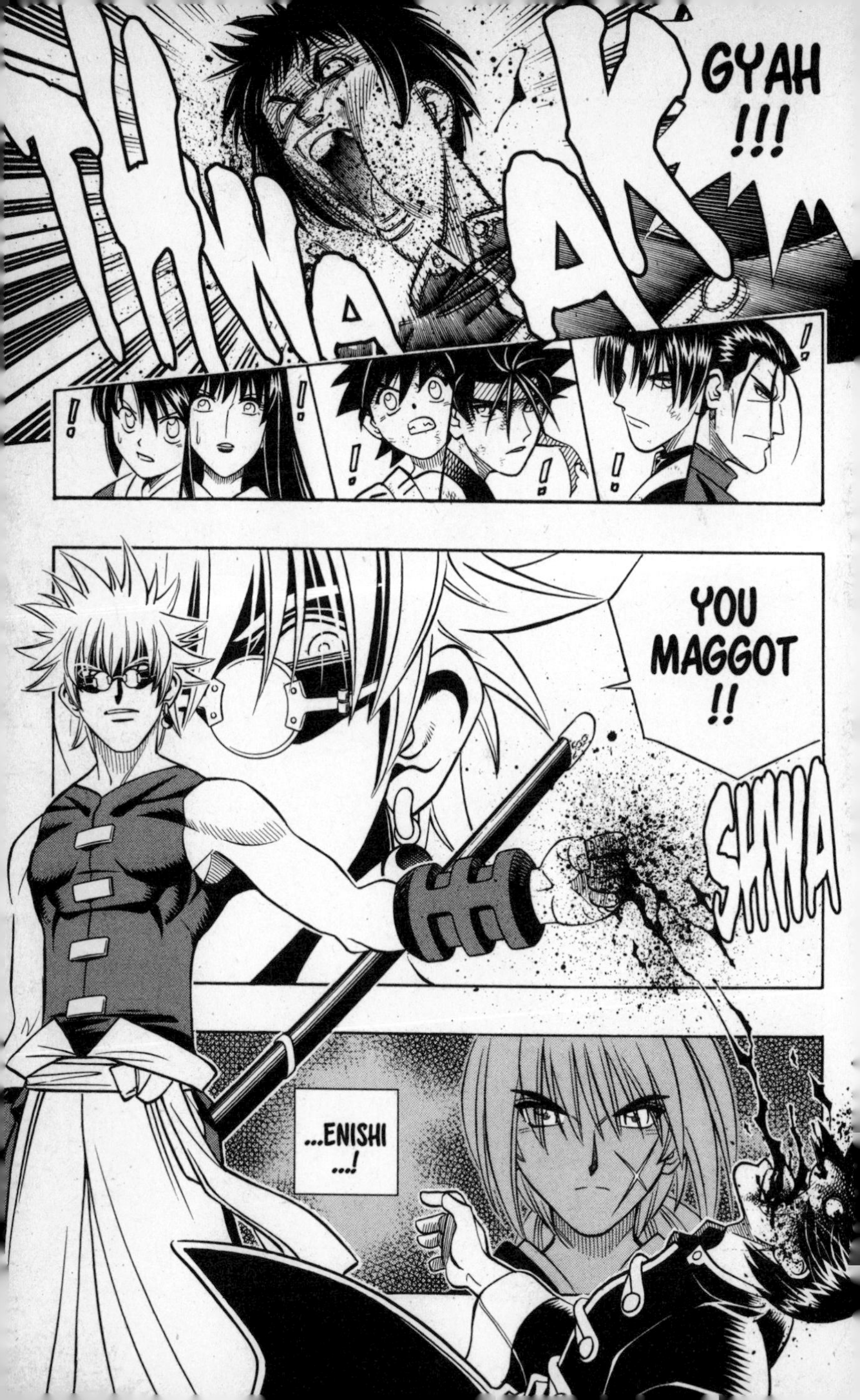
GYAH !!!
THWAAK
!
!
!
!
!
!
YOU MAGGOT !!
SHWA
...ENISHI ...!

The Secret Life of Characters (51)

—Sū-shin (Four Stars), Sū-shin (Four Gods)—

There is no model for their personalities. Actually, they have none...the *Sū-shin* were just made to fill out the numbers.

As the story advanced to the final battle, I realized "If it keeps going like this, Sanosuke and the rest will have no glamour," and I made these guys up on the spot. Because they were so irresponsibly made, I named them *Sū-shin* (Four Stars), but then changed their names to *Sū-shin* (Four Gods), giving them names according to the four godly beasts. Later I realized what I had done, and tried to patch up the dialogue to make it work, but it got weird. And the battles were not as glamorous as I had hoped for, either. It made me realize that "Having the scenes and plot made way in advance is very important."

There are no models in terms of design either. It was simply an "easy to draw" design, turning them into quadruplets in Chinese costumes without any tone or anything. You can at least tell them apart by the tattoos on their heads and their weapons, but that's it. Misao's comments about "mass produced" hits the bull's eye.

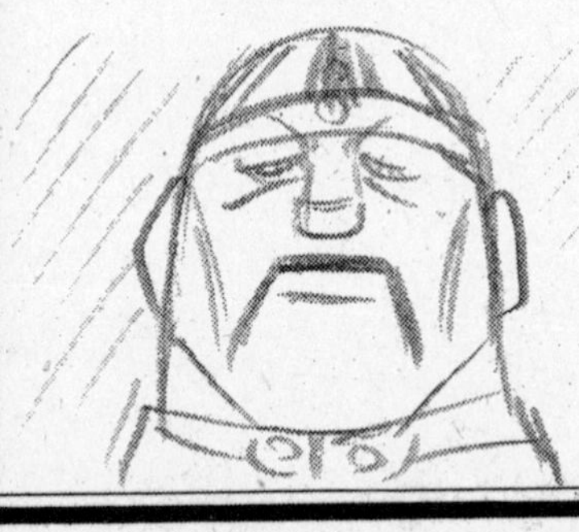

伸宏
和月

Act 243
The Dragon and the Tiger Meet Again

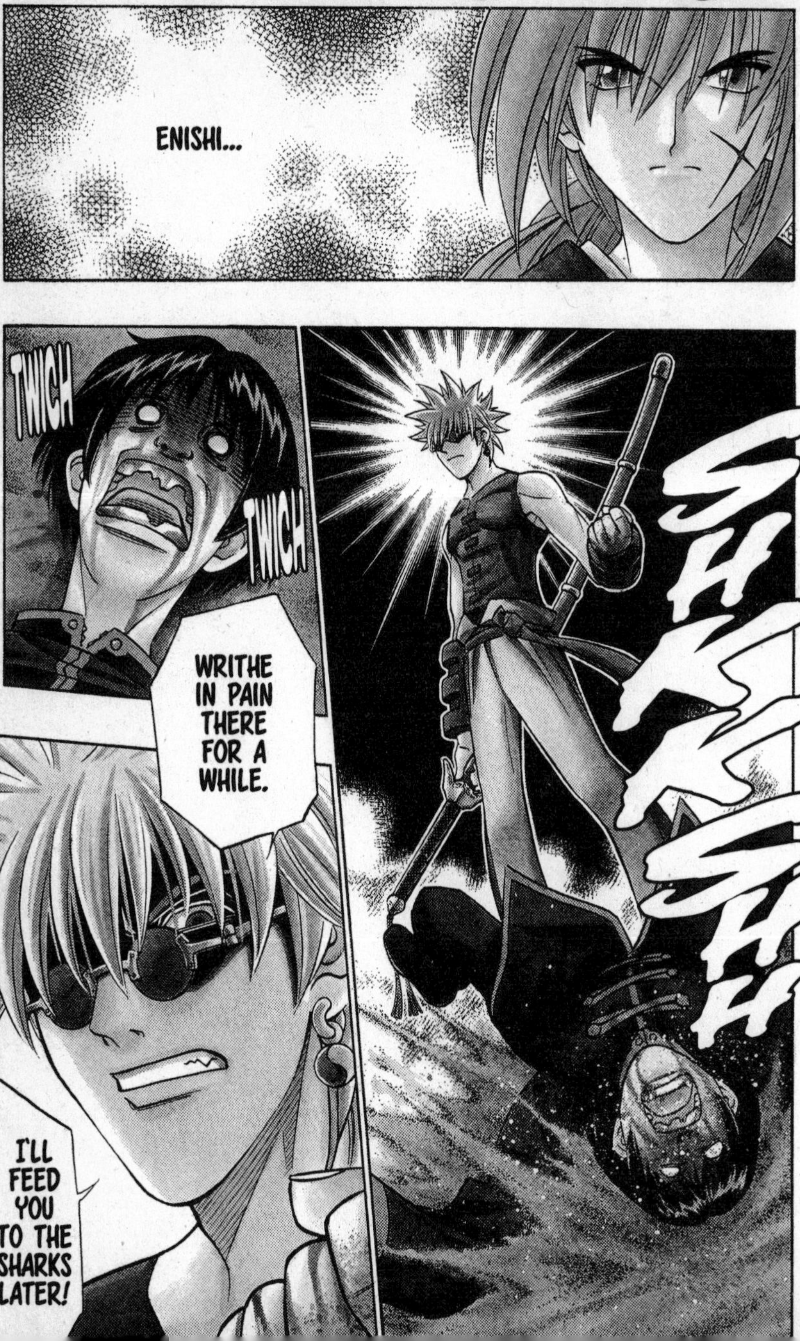

ENISHI...
TWICH
TWICH
WRITHE IN PAIN THERE FOR A WHILE.
I'LL FEED YOU TO THE SHARKS LATER!

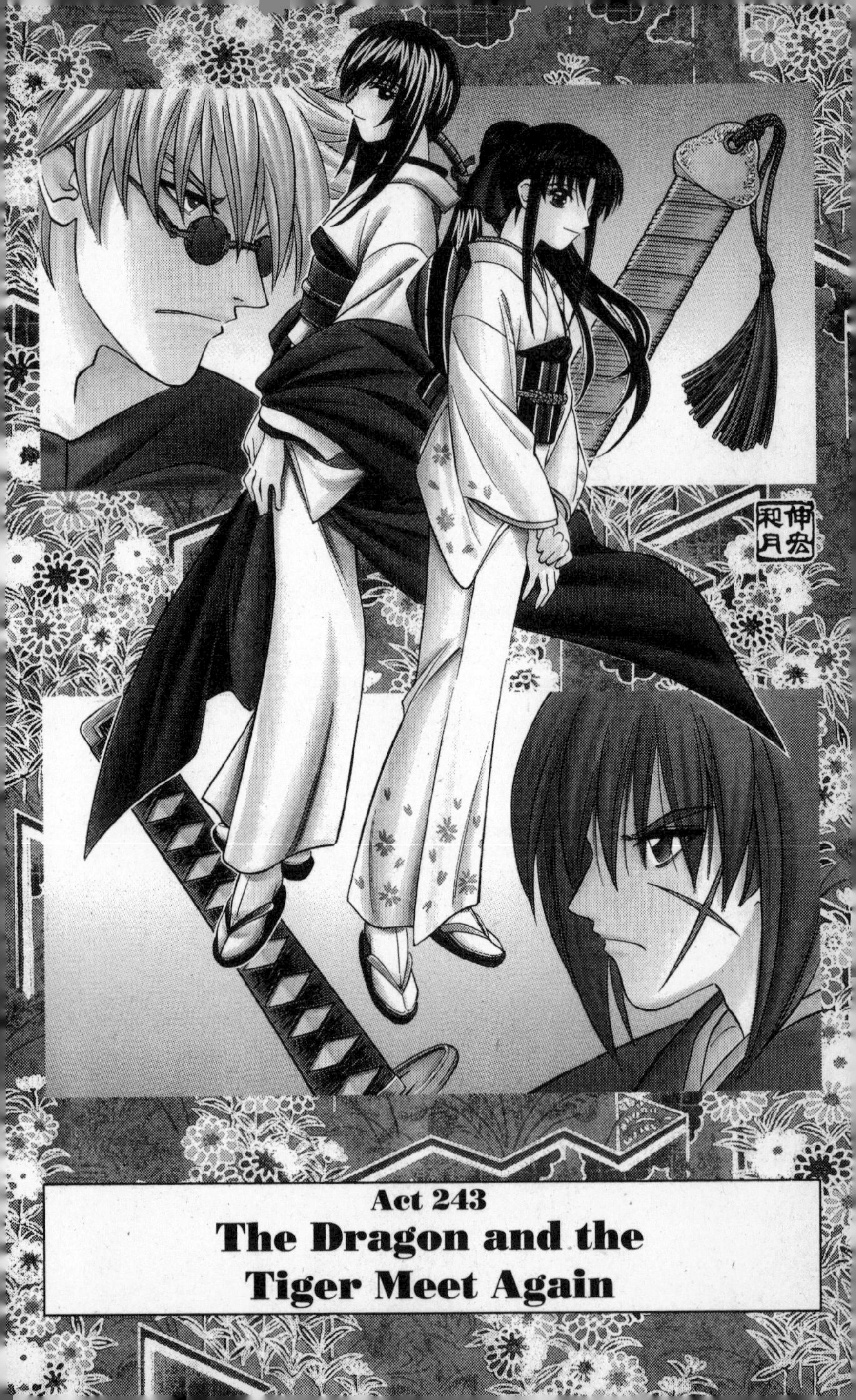

Act 243
The Dragon and the Tiger Meet Again

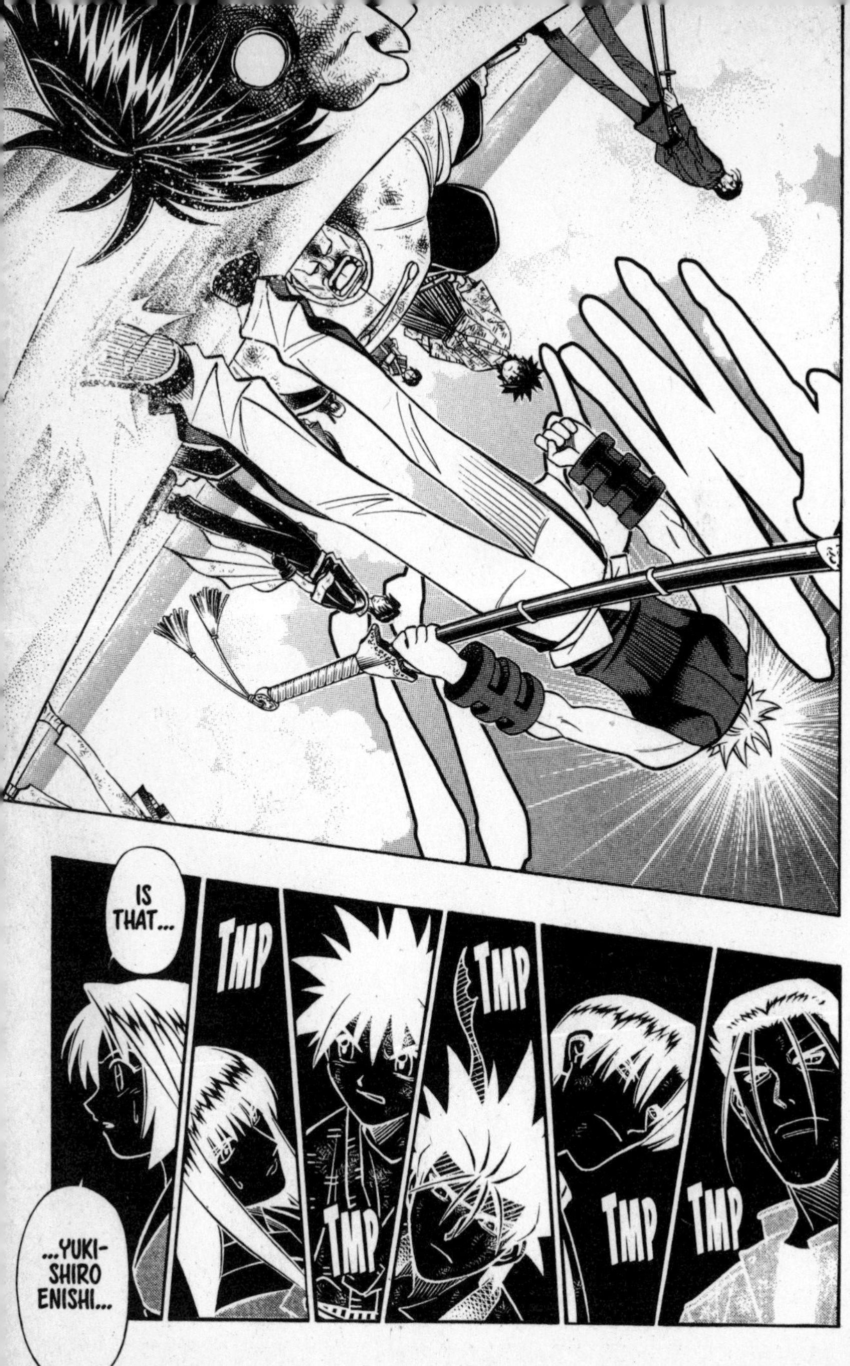
TMP
TMP
TMP
TMP
TMP
IS THAT...
...YUKI-SHIRO ENISHI...

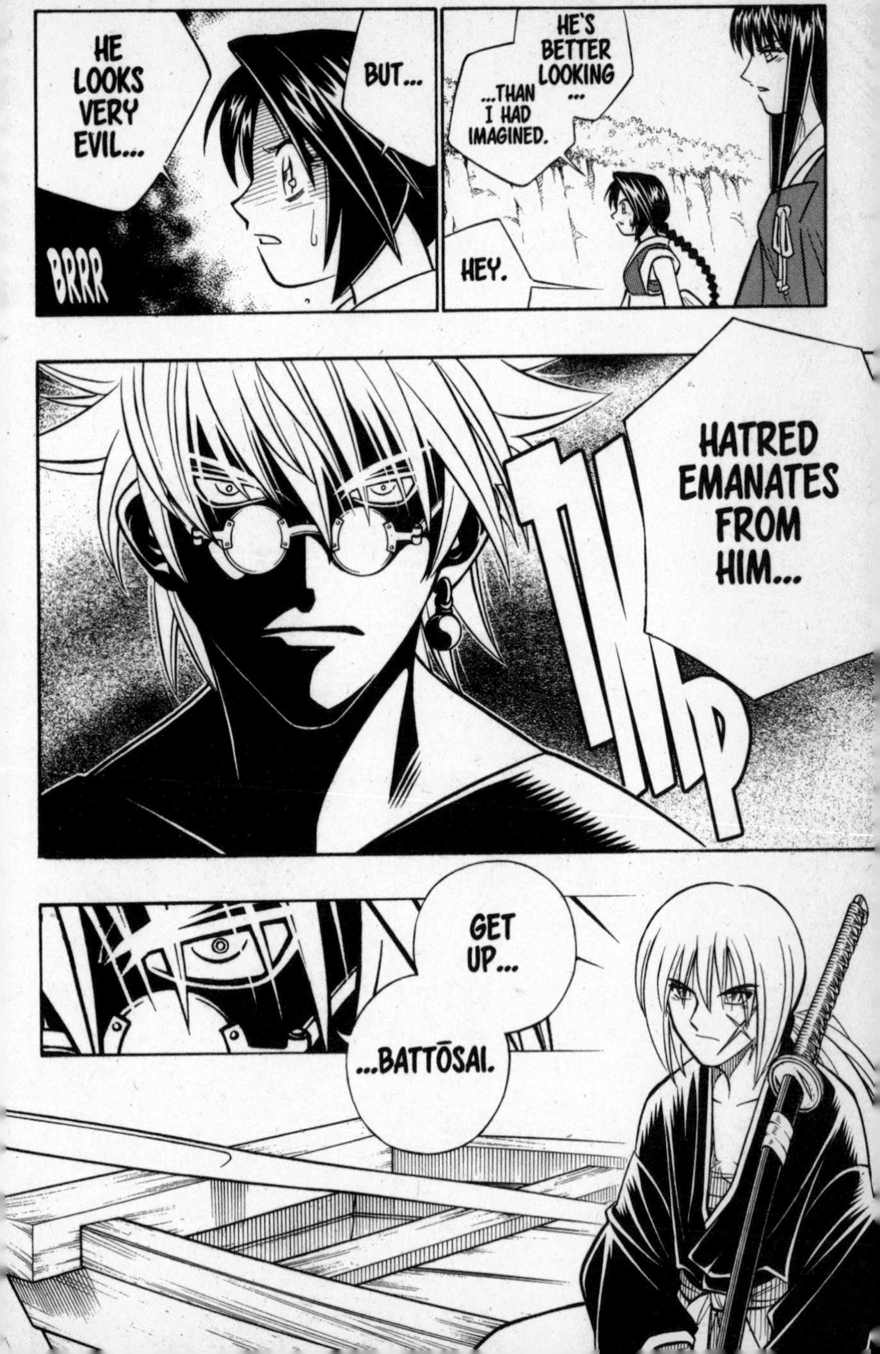
HE'S BETTER LOOKING ...
...THAN I HAD IMAGINED.
HEY.
BUT...
HE LOOKS VERY EVIL...
BRRR
HATRED EMANATES FROM HIM...
THMP
GET UP...
...BATTŌSAI.

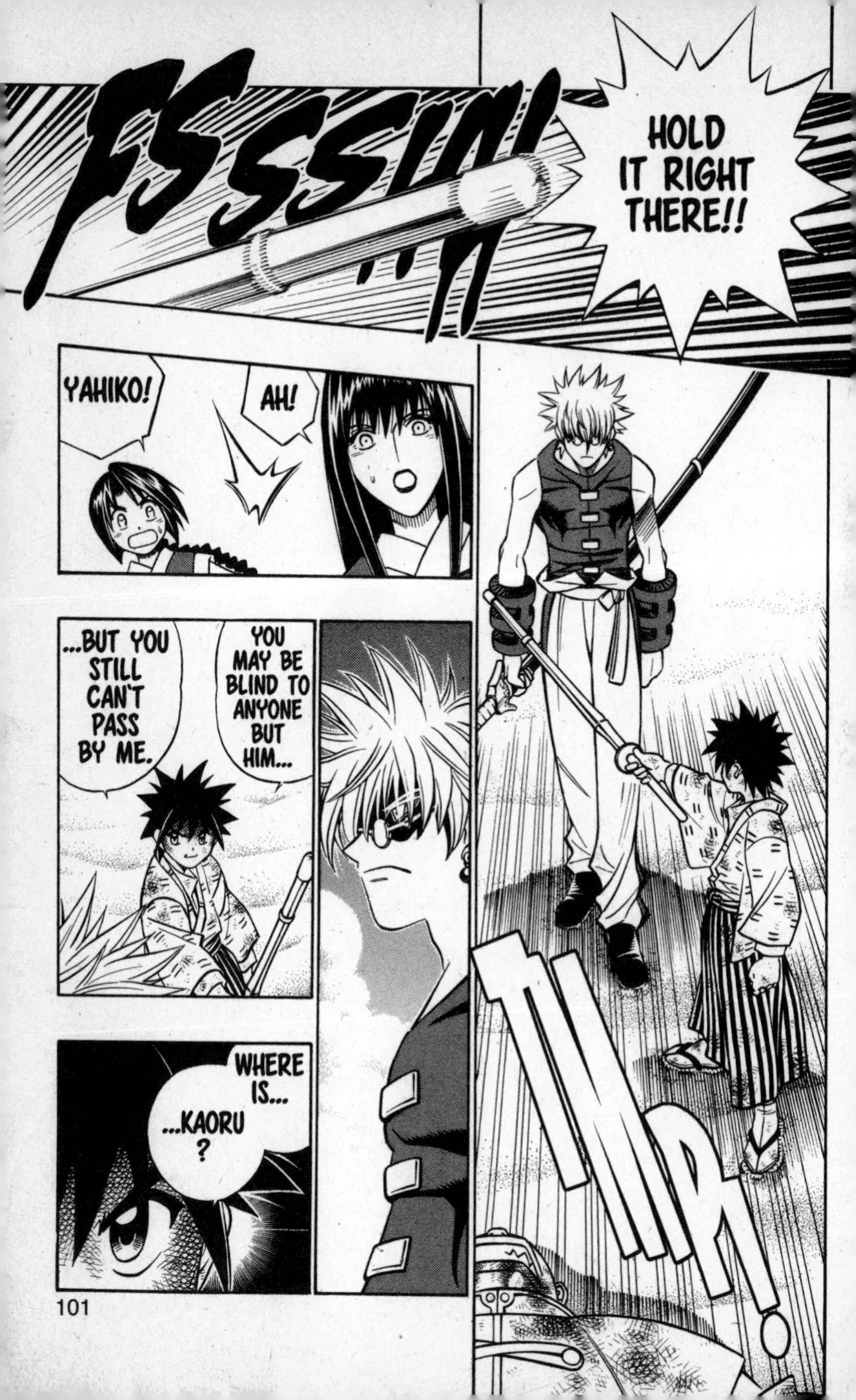
HOLD IT RIGHT THERE!!
AH!
YAHIKO!
YOU MAY BE BLIND TO ANYONE BUT HIM...
...BUT YOU STILL CAN'T PASS BY ME.
WHERE IS...
...KAORU?

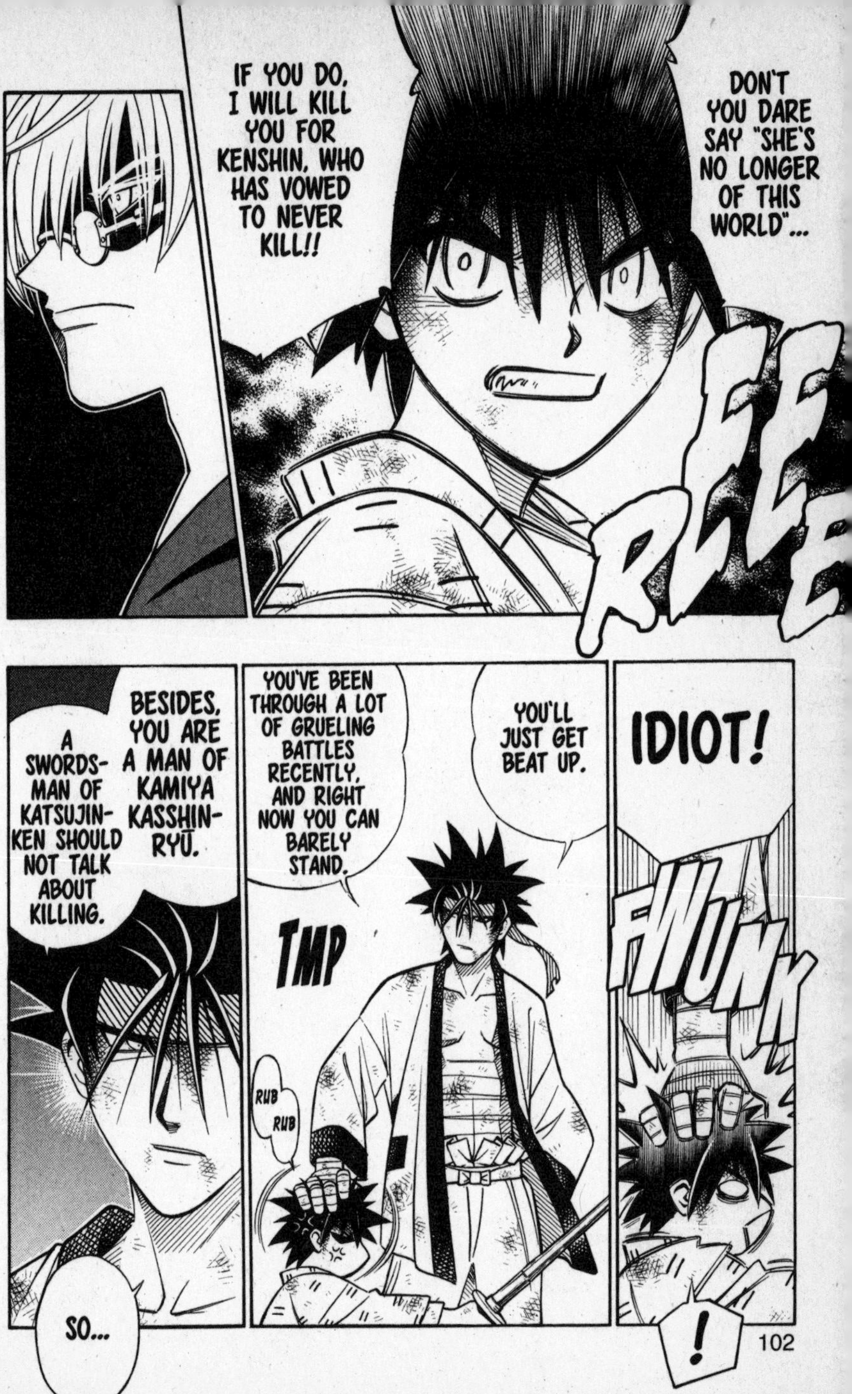
DON'T YOU DARE SAY "SHE'S NO LONGER OF THIS WORLD"...
IF YOU DO, I WILL KILL YOU FOR KENSHIN, WHO HAS VOWED TO NEVER KILL!!
IDIOT!
FWUNK
!
YOU'LL JUST GET BEAT UP.
YOU'VE BEEN THROUGH A LOT OF GRUELING BATTLES RECENTLY, AND RIGHT NOW YOU CAN BARELY STAND.
TMP
RUB RUB
BESIDES, YOU ARE A MAN OF KAMIYA KASSHIN-RYŪ.
A SWORDS-MAN OF KATSUJIN-KEN SHOULD NOT TALK ABOUT KILLING.
SO...

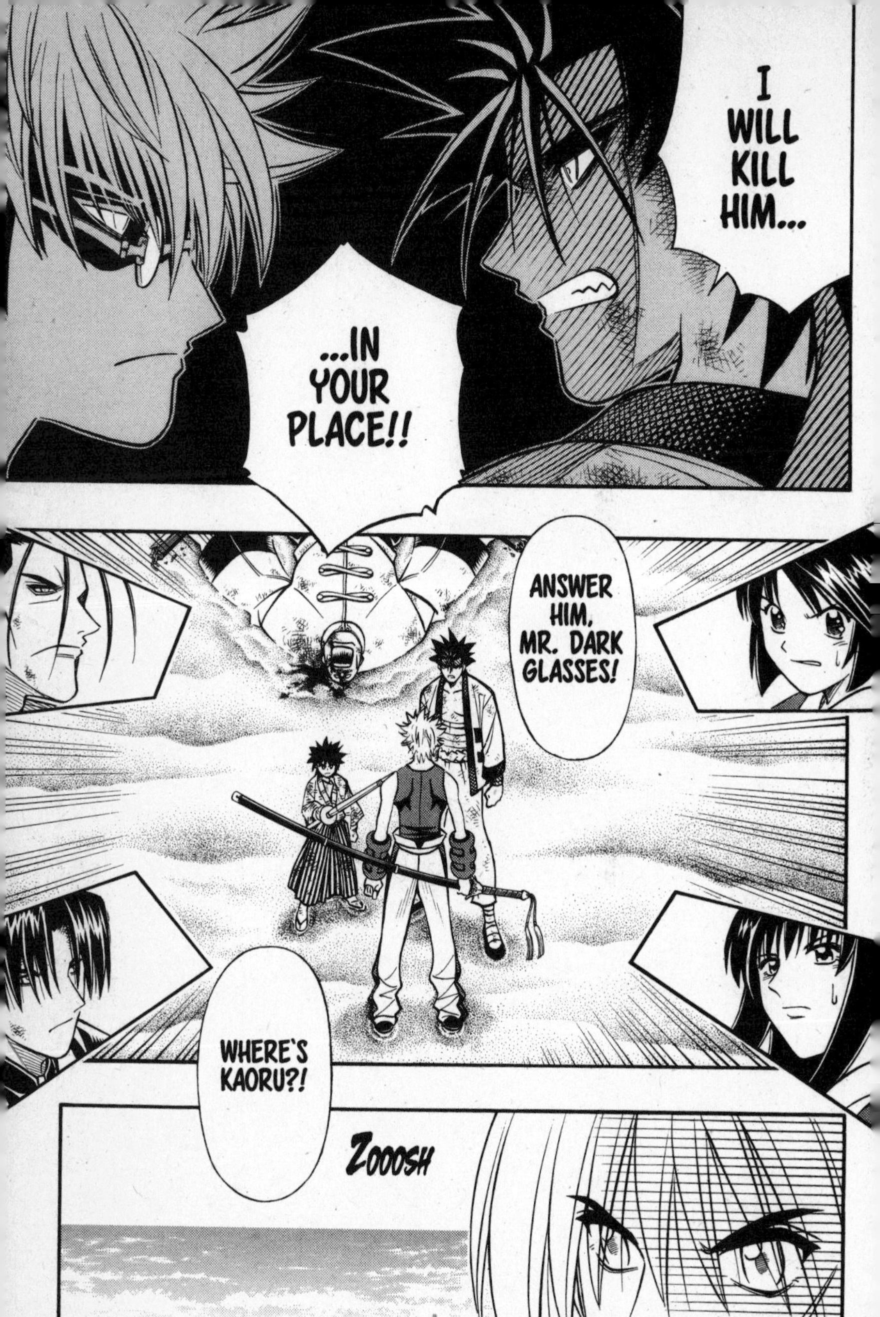
I WILL KILL HIM...
...IN YOUR PLACE!!
ANSWER HIM, MR. DARK GLASSES!
WHERE'S KAORU?!
ZOOOSH

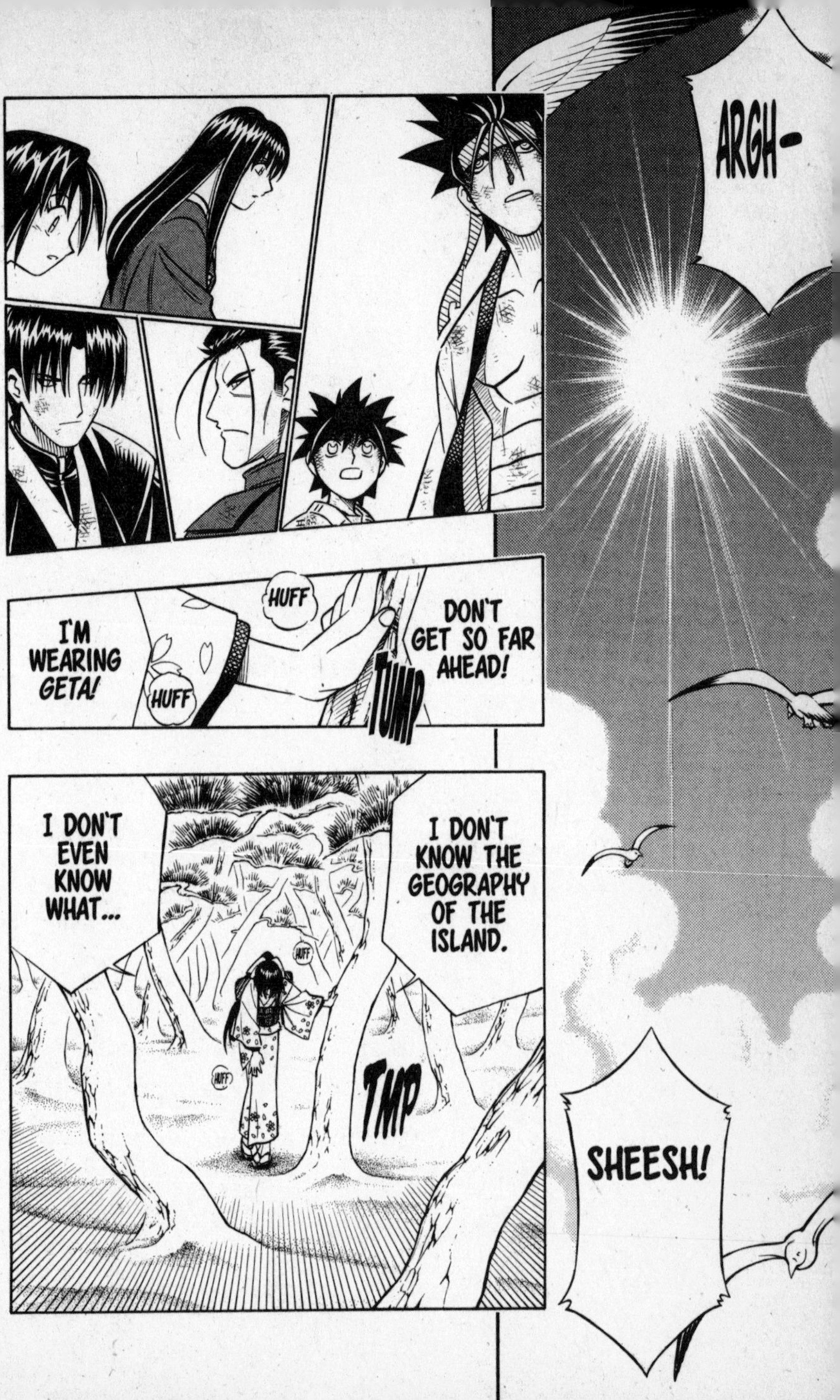
ARGH-
SHEESH!
DON'T GET SO FAR AHEAD!
HUFF
TUMP
I'M WEARING GETA!
HUFF
I DON'T KNOW THE GEOGRAPHY OF THE ISLAND.
I DON'T EVEN KNOW WHAT...
HUFF
TMP
HUFF

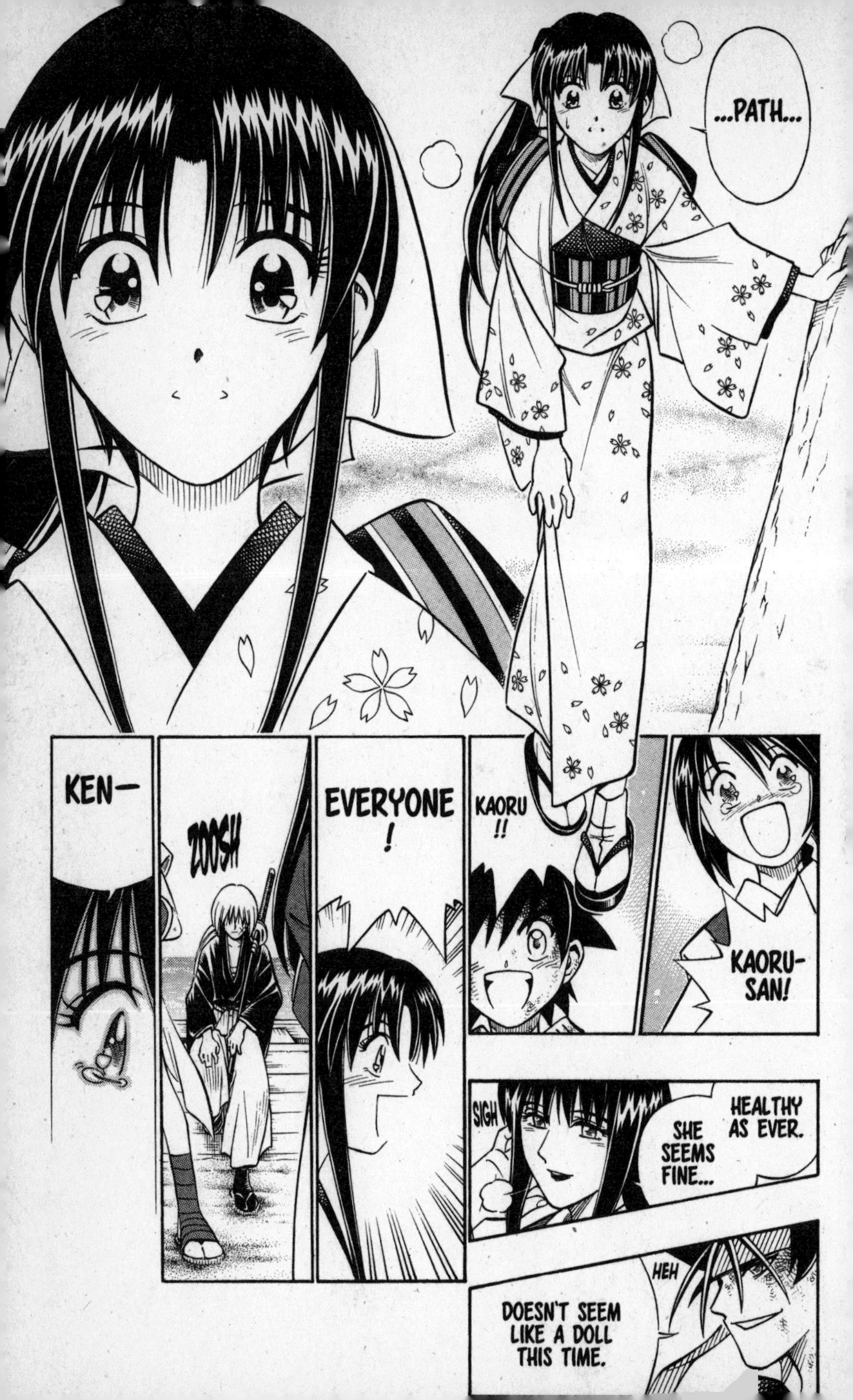
...PATH...
KAORU-SAN!
KAORU !!
SIGH
HEALTHY AS EVER.
SHE SEEMS FINE...
HEH
DOESN'T SEEM LIKE A DOLL THIS TIME.
EVERYONE !
ZOOSH
KEN—

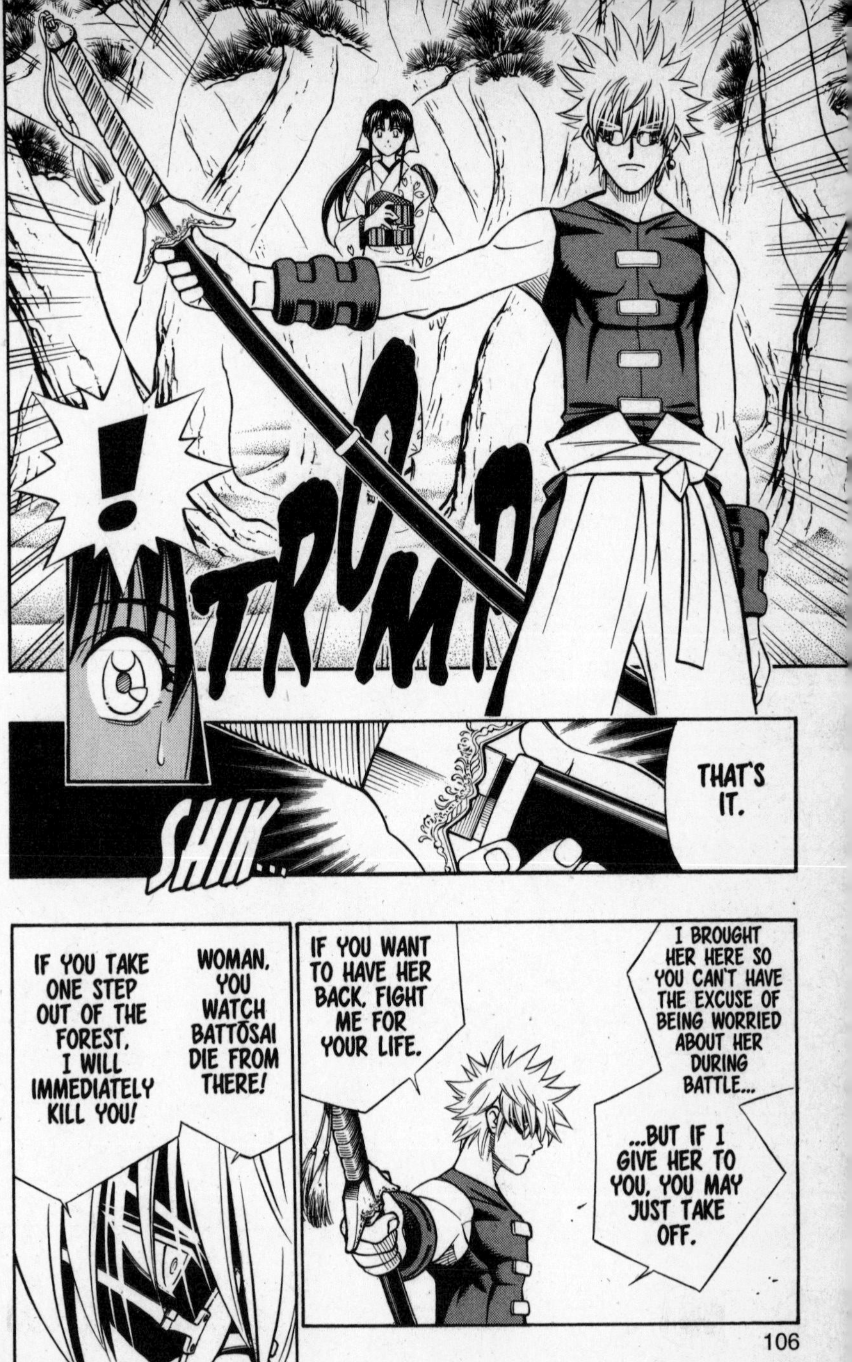
TRUMP
!
THAT'S IT.
SHIK...
I BROUGHT HER HERE SO YOU CAN'T HAVE THE EXCUSE OF BEING WORRIED ABOUT HER DURING BATTLE...
...BUT IF I GIVE HER TO YOU, YOU MAY JUST TAKE OFF.
IF YOU WANT TO HAVE HER BACK, FIGHT ME FOR YOUR LIFE.
WOMAN, YOU WATCH BATTŌSAI DIE FROM THERE!
IF YOU TAKE ONE STEP OUT OF THE FOREST, I WILL IMMEDIATELY KILL YOU!

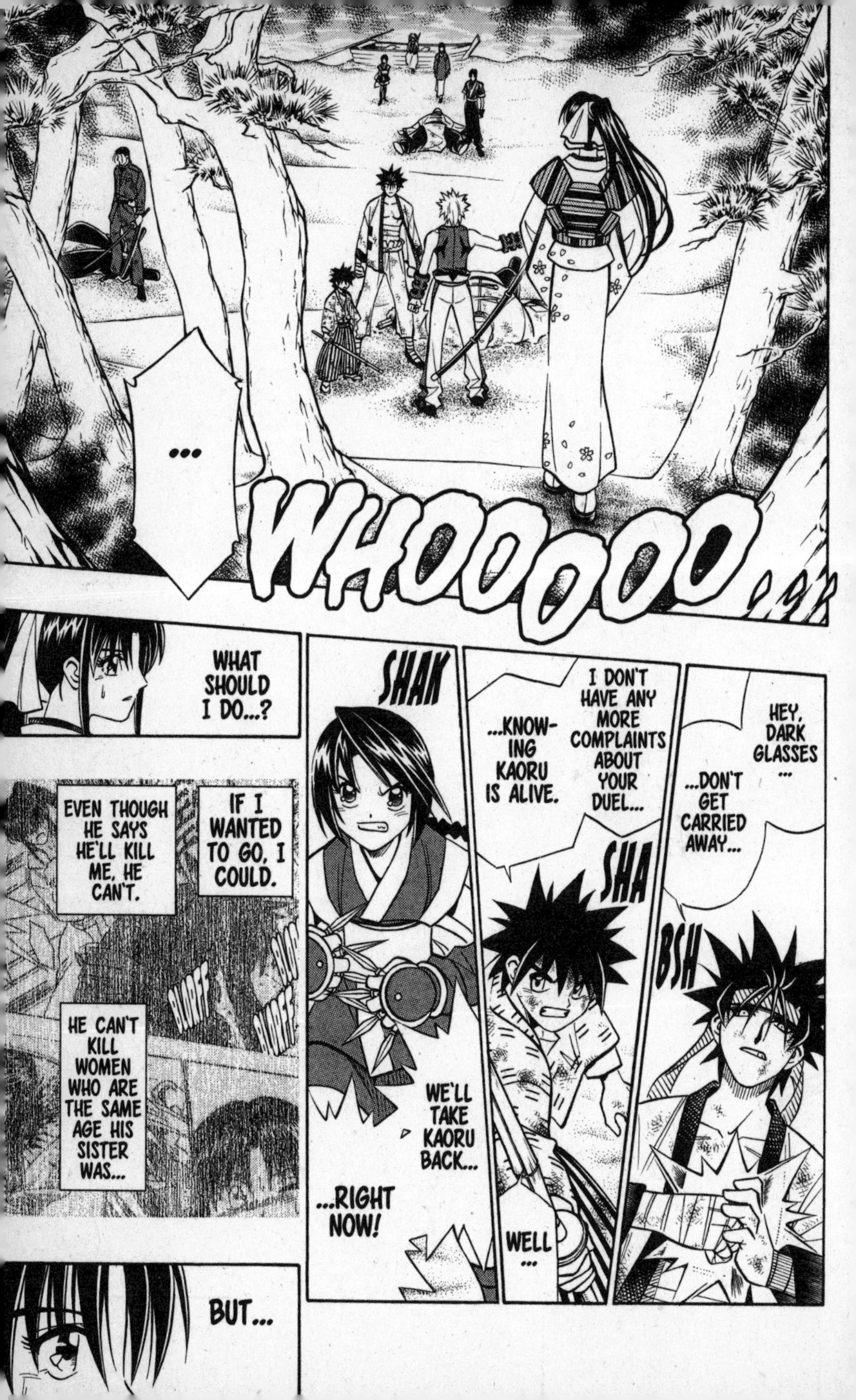
...
WHOOOOOO...
HEY, DARK GLASSES...
...DON'T GET CARRIED AWAY...
BSH
I DON'T HAVE ANY MORE COMPLAINTS ABOUT YOUR DUEL...
...KNOWING KAORU IS ALIVE.
SHA
WELL...
SHAK
WE'LL TAKE KAORU BACK...
...RIGHT NOW!
WHAT SHOULD I DO...?
IF I WANTED TO GO, I COULD.
EVEN THOUGH HE SAYS HE'LL KILL ME, HE CAN'T.
HE CAN'T KILL WOMEN WHO ARE THE SAME AGE HIS SISTER WAS...
BUT...

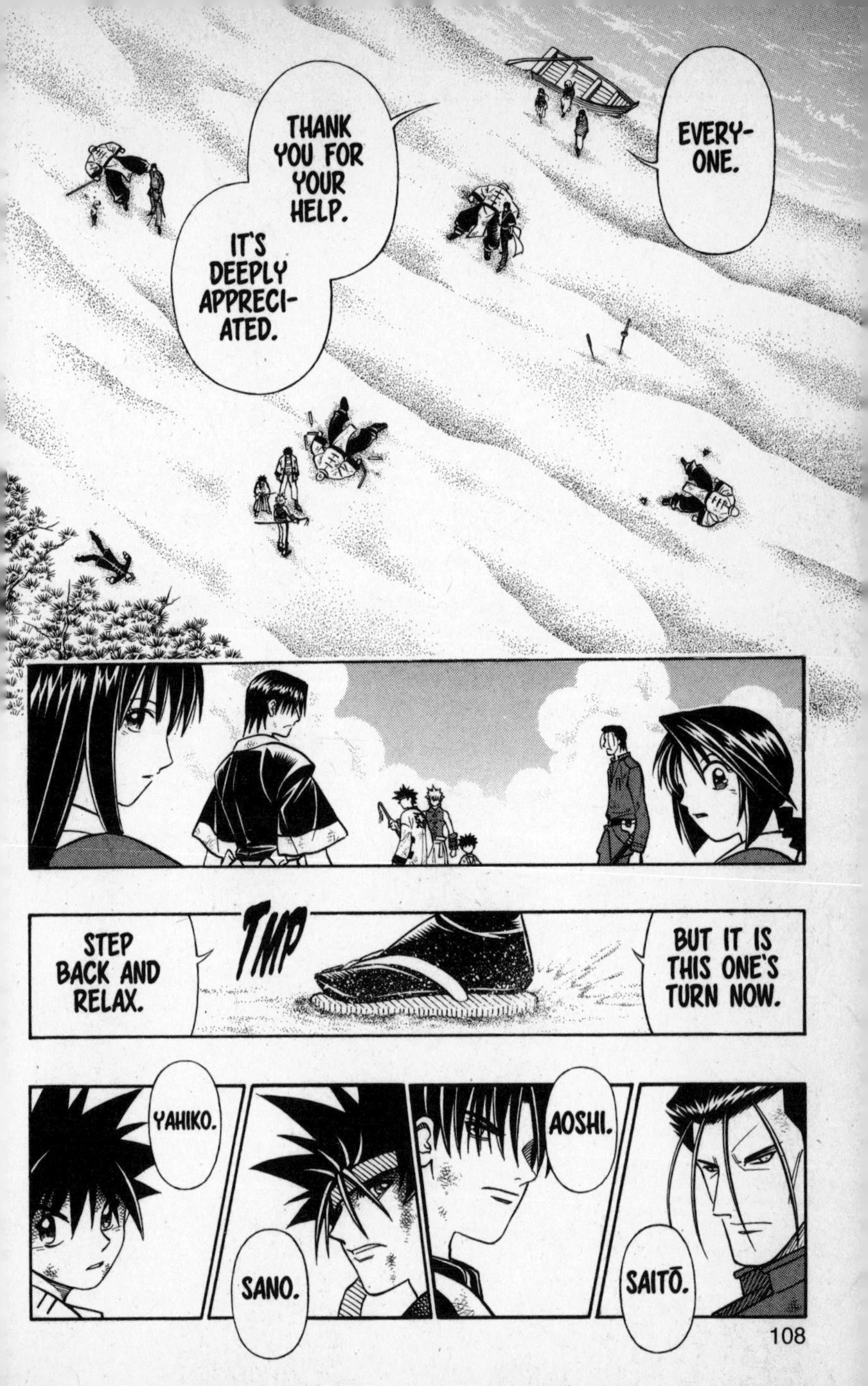
EVERY-ONE.
THANK YOU FOR YOUR HELP.
IT'S DEEPLY APPRECIATED.
BUT IT IS THIS ONE'S TURN NOW.
TMP
STEP BACK AND RELAX.
SAITŌ.
AOSHI.
SANO.
YAHIKO.

READ THIS WAY

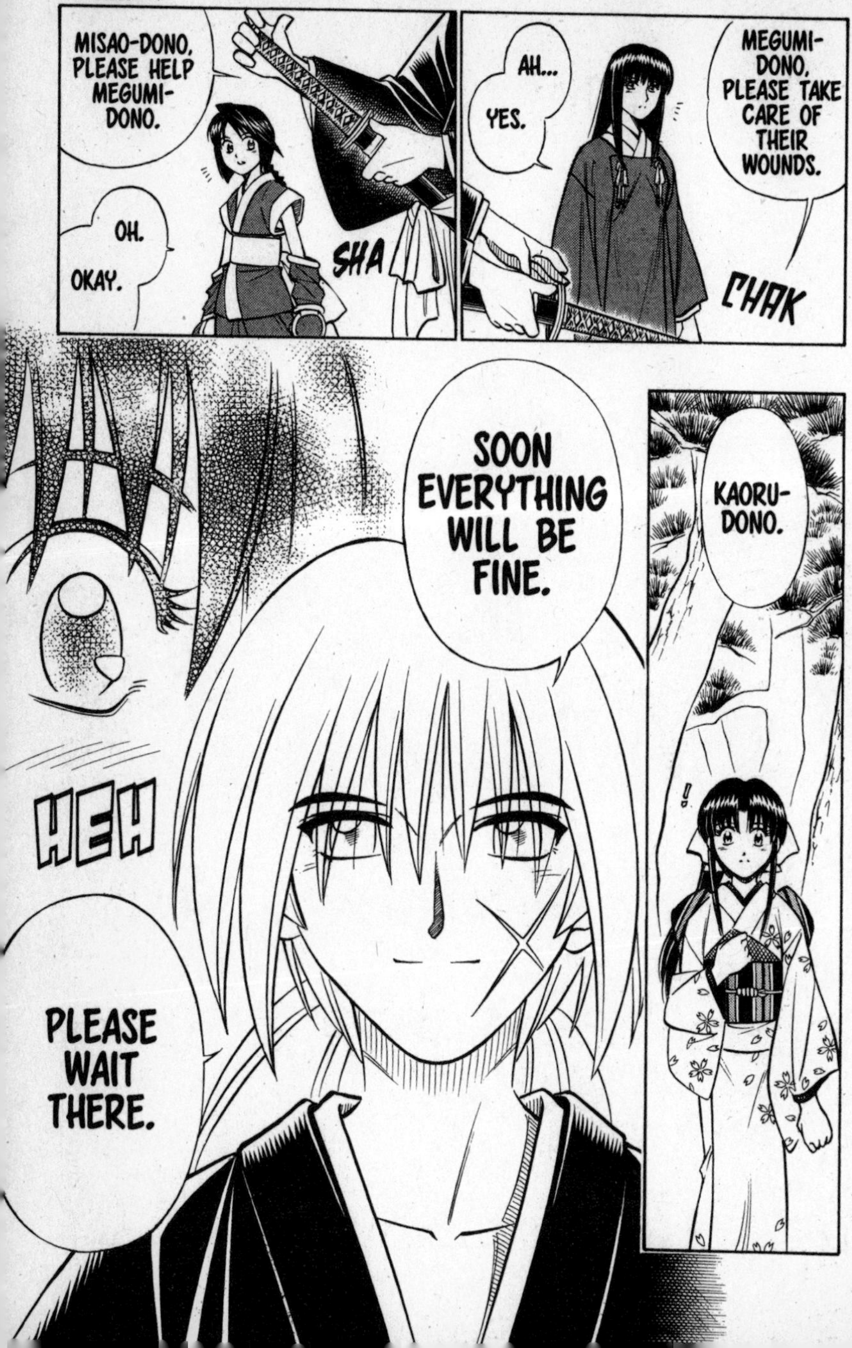
MEGUMI-DONO, PLEASE TAKE CARE OF THEIR WOUNDS.
AH... YES.
CHAK
MISAO-DONO, PLEASE HELP MEGUMI-DONO.
SHA
OH. OKAY.
KAORU-DONO.
!
SOON EVERYTHING WILL BE FINE.
HEH
PLEASE WAIT THERE.

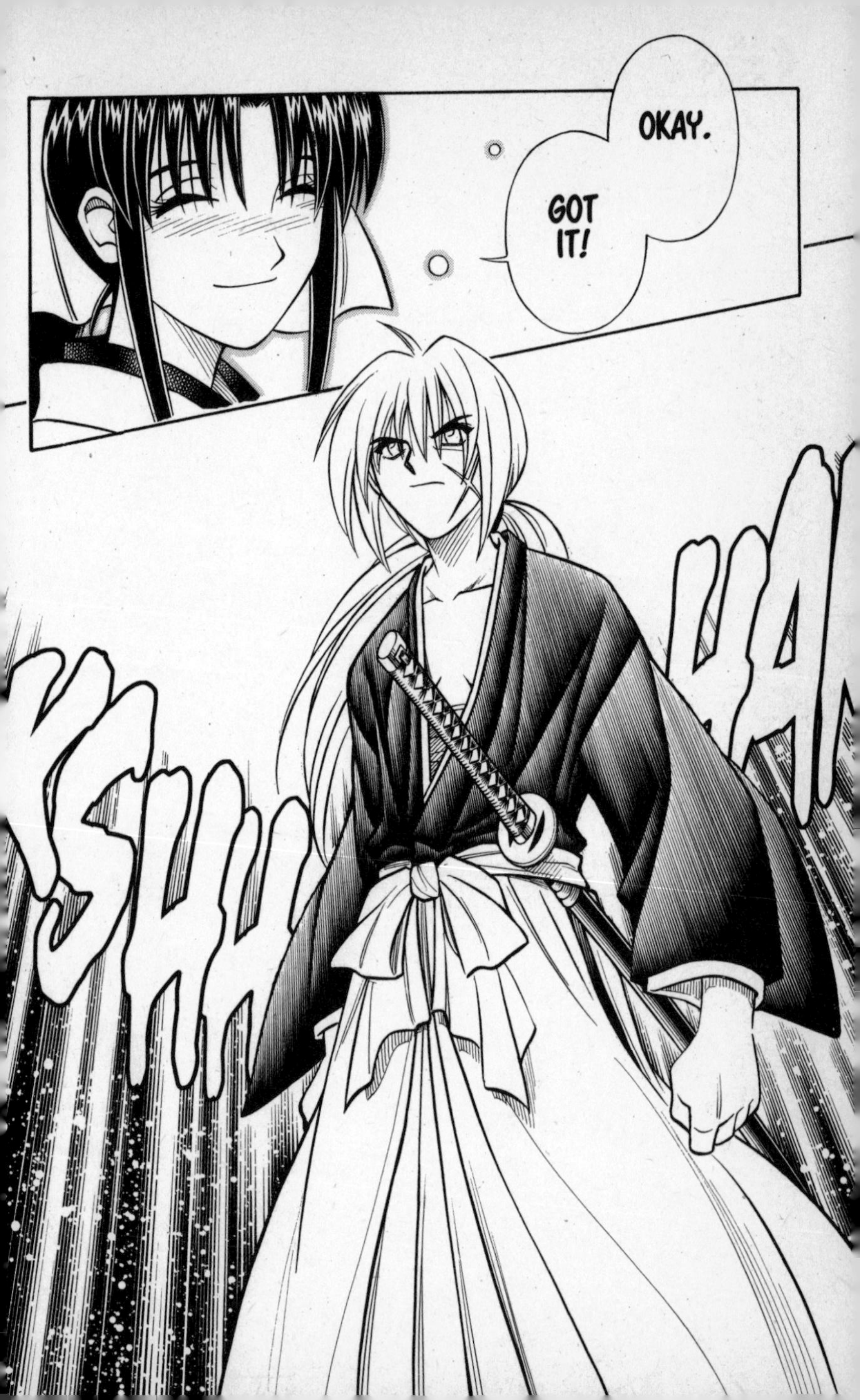
OKAY.
GOT IT!
SHHA

READ THIS WAY

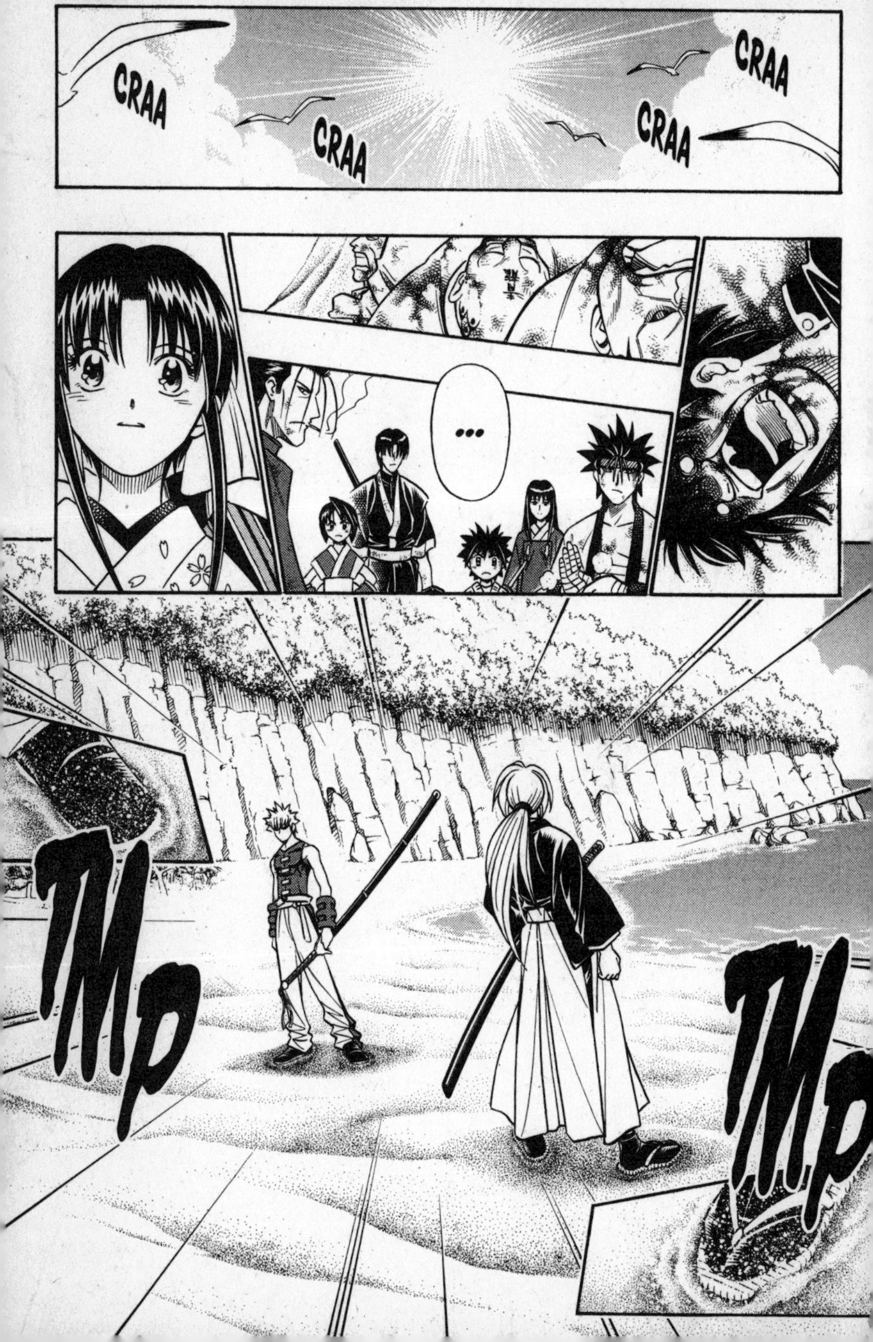
CRAA
CRAA
CRAA
CRAA
...
TMP
TMP

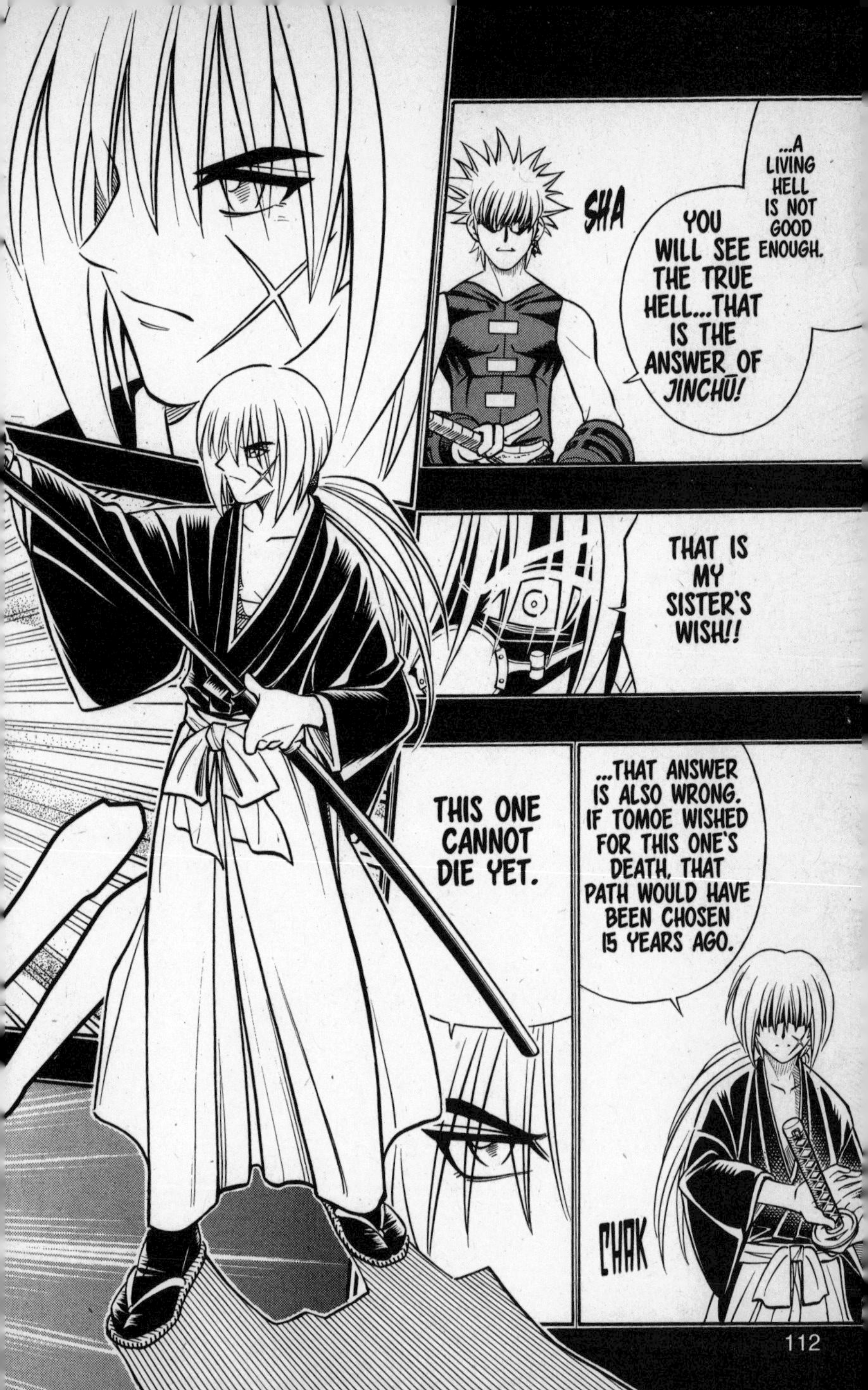
...A LIVING HELL IS NOT GOOD ENOUGH.
SHA
YOU WILL SEE THE TRUE HELL...THAT IS THE ANSWER OF JINCHŪ!
THAT IS MY SISTER'S WISH!!
...THAT ANSWER IS ALSO WRONG. IF TOMOE WISHED FOR THIS ONE'S DEATH, THAT PATH WOULD HAVE BEEN CHOSEN 15 YEARS AGO.
CHAK
THIS ONE CANNOT DIE YET.

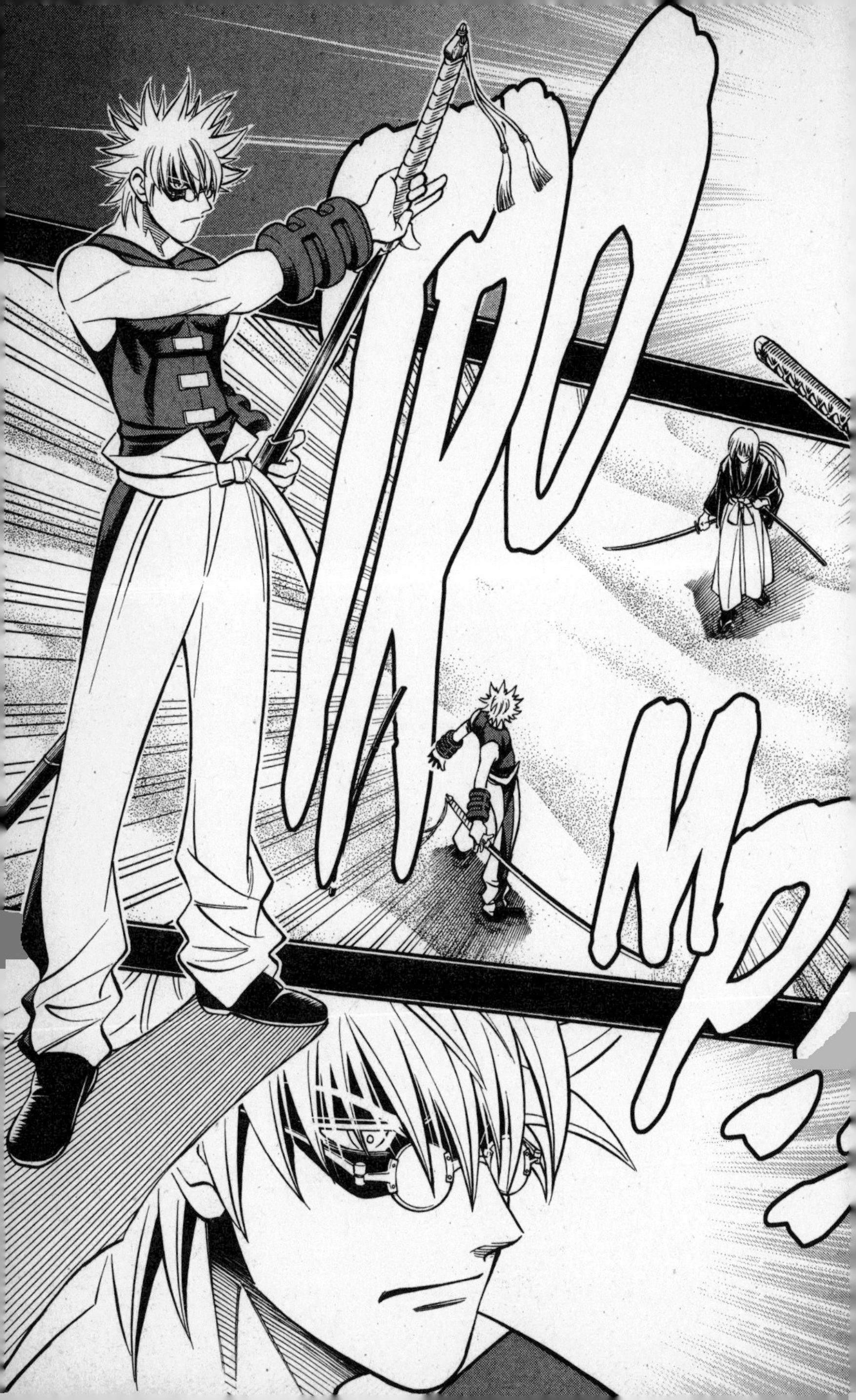
WHOMP!

The Secret Life of Characters (52)

—Woo Heishin—

There is no model for him. He was created after the editor's feedback to put some more depth into the "Black Market Weapons Organization." But the organization itself was only created to explain Enishi's financial situation, so adding Heishin didn't seem to change anything. We brought him out as the number two of the organization, but chapters just went by without being able to set his personality, and he became this pathetic creature. Although he was Watsuki's favorite "#2," he turned into an unattractive character. There is one more place where he makes an appearance, but I regret how this character turned out. This pertains to more than just Woo Heishin, because all of the characters in the *Jinchū* chapters show Watsuki's immaturity, so I regret it all.

I'd like to reflect upon this a lot and use the experience towards character creation in my next work.

There is also no model in terms of design. I designed Woo Heishin around the time of the Tomoe episode, and I felt that "Originality is a writer's best weapon!" (I felt it like a body blow occasionally throughout the five years, but this was the decisive blow. I'm so stupid. I would like to retrain and come back.) That made me head in the opposite direction of my influences, creating characters that did not obviously look like others. Woo Heishin was designed to be heavy on the black, as a contrast to the whiteness of Enishi.

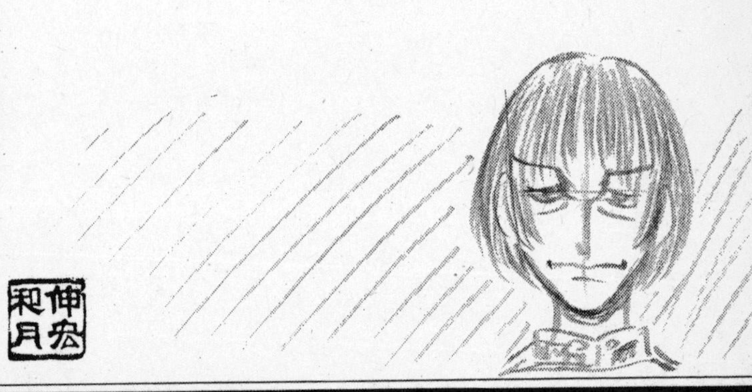

伸宏
和月

Act 244—Sword Strikes

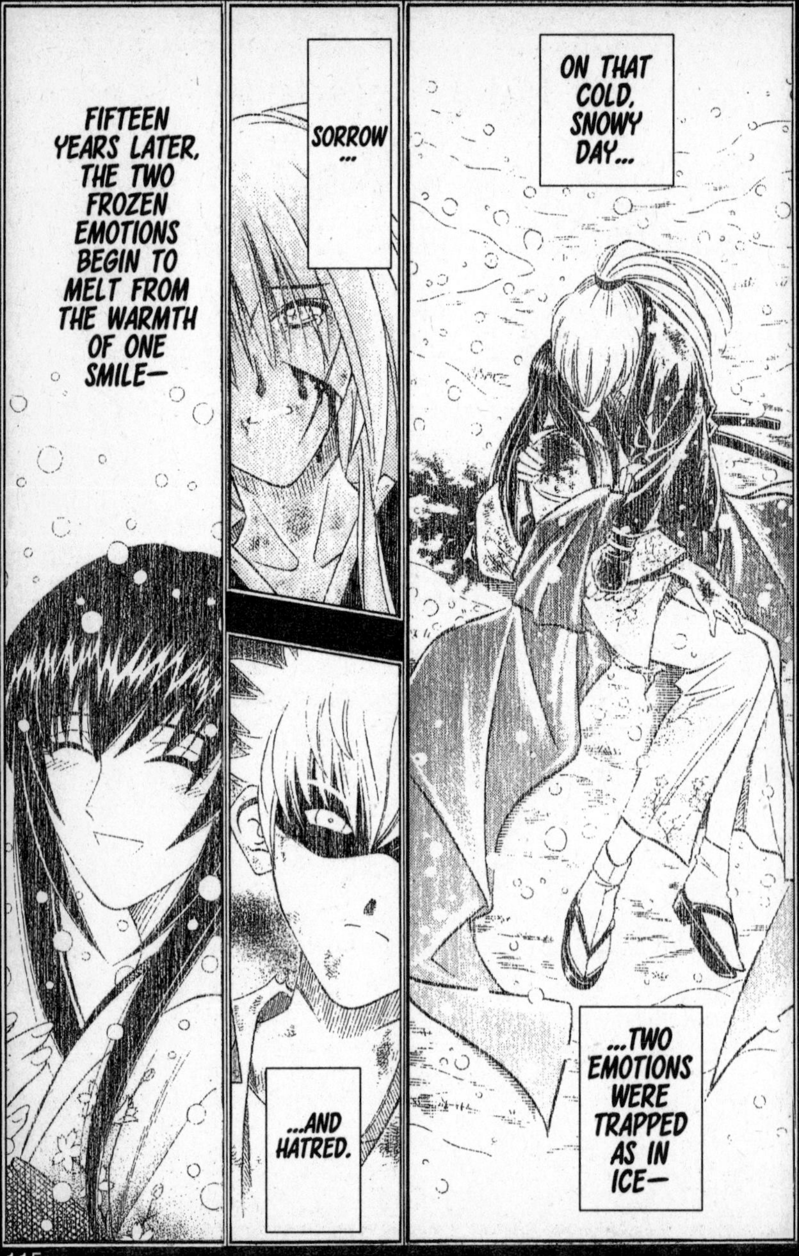
ON THAT COLD, SNOWY DAY...
...TWO EMOTIONS WERE TRAPPED AS IN ICE—
SORROW...
...AND HATRED.
FIFTEEN YEARS LATER, THE TWO FROZEN EMOTIONS BEGIN TO MELT FROM THE WARMTH OF ONE SMILE—

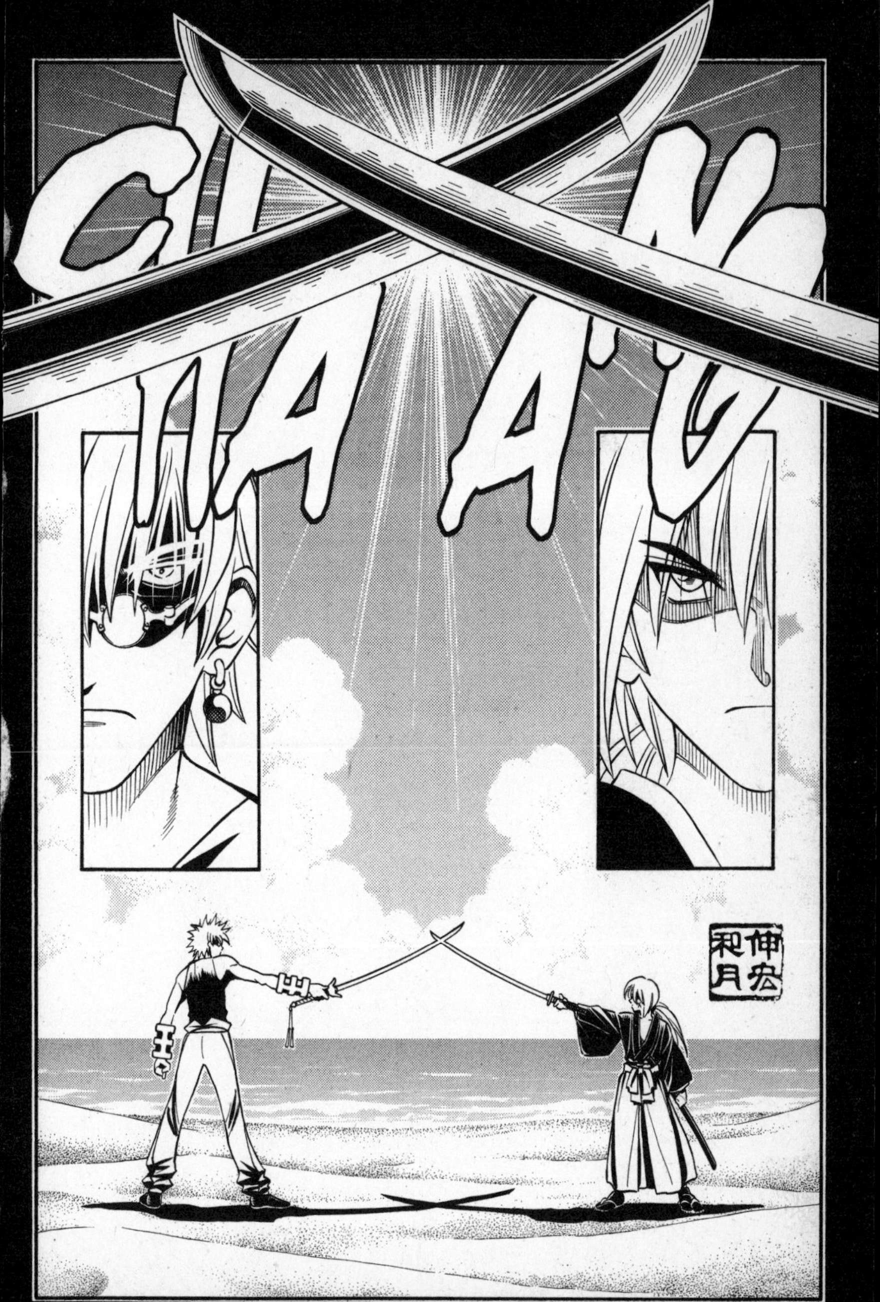
伸宏
和月

Act 244—Sword Strikes

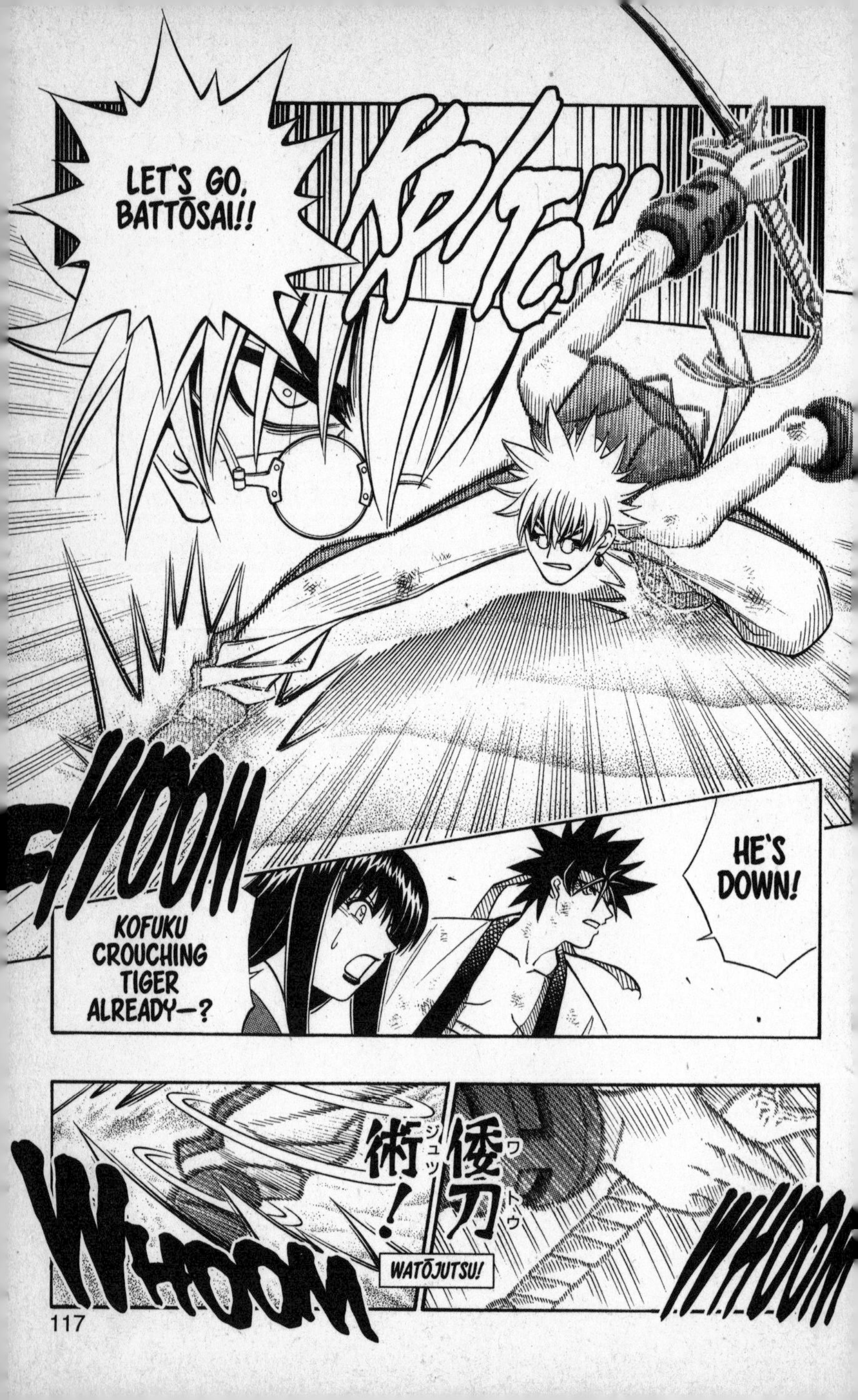
LET'S GO, BATTŌSAI!!
HE'S DOWN!
KOFUKU CROUCHING TIGER ALREADY—?
倭刀術！
WATŌJUTSU!

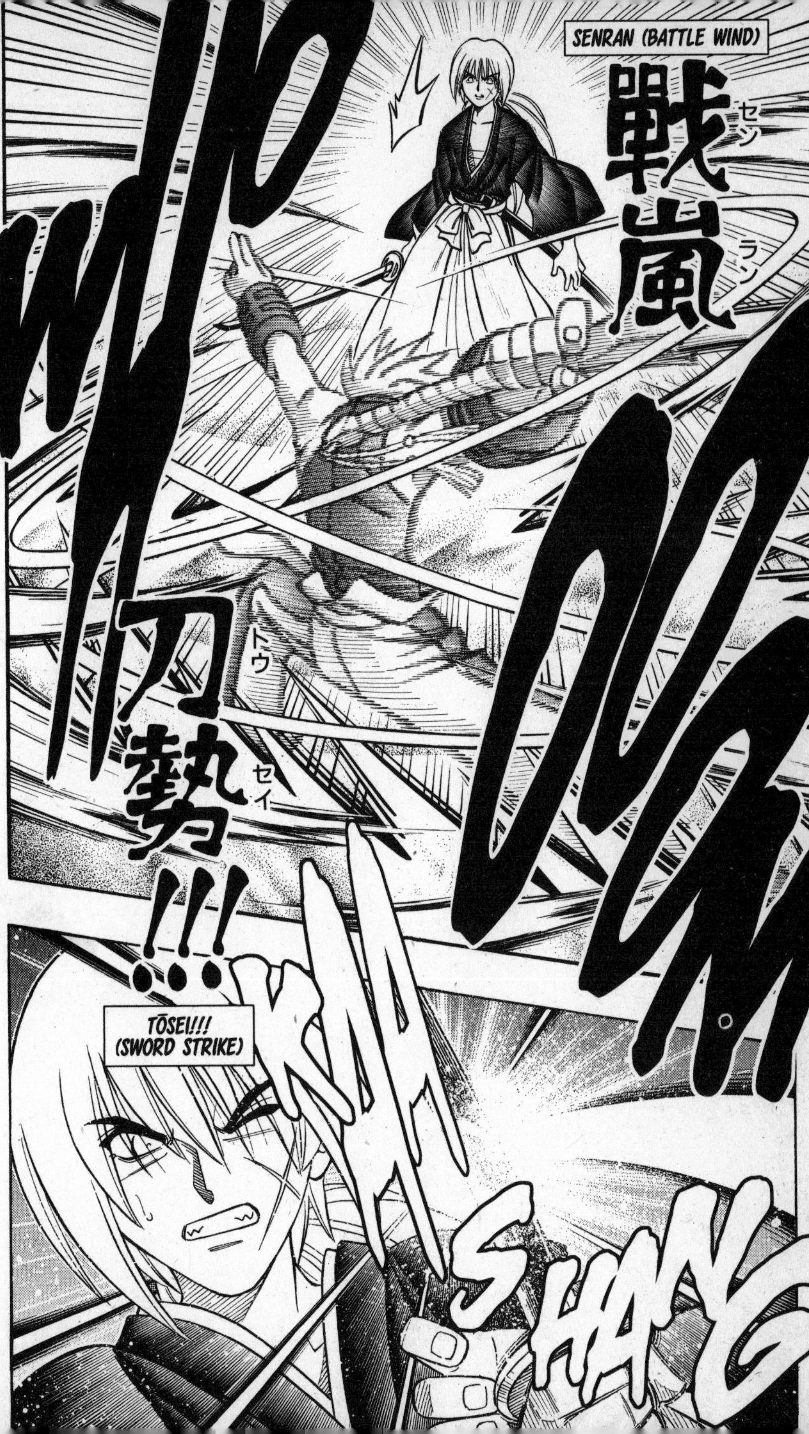
SENRAN (BATTLE WIND)
戦嵐（セン ラン）
刀勢（トウ セイ）!!!
TŌSEI!!! (SWORD STRIKE)
SHANG

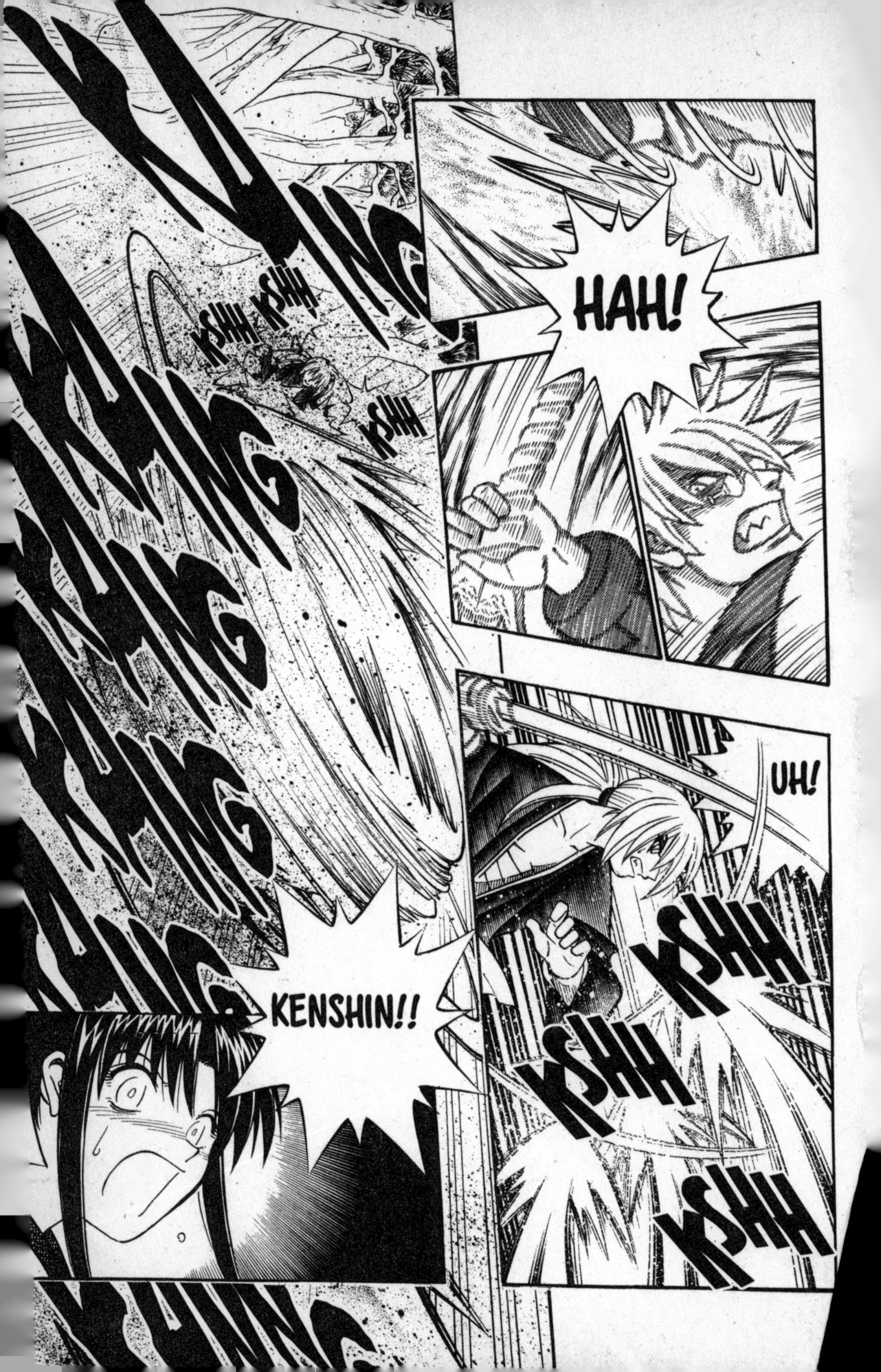
HAH!
UH!
KSHH
KSHH
KSHH
KSHH
KSHH
KSHH
KSHH
KENSHIN!!

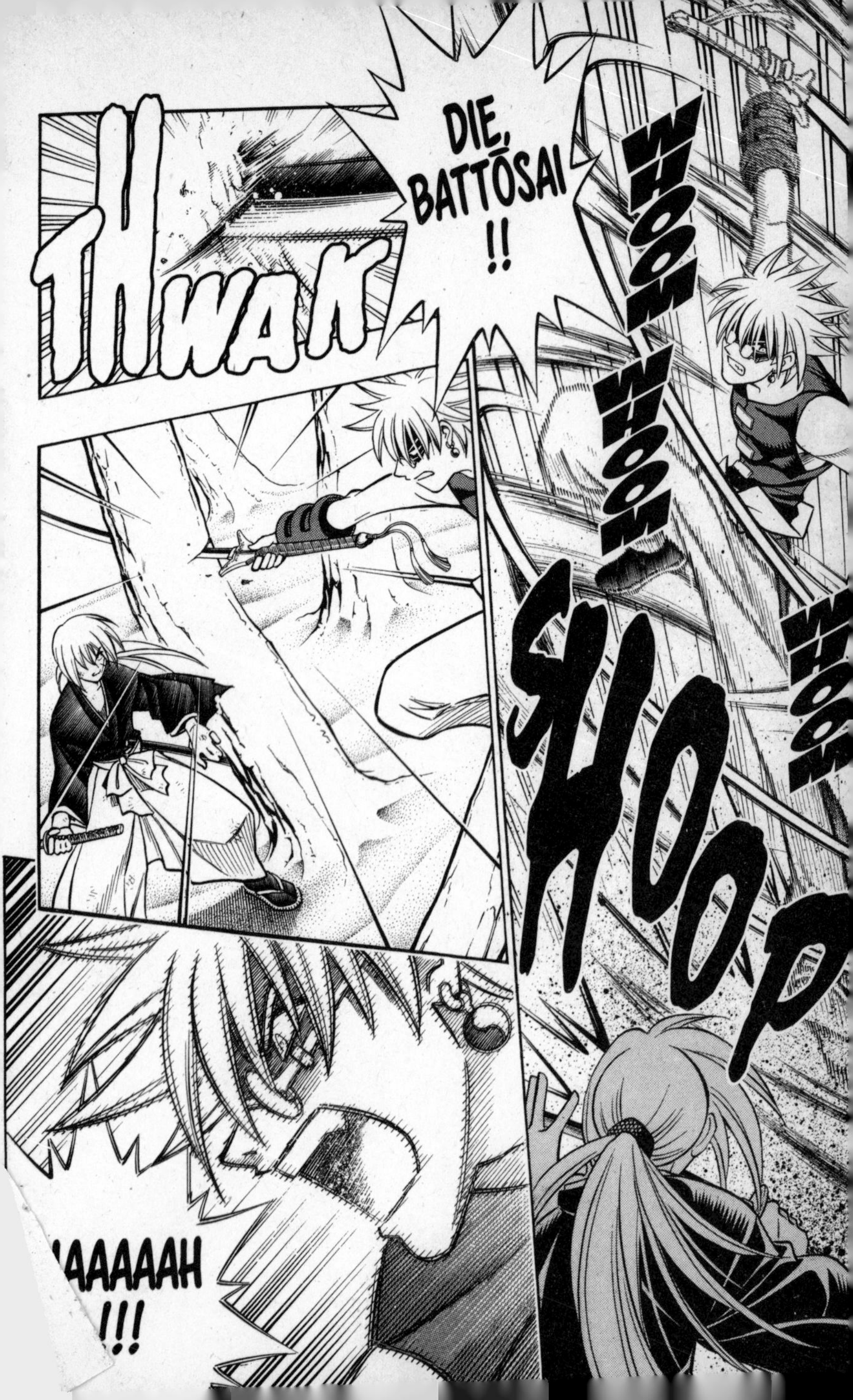
WHOOM WHOOM
DIE, BATTŌSAI !!
THWAK
WHOOM
SHOOP
AAAAAH !!!

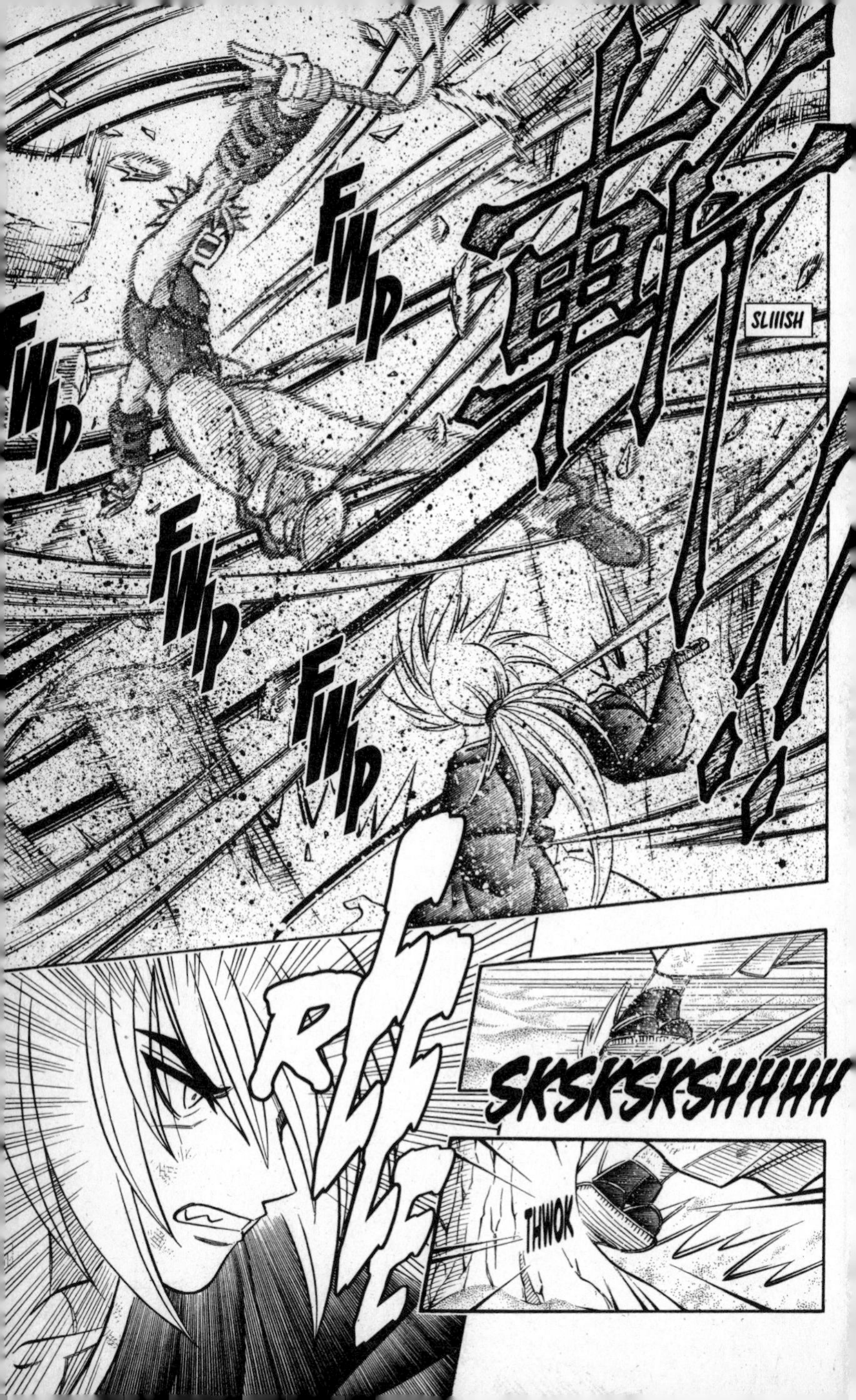
SLIIISH
FWIP
FWIP
FWIP
FWIP
SKSKSKSHHHH
THWOK

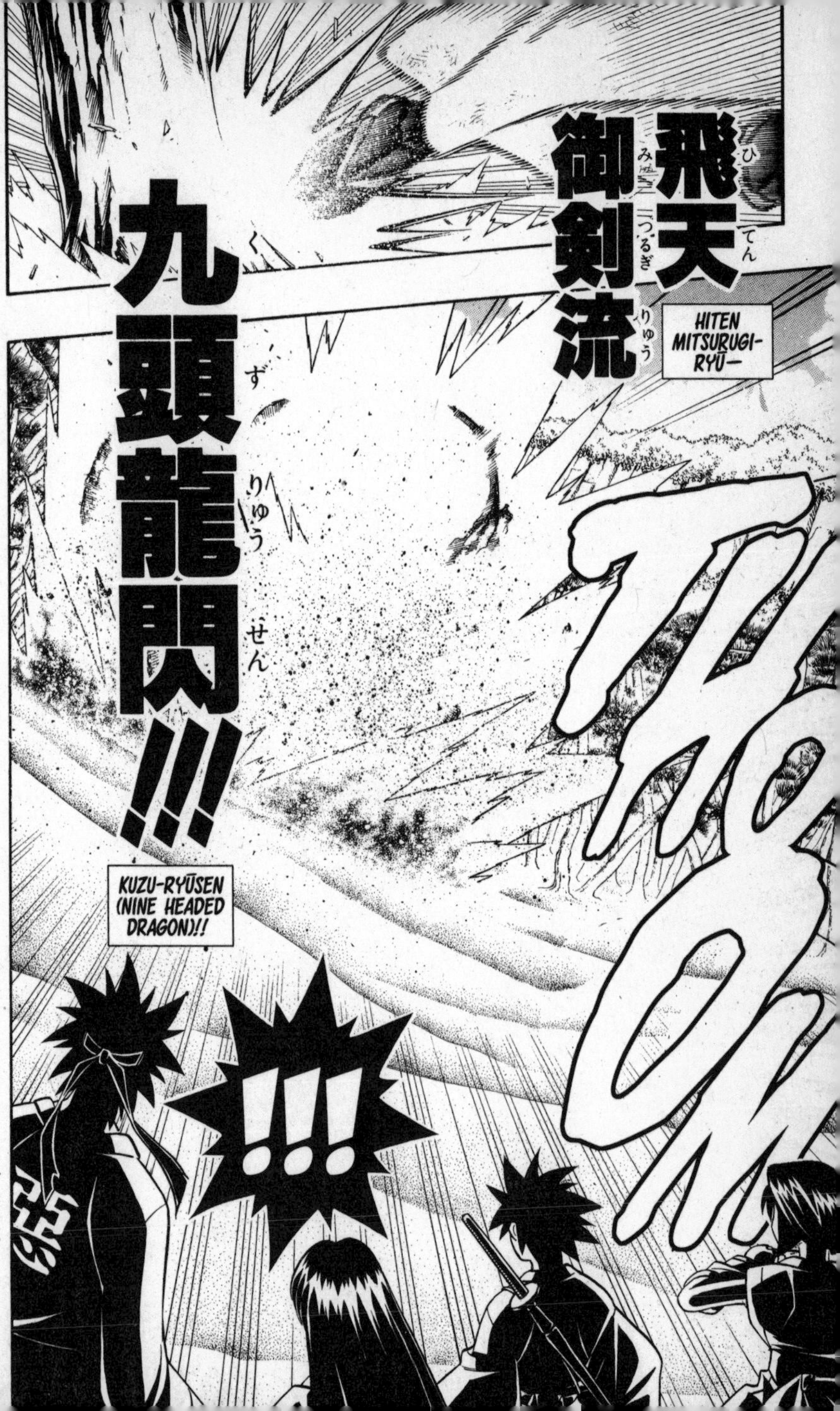
飛天御剣流
HITEN MITSURUGI-RYŪ—
九頭龍閃!!
KUZU-RYŪSEN (NINE HEADED DRAGON)!!
!!!

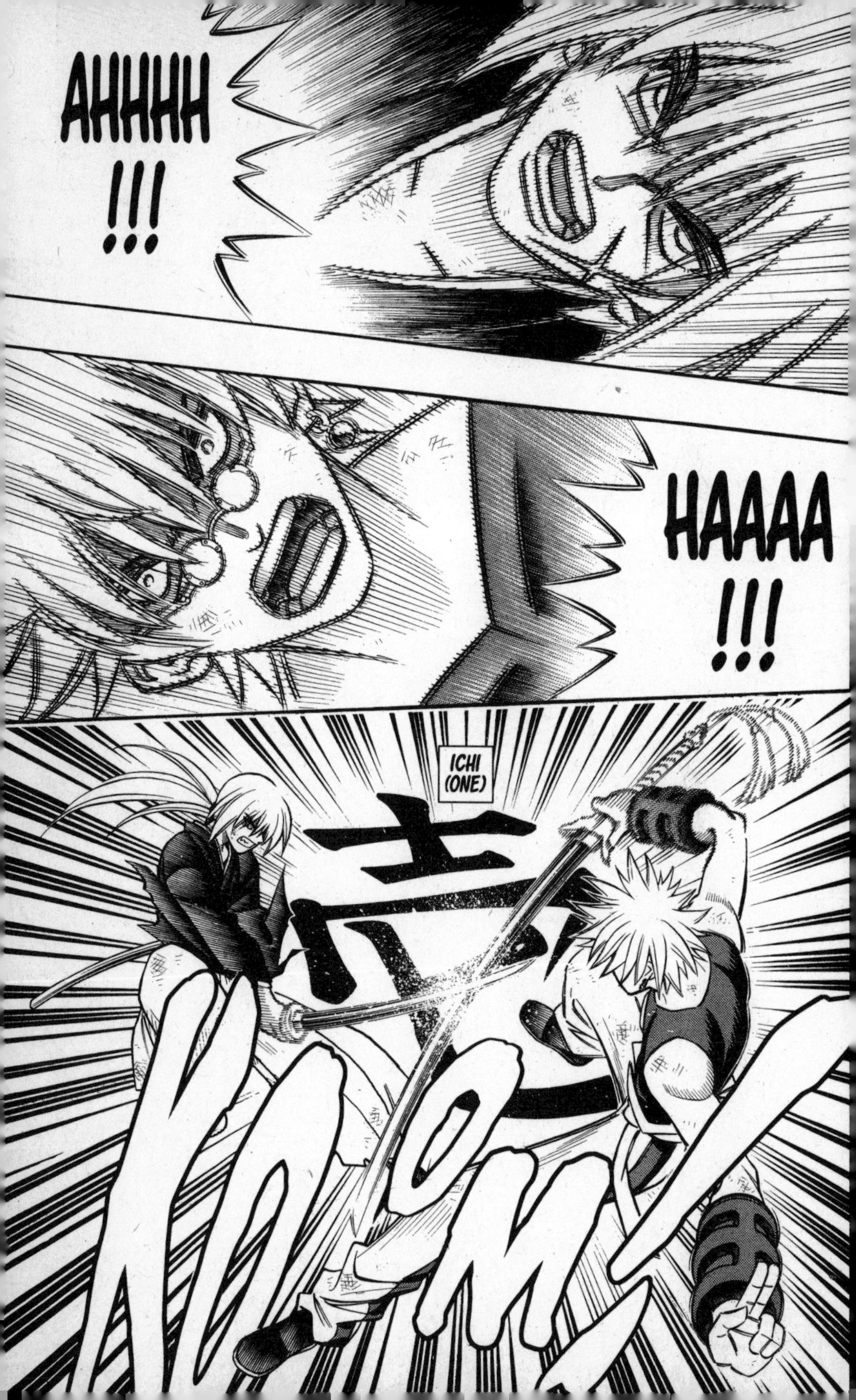
AHHHH !!!
HAAAA !!!
ICHI (ONE)
壱

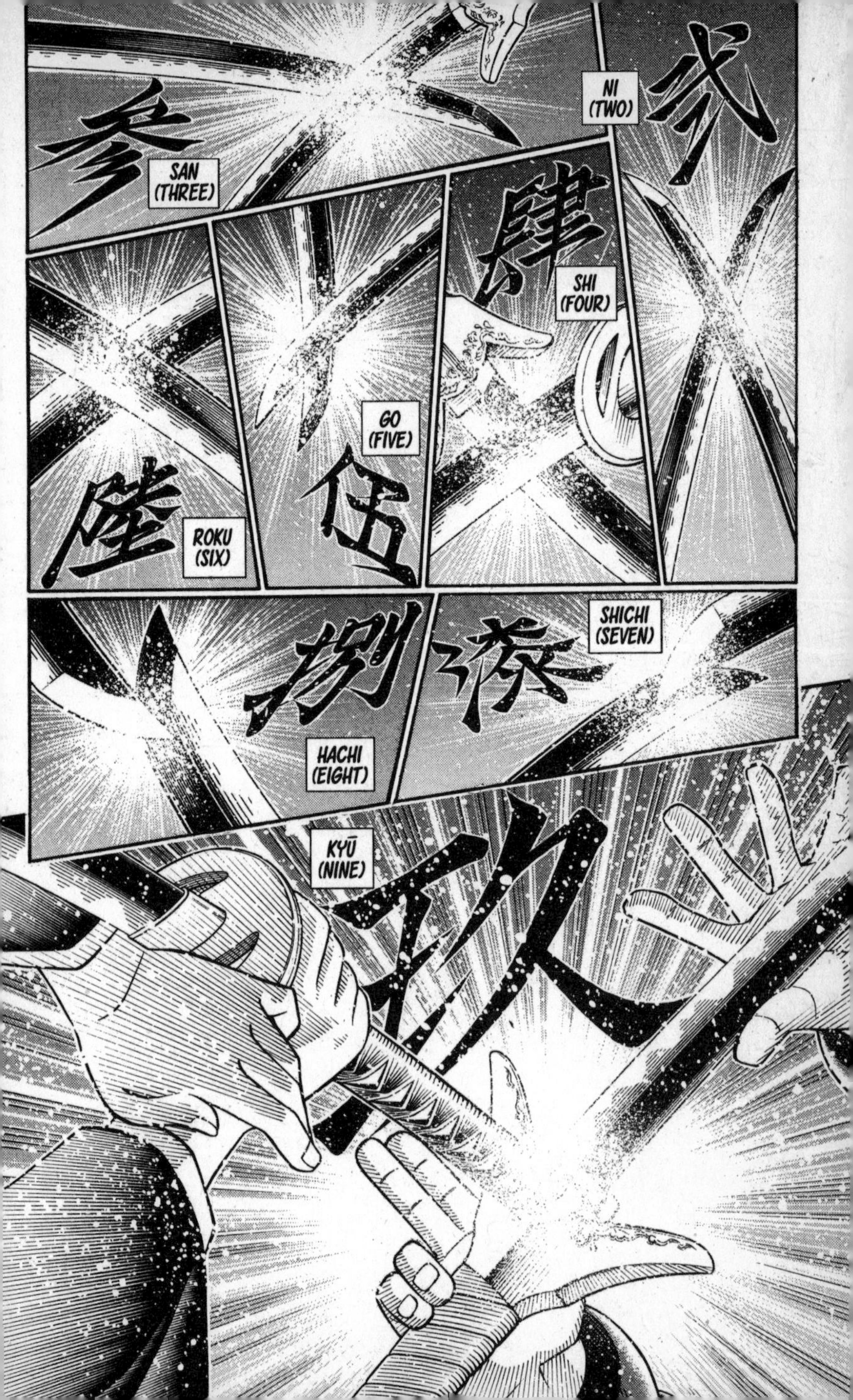

弐
NI (TWO)
参
SAN (THREE)
肆
SHI (FOUR)
伍
GO (FIVE)
陸
ROKU (SIX)
漆
SHICHI (SEVEN)
捌
HACHI (EIGHT)
玖
KYŪ (NINE)

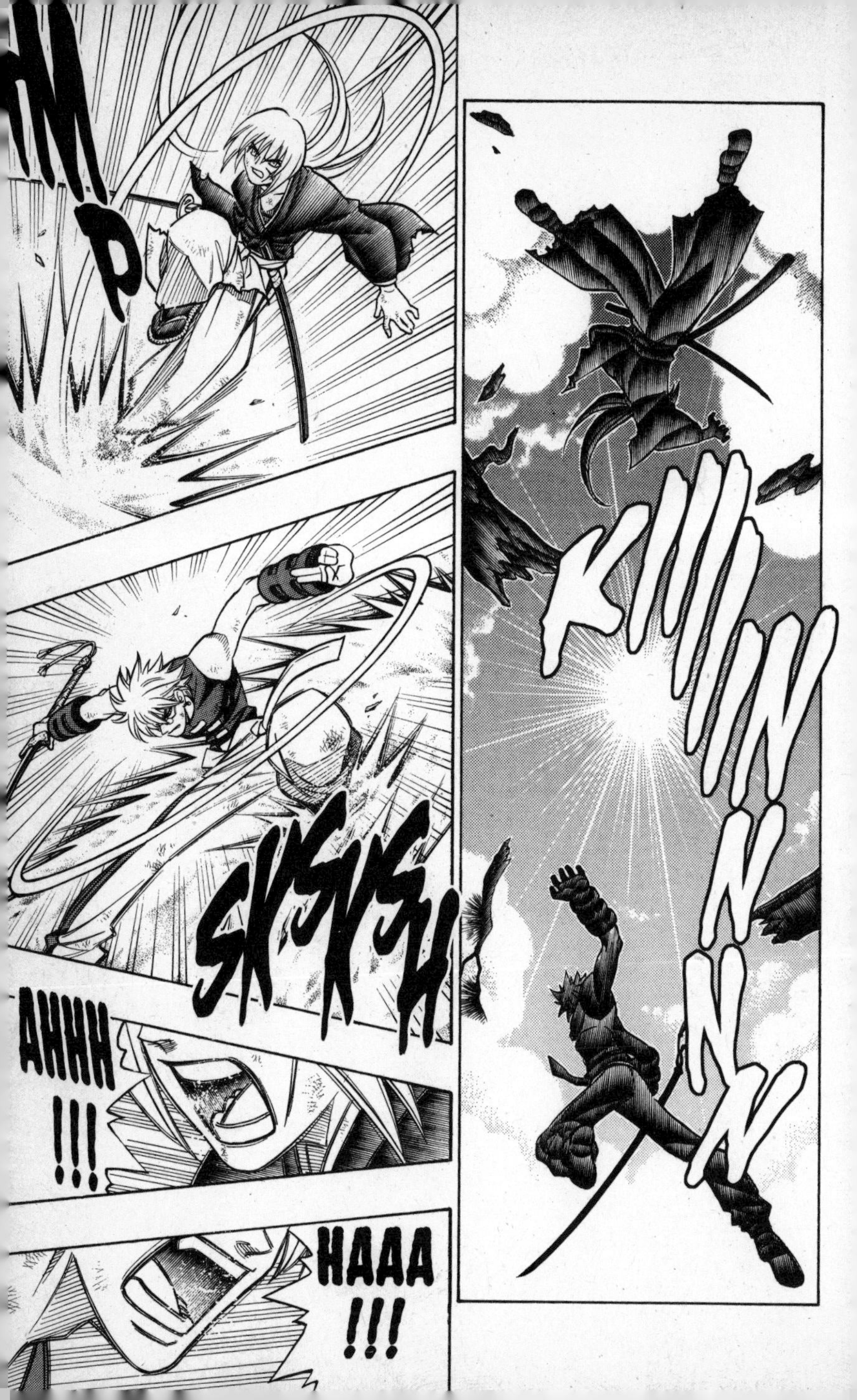
AHHH!!!
HAAA!!!

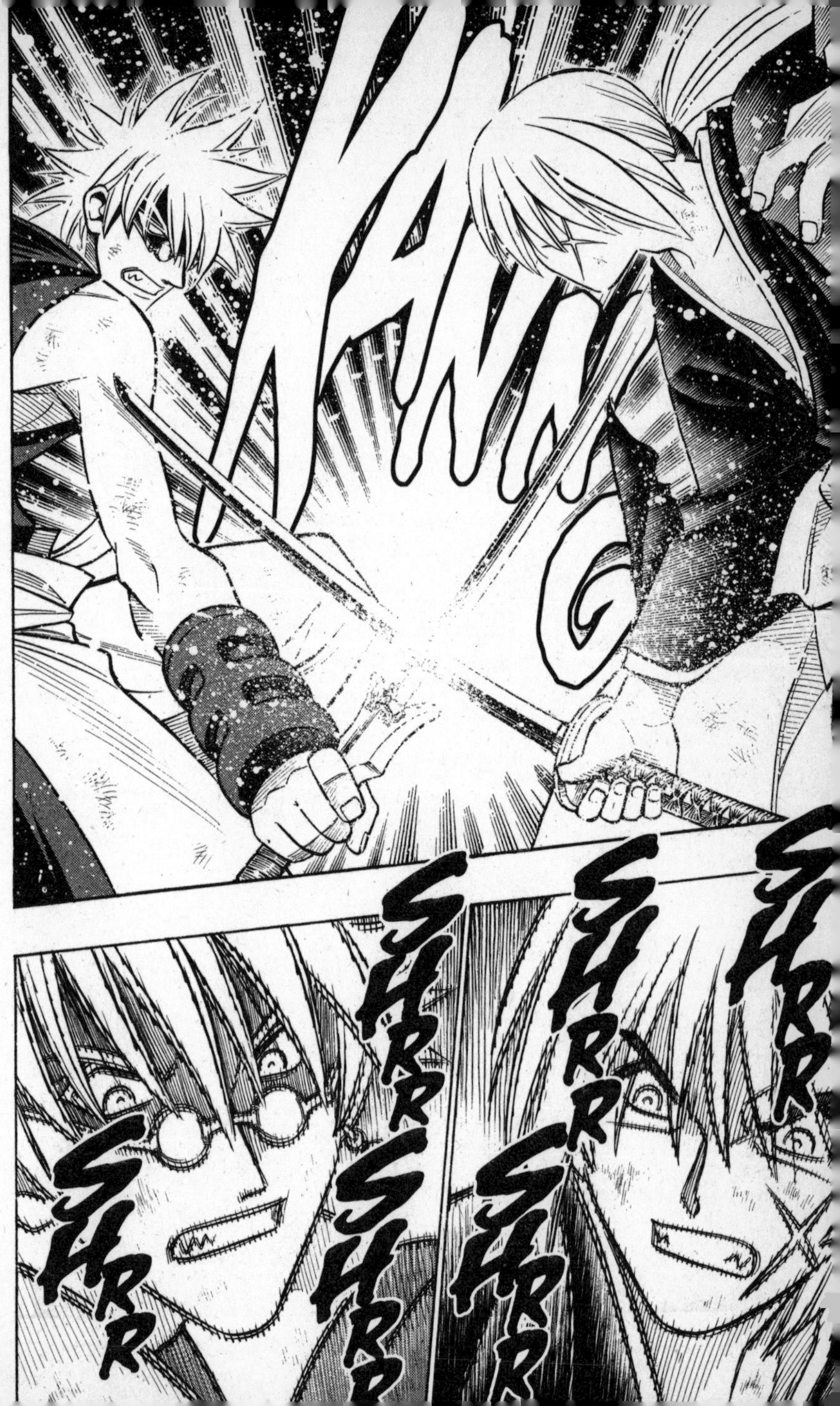
SHRR
SHRR
SHRR
SHRR
SHRR
SHRR

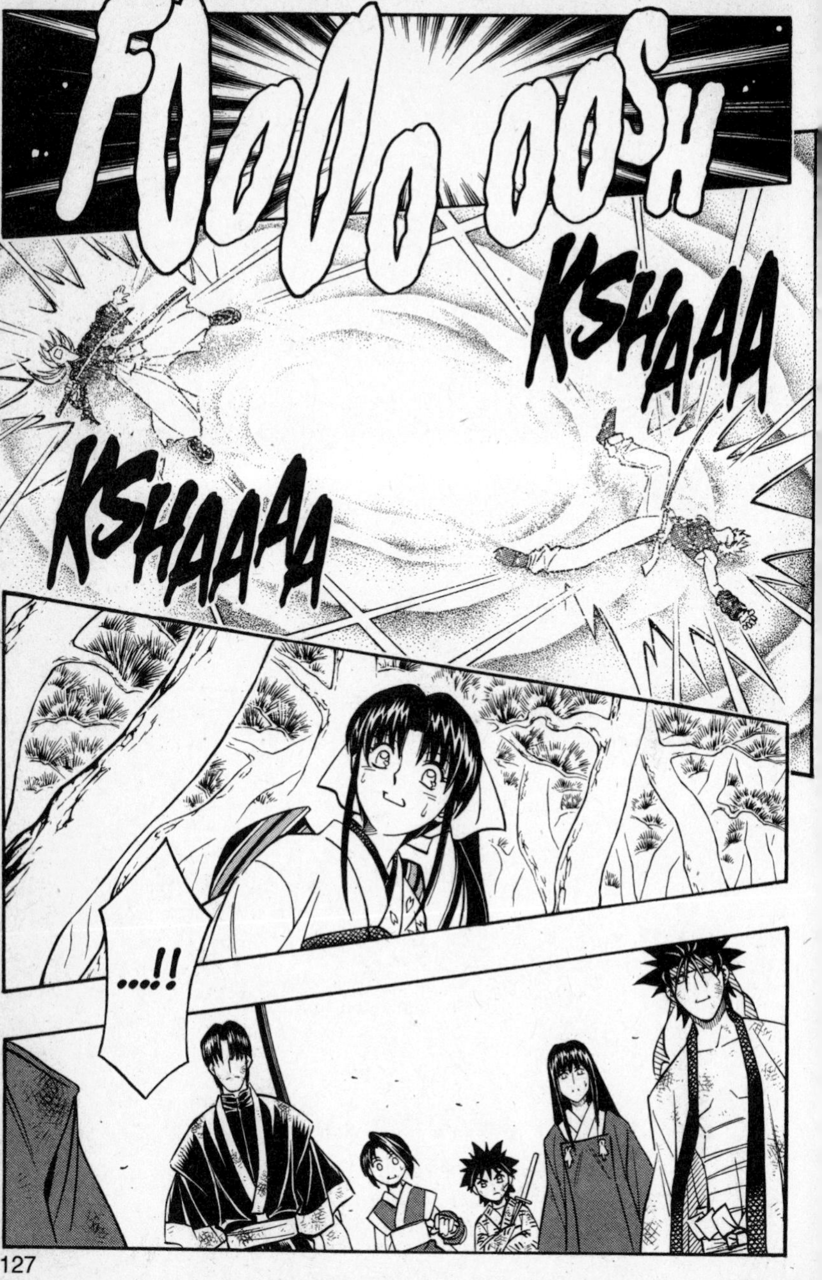
FOOOO OOSH
KSHAAA
KSHAAAA
...!!

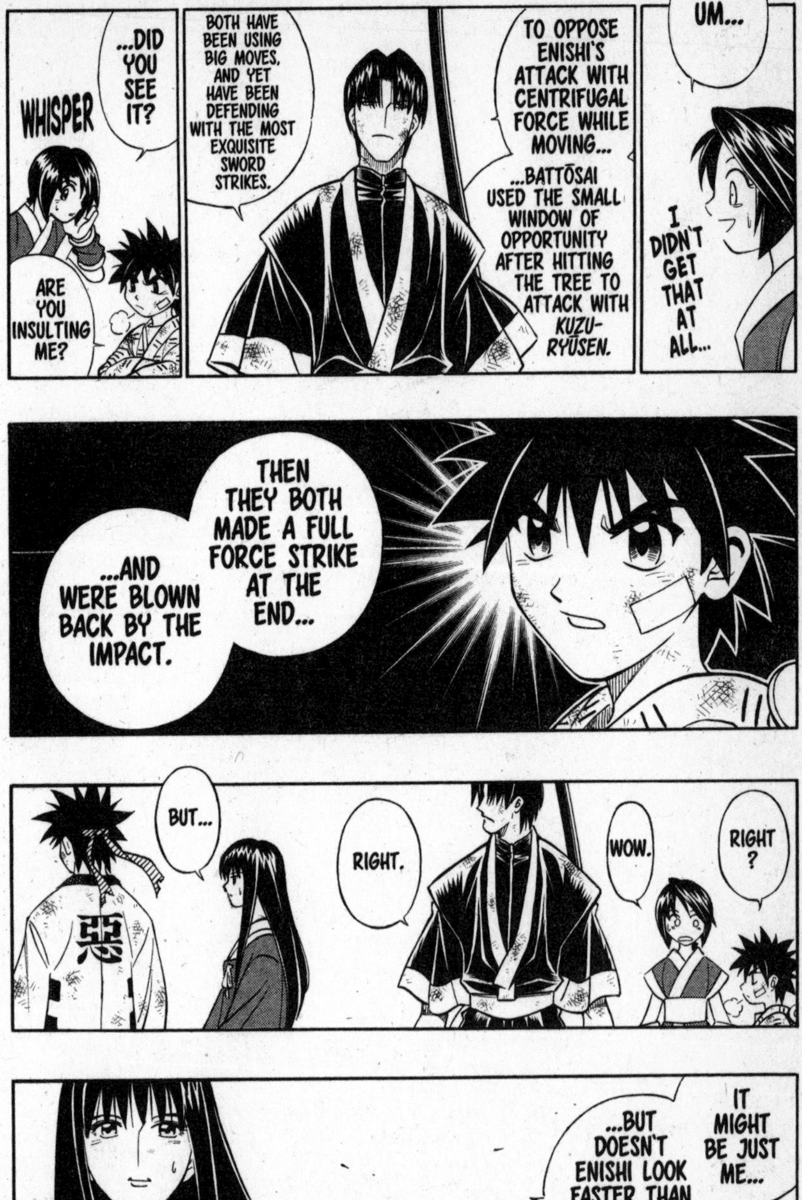
UM...
I DIDN'T GET THAT AT ALL...
TO OPPOSE ENISHI'S ATTACK WITH CENTRIFUGAL FORCE WHILE MOVING...
...BATTŌSAI USED THE SMALL WINDOW OF OPPORTUNITY AFTER HITTING THE TREE TO ATTACK WITH *KUZU-RYŪSEN.*
BOTH HAVE BEEN USING BIG MOVES, AND YET HAVE BEEN DEFENDING WITH THE MOST EXQUISITE SWORD STRIKES.
...DID YOU SEE IT?
WHISPER
ARE YOU INSULTING ME?
THEN THEY BOTH MADE A FULL FORCE STRIKE AT THE END...
...AND WERE BLOWN BACK BY THE IMPACT.
RIGHT?
WOW.
RIGHT.
BUT...
IT MIGHT BE JUST ME...
...BUT DOESN'T ENISHI LOOK FASTER THAN BEFORE?

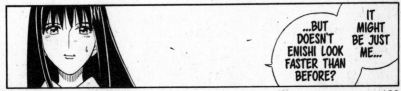

READ THIS WAY

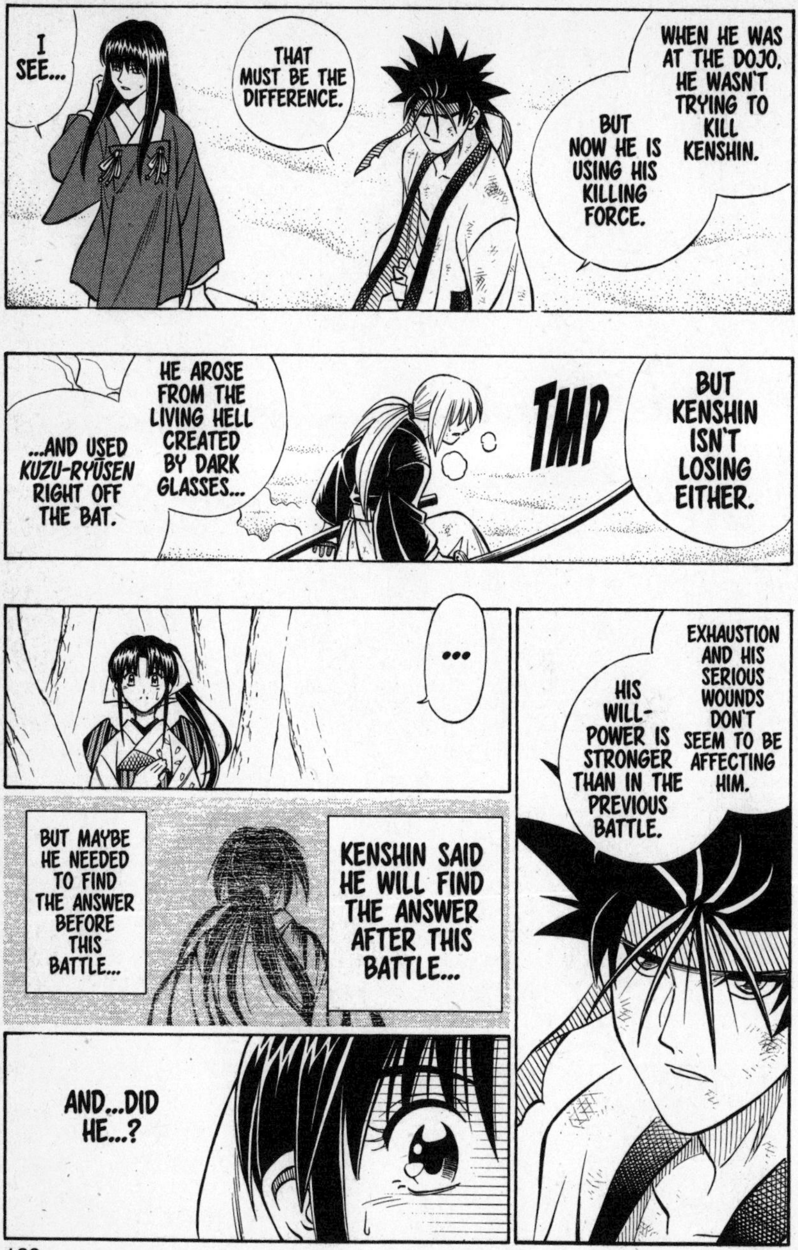

WHEN HE WAS AT THE DOJO, HE WASN'T TRYING TO KILL KENSHIN.
BUT NOW HE IS USING HIS KILLING FORCE.
THAT MUST BE THE DIFFERENCE.
I SEE...
BUT KENSHIN ISN'T LOSING EITHER.
TMP
HE AROSE FROM THE LIVING HELL CREATED BY DARK GLASSES...
...AND USED KUZU-RYŪSEN RIGHT OFF THE BAT.
EXHAUSTION AND HIS SERIOUS WOUNDS DON'T SEEM TO BE AFFECTING HIM.
HIS WILL-POWER IS STRONGER THAN IN THE PREVIOUS BATTLE.
...
KENSHIN SAID HE WILL FIND THE ANSWER AFTER THIS BATTLE...
BUT MAYBE HE NEEDED TO FIND THE ANSWER BEFORE THIS BATTLE...
AND...DID HE...?

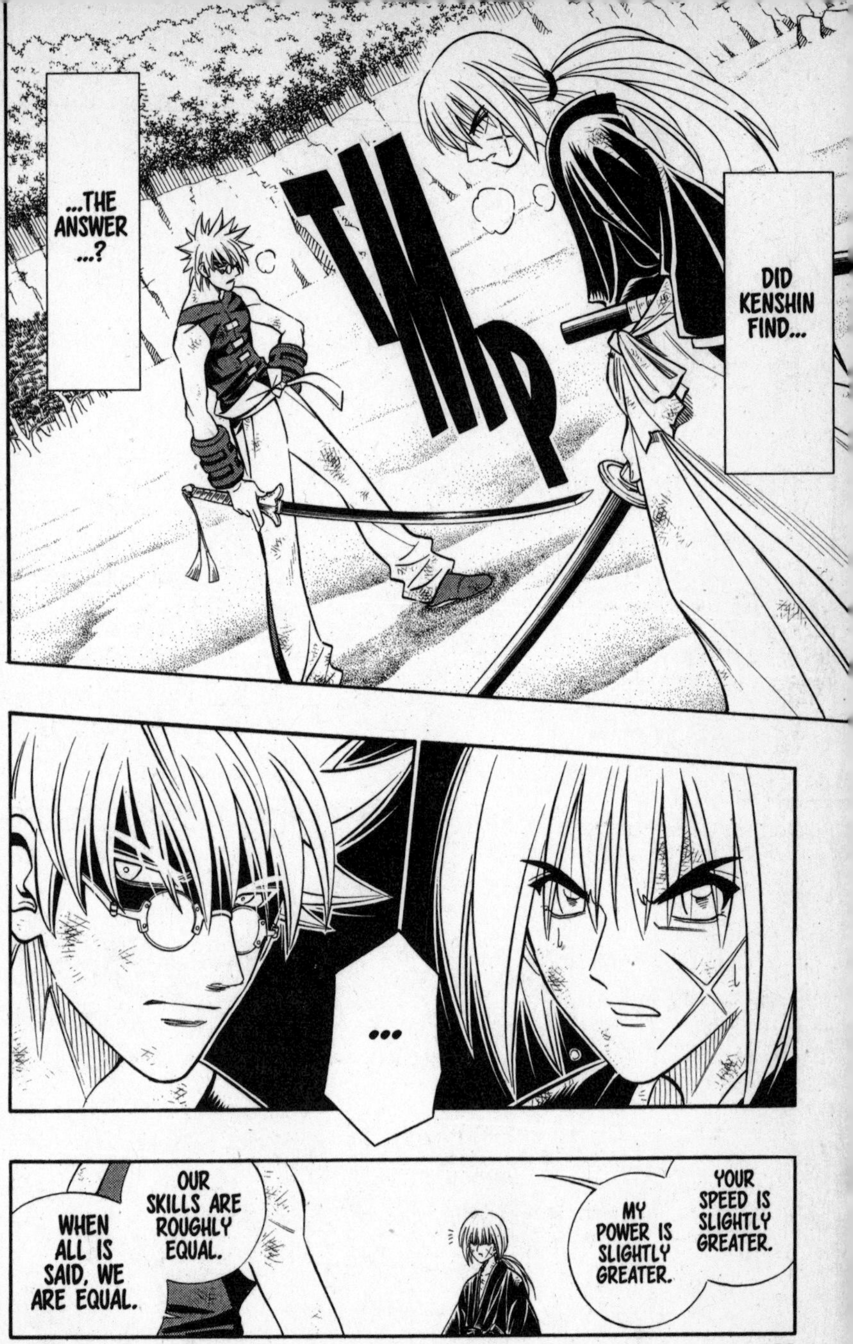
DID KENSHIN FIND...
THMP
...THE ANSWER ...?
...
YOUR SPEED IS SLIGHTLY GREATER.
MY POWER IS SLIGHTLY GREATER.
OUR SKILLS ARE ROUGHLY EQUAL.
WHEN ALL IS SAID, WE ARE EQUAL.

READ THIS WAY

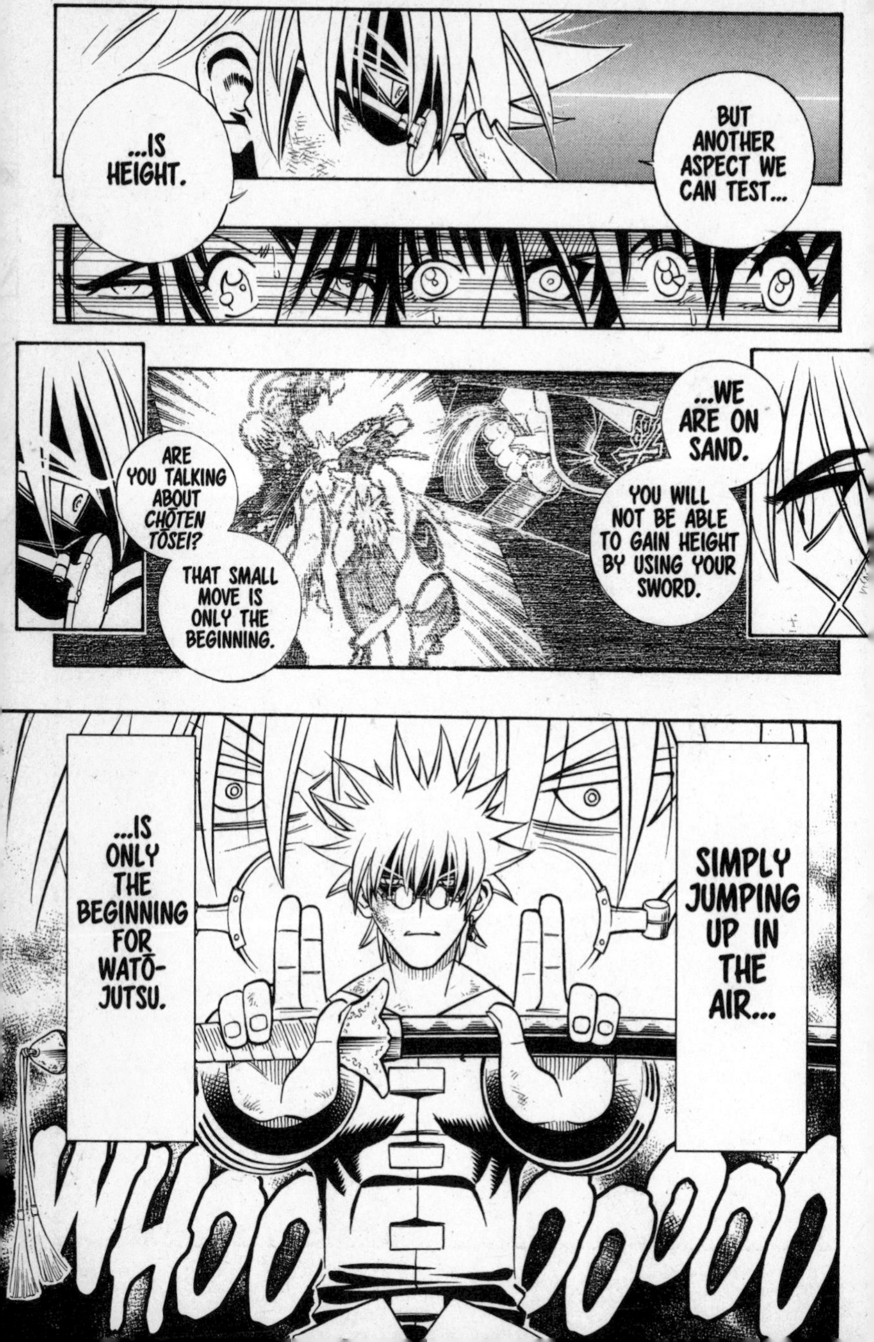
BUT ANOTHER ASPECT WE CAN TEST...
...IS HEIGHT.
...WE ARE ON SAND.
YOU WILL NOT BE ABLE TO GAIN HEIGHT BY USING YOUR SWORD.
ARE YOU TALKING ABOUT CHŌTEN TŌSEI?
THAT SMALL MOVE IS ONLY THE BEGINNING.
SIMPLY JUMPING UP IN THE AIR...
...IS ONLY THE BEGINNING FOR WATŌ-JUTSU.
WHOOOOOOOO

Rurouni Kenshin

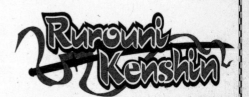

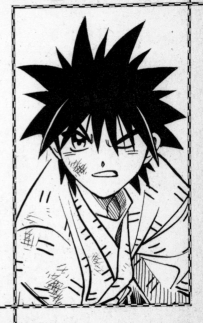

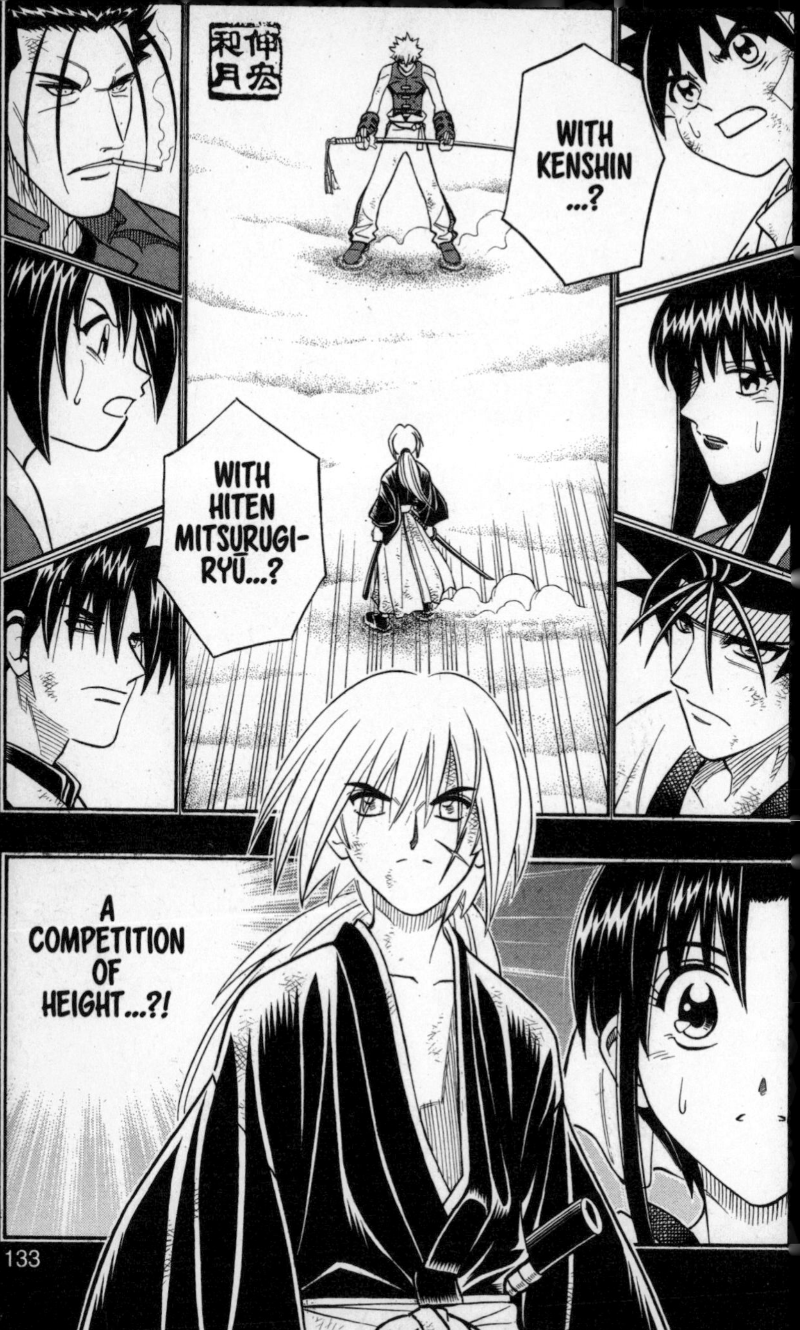
伸宏和月
WITH KENSHIN ...?
WITH HITEN MITSURUGI-RYŪ...?
A COMPETITION OF HEIGHT...?!

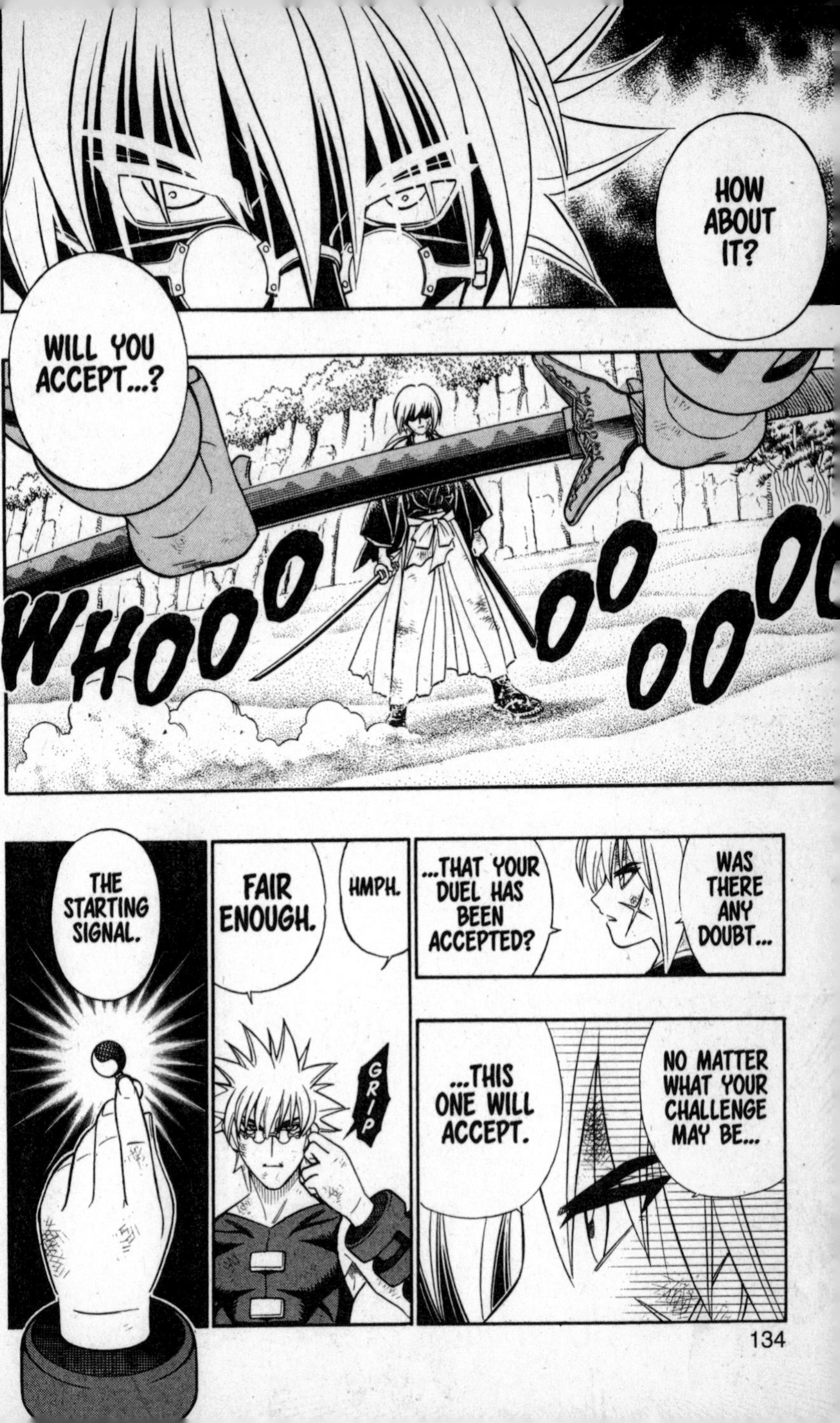
HOW ABOUT IT?
WILL YOU ACCEPT...?
WHOOOOOOOOOO
WAS THERE ANY DOUBT...
...THAT YOUR DUEL HAS BEEN ACCEPTED?
NO MATTER WHAT YOUR CHALLENGE MAY BE...
...THIS ONE WILL ACCEPT.
HMPH.
FAIR ENOUGH.
GRIP
THE STARTING SIGNAL.

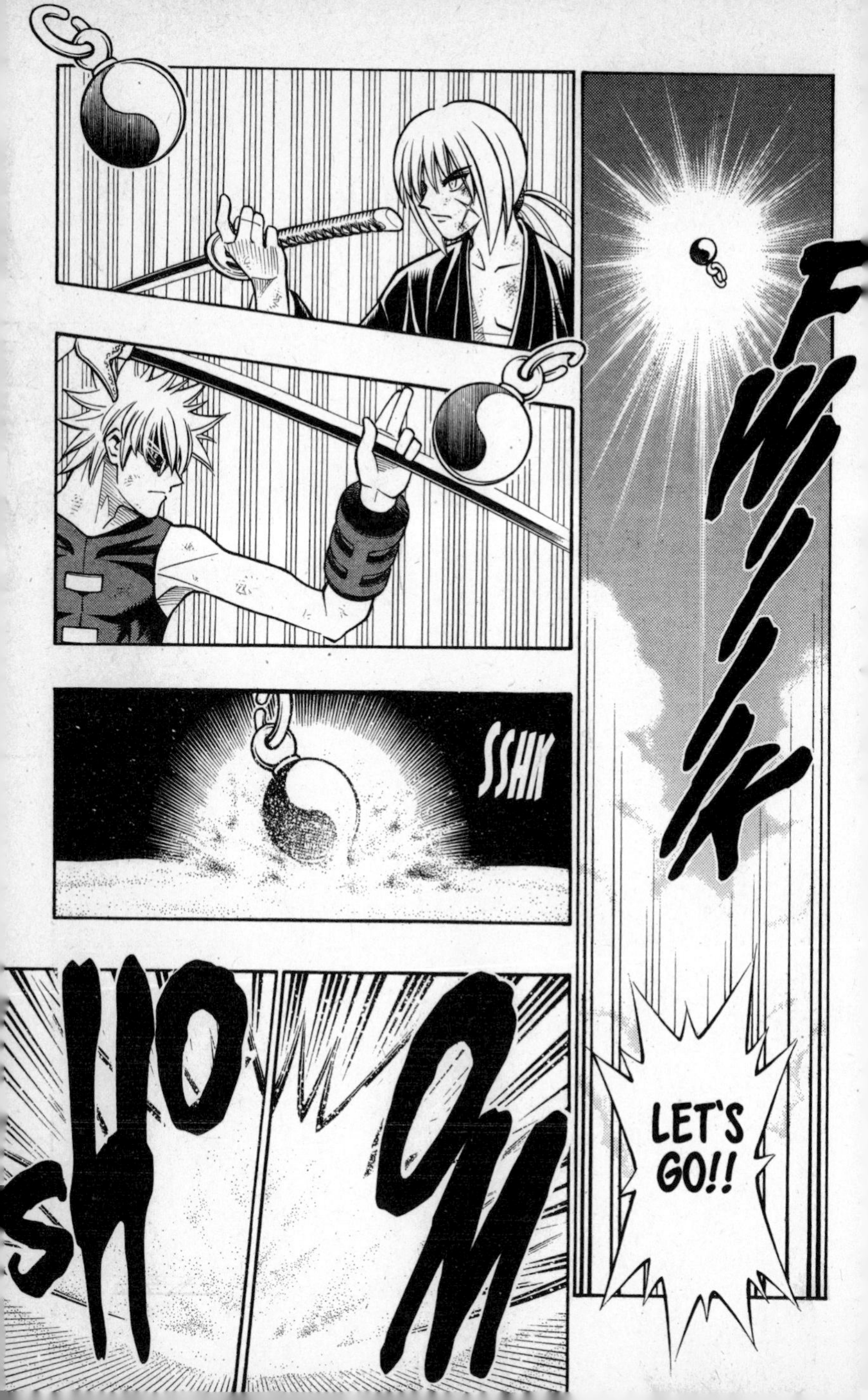
FWIIIK
LET'S GO!!
SSHK
SHOOM

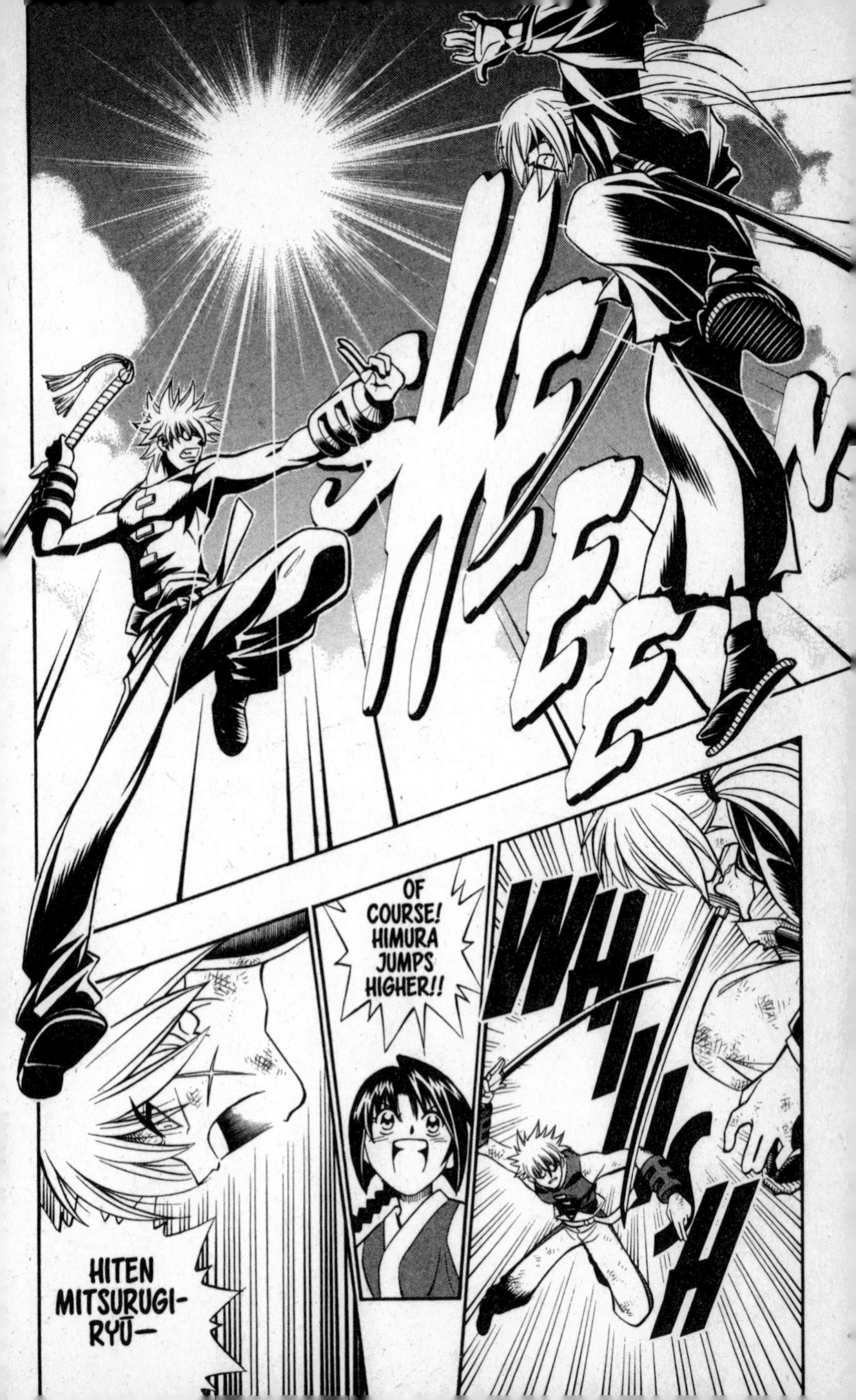
OF COURSE! HIMURA JUMPS HIGHER!!
HITEN MITSURUGI-RYŪ—

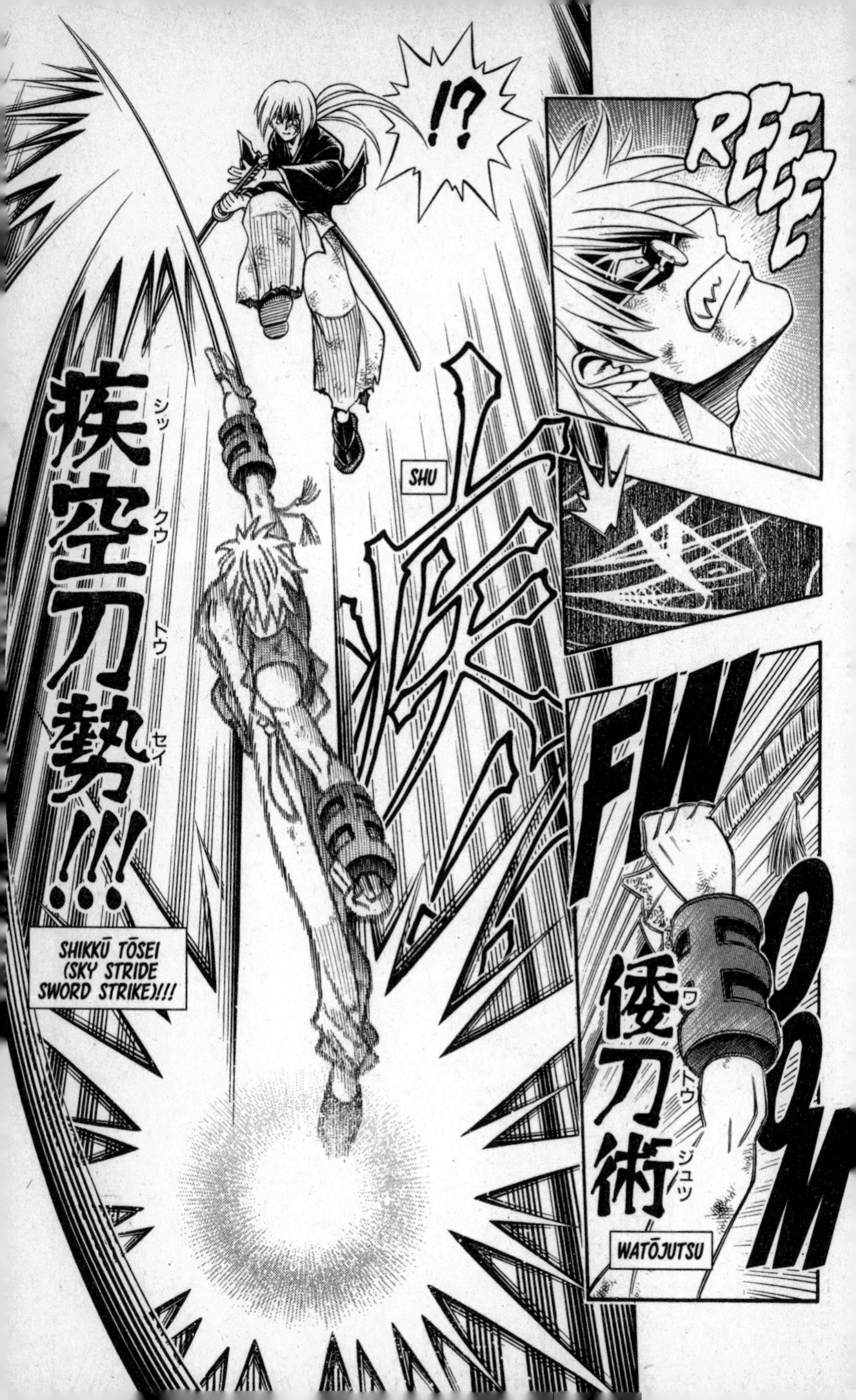
REEEE
FWOOM
倭刀術
ワトウジュツ
WATŌJUTSU
!?
SHU
疾空刀勢!!!
シックウトウセイ
SHIKKŪ TŌSEI (SKY STRIDE SWORD STRIKE)!!!

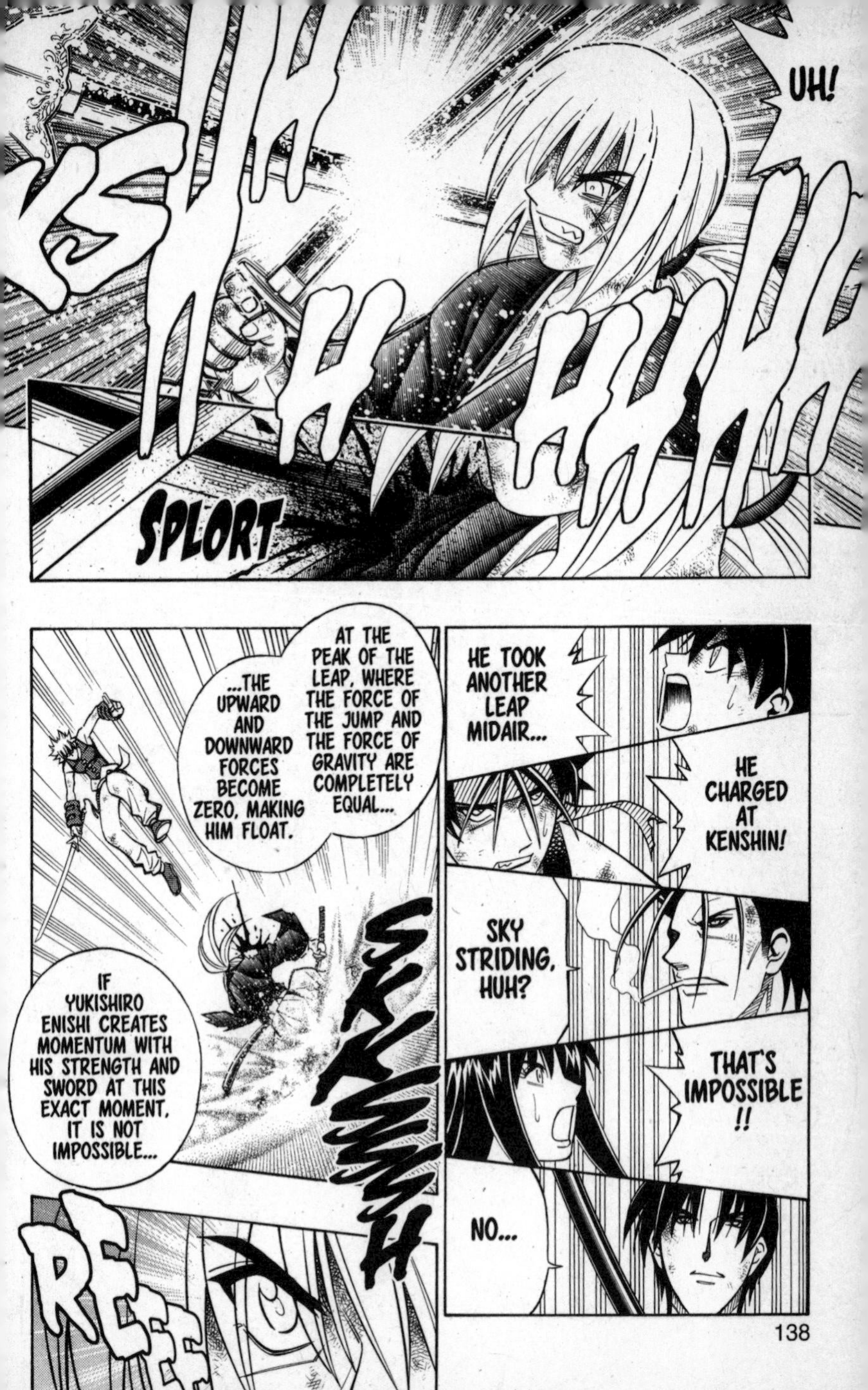
UH!
SPLORT
HE TOOK ANOTHER LEAP MIDAIR...
HE CHARGED AT KENSHIN!
SKY STRIDING, HUH?
THAT'S IMPOSSIBLE !!
NO...
AT THE PEAK OF THE LEAP, WHERE THE FORCE OF THE JUMP AND THE FORCE OF GRAVITY ARE COMPLETELY EQUAL...
...THE UPWARD AND DOWNWARD FORCES BECOME ZERO, MAKING HIM FLOAT.
IF YUKISHIRO ENISHI CREATES MOMENTUM WITH HIS STRENGTH AND SWORD AT THIS EXACT MOMENT, IT IS NOT IMPOSSIBLE...

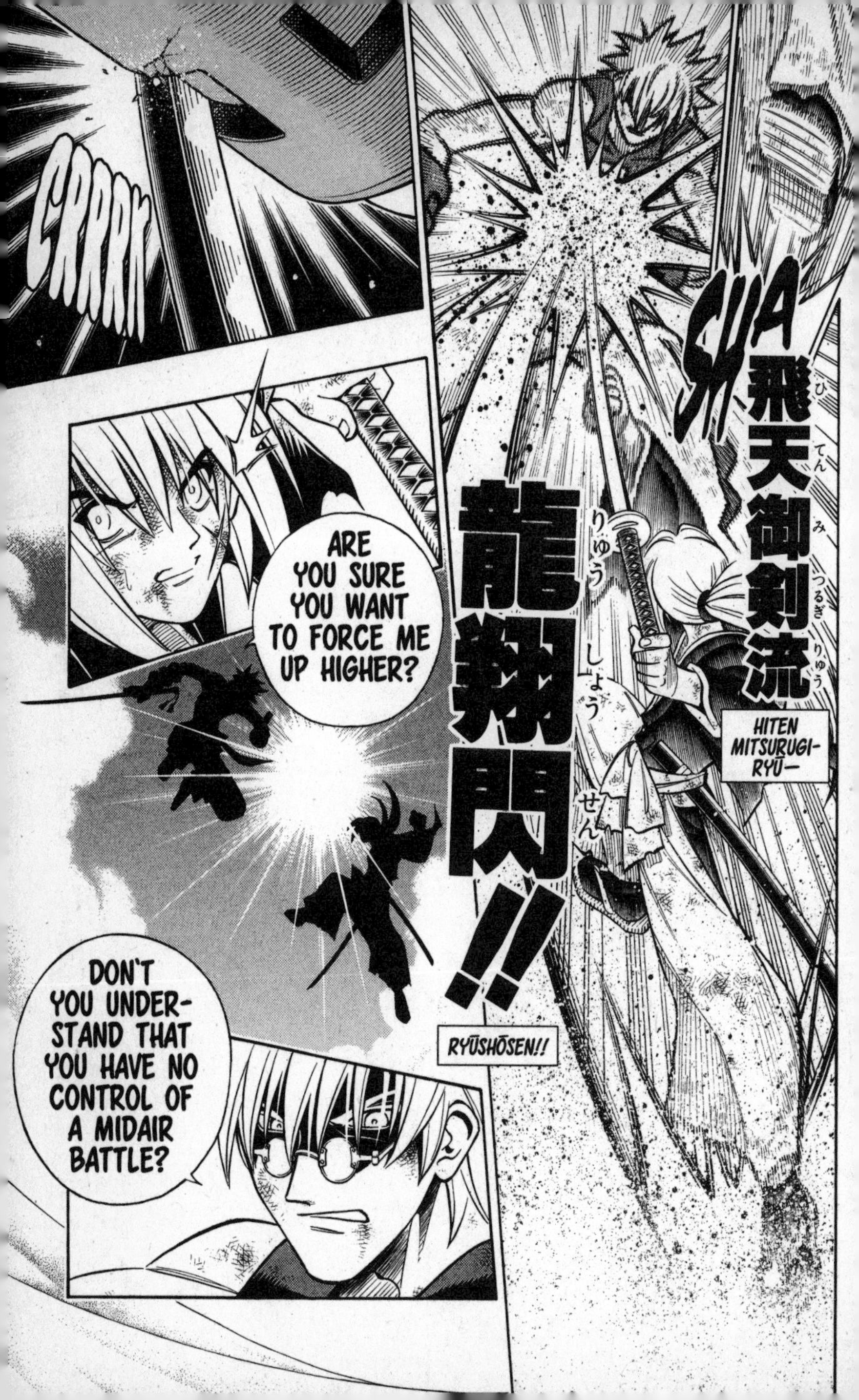
SHA
飛天御剣流
HITEN MITSURUGI-RYŪ—
龍翔閃!!
RYŪSHŌSEN!!
CRRRK
ARE YOU SURE YOU WANT TO FORCE ME UP HIGHER?
DON'T YOU UNDER-STAND THAT YOU HAVE NO CONTROL OF A MIDAIR BATTLE?

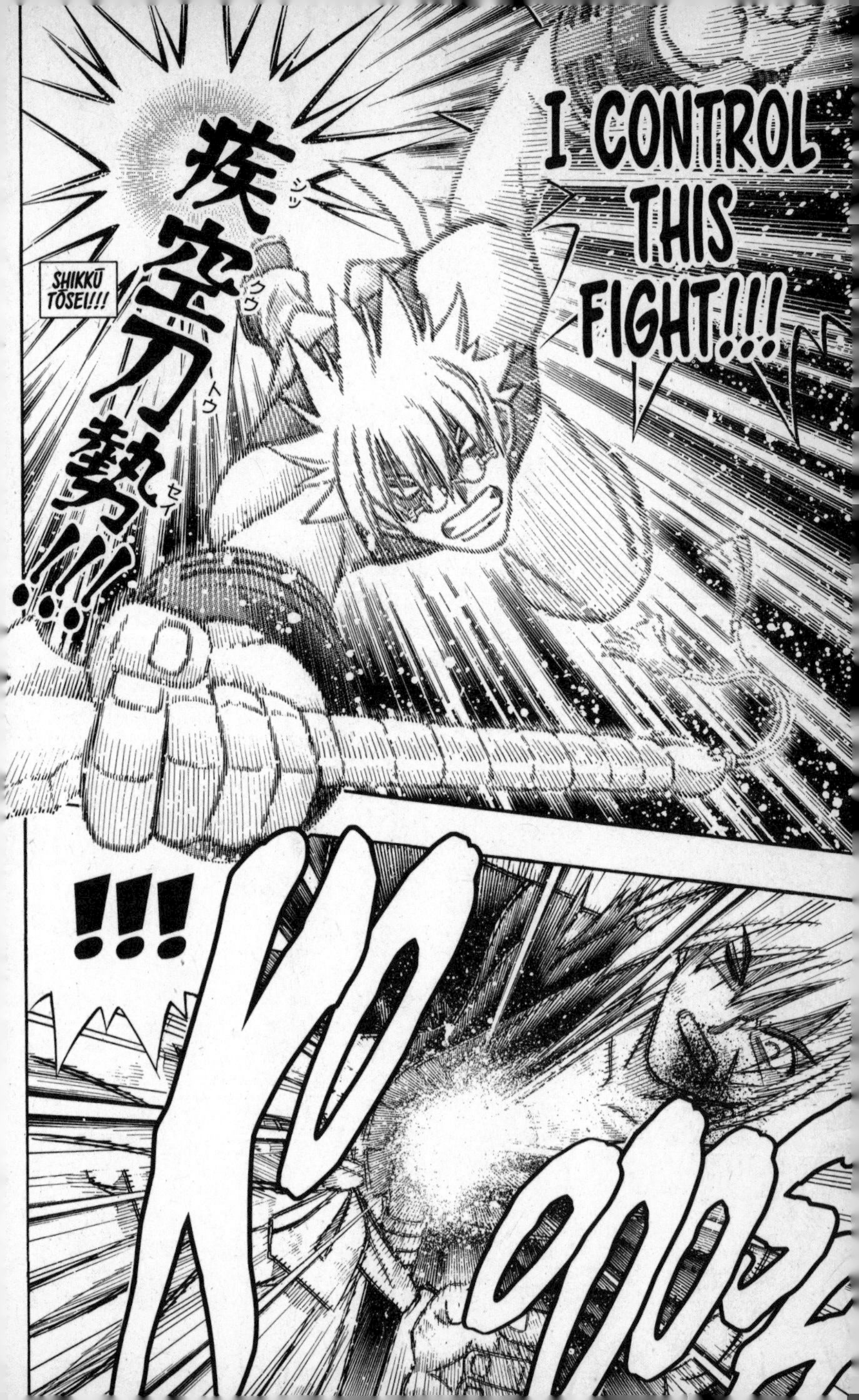
I CONTROL THIS FIGHT!!!
疾空刀勢!!!!
SHIKKŪ TŌSEI!!!
!!!

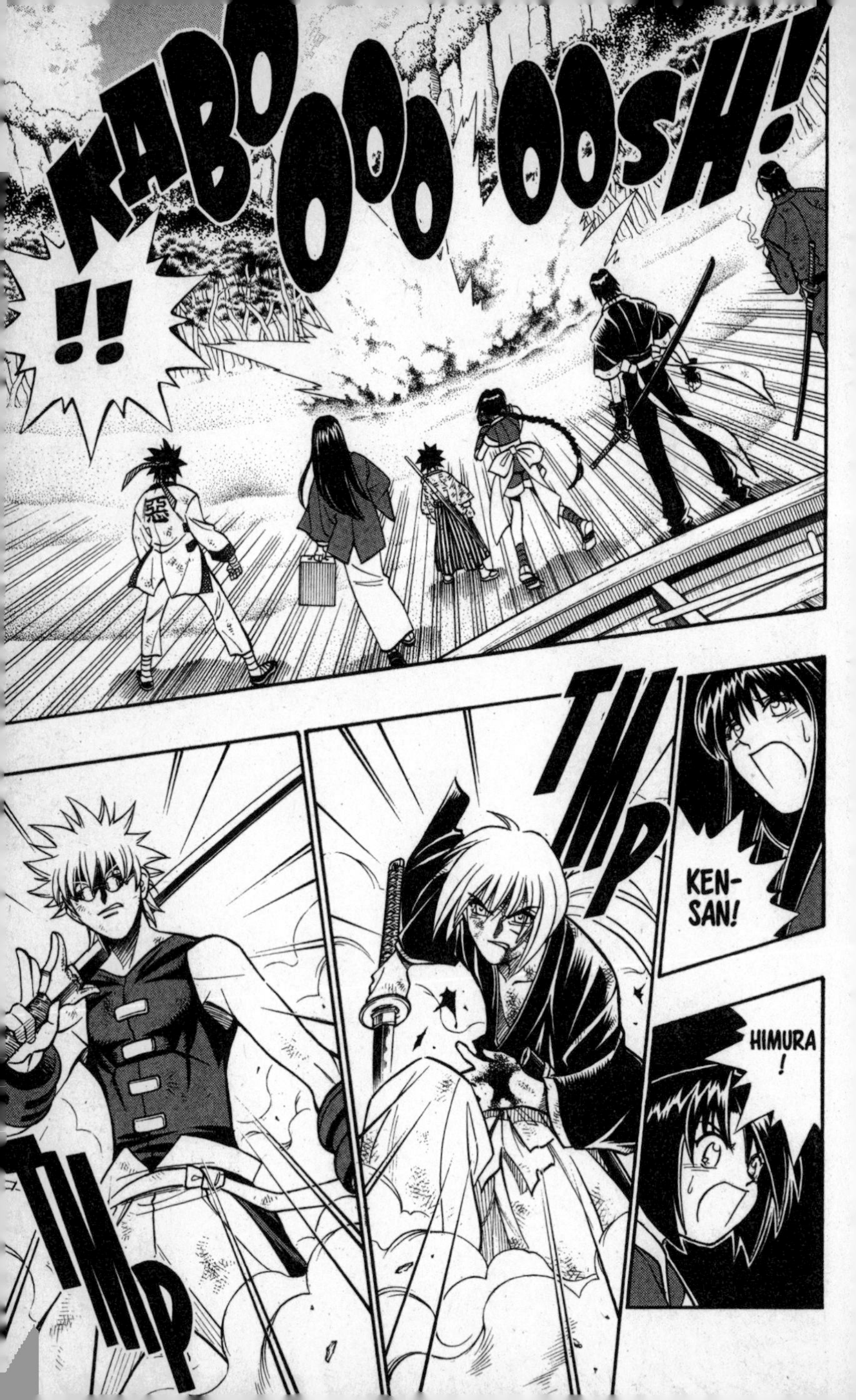
KABOOOOOOOSH!!
!!
KEN-SAN!
HIMURA!
TMP
TMP

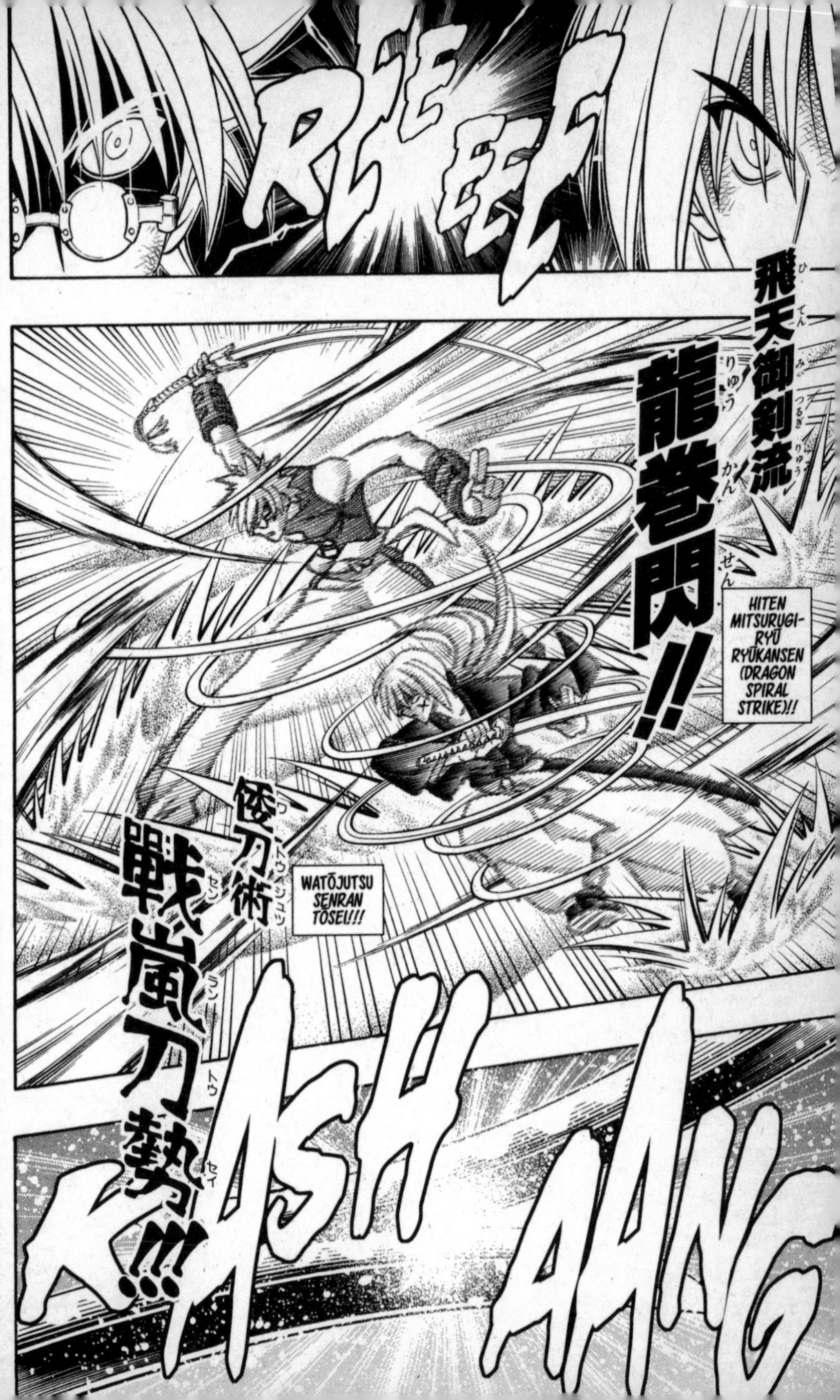
飛天御剣流龍巻閃!!
HITEN MITSURUGI-RYŪ RYŪKANSEN (DRAGON SPIRAL STRIKE)!!
倭刀術戦嵐刀勢!!!
WATŌJUTSU SENRAN TŌSEI!!!

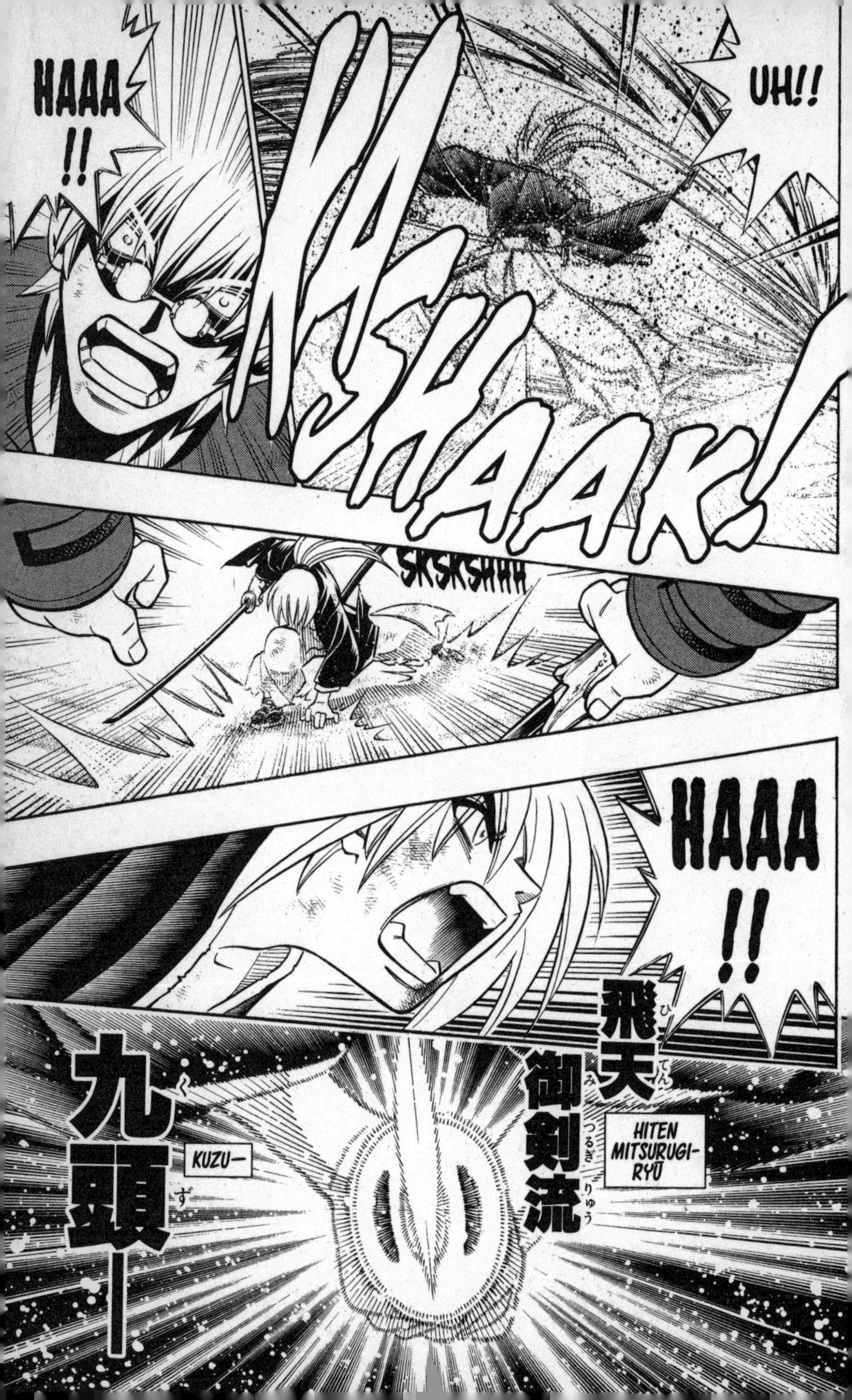
UH!!
WHHAAK!
HAAA!!
SKSKSHHH
HAAA!!
飛天御剣流
HITEN MITSURUGI-RYŪ
九頭—
KUZU—

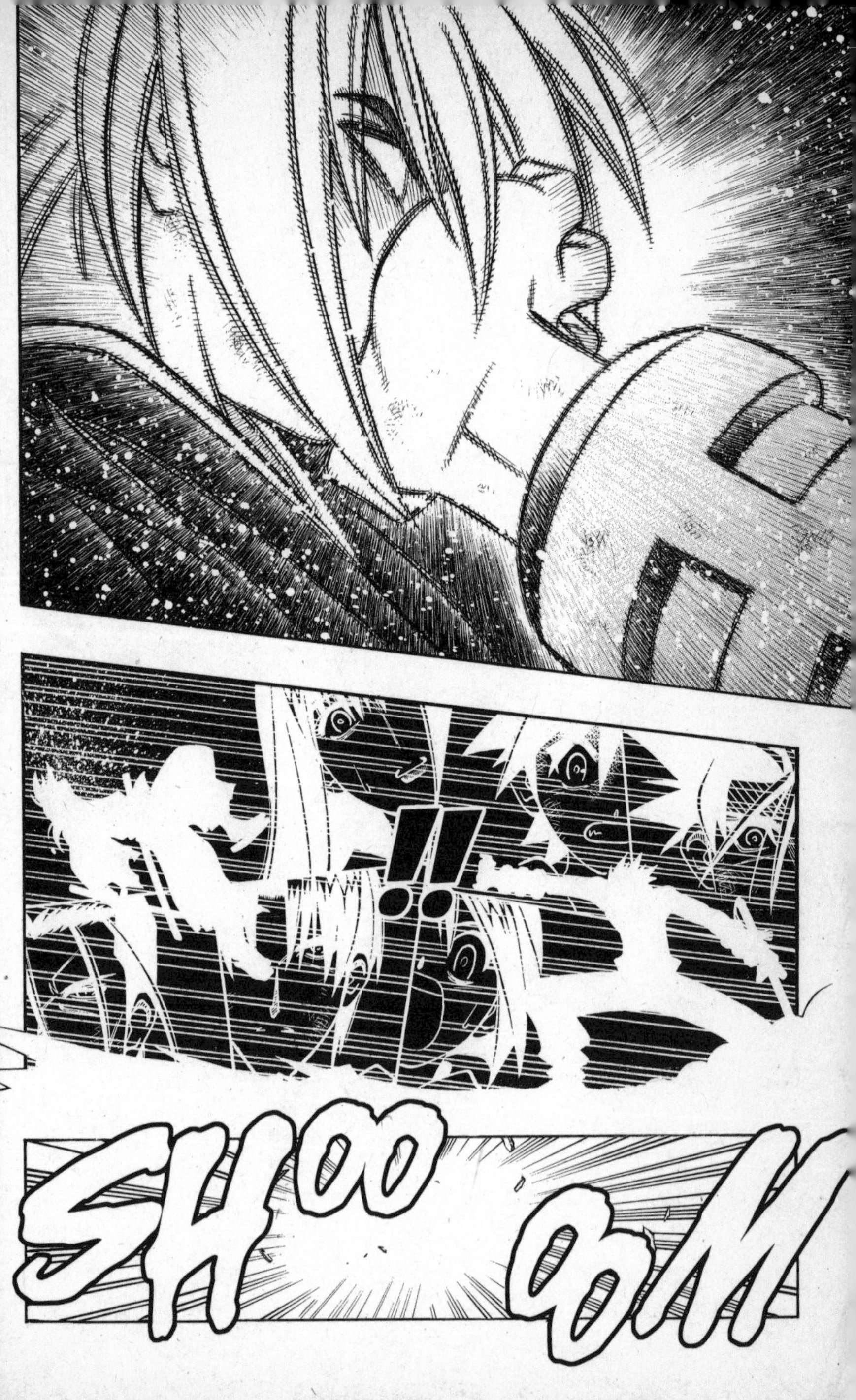
!!
SHOOOOM

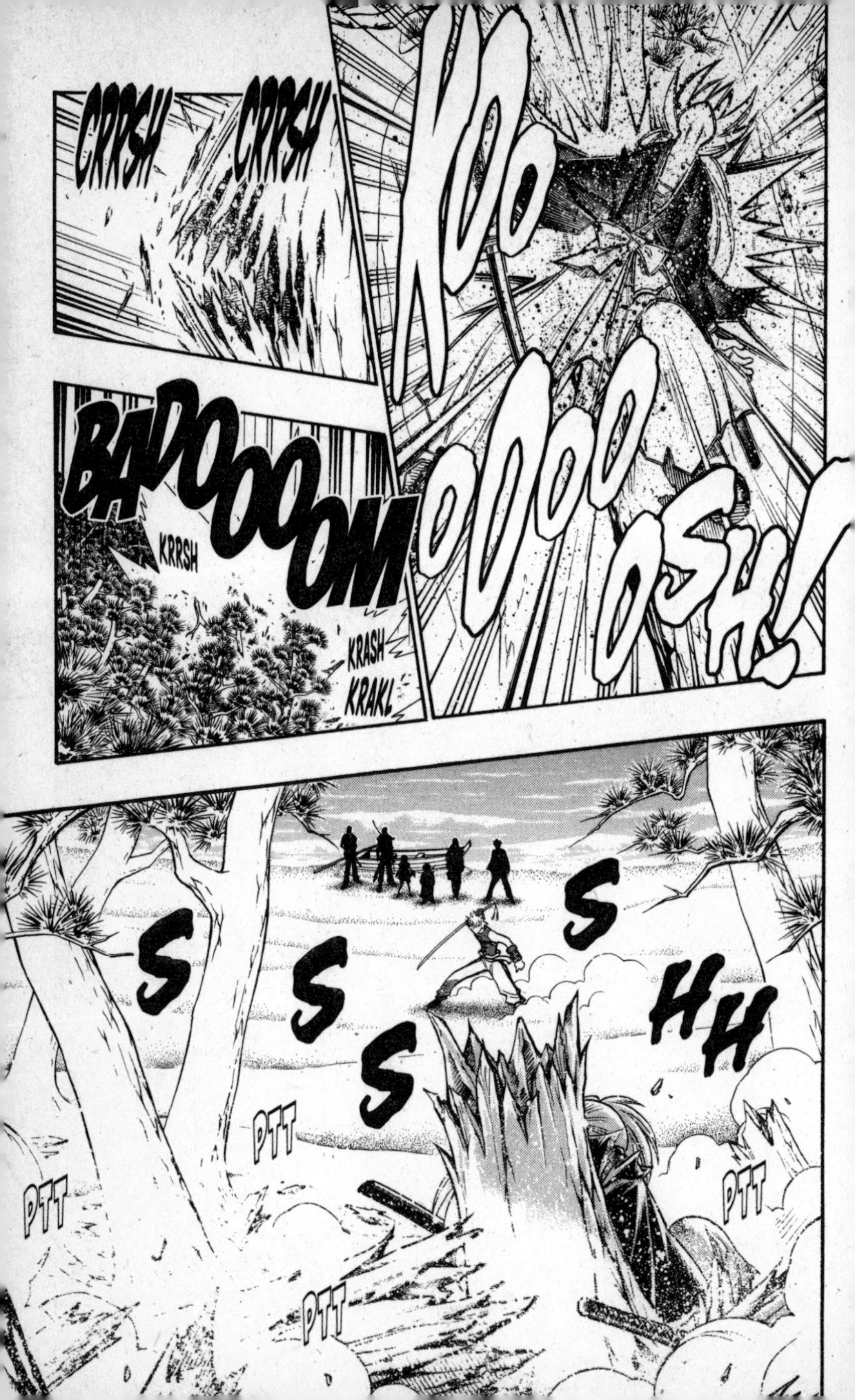
WOOOOOOOOSH!
CRRSH
CRRSH
BADOOOOM
KRRSH
KRASH
KRAKL
SSSSHH
PTT
PTT
PTT
PTT

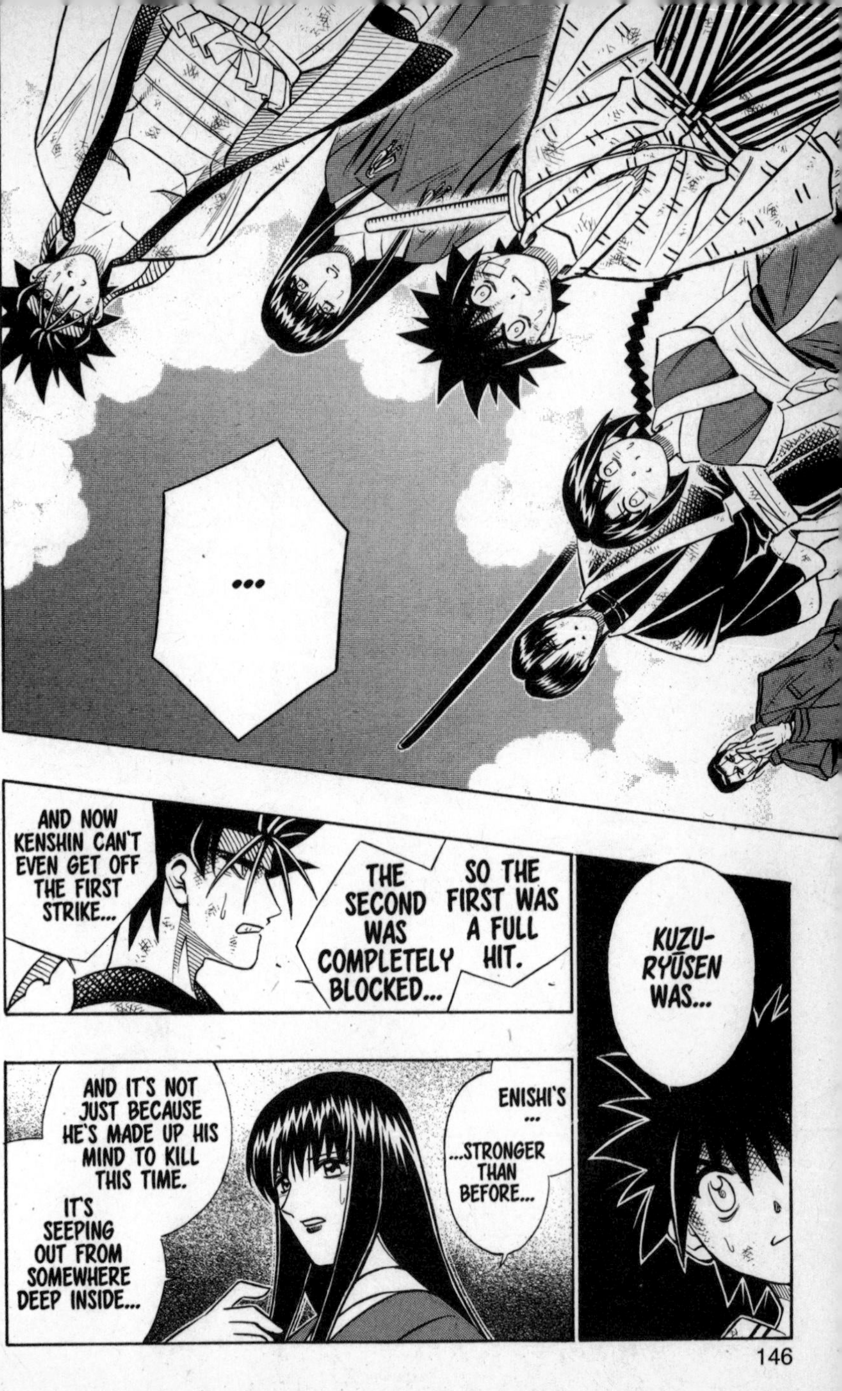
...
KUZU-RYŪSEN WAS...
SO THE FIRST WAS A FULL HIT.
THE SECOND WAS COMPLETELY BLOCKED...
AND NOW KENSHIN CAN'T EVEN GET OFF THE FIRST STRIKE...
ENISHI'S ...
...STRONGER THAN BEFORE...
AND IT'S NOT JUST BECAUSE HE'S MADE UP HIS MIND TO KILL THIS TIME.
IT'S SEEPING OUT FROM SOMEWHERE DEEP INSIDE...

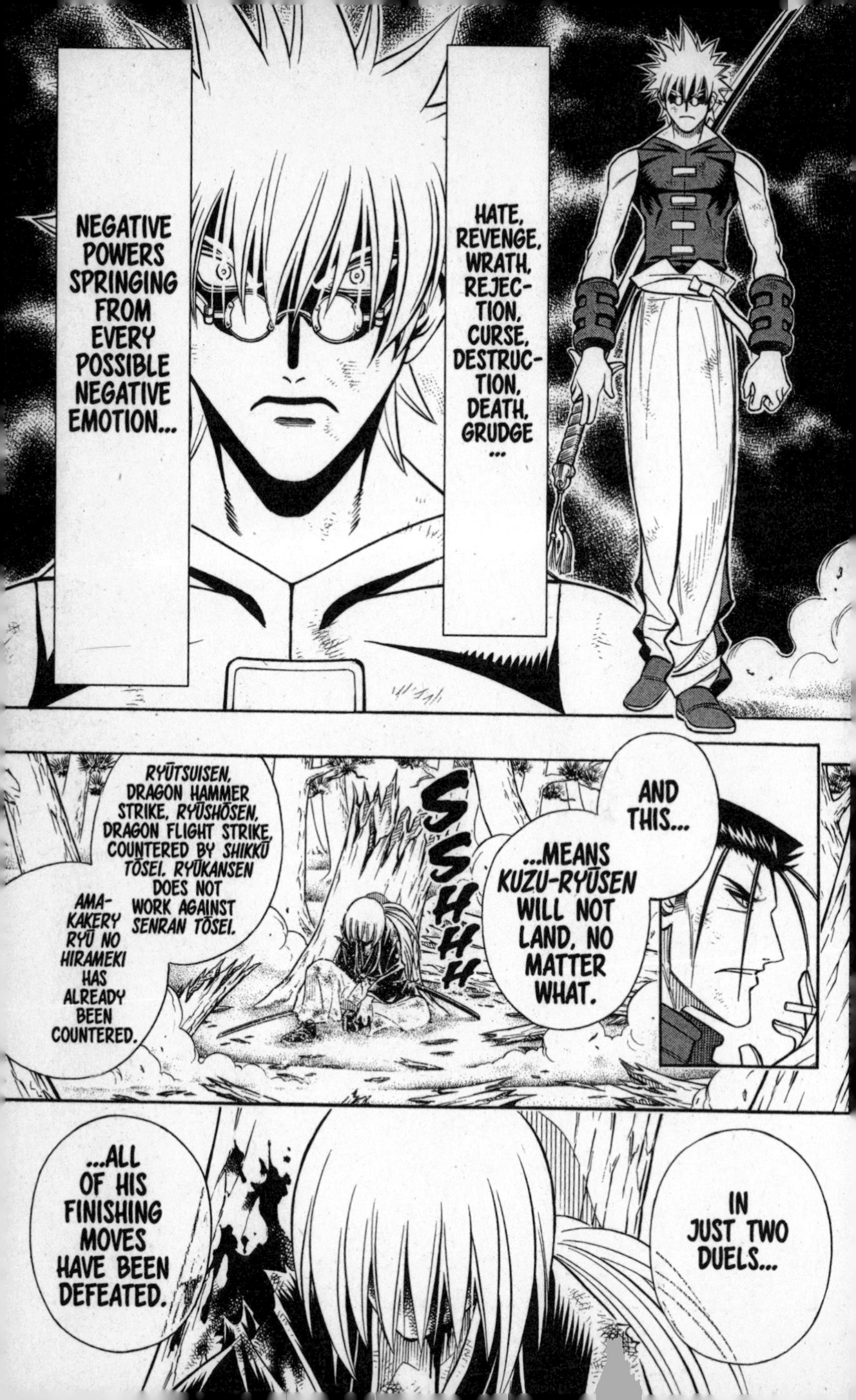
HATE, REVENGE, WRATH, REJECTION, CURSE, DESTRUCTION, DEATH, GRUDGE...
NEGATIVE POWERS SPRINGING FROM EVERY POSSIBLE NEGATIVE EMOTION...
AND THIS...
...MEANS KUZU-RYŪSEN WILL NOT LAND, NO MATTER WHAT.
SSHHH
RYŪTSUISEN, DRAGON HAMMER STRIKE, RYŪSHŌSEN, DRAGON FLIGHT STRIKE, COUNTERED BY SHIKKŪ TŌSEI. RYŪKANSEN DOES NOT WORK AGAINST SENRAN TŌSEI.
AMAKAKERY RYŪ NO HIRAMEKI HAS ALREADY BEEN COUNTERED.
IN JUST TWO DUELS...
...ALL OF HIS FINISHING MOVES HAVE BEEN DEFEATED.

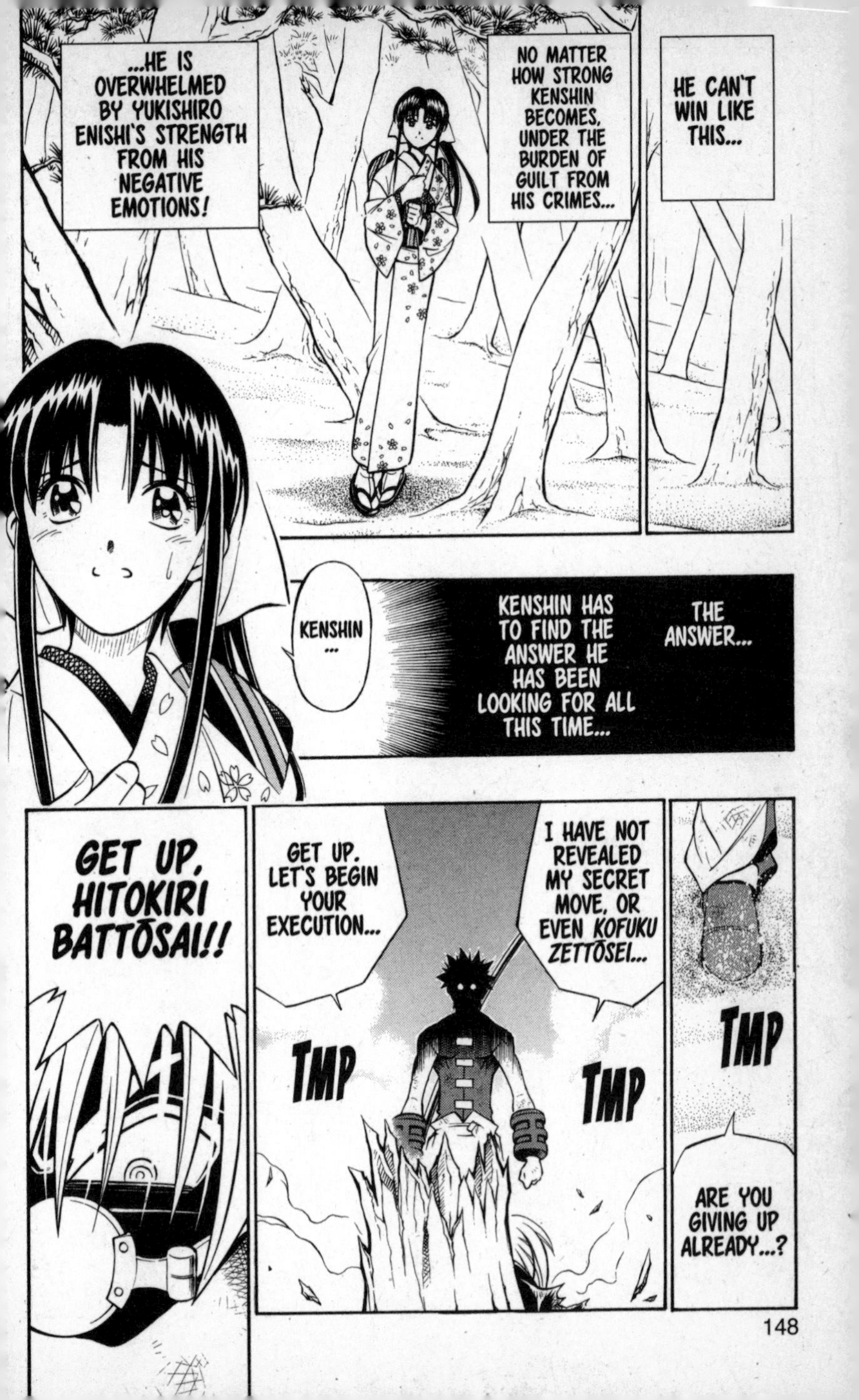
HE CAN'T WIN LIKE THIS...
NO MATTER HOW STRONG KENSHIN BECOMES, UNDER THE BURDEN OF GUILT FROM HIS CRIMES...
...HE IS OVERWHELMED BY YUKISHIRO ENISHI'S STRENGTH FROM HIS NEGATIVE EMOTIONS!
THE ANSWER...
KENSHIN HAS TO FIND THE ANSWER HE HAS BEEN LOOKING FOR ALL THIS TIME...
KENSHIN...
TMP
ARE YOU GIVING UP ALREADY...?
I HAVE NOT REVEALED MY SECRET MOVE, OR EVEN KOFUKU ZETTŌSEI...
GET UP. LET'S BEGIN YOUR EXECUTION...
TMP
TMP
GET UP, HITOKIRI BATTŌSAI!!

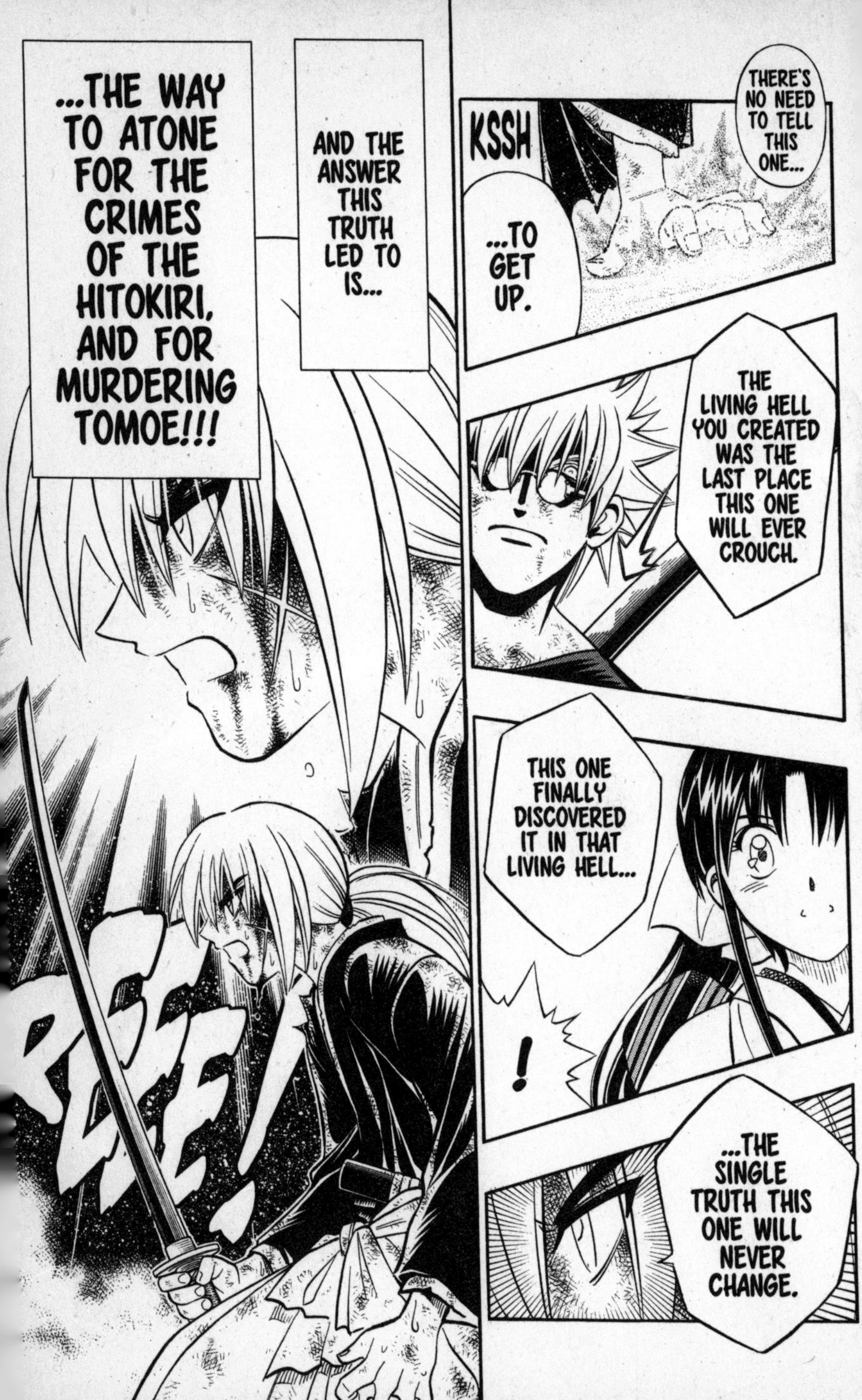
THERE'S NO NEED TO TELL THIS ONE...
KSSH
...TO GET UP.
THE LIVING HELL YOU CREATED WAS THE LAST PLACE THIS ONE WILL EVER CROUCH.
THIS ONE FINALLY DISCOVERED IT IN THAT LIVING HELL...
!
...THE SINGLE TRUTH THIS ONE WILL NEVER CHANGE.
AND THE ANSWER THIS TRUTH LED TO IS...
...THE WAY TO ATONE FOR THE CRIMES OF THE HITOKIRI, AND FOR MURDERING TOMOE!!!

Rurouni Kenshin

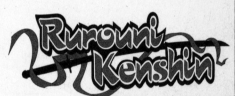

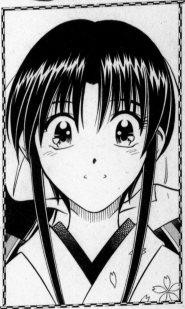

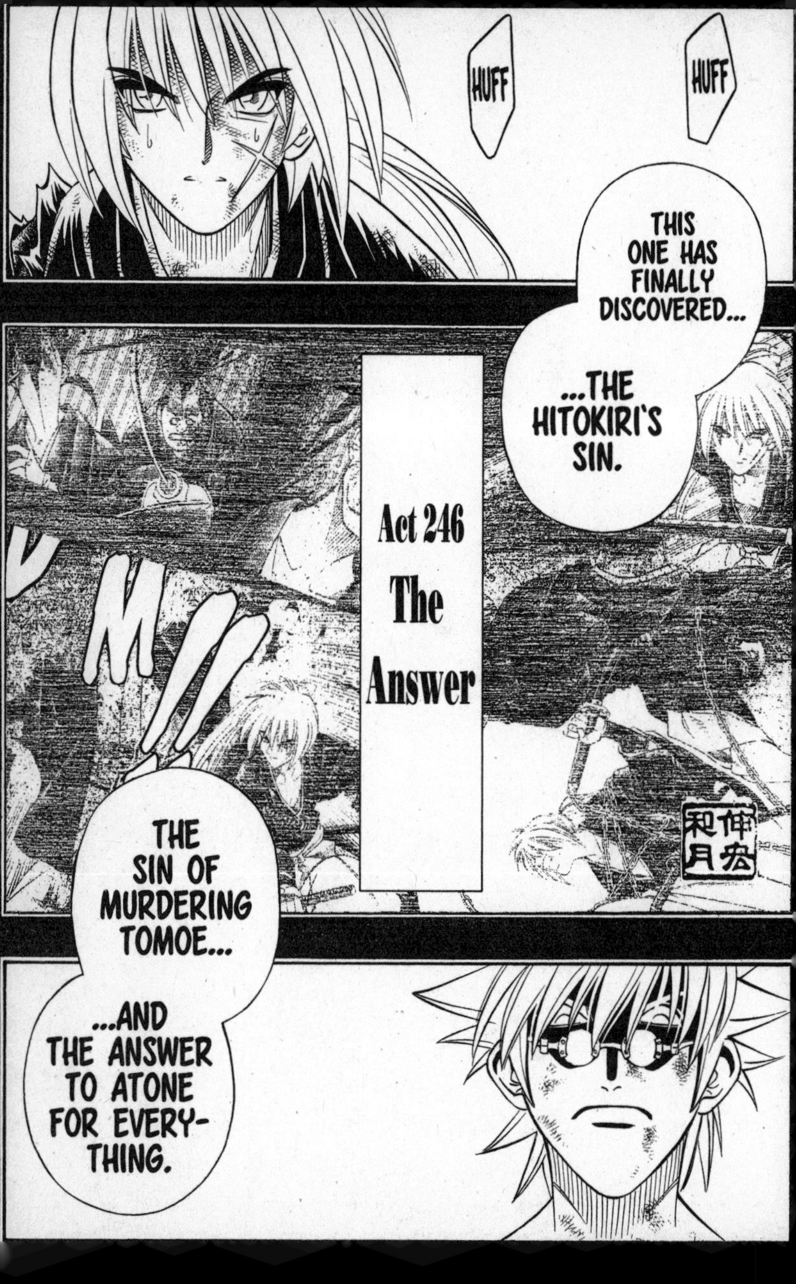
HUFF
HUFF
THIS ONE HAS FINALLY DISCOVERED...
...THE HITOKIRI'S SIN.
Act 246 The Answer
伸宏和月
THE SIN OF MURDERING TOMOE...
...AND THE ANSWER TO ATONE FOR EVERY-THING.

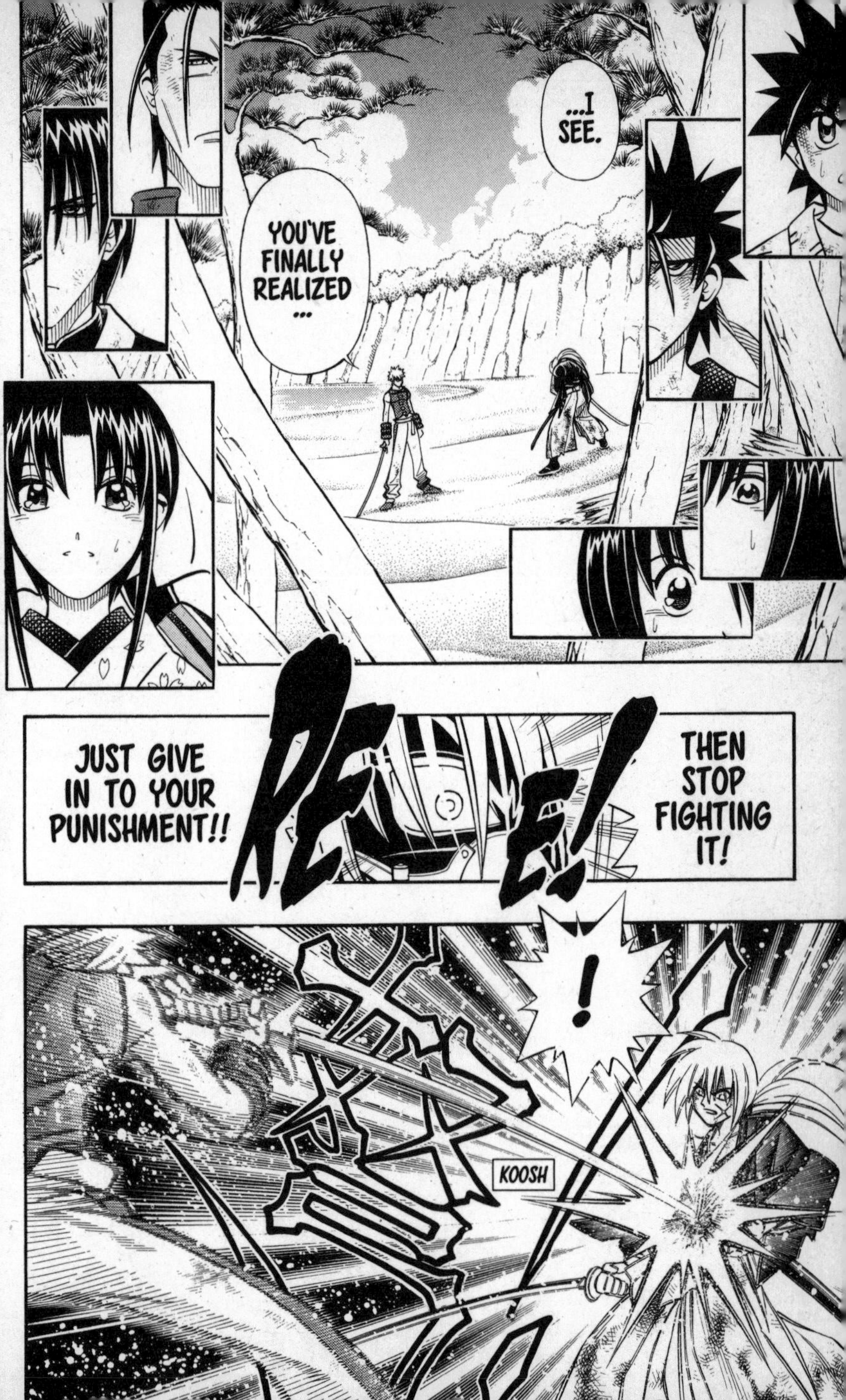
...I SEE.
YOU'VE FINALLY REALIZED...
THEN STOP FIGHTING IT!
JUST GIVE IN TO YOUR PUNISHMENT!!
!
KOOSH

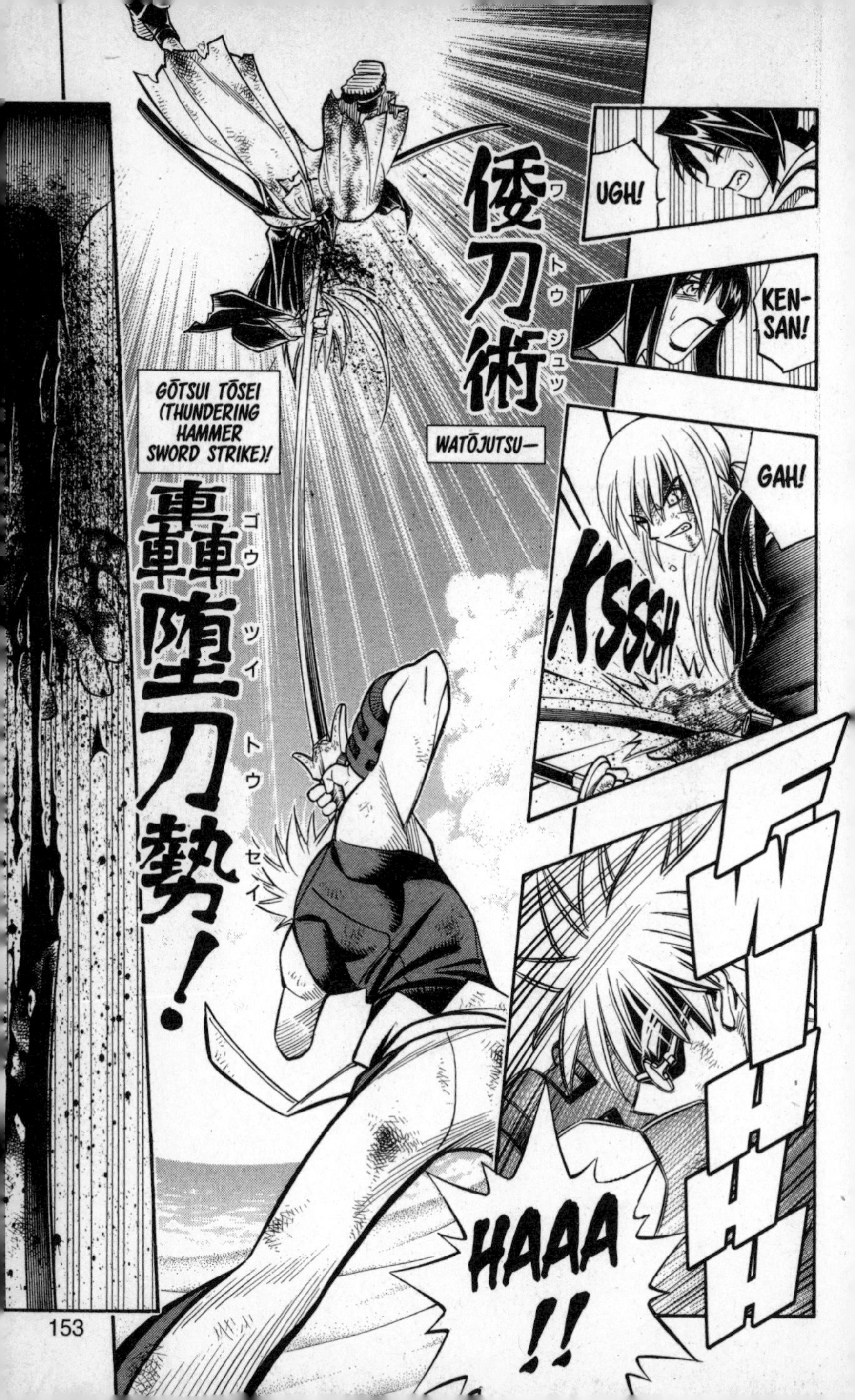
UGH!
KEN-SAN!
GAH!
KSSSH
倭刀術
WATŌJUTSU—
GŌTSUI TŌSEI (THUNDERING HAMMER SWORD STRIKE)!
轟墮刀勢！
FWHHHH
HAAA!!

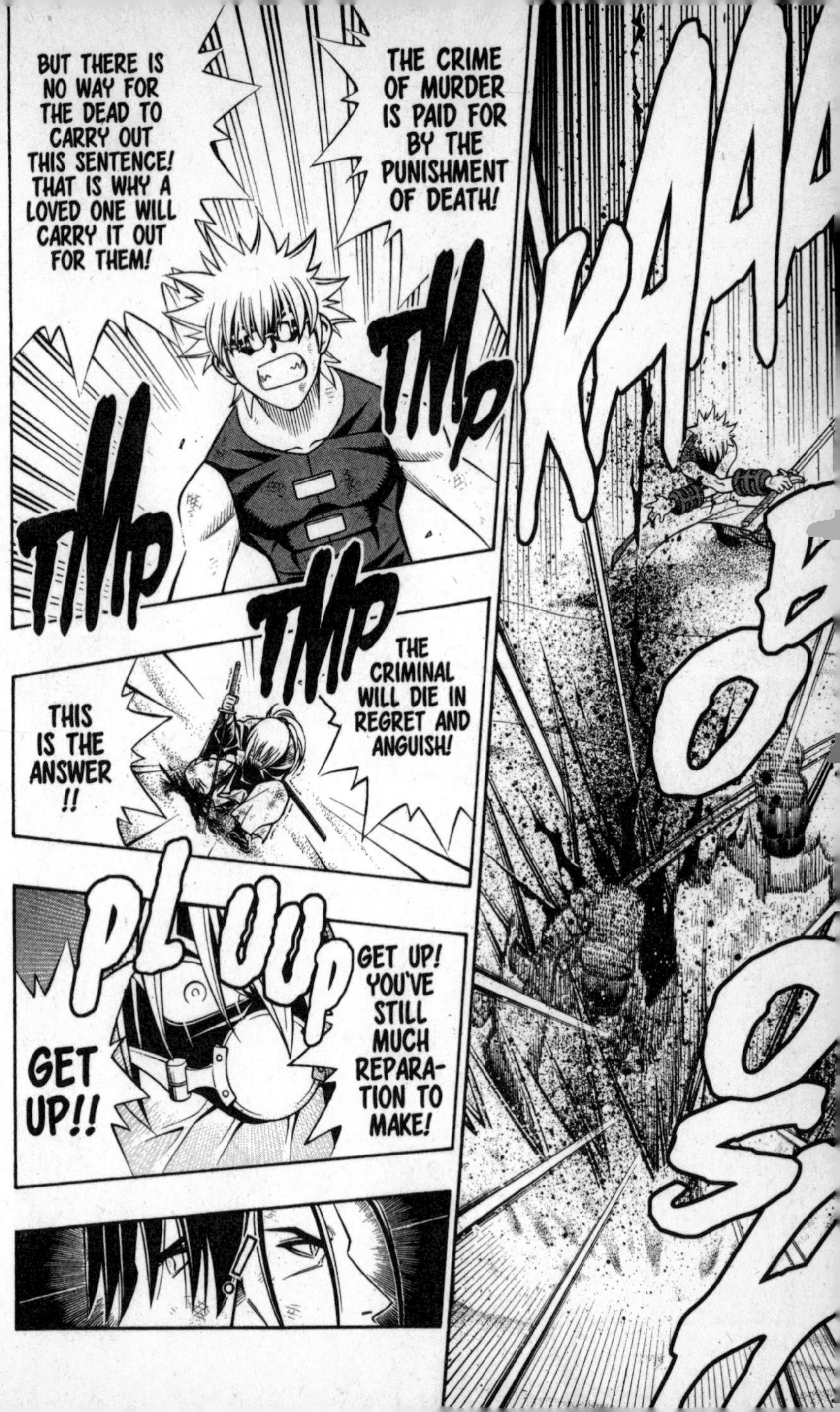
THE CRIME OF MURDER IS PAID FOR BY THE PUNISHMENT OF DEATH!
BUT THERE IS NO WAY FOR THE DEAD TO CARRY OUT THIS SENTENCE! THAT IS WHY A LOVED ONE WILL CARRY IT OUT FOR THEM!
TMP
TMP
TMP
THE CRIMINAL WILL DIE IN REGRET AND ANGUISH!
THIS IS THE ANSWER !!
PLUUP
GET UP! YOU'VE STILL MUCH REPARA-TION TO MAKE!
GET UP!!

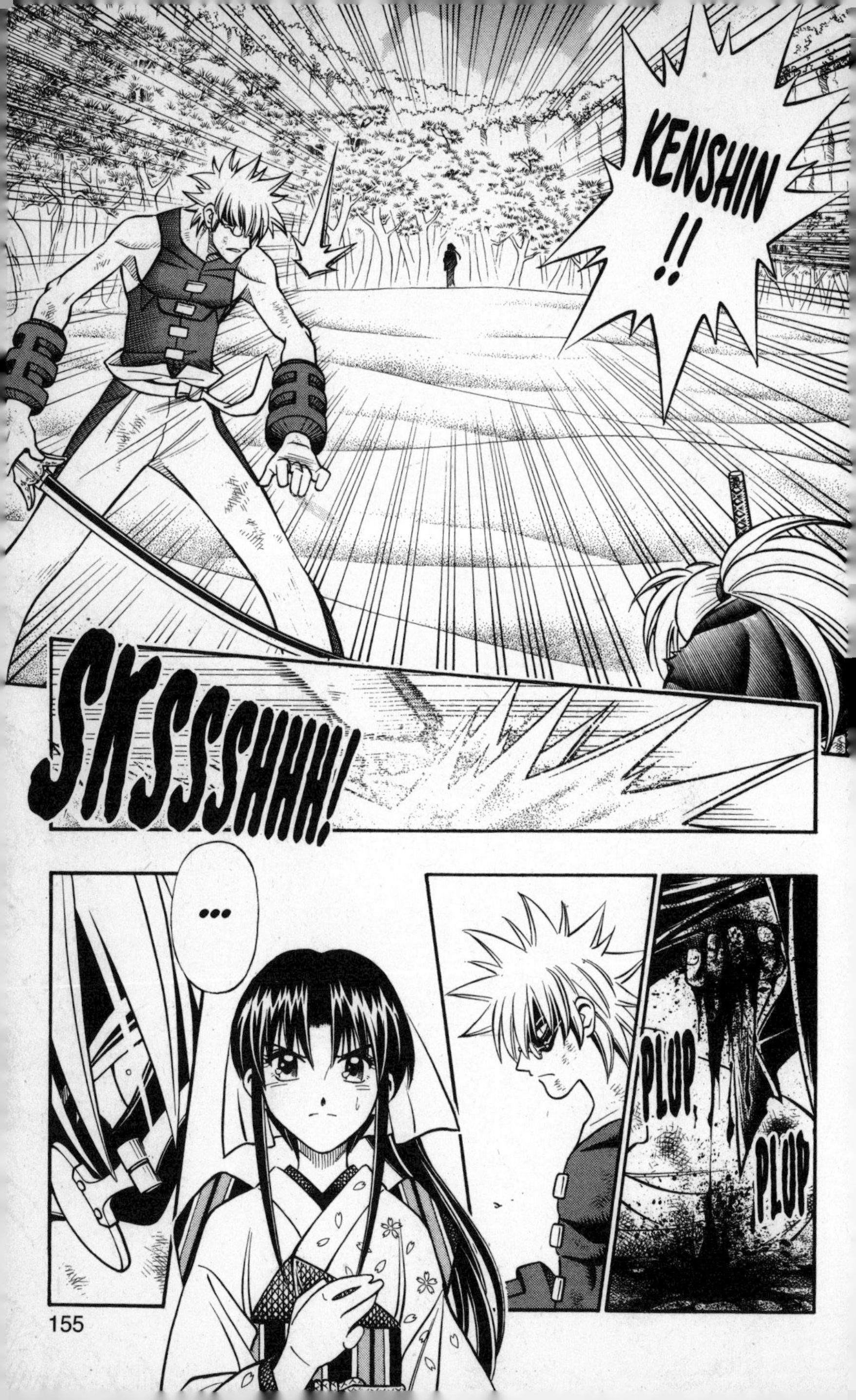
KENSHIN !!
SHSSSHHH!
PLUP, PLUP
...

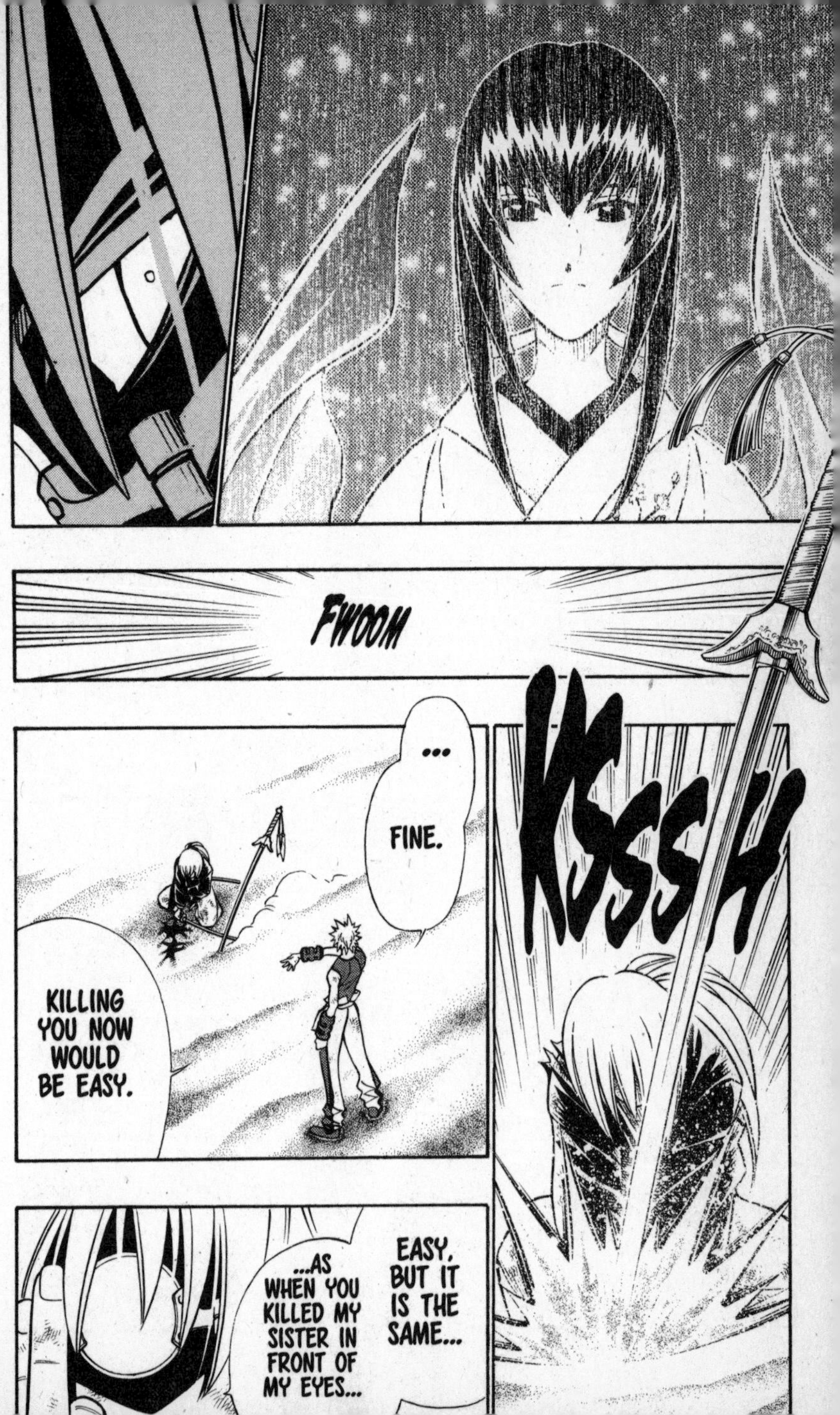
FWOOM
KSSH
...
FINE.
KILLING YOU NOW WOULD BE EASY.
EASY, BUT IT IS THE SAME...
...AS WHEN YOU KILLED MY SISTER IN FRONT OF MY EYES...

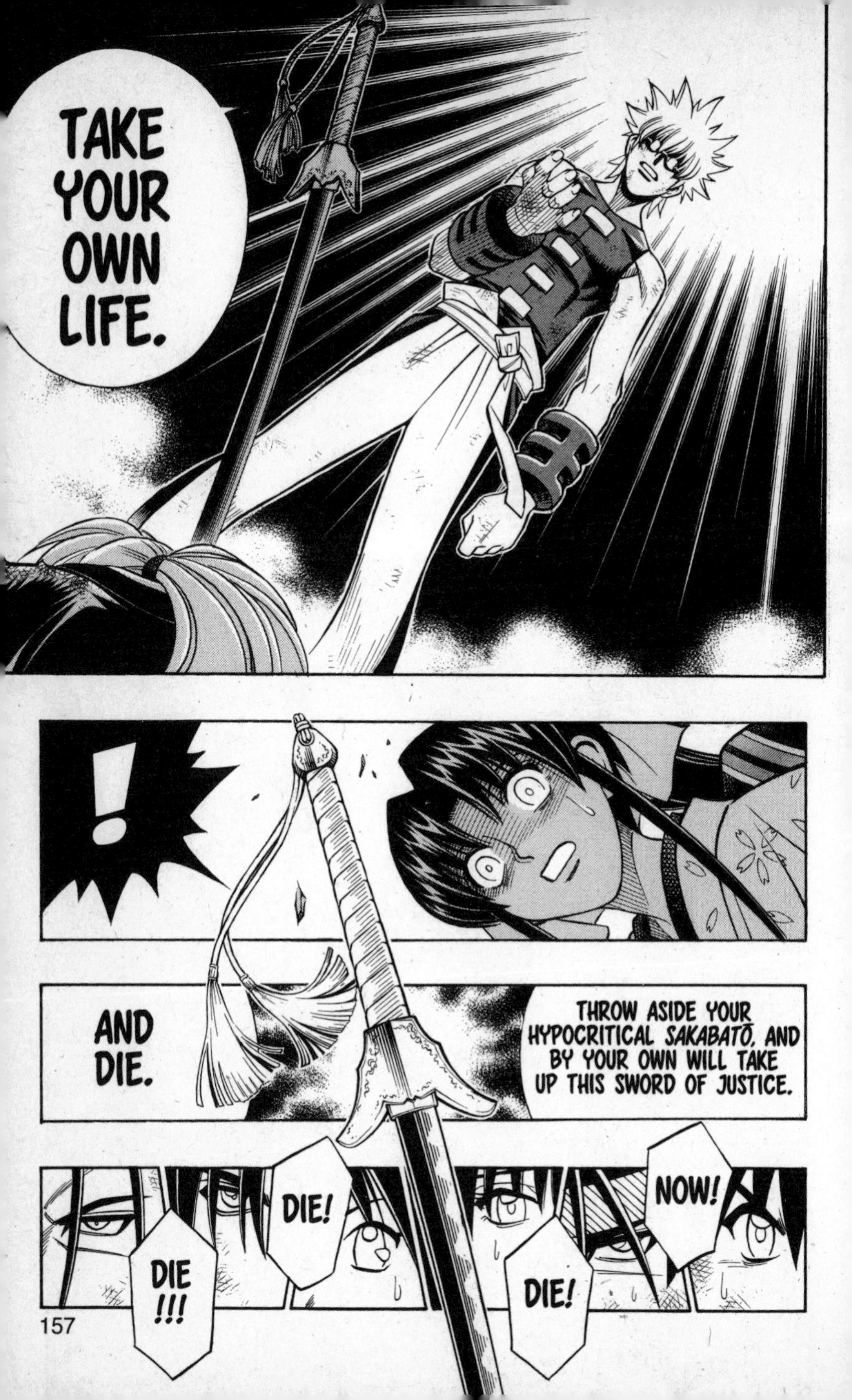
TAKE YOUR OWN LIFE.
!
THROW ASIDE YOUR HYPOCRITICAL *SAKABATŌ*, AND BY YOUR OWN WILL TAKE UP THIS SWORD OF JUSTICE.
AND DIE.
NOW!
DIE!
DIE!
DIE !!!

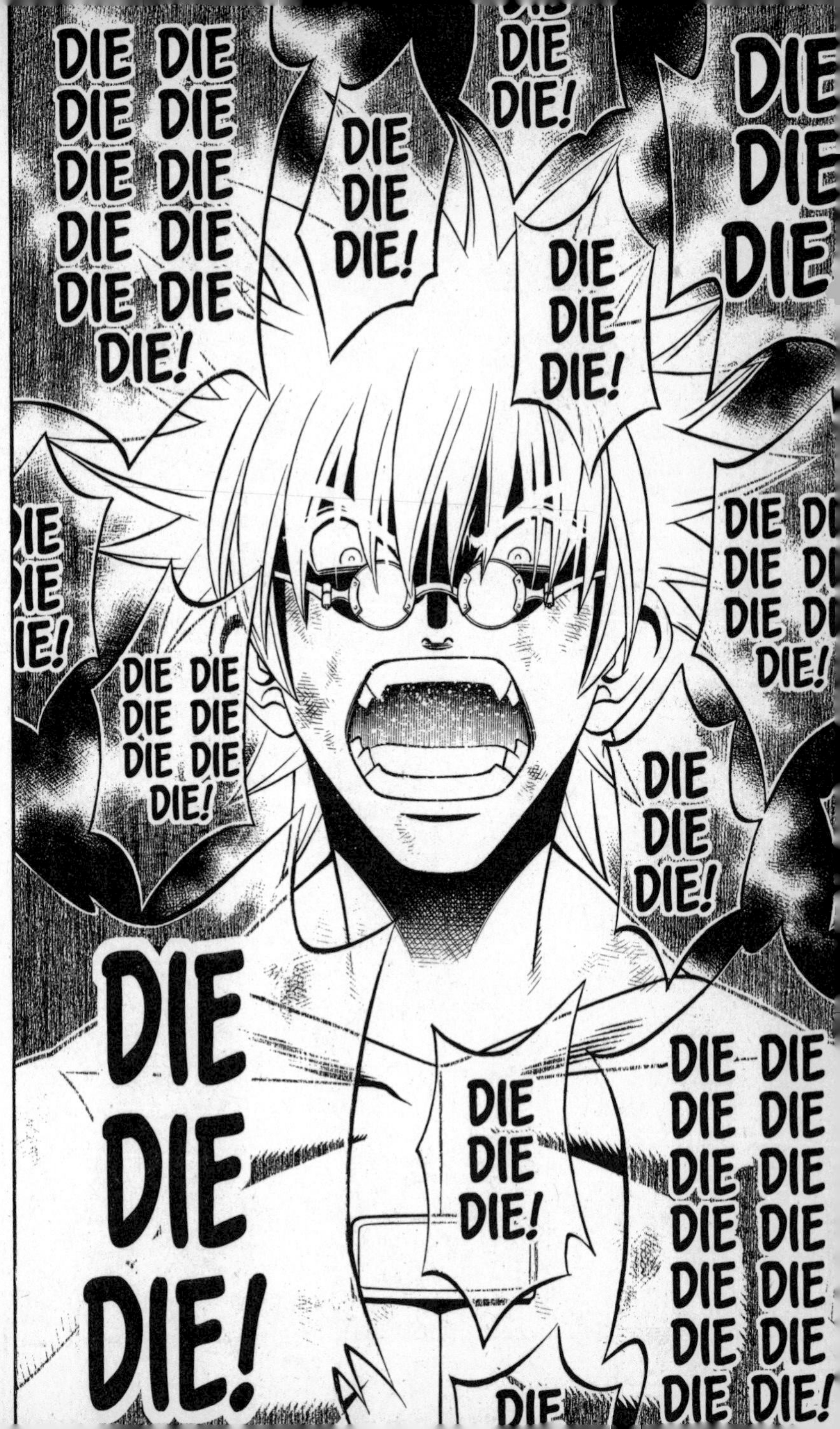
DIE DIE DIE
DIE DIE!
DIE DIE DIE!
DIE DIE DIE!
DIE DIE DIE DIE DIE DIE DIE DIE DIE DIE DIE!
DIE DIE DIE!
DIE DIE DIE DIE DIE DIE DIE!
DIE DIE DIE DIE DIE DIE DIE DIE DIE DIE DIE DIE DIE DIE DIE DIE!
DIE DIE DIE!
DIE DIE DIE!

READ THIS WAY

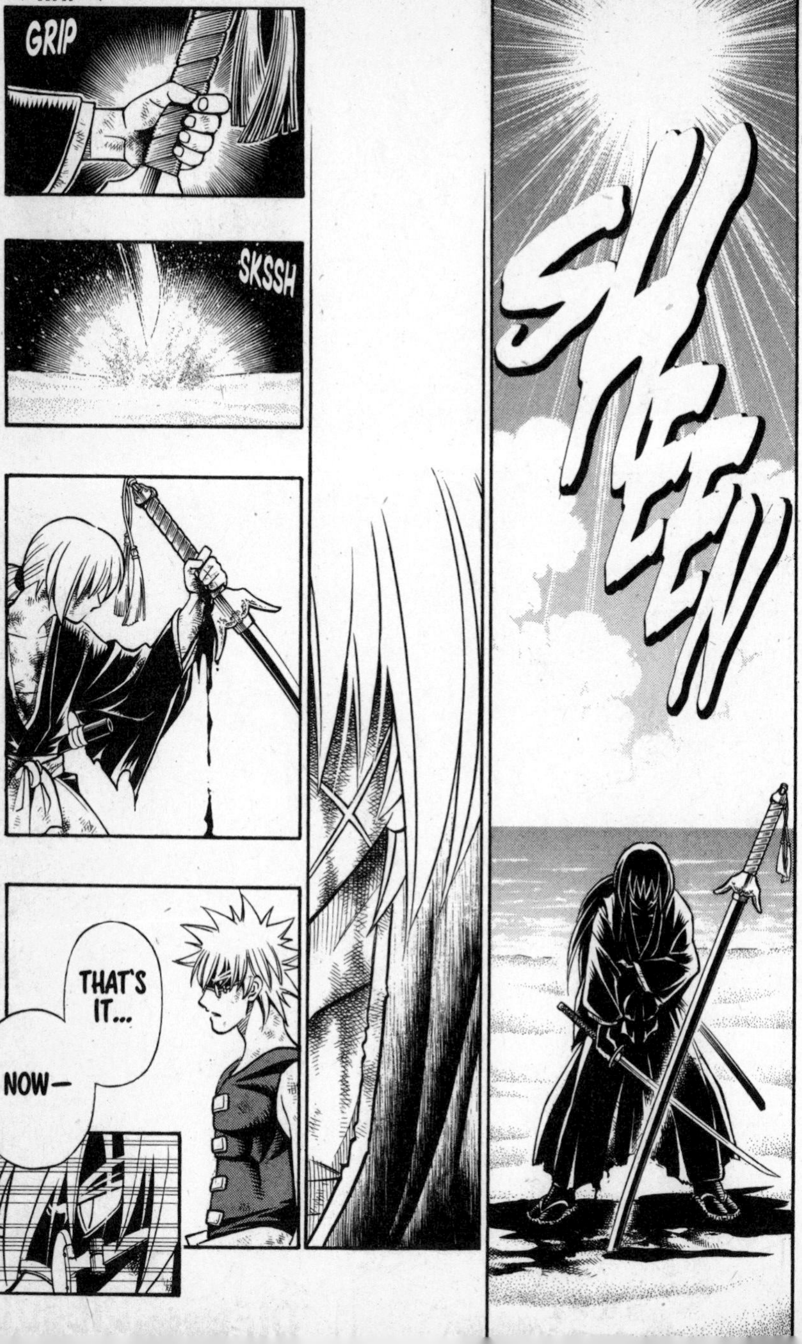
SHEEN
GRIP
SKSSH
THAT'S IT...
NOW—

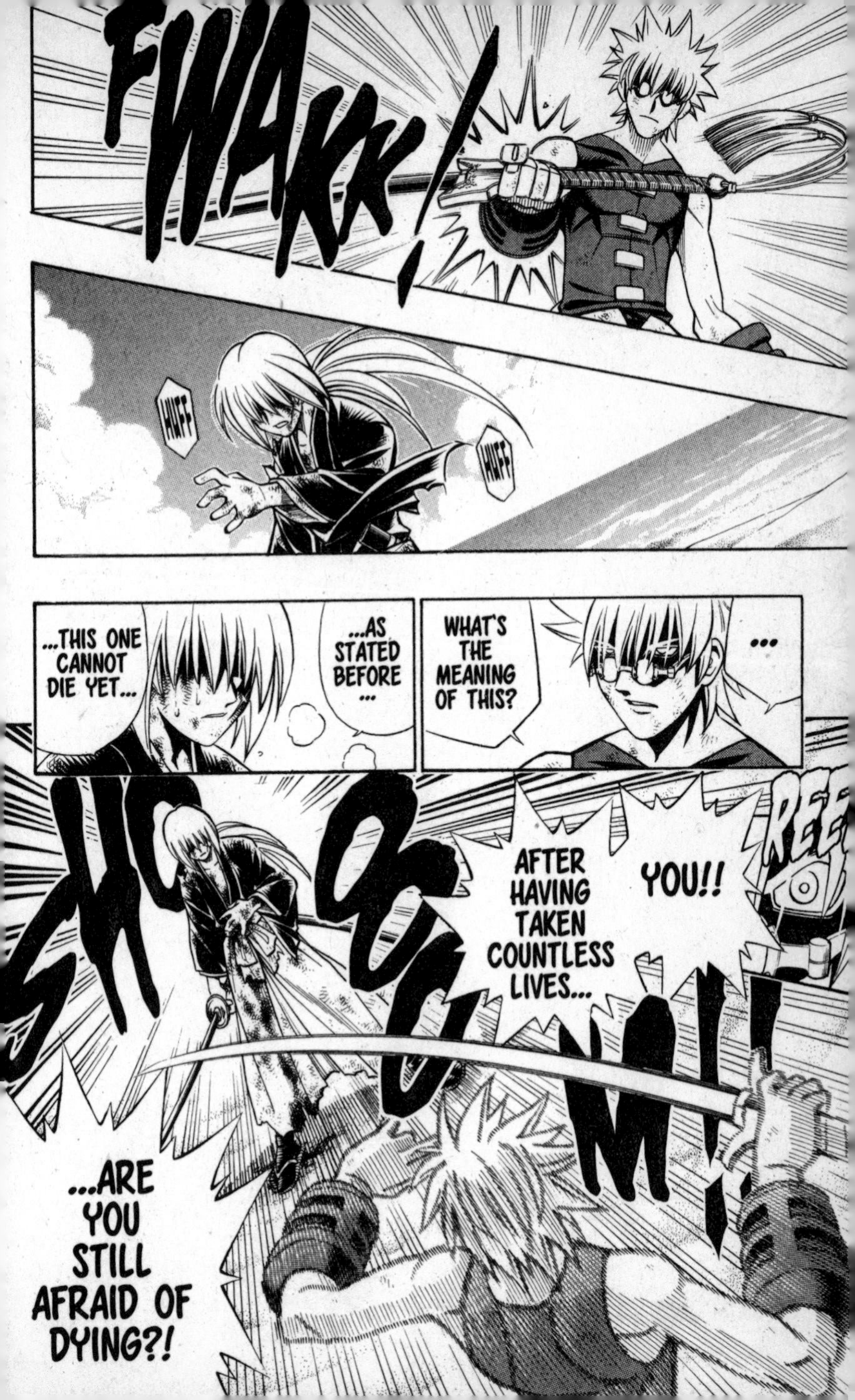
FWAKK!
HUFF
HUFF
...
WHAT'S THE MEANING OF THIS?
...AS STATED BEFORE ...
...THIS ONE CANNOT DIE YET...
REE
YOU!!
AFTER HAVING TAKEN COUNTLESS LIVES...
SHOOOM!!
...ARE YOU STILL AFRAID OF DYING?!

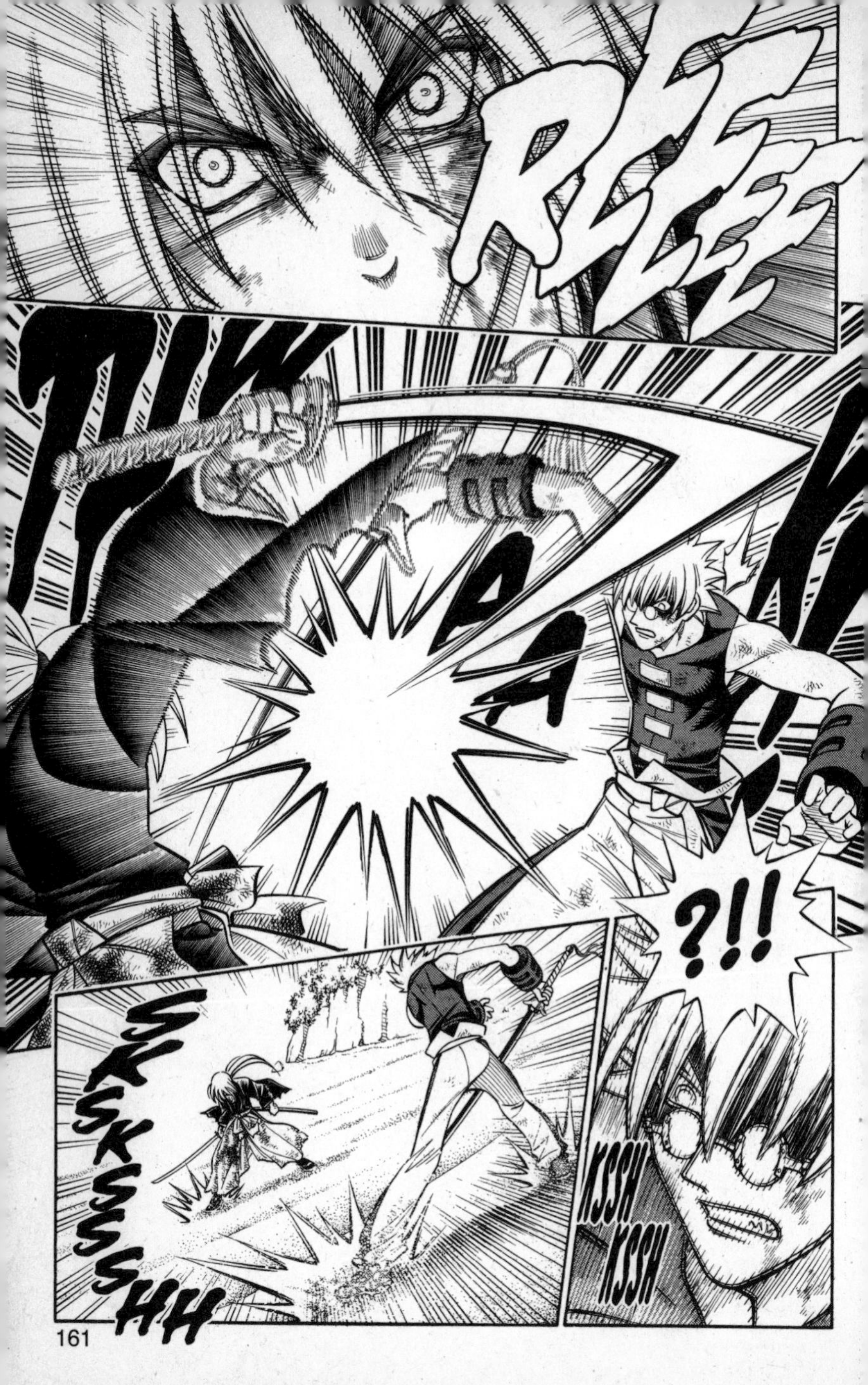
?!!
KSH KSH
SKSKSSSSHH

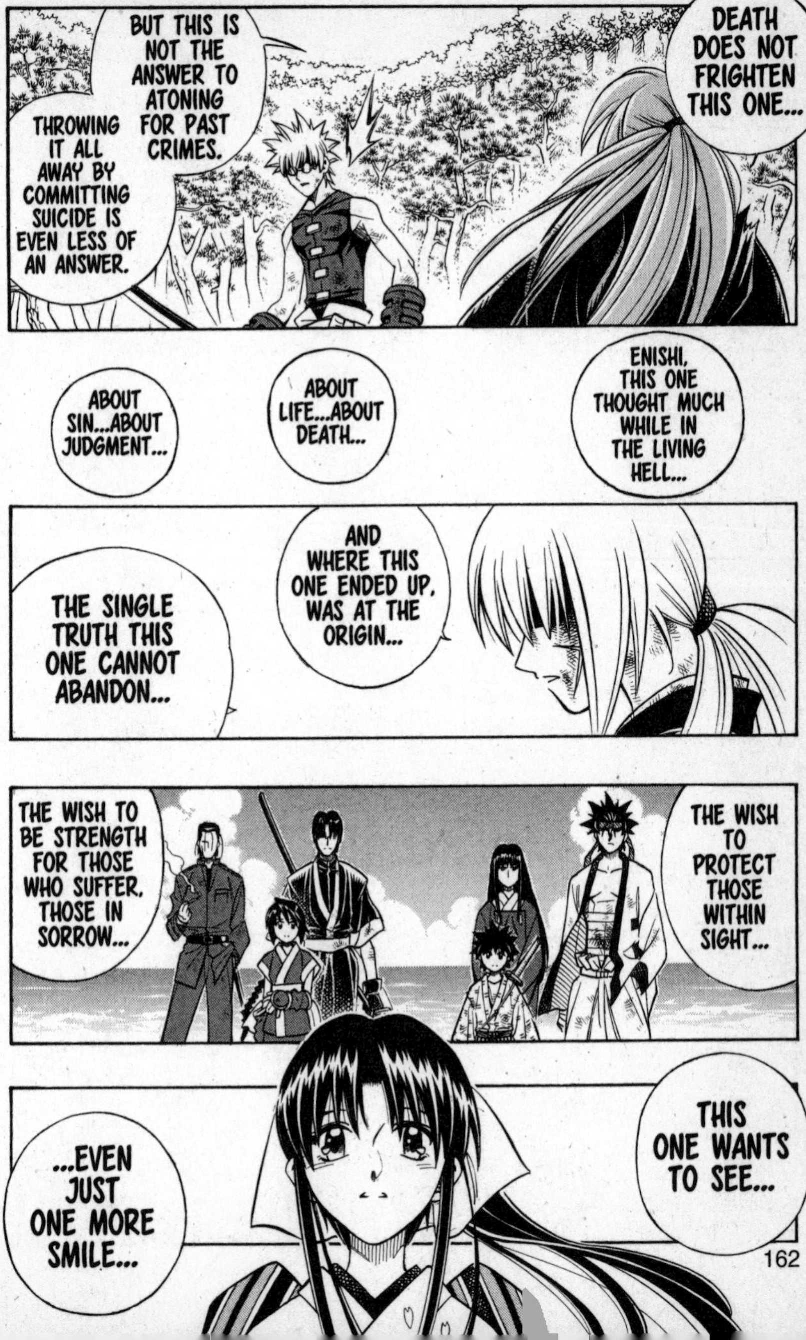
DEATH DOES NOT FRIGHTEN THIS ONE...
BUT THIS IS NOT THE ANSWER TO ATONING FOR PAST CRIMES.
THROWING IT ALL AWAY BY COMMITTING SUICIDE IS EVEN LESS OF AN ANSWER.
ENISHI, THIS ONE THOUGHT MUCH WHILE IN THE LIVING HELL...
ABOUT LIFE...ABOUT DEATH...
ABOUT SIN...ABOUT JUDGMENT...
AND WHERE THIS ONE ENDED UP, WAS AT THE ORIGIN...
THE SINGLE TRUTH THIS ONE CANNOT ABANDON...
THE WISH TO PROTECT THOSE WITHIN SIGHT...
THE WISH TO BE STRENGTH FOR THOSE WHO SUFFER, THOSE IN SORROW...
THIS ONE WANTS TO SEE...
...EVEN JUST ONE MORE SMILE...

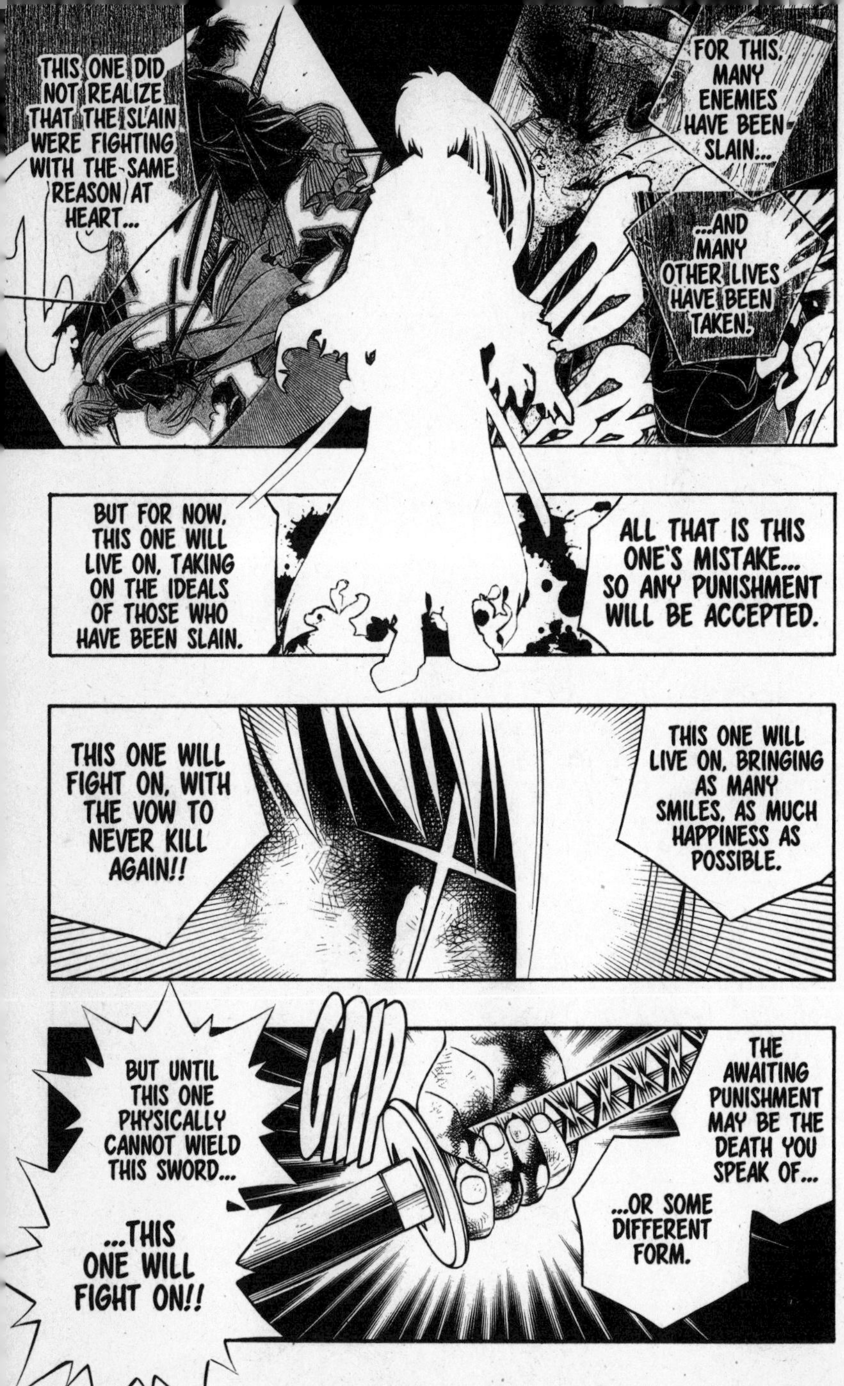
FOR THIS, MANY ENEMIES HAVE BEEN SLAIN...
...AND MANY OTHER LIVES HAVE BEEN TAKEN.
THIS ONE DID NOT REALIZE THAT THE SLAIN WERE FIGHTING WITH THE SAME REASON AT HEART...
ALL THAT IS THIS ONE'S MISTAKE... SO ANY PUNISHMENT WILL BE ACCEPTED.
BUT FOR NOW, THIS ONE WILL LIVE ON, TAKING ON THE IDEALS OF THOSE WHO HAVE BEEN SLAIN.
THIS ONE WILL LIVE ON, BRINGING AS MANY SMILES, AS MUCH HAPPINESS AS POSSIBLE.
THIS ONE WILL FIGHT ON, WITH THE VOW TO NEVER KILL AGAIN!!
THE AWAITING PUNISHMENT MAY BE THE DEATH YOU SPEAK OF...
...OR SOME DIFFERENT FORM.
GRIP
BUT UNTIL THIS ONE PHYSICALLY CANNOT WIELD THIS SWORD...
...THIS ONE WILL FIGHT ON!!

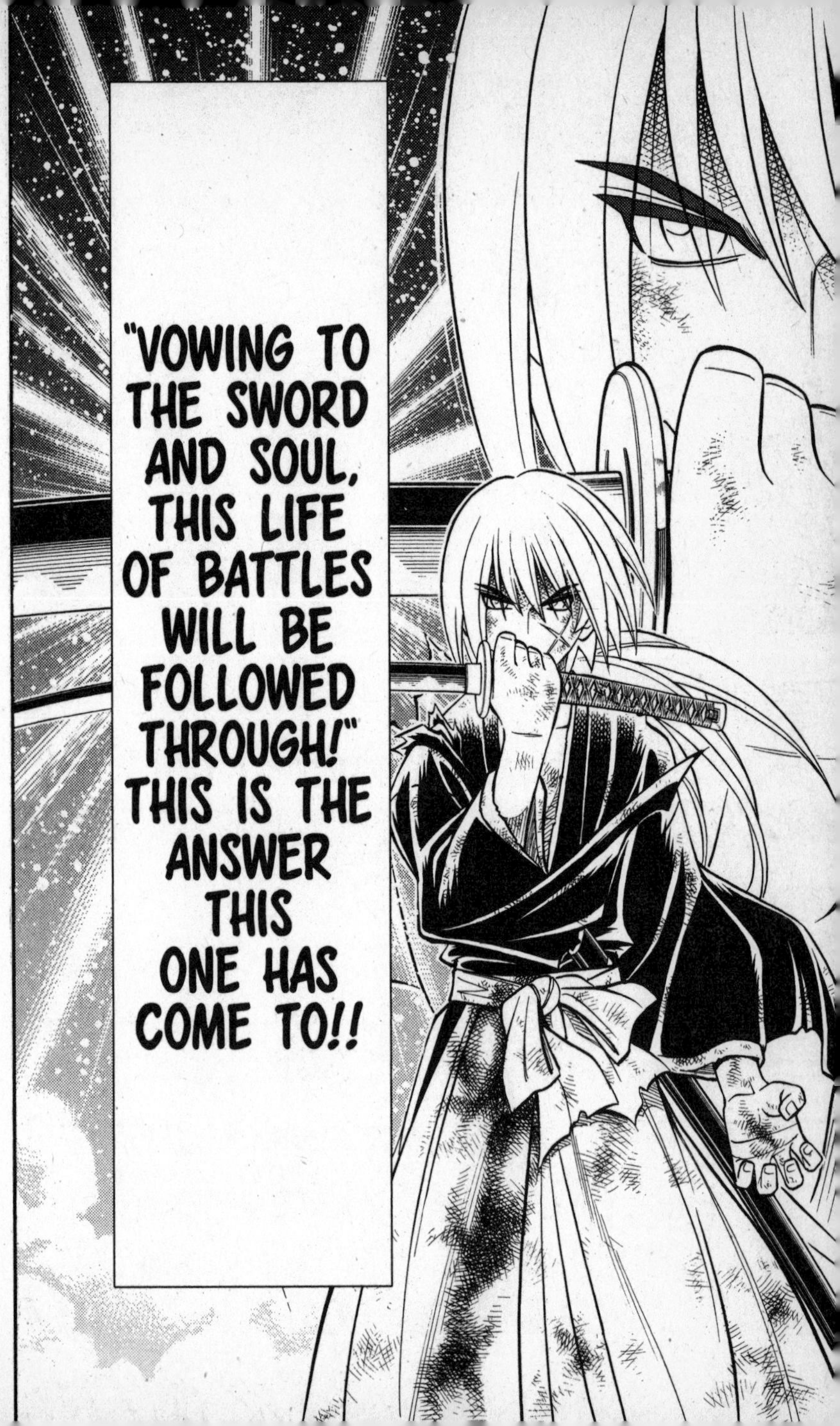
"VOWING TO THE SWORD AND SOUL, THIS LIFE OF BATTLES WILL BE FOLLOWED THROUGH!" THIS IS THE ANSWER THIS ONE HAS COME TO!!

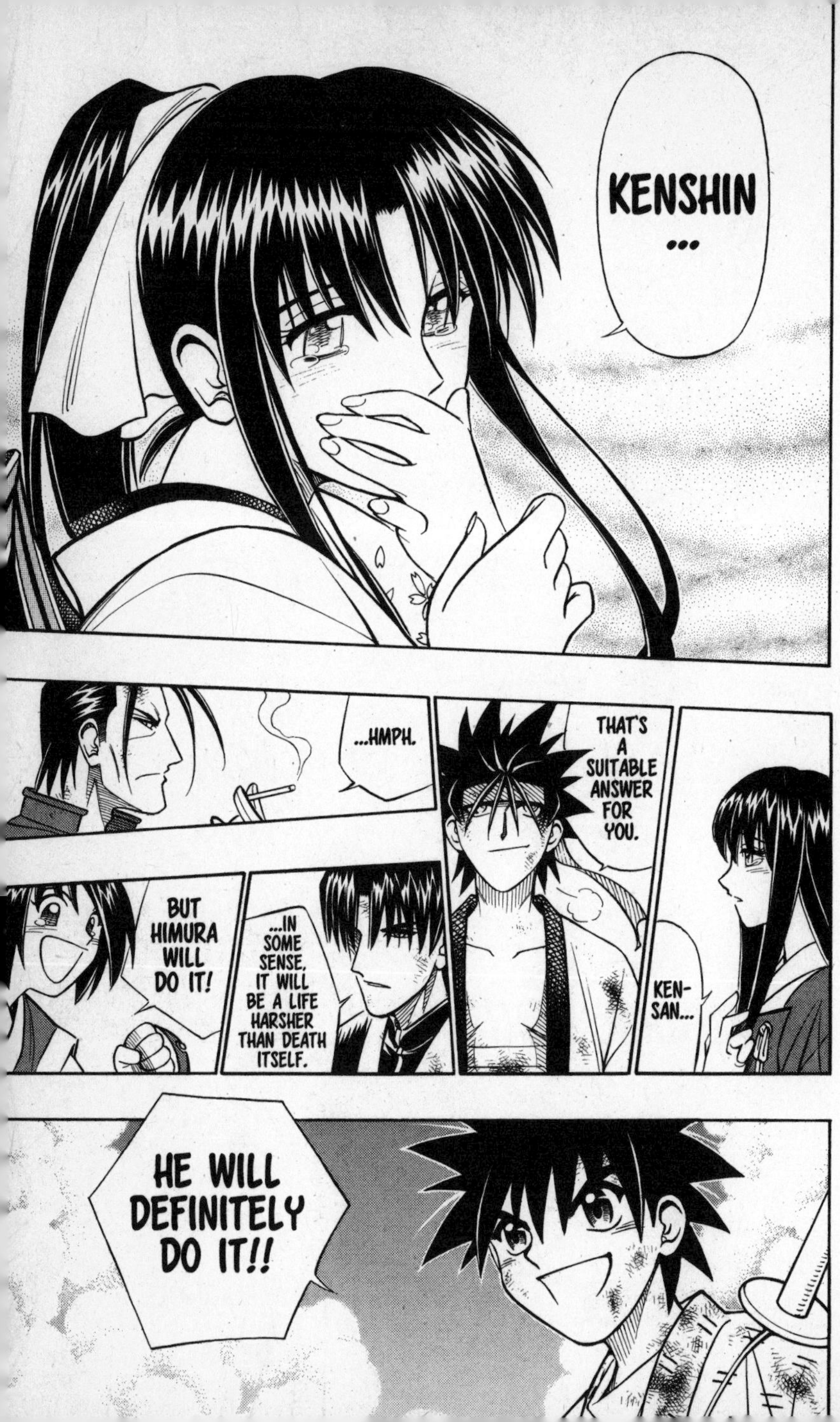
KENSHIN ...
KEN-SAN...
THAT'S A SUITABLE ANSWER FOR YOU.
...HMPH.
...IN SOME SENSE, IT WILL BE A LIFE HARSHER THAN DEATH ITSELF.
BUT HIMURA WILL DO IT!
HE WILL DEFINITELY DO IT!!

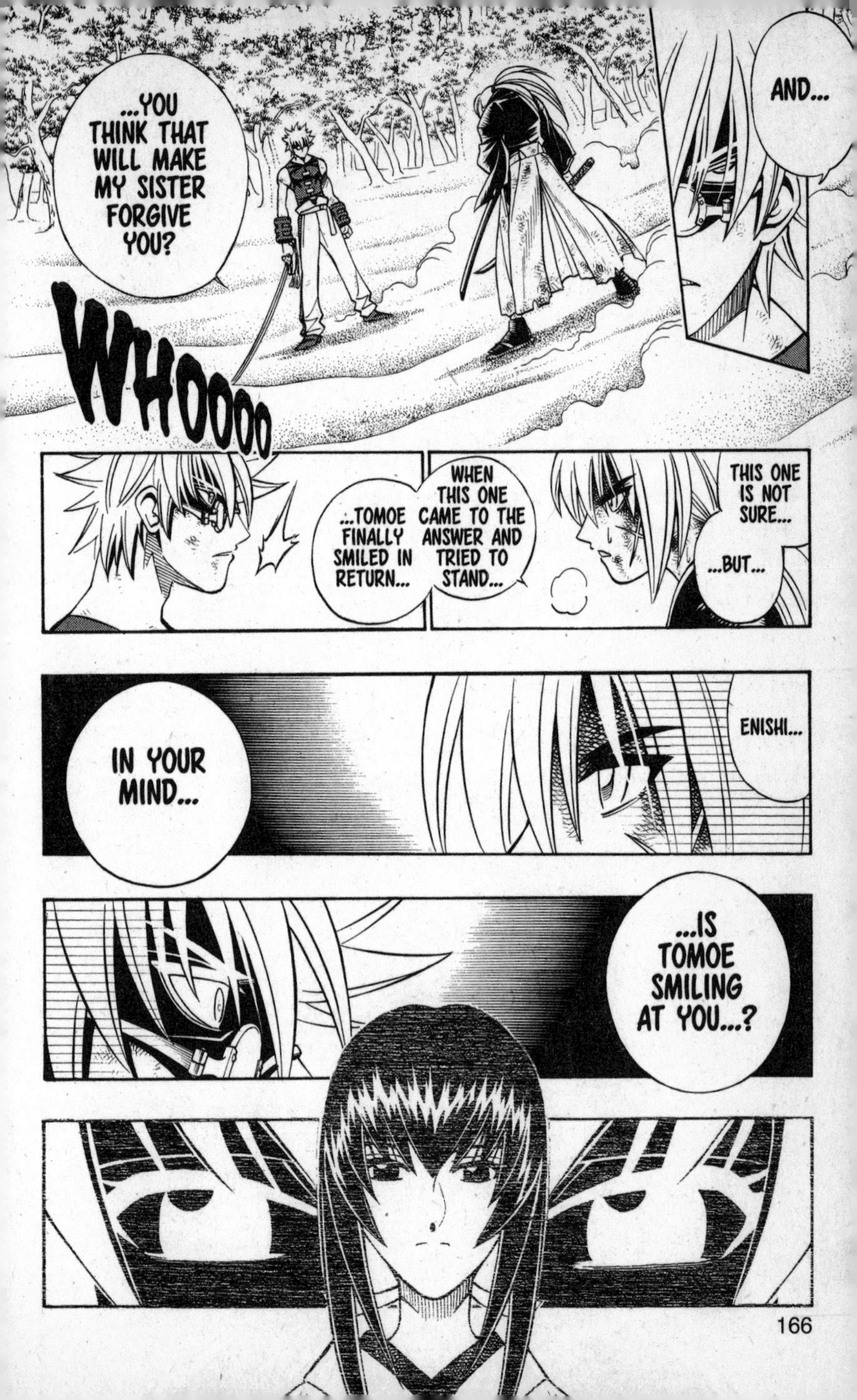
AND...
...YOU THINK THAT WILL MAKE MY SISTER FORGIVE YOU?
WHOOOO
THIS ONE IS NOT SURE...
...BUT...
WHEN THIS ONE CAME TO THE ANSWER AND TRIED TO STAND...
...TOMOE FINALLY SMILED IN RETURN...
ENISHI...
IN YOUR MIND...
...IS TOMOE SMILING AT YOU...?

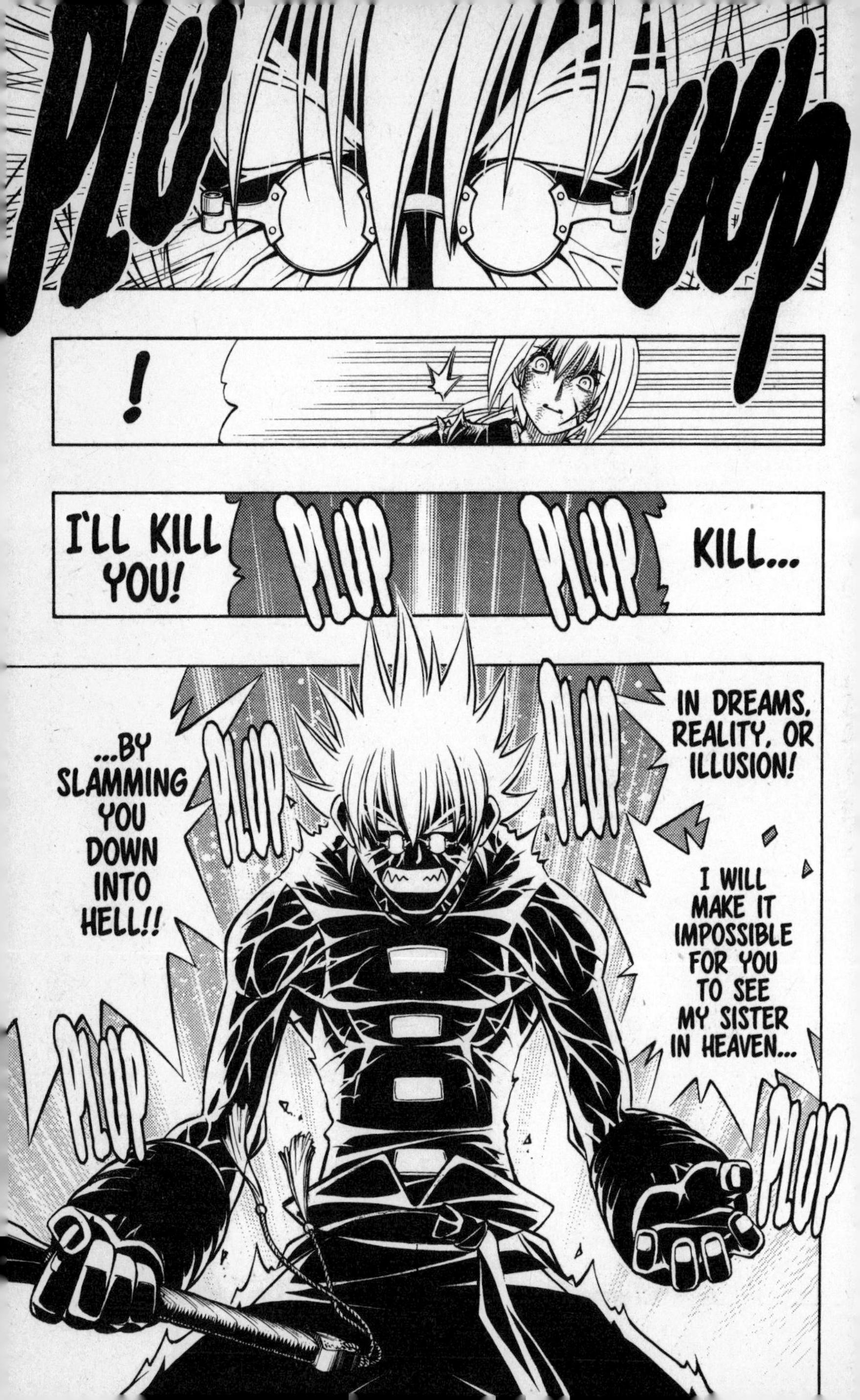
!
KILL...
PLUP
PLUP
I'LL KILL YOU!
IN DREAMS, REALITY, OR ILLUSION!
PLUP
I WILL MAKE IT IMPOSSIBLE FOR YOU TO SEE MY SISTER IN HEAVEN...
PLUP
...BY SLAMMING YOU DOWN INTO HELL!!
PLUP
PLUP

"FREE TALK"

Long time no see. This is Watsuki, who was told by an ex-assistant who read this column in the previous volume that I am "over." A friend also said "Hmm" in a very cold manner.

Undeterred by the rain or wind of society, let's talk about figures and games again.

In terms of figures, I have not bought a single European toy for three months. What happened to Watsuki? I am looking forward to the already pre-ordered complete transformation *Getter Robo* (Studio Half-Eye). I have stated before that "it is not my taste to spend $300-400 for figures," but this one is a reward to myself for hitting five years in publication. And look, it transforms into Getter 1, 2, and 3 separately, so each of them would be about $100 (what a crappy argument). In terms of "Gachapon," there's always something I want, so I'm having lots of fun there.

In games, it's *Raising Zan* (UEP Sytems, Playstation) and *To Heart* (Aquaplus, Playstation). Right now, I'm at the climax of writing the manga, so both games have been left off about half way through. And as can be seen above, they've had some influence. Isn't *To Heart* quite fitting for Watsuki...? Well, I guess I would be worried if it was fitting. Okay, I'm "over"?!! "Hmm" is okay!!! But false rumors are not okay. Watsuki has never played any girly game other than *To Heart*, and is not collecting all the toys related to it. I am actually more of a "passionate" type of person rather than an "infatuated" type of person (or else *Ruro-Ken* would be a "Meiji Love Story" rather than a "Meiji Swordsman Story"). I am not that deep into it.

I really have no time these days. It is often said that time is money, but this is incorrect. Time is more valuable than money. Right now, I really want some time to rest my brain. I would like to just vegetate and reset my operating system. There are differences between how I think now and five years ago, but it's all mixed up and disorganized, so I'd like to have some time to take care of this soon. So, the theme for Watsuki in the second half of this year is "Change time priorities."

In terms of manga, we'll just pass this time. If you can, please read the magazines. See you in the next volume.

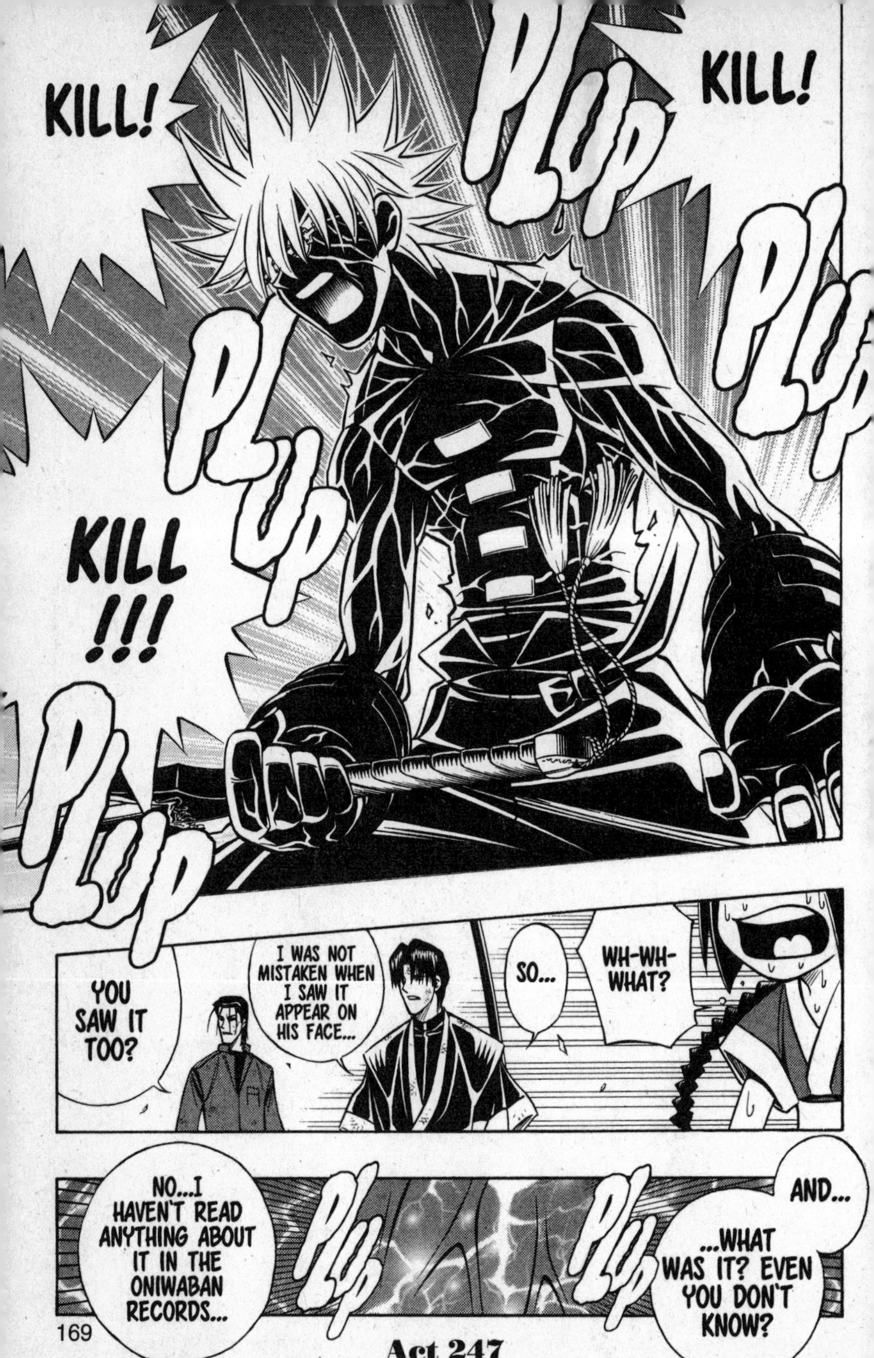
KILL!
PLOP
KILL!
PLOP
PLOP
KILL !!!
PLOP
PLOP
WH-WH-WHAT?
SO...
I WAS NOT MISTAKEN WHEN I SAW IT APPEAR ON HIS FACE...
YOU SAW IT TOO?
AND...
...WHAT WAS IT? EVEN YOU DON'T KNOW?
PLOP
PLOP
NO...I HAVEN'T READ ANYTHING ABOUT IT IN THE ONIWABAN RECORDS...

Act 247

Kyōkeimyaku (Frenzied Nerves)

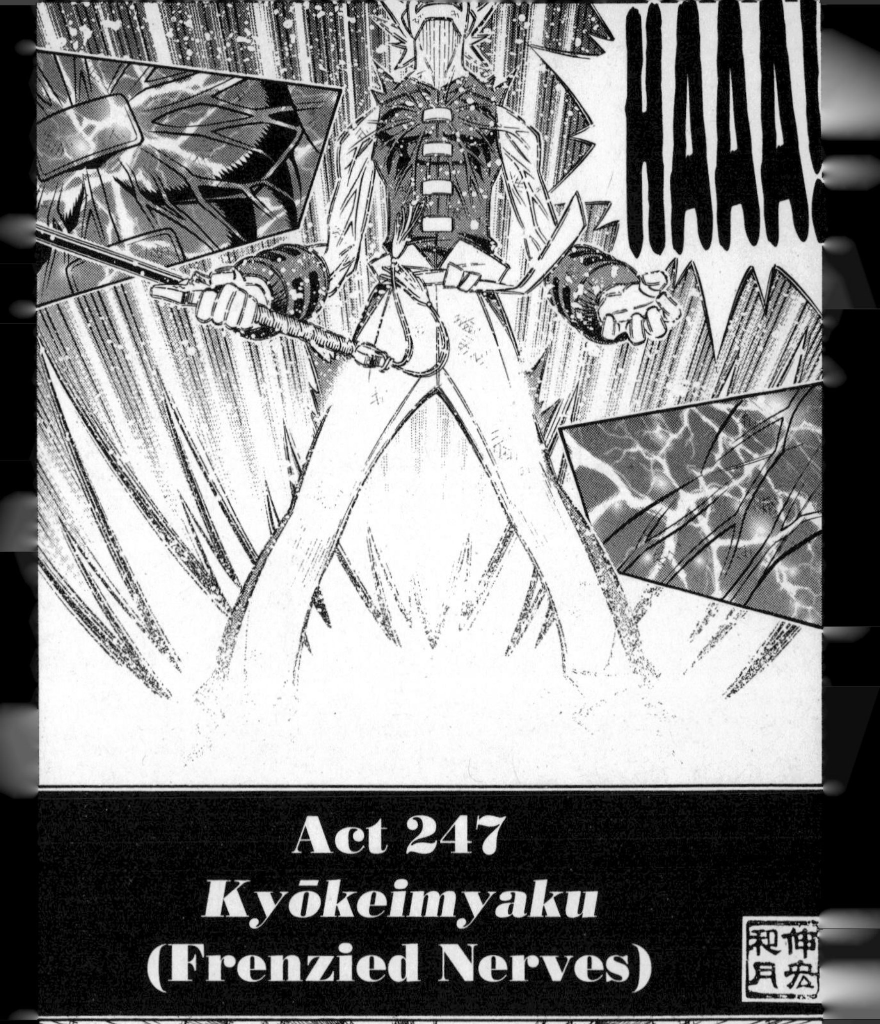
HAAA!

Act 247
Kyōkeimyaku (Frenzied Nerves)

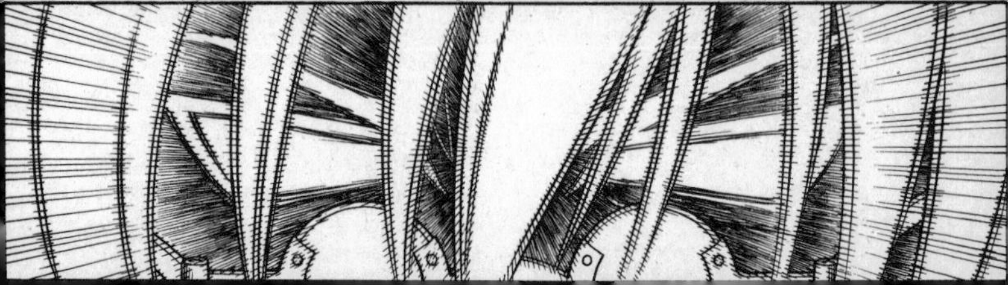

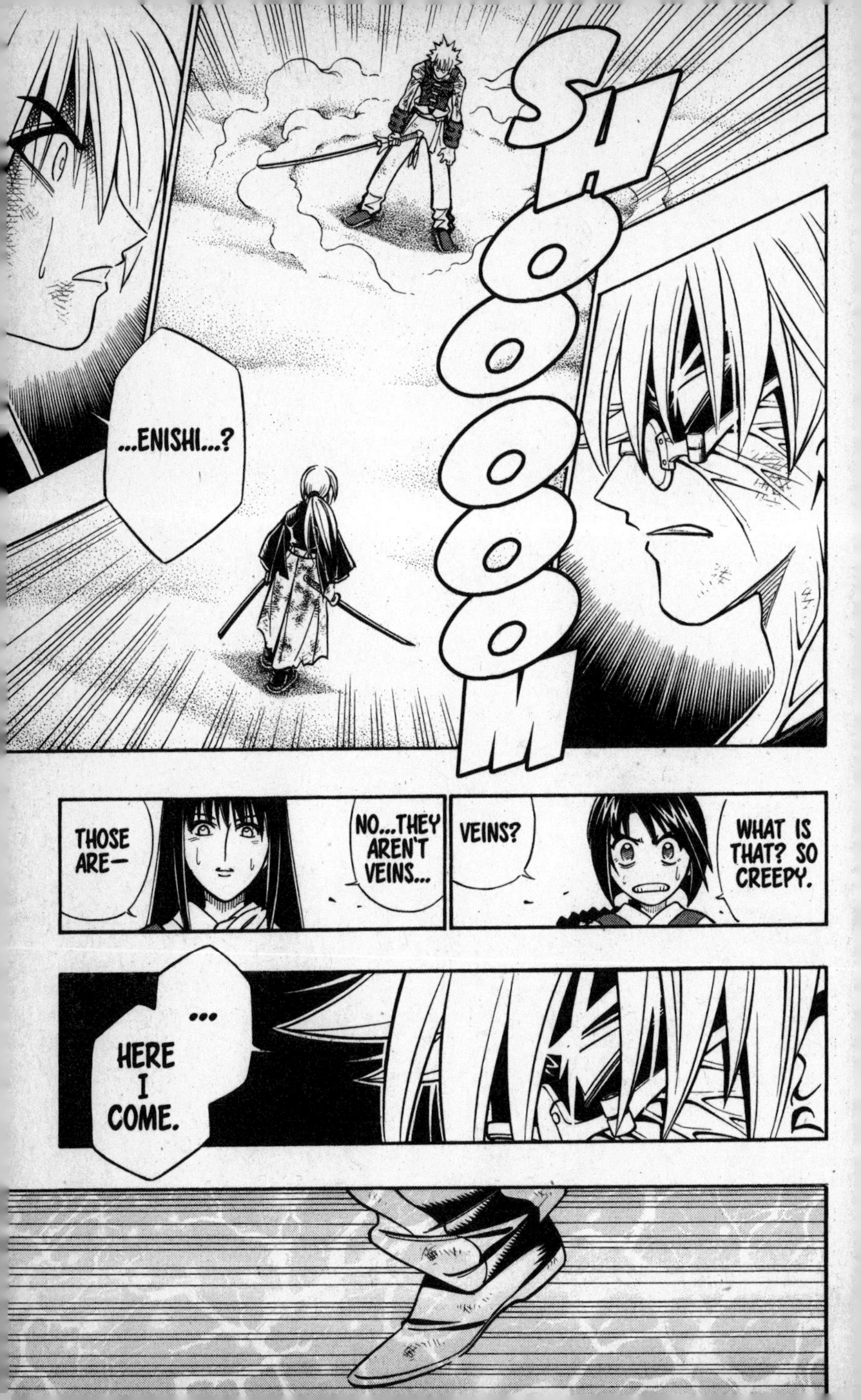
SHOOOOOOOM
...ENISHI...?
WHAT IS THAT? SO CREEPY.
VEINS?
NO...THEY AREN'T VEINS...
THOSE ARE—
... HERE I COME.

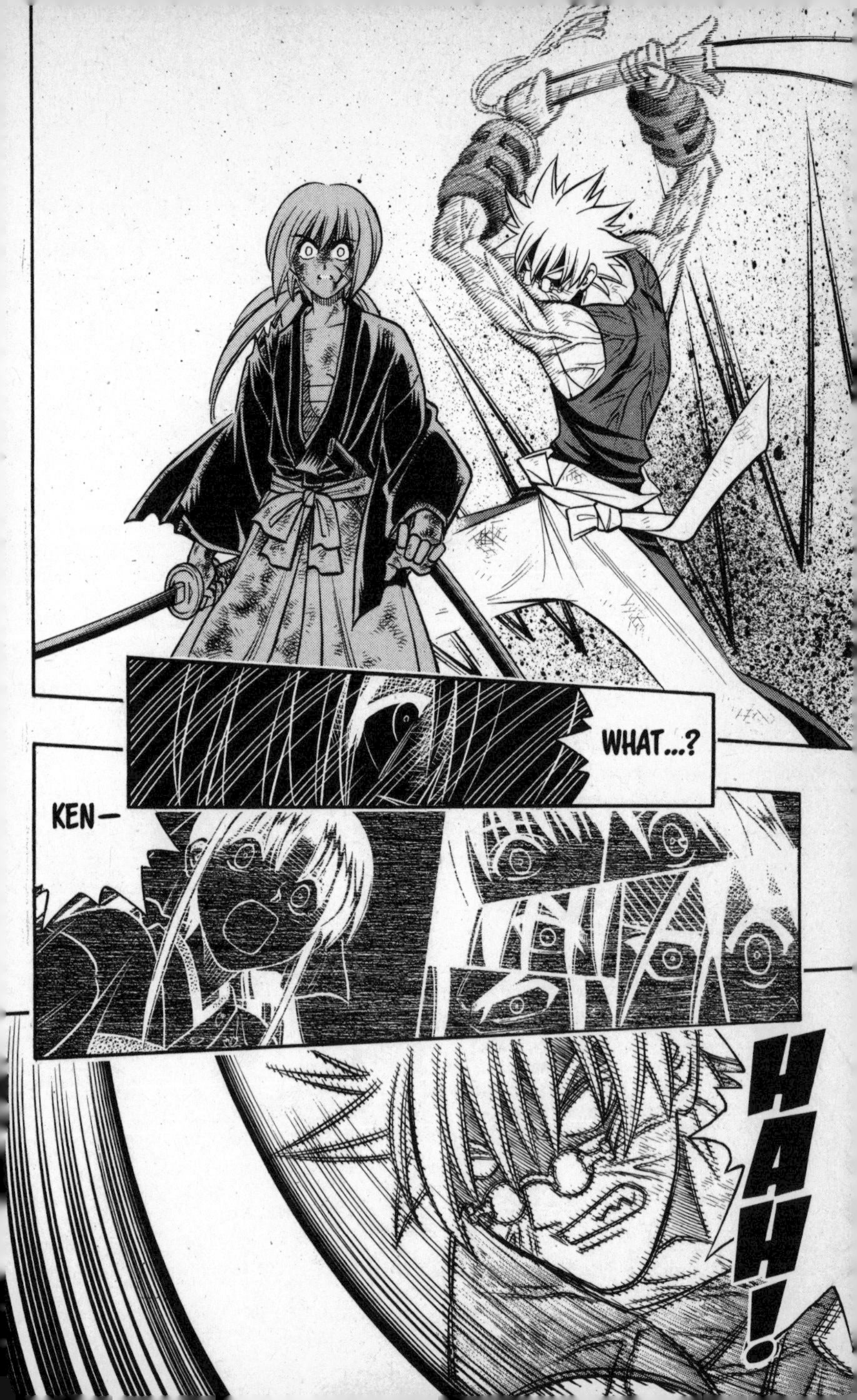
WHAT...?
KEN—
HAAH!

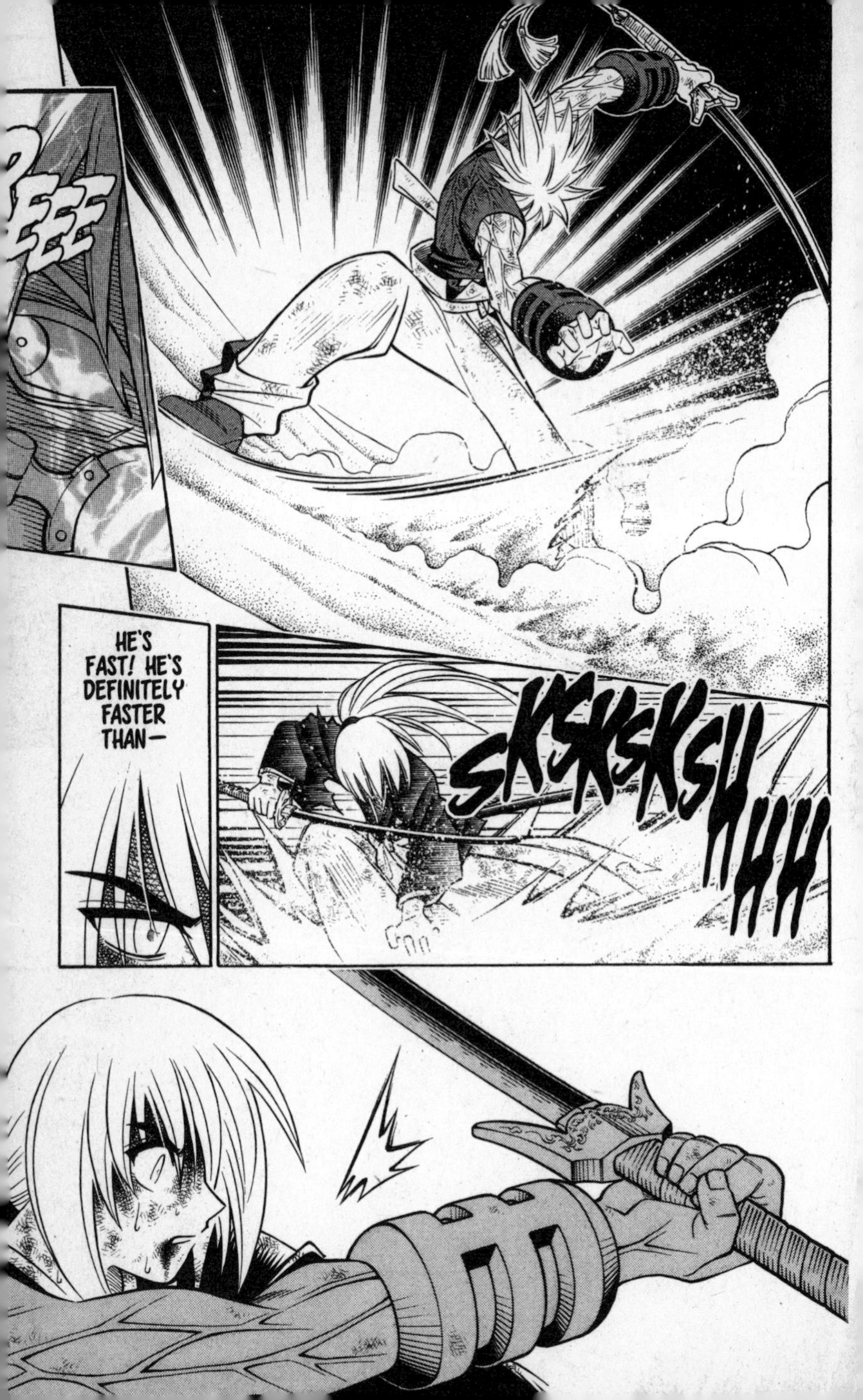
EEE
SKSKSKSHHHH
HE'S FAST! HE'S DEFINITELY FASTER THAN—

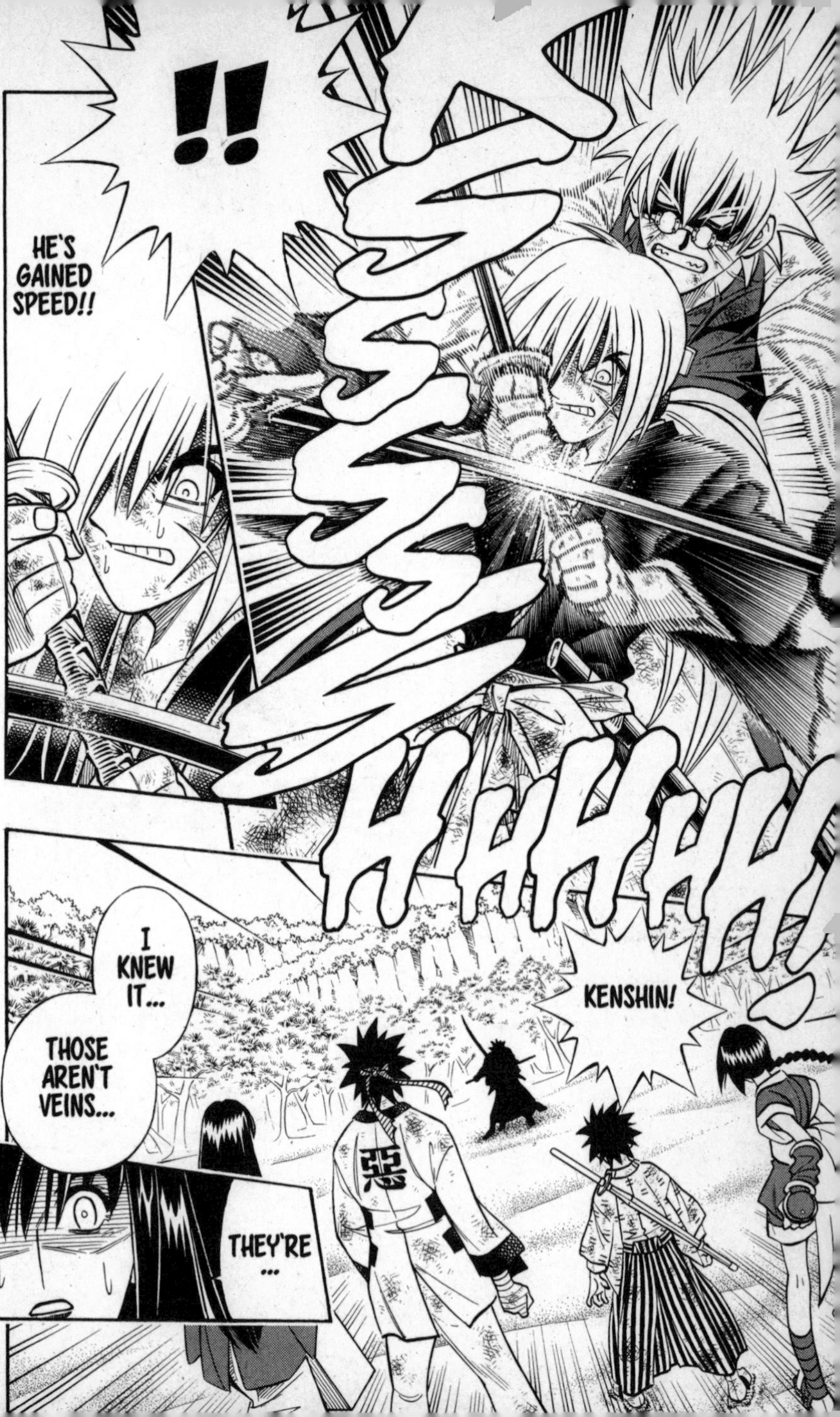
!!
HE'S GAINED SPEED!!
I KNEW IT...
THOSE AREN'T VEINS...
THEY'RE ...
KENSHIN!

READ THIS WAY

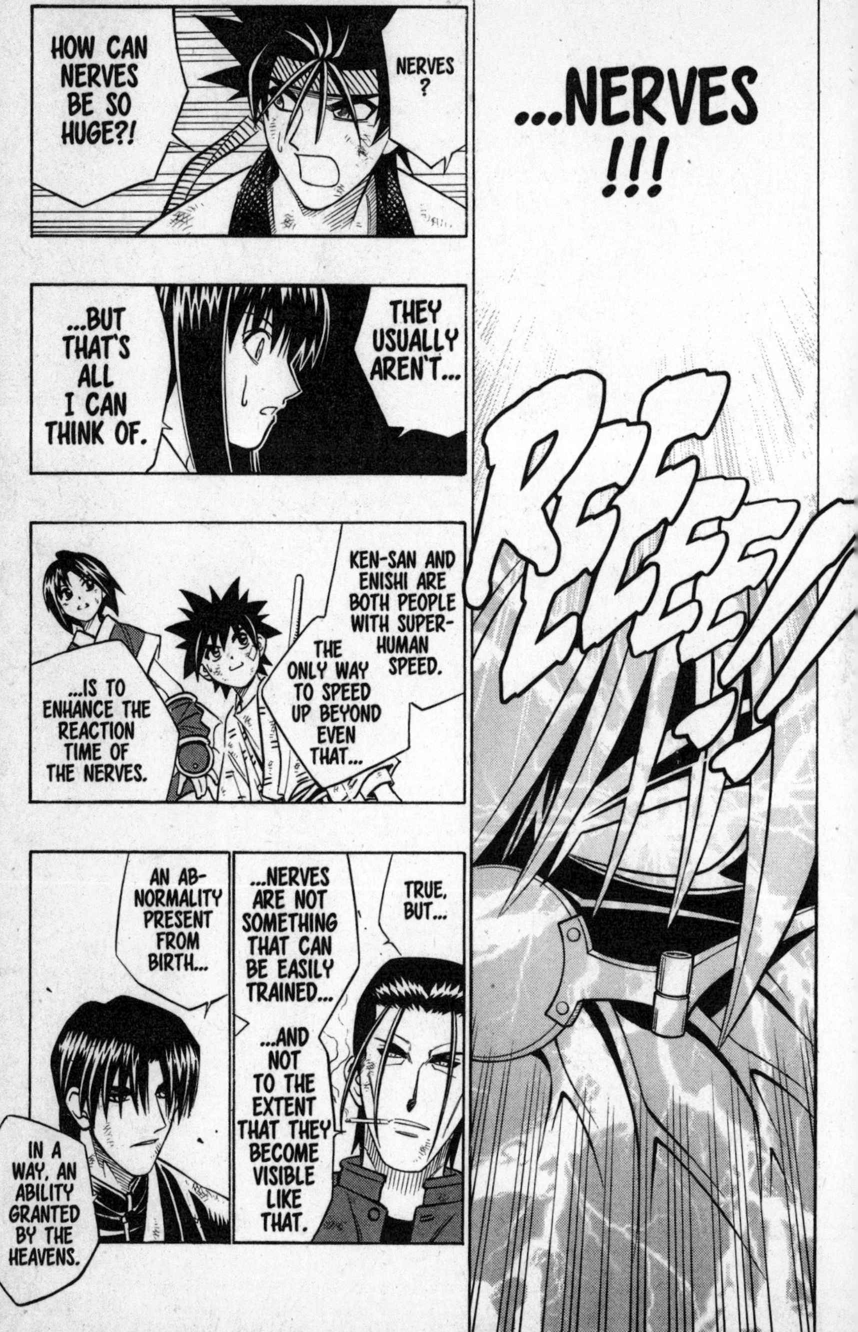
...NERVES !!!
NERVES ?
HOW CAN NERVES BE SO HUGE?!
THEY USUALLY AREN'T...
...BUT THAT'S ALL I CAN THINK OF.
KEN-SAN AND ENISHI ARE BOTH PEOPLE WITH SUPER-HUMAN SPEED.
THE ONLY WAY TO SPEED UP BEYOND EVEN THAT...
...IS TO ENHANCE THE REACTION TIME OF THE NERVES.
TRUE, BUT...
...NERVES ARE NOT SOMETHING THAT CAN BE EASILY TRAINED...
...AND NOT TO THE EXTENT THAT THEY BECOME VISIBLE LIKE THAT.
AN AB-NORMALITY PRESENT FROM BIRTH...
IN A WAY, AN ABILITY GRANTED BY THE HEAVENS.

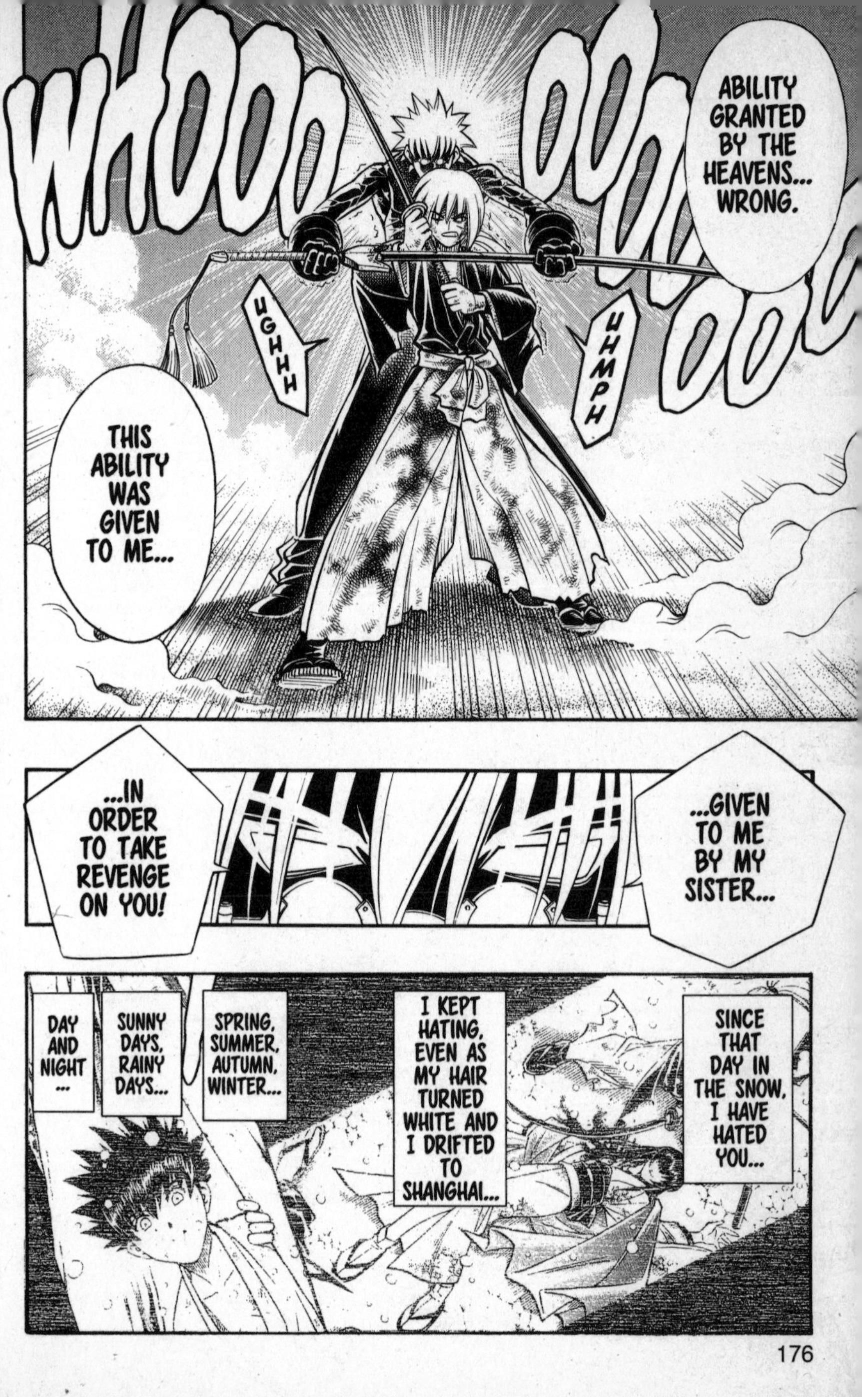
ABILITY GRANTED BY THE HEAVENS... WRONG.
WHOOOOOOOOOOO
UHMPH
UGHHH
THIS ABILITY WAS GIVEN TO ME...
...GIVEN TO ME BY MY SISTER...
...IN ORDER TO TAKE REVENGE ON YOU!
SINCE THAT DAY IN THE SNOW, I HAVE HATED YOU...
I KEPT HATING, EVEN AS MY HAIR TURNED WHITE AND I DRIFTED TO SHANGHAI...
SPRING, SUMMER, AUTUMN, WINTER...
SUNNY DAYS, RAINY DAYS...
DAY AND NIGHT ...

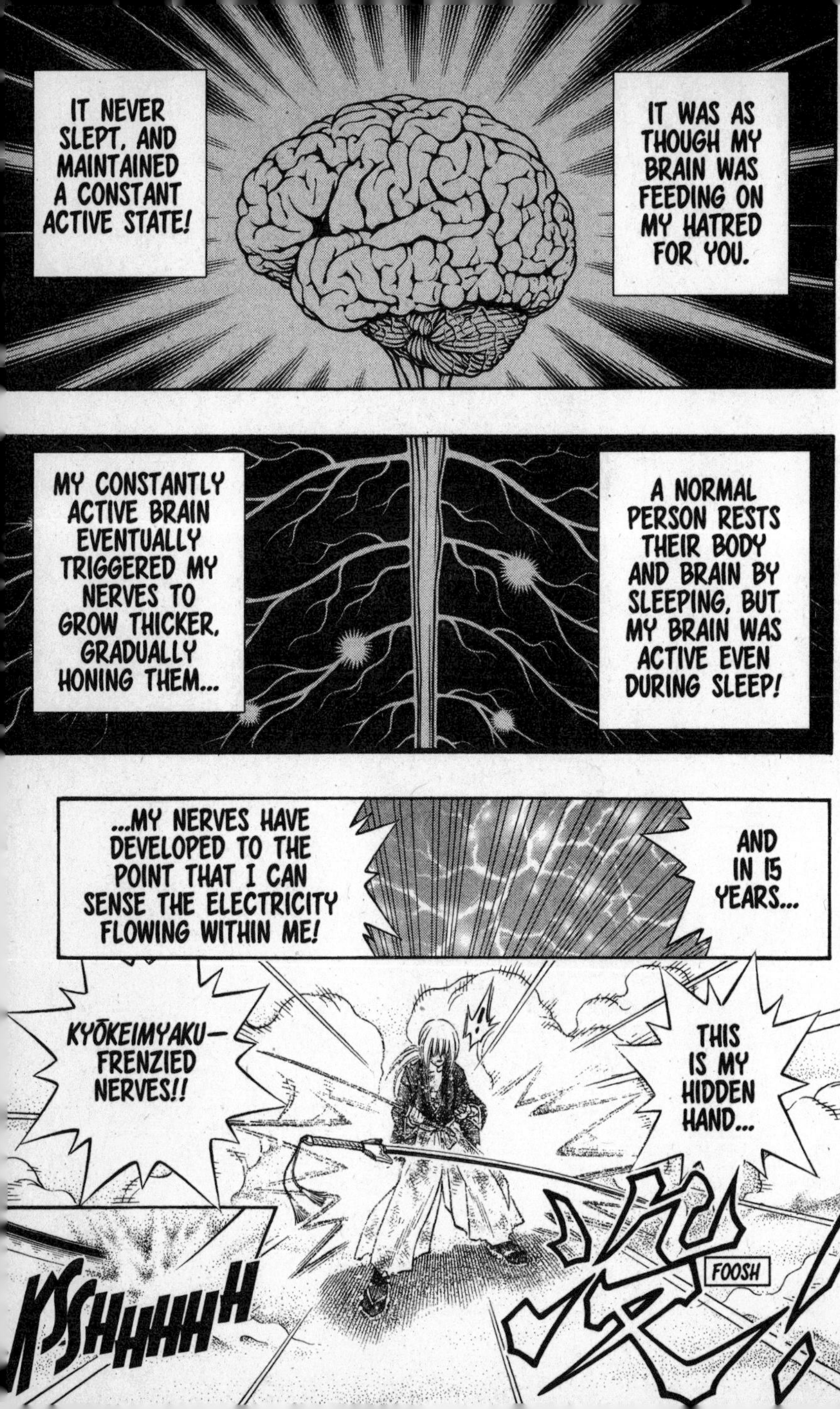
IT WAS AS THOUGH MY BRAIN WAS FEEDING ON MY HATRED FOR YOU.
IT NEVER SLEPT, AND MAINTAINED A CONSTANT ACTIVE STATE!
A NORMAL PERSON RESTS THEIR BODY AND BRAIN BY SLEEPING, BUT MY BRAIN WAS ACTIVE EVEN DURING SLEEP!
MY CONSTANTLY ACTIVE BRAIN EVENTUALLY TRIGGERED MY NERVES TO GROW THICKER, GRADUALLY HONING THEM...
AND IN 15 YEARS...
...MY NERVES HAVE DEVELOPED TO THE POINT THAT I CAN SENSE THE ELECTRICITY FLOWING WITHIN ME!
THIS IS MY HIDDEN HAND...
KYŌKEIMYAKU— FRENZIED NERVES!!
FOOSH
KSHHHHHH

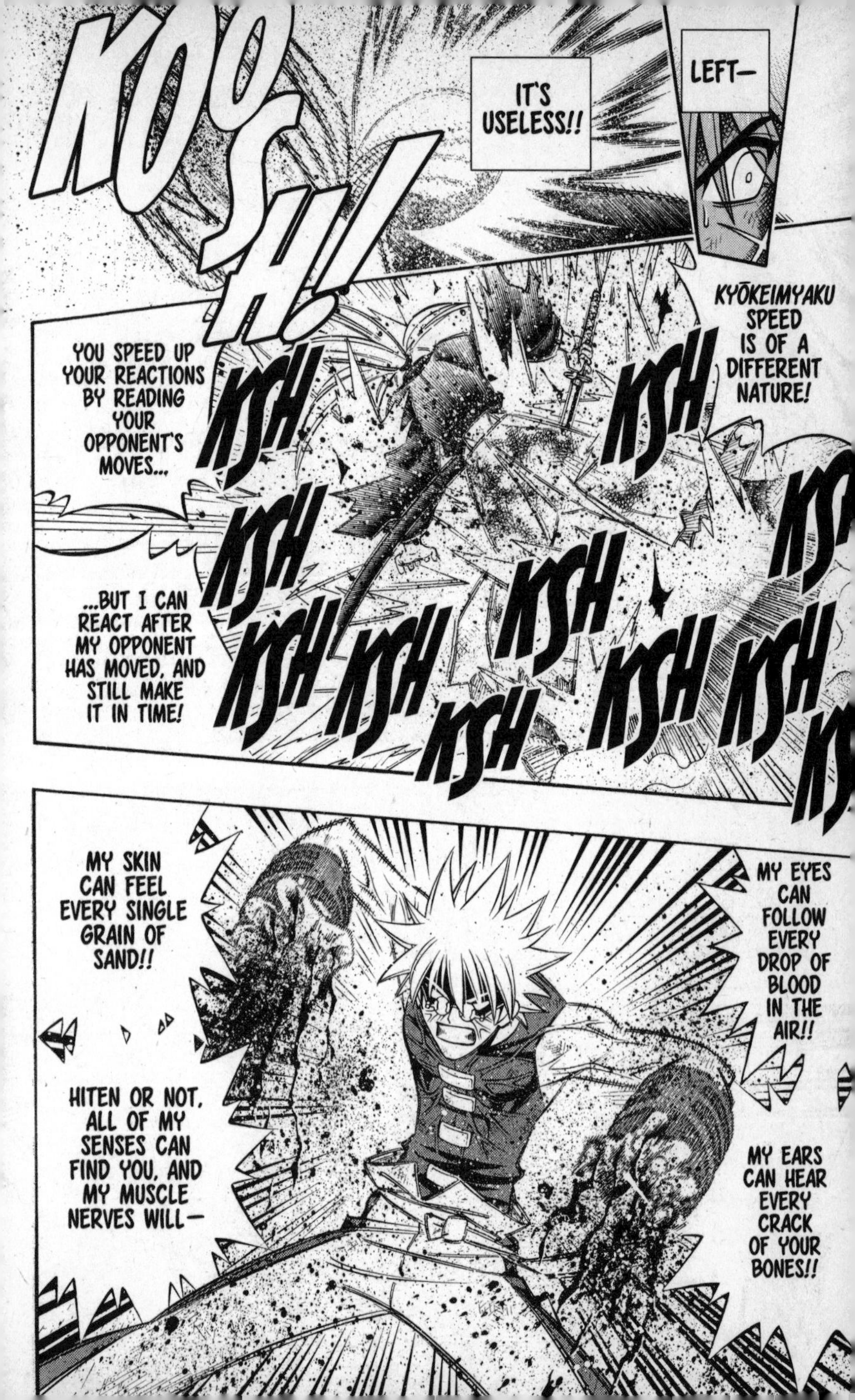
LEFT—
IT'S USELESS!!
KOOSH!
KYŌKEIMYAKU SPEED IS OF A DIFFERENT NATURE!
YOU SPEED UP YOUR REACTIONS BY READING YOUR OPPONENT'S MOVES...
...BUT I CAN REACT AFTER MY OPPONENT HAS MOVED, AND STILL MAKE IT IN TIME!
KSH KSH KSH KSH KSH KSH KSH KSH KSH KSH
MY EYES CAN FOLLOW EVERY DROP OF BLOOD IN THE AIR!!
MY EARS CAN HEAR EVERY CRACK OF YOUR BONES!!
MY SKIN CAN FEEL EVERY SINGLE GRAIN OF SAND!!
HITEN OR NOT, ALL OF MY SENSES CAN FIND YOU, AND MY MUSCLE NERVES WILL—

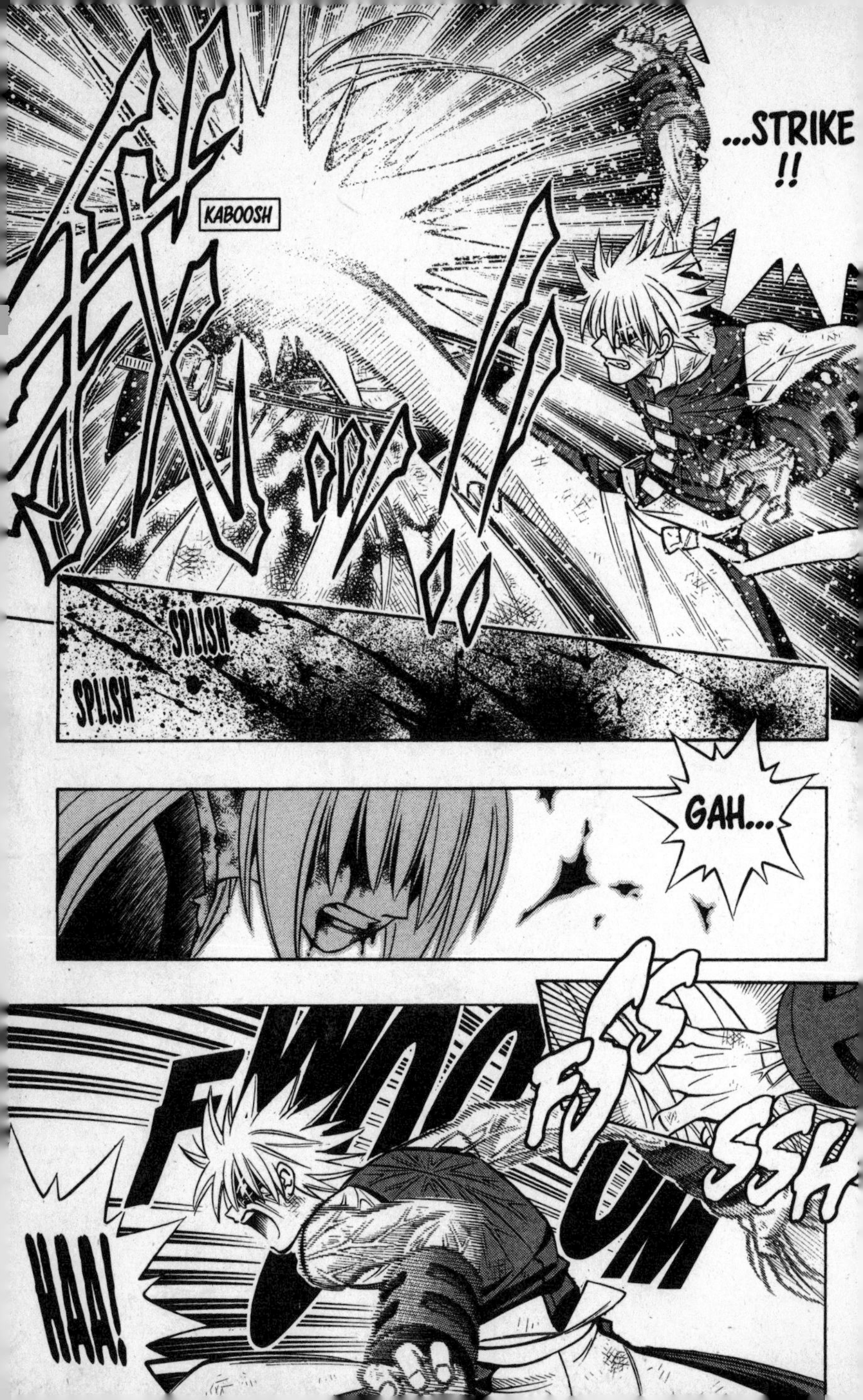
...STRIKE !!
KABOOSH
SPLISH
SPLISH
GAH...
HAA!

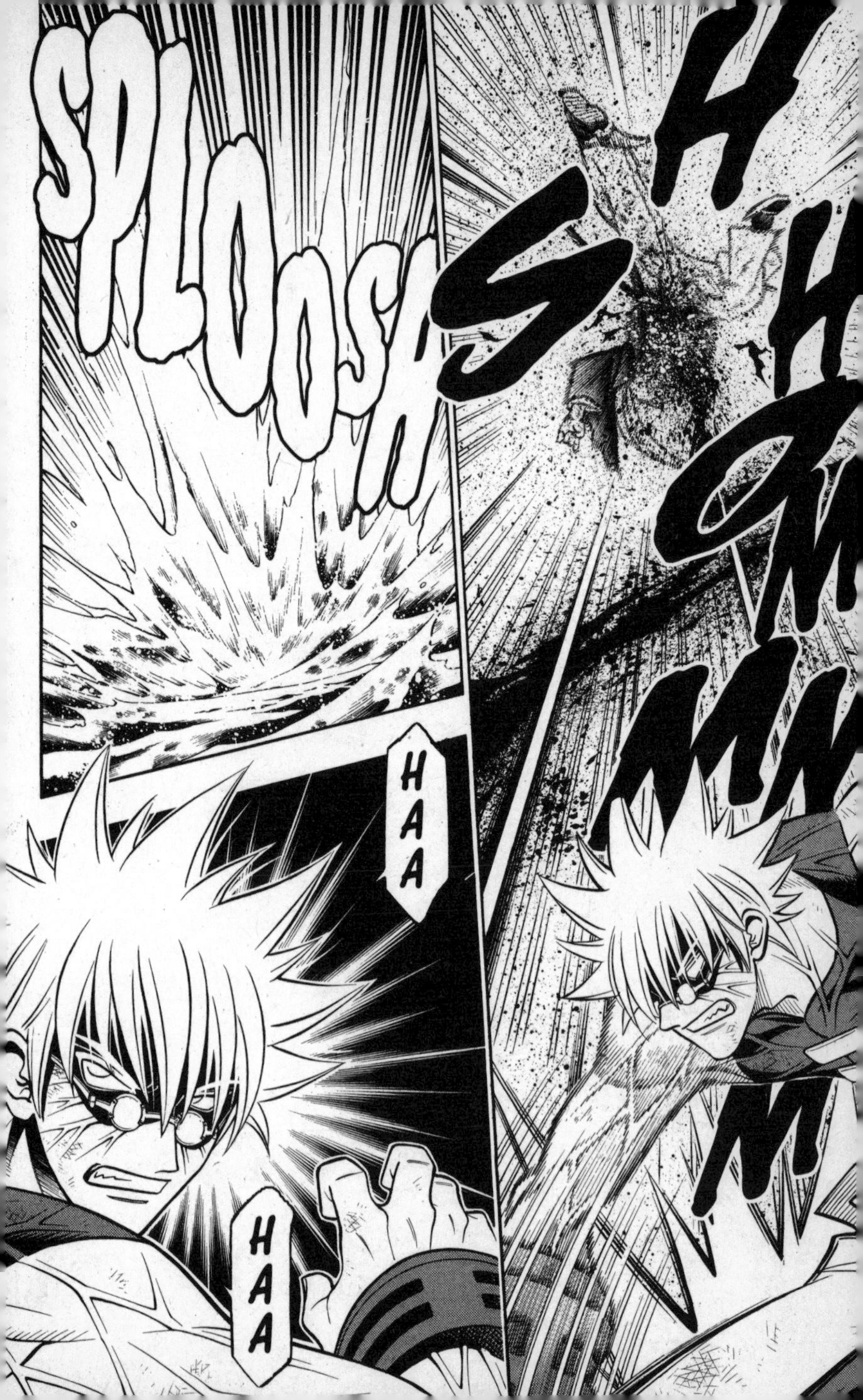
SPLOOSH
HAA
HAA

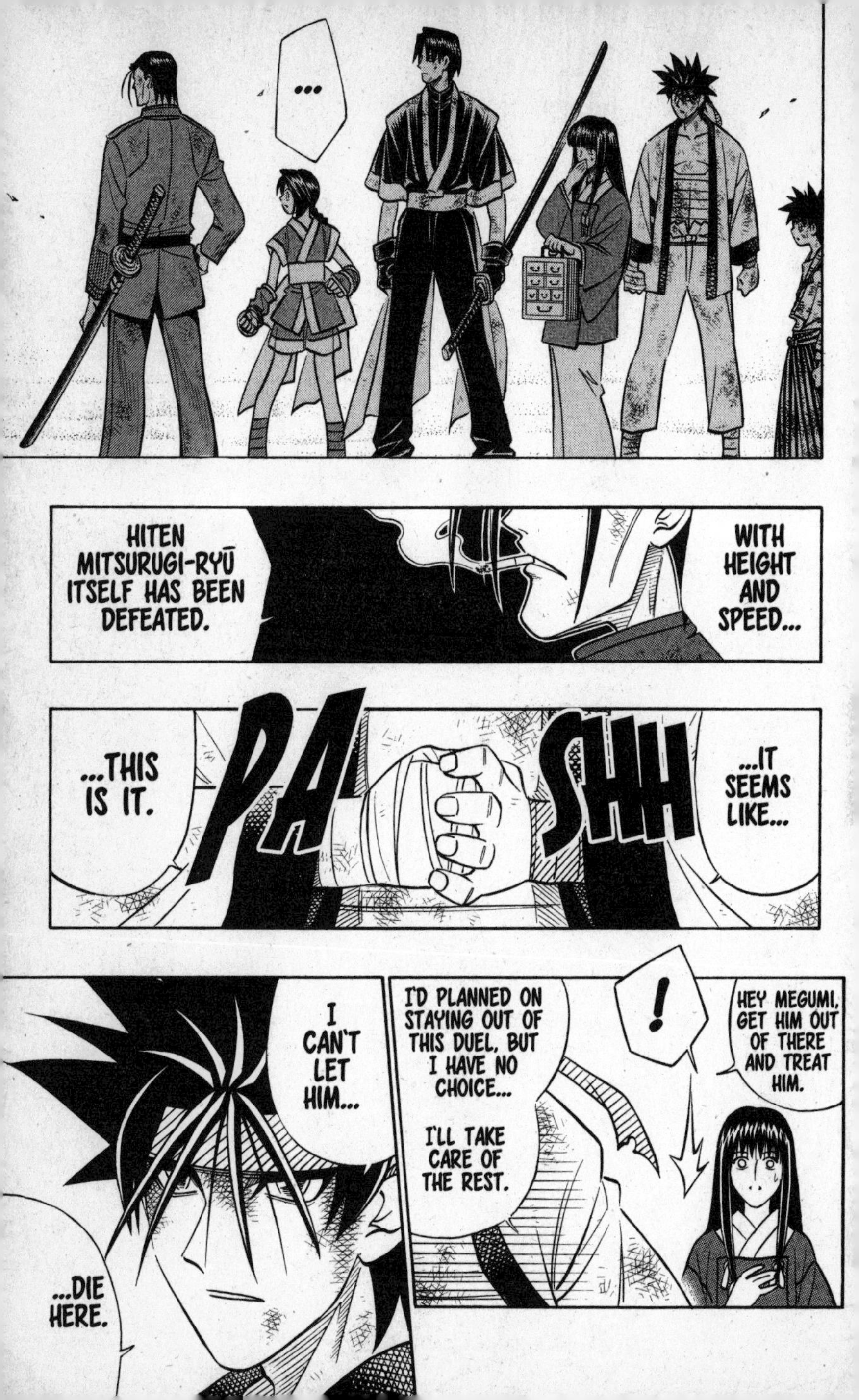
...
WITH HEIGHT AND SPEED...
HITEN MITSURUGI-RYŪ ITSELF HAS BEEN DEFEATED.
...IT SEEMS LIKE...
PASHH
...THIS IS IT.
HEY MEGUMI, GET HIM OUT OF THERE AND TREAT HIM.
!
I'D PLANNED ON STAYING OUT OF THIS DUEL, BUT I HAVE NO CHOICE...
I'LL TAKE CARE OF THE REST.
I CAN'T LET HIM...
...DIE HERE.

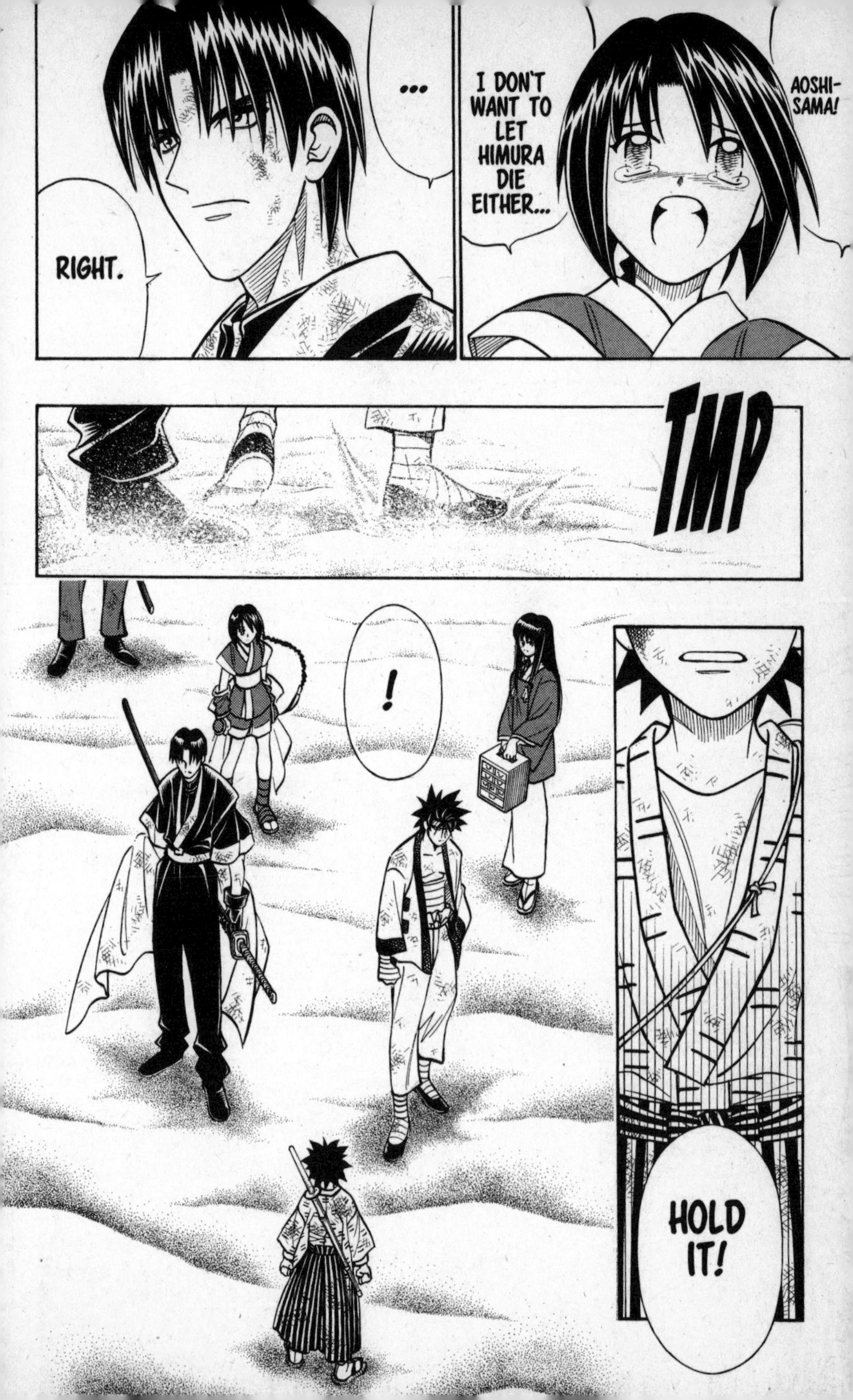
AOSHI-SAMA!
I DON'T WANT TO LET HIMURA DIE EITHER...
...
RIGHT.
TMP
HOLD IT!
!

READ THIS WAY

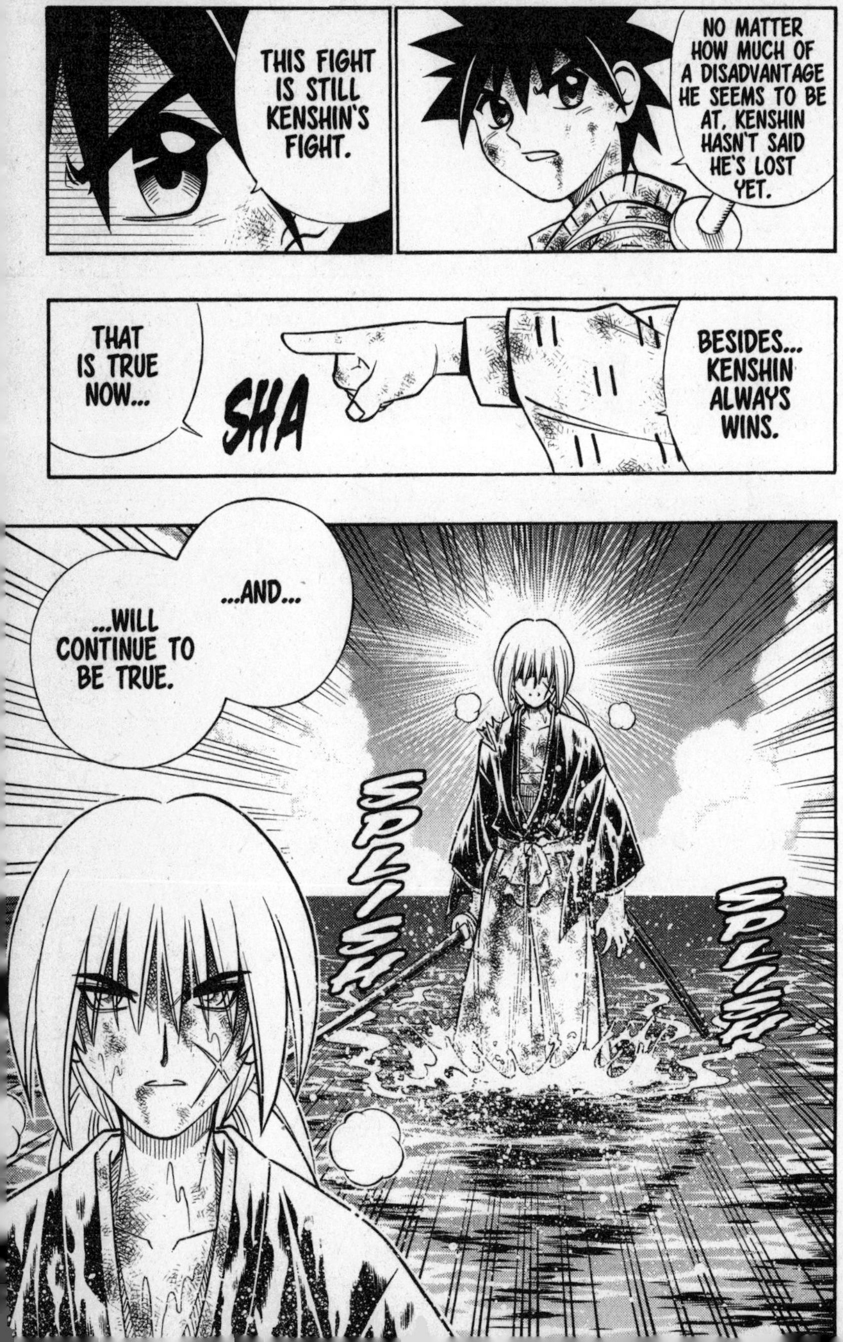
NO MATTER HOW MUCH OF A DISADVANTAGE HE SEEMS TO BE AT, KENSHIN HASN'T SAID HE'S LOST YET.
THIS FIGHT IS STILL KENSHIN'S FIGHT.
BESIDES... KENSHIN ALWAYS WINS.
SHA
THAT IS TRUE NOW...
SPLISH
SPLISH
...AND...
...WILL CONTINUE TO BE TRUE.

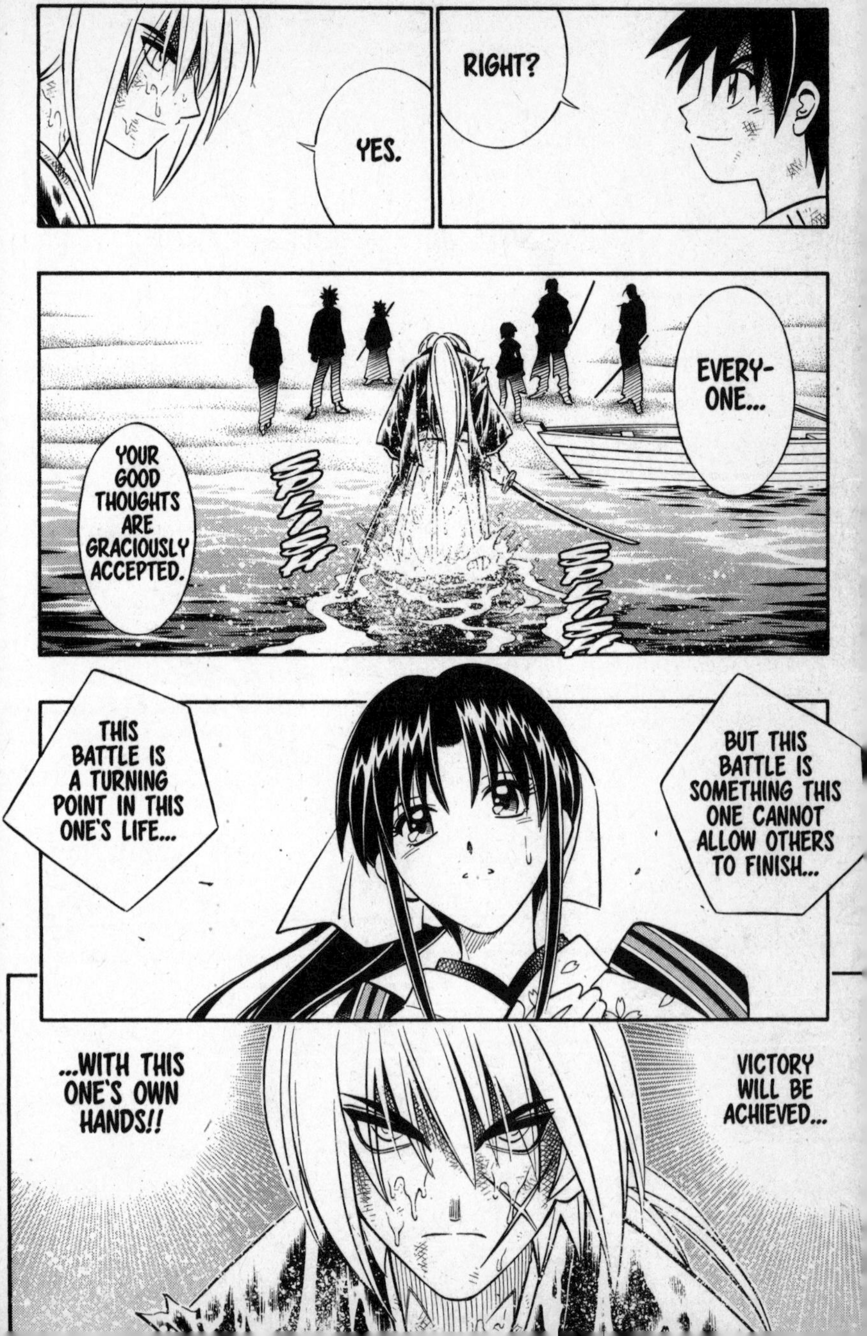

RIGHT?
YES.
EVERY-ONE...
YOUR GOOD THOUGHTS ARE GRACIOUSLY ACCEPTED.
THIS BATTLE IS A TURNING POINT IN THIS ONE'S LIFE...
BUT THIS BATTLE IS SOMETHING THIS ONE CANNOT ALLOW OTHERS TO FINISH...
VICTORY WILL BE ACHIEVED...
...WITH THIS ONE'S OWN HANDS!!

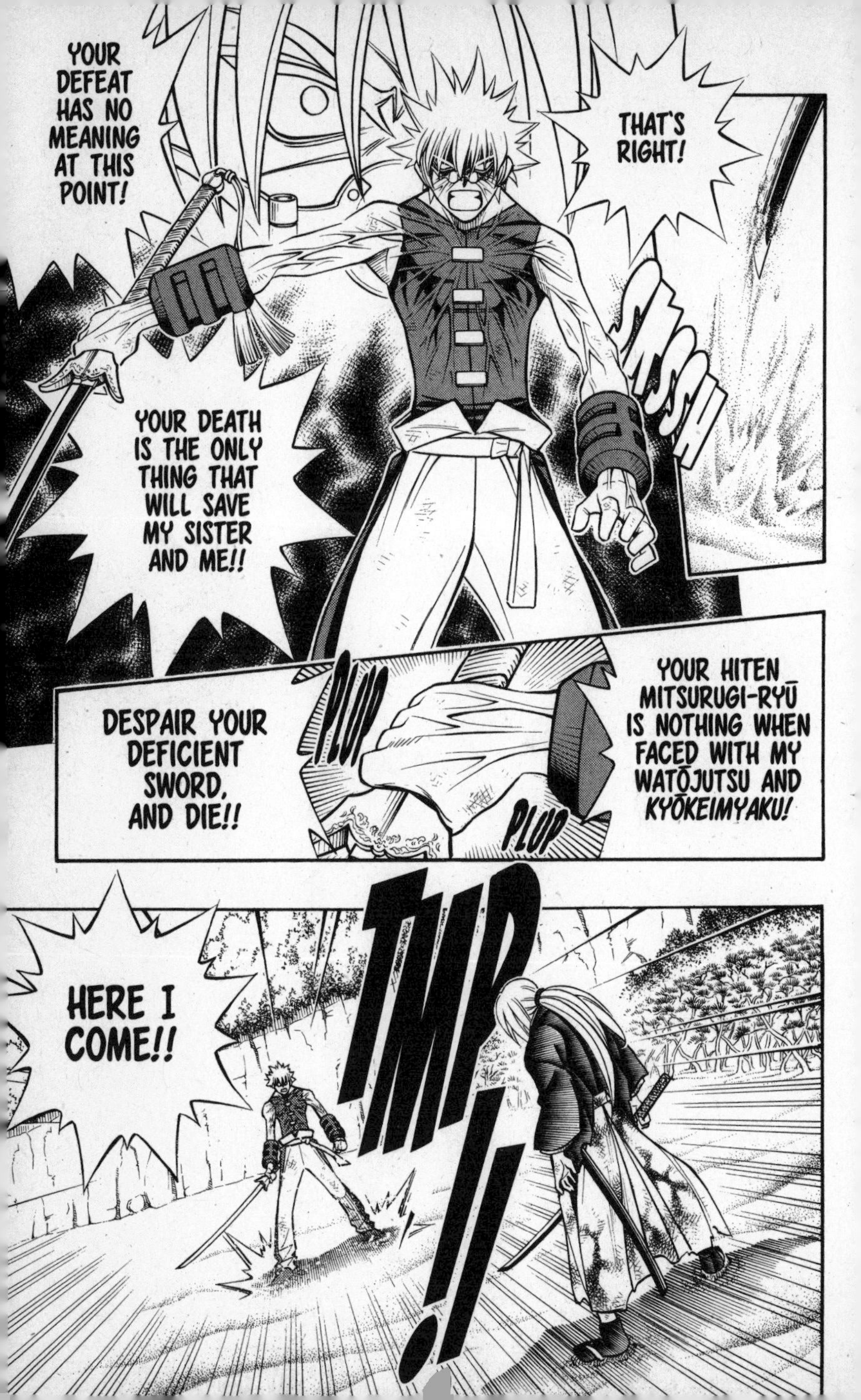
THAT'S RIGHT!
YOUR DEFEAT HAS NO MEANING AT THIS POINT!
SWSSH
YOUR DEATH IS THE ONLY THING THAT WILL SAVE MY SISTER AND ME!!
YOUR HITEN MITSURUGI-RYŪ IS NOTHING WHEN FACED WITH MY WATŌJUTSU AND KYŌKEIMYAKU!
PLUP
PLUP
DESPAIR YOUR DEFICIENT SWORD, AND DIE!!
THP!!
HERE I COME!!

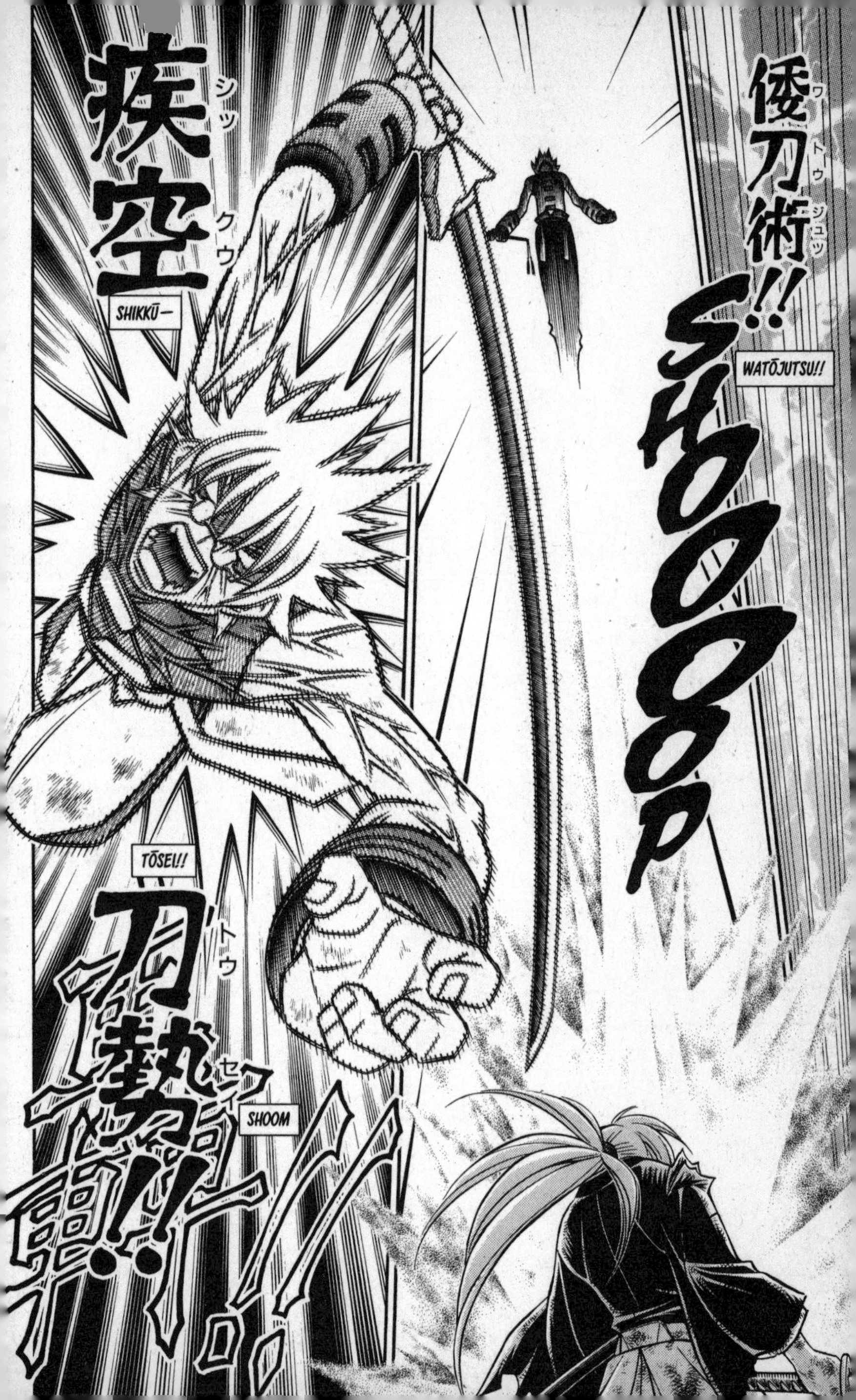
倭刀術!!
WATŌJUTSU!!
SWOOOOP
疾空
SHIKKŪ—
刀勢!!
TŌSEI!!
SHOOM

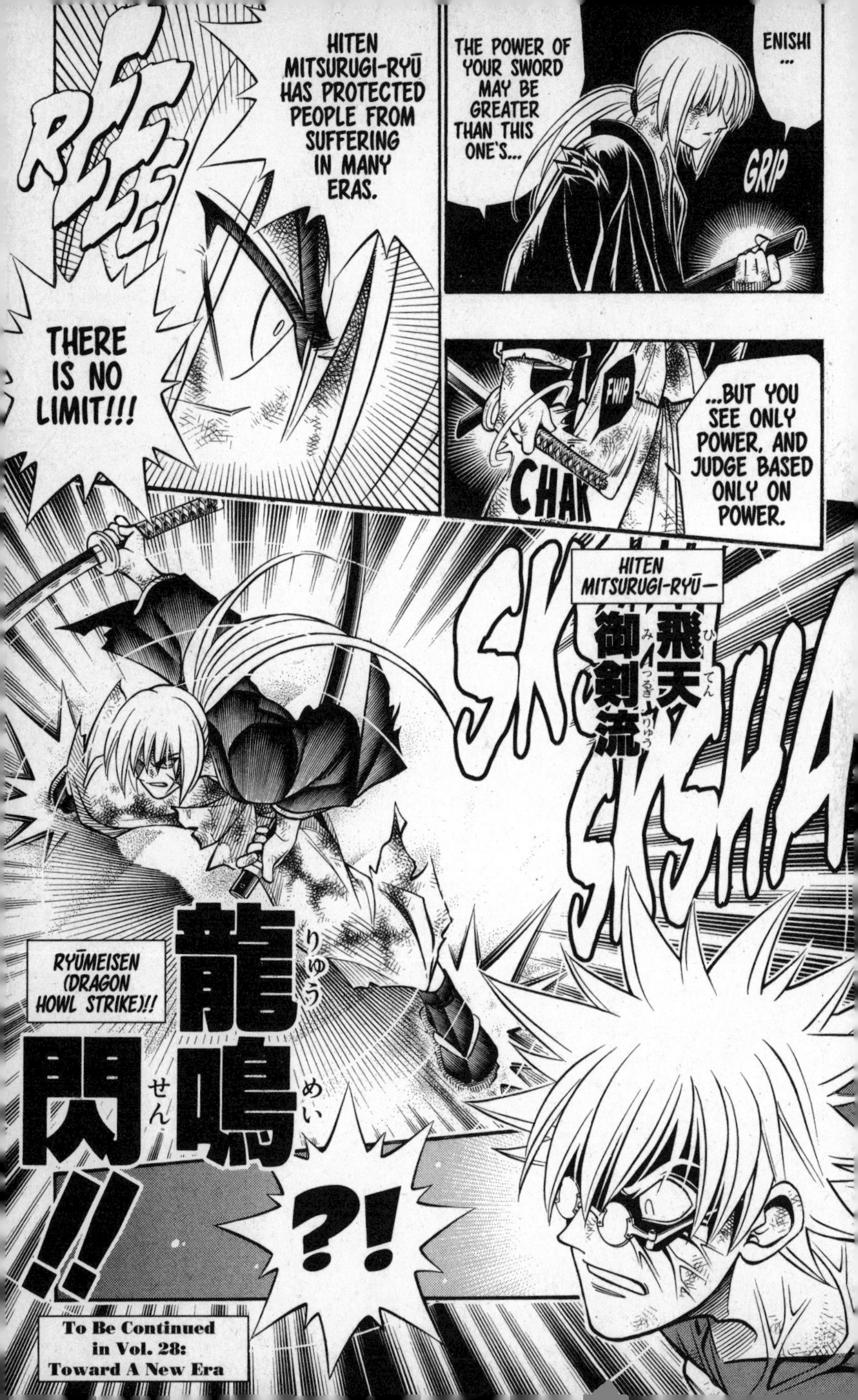
ENISHI ...
THE POWER OF YOUR SWORD MAY BE GREATER THAN THIS ONE'S...
GRIP
...BUT YOU SEE ONLY POWER, AND JUDGE BASED ONLY ON POWER.
FWIP
CHAK
HITEN MITSURUGI-RYŪ HAS PROTECTED PEOPLE FROM SUFFERING IN MANY ERAS.
THERE IS NO LIMIT!!!
HITEN MITSURUGI-RYŪ—
飛天御剣流
RYŪMEISEN (DRAGON HOWL STRIKE)!!
龍鳴閃!!
?!

To Be Continued in Vol. 28: Toward A New Era

GLOSSARY of the RESTORATION

*A brief guide to select Japanese terms used in **Rurouni Kenshin**. Note that, both here and within the story itself, all names are Japanese style—i.e., last or "family" name first, with personal or "given" name following. This is both because **Kenshin** is a "period" story, as well as to decrease confusion—if we were to take the example of Kenshin's* sakabatô *and "reverse" the format of the historically established assassin-name "Hitokiri Battôsai," for example, it would make little sense to then call him "Battôsai Himura."*

Himura Kenshin
Kenshin's "real" name, revealed to Kaoru only at her urging

Hiten Mitsurugi-ryû
Kenshin's sword technique, used more for defense than offense. An "ancient style that pits one against many," it requires exceptional speed and agility to master.

hitokiri
An assassin. Famous swordsmen of the period were sometimes thus known to adopt "professional" names—**Kawakami Gensai**, for example, was also known as "Hitokiri Gensai."

Ishin Shishi
Loyalist or pro-Imperialist **patriots** who fought to restore the Emperor to his ancient seat of power

jinchû
Hitokiri were fond of the word *tenchû*, or "judgment from the heavens," which expressed their belief that judgment lay in their hands. Enishi calls his form of revenge *jinchû*, meaning that if the heavens won't cast judgment on Kenshin, he will with his own brand of justice.

Kamiya Kasshin-ryû
Sword-arts or *kenjutsu* school established by Kaoru's father, who rejected the ethics of **Satsujin-ken** for **Katsujin-ken**

Bakumatsu
Final, chaotic days of the Tokugawa regime

-chan
Honorific. Can be used either as a diminutive (e.g., with a small child— "Little Hanako or Kentarô"), or with those who are grown, to indicate affection ("My dear...").

-dono
Honorific. Even more respectful than **-san**; the effect in modern-day Japanese conversation would be along the lines of "Milord So-and-So." As used by Kenshin, it indicates both respect and humility.

Edo
Capital city of the **Tokugawa Bakufu**; renamed **Tokyo** ("Eastern Capital") after the Meiji Restoration

Gatotsu
The signature move of Saitô Hajime, series creator Watsuki reportedly based his (fictional) version on an actual, historical, horizontal (or "flat") sword-technique. There are four "types" of **Gatotsu**: *Isshiki*, *Nishiki*, and *Sanshiki* (Variants One, Two and Three), as well as *Gatotsu Zeroshiki*—the final technique which doubles or even triples the power of the original thrust.

geta
Japanese wooden sandals. They are named for the noise they make when walking.

sakabatô
Reversed-edge sword (the dull edge on the side the sharp should be, and vice versa); carried by Kenshin as a symbol of his resolution never to kill again

-sama
Honorific. The respectful equivalent of *-san*, *-sama* is used primarily in addressing persons of much higher rank than one's self...or, in a romantic sense, in addressing those upon whom one is crushing, wicked hard.

-san
Honorific. Carries the meaning of "Mr.," "Ms.," "Miss," etc., but used more extensively in Japanese than its English equivalent (note that even an enemy may be addressed as "*-san*").

Satsujin-ken
"Swords that give death"; a style of swordsmanship rejected by Kaoru's father

shôgun
Feudal military ruler of Japan

shôgunate
See *Tokugawa Bakufu*

"Swift Death to Evil!"
Although there is some debate on who originated the term (some say it was the personal slogan of Saitô Hajime; others hold it to be a more general motto of the Shinsengumi itself), a more liberal translation of "*Aku • Soku • Zan*" might be "Evil Unto Evil"...where, in this case, the "evil" would be beheading, or death.

Tokugawa Bakufu
Military feudal government which dominated Japan from 1603 to 1867

Tokyo
The renaming of "*Edo*" to "*Tokyo*" is a marker of the start of the *Meiji Restoration*

Katsujin-ken
"Swords that give life"; the sword-arts style developed over ten years by Kaoru's father and founding principle of *Kamiya Kasshin-ryû*

Kawakami Gensai
Real-life, historical inspiration for the character of *Himura Kenshin*

kodachi
Medium-length sword, shorter than the *katana* but longer than the *wakizashi*. Its easy maneuverability also makes for higher defensive capability.

-kun
Honorific. Used in the modern day among male students, or those who grew up together, but another usage—the one you're more likely to find in *Rurouni Kenshin*—is the "superior-to- inferior" form, intended as a way to emphasize a difference in status or rank, as well as to indicate familiarity or affection.

Kyoto
Home of the Emperor and imperial court from A.D. 794 until shortly after the *Meiji Restoration* in 1868

loyalists
Those who supported the return of the Emperor to power; *Ishin Shishi*

Meiji Restoration
1853-1868; culminated in the collapse of the *Tokugawa Bakufu* and the restoration of imperial rule. So called after Emperor Meiji, whose chosen name was written with the characters for "culture and enlightenment."

patriots
Another term for *Ishin Shishi*... and, when used by Sano, not a flattering one

rurouni
Wanderer, vagabond

IN THE NEXT VOLUME...

Kenshin's battle with the relentless and monstrously powerful Enishi has entered its final stage. During the Bakumatsu, Kenshin used his bloodstained sword to fight for a new era, where peace and prosperity could flourish. As a *rurouni* of the Meiji era, Kenshin used his *sakabatô* to continue this mission—but has it all been a naïve lie? Can Kenshin atone for his past crimes without laying down his, or Enishi's, life? Find out in the exciting, unforgettable conclusion of **Rurouni Kenshin**!

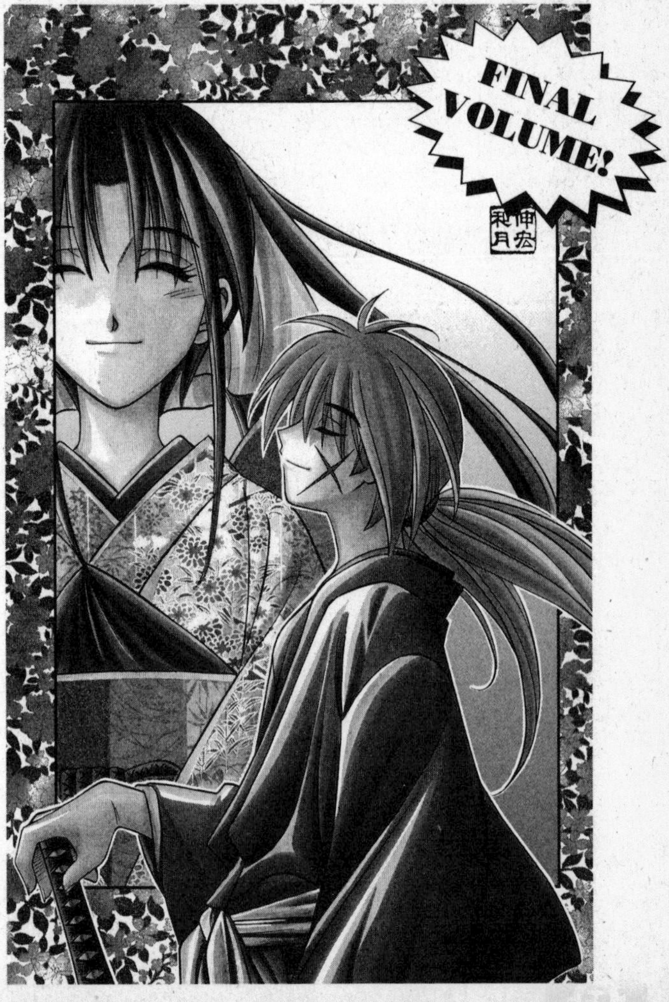
FINAL VOLUME!

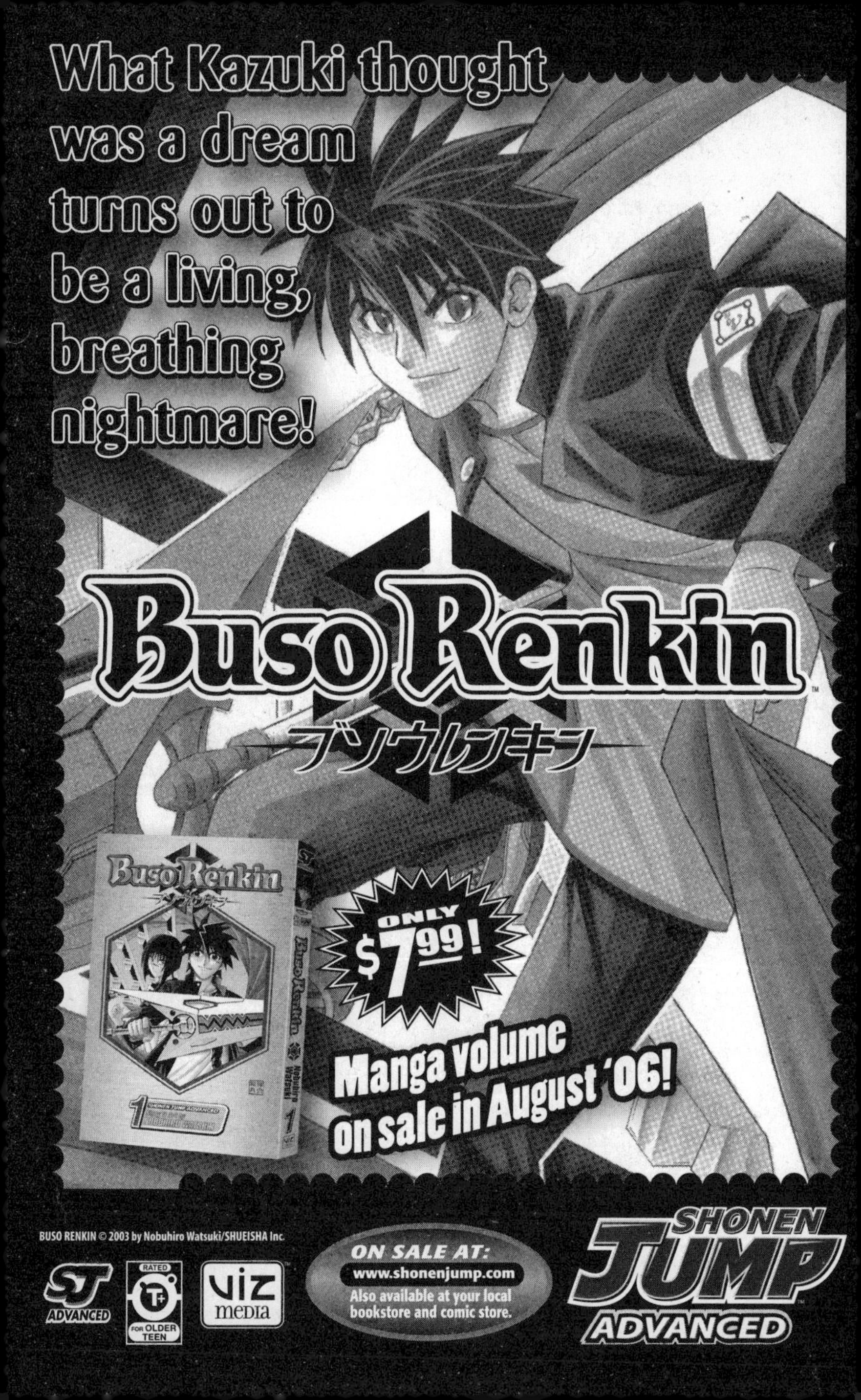
What Kazuki thought was a dream turns out to be a living, breathing nightmare!
Buso Renkin
ブソウレンキン
ONLY $7.99!
Manga volume on sale in August '06!
BUSO RENKIN © 2003 by Nobuhiro Watsuki/SHUEISHA Inc.
ON SALE AT:
www.shonenjump.com
Also available at your local bookstore and comic store.
SHONEN JUMP ADVANCED

VOLS. 1-5 ON SALE NOW!

In the battle between Light and L, will love make the difference between life and death?

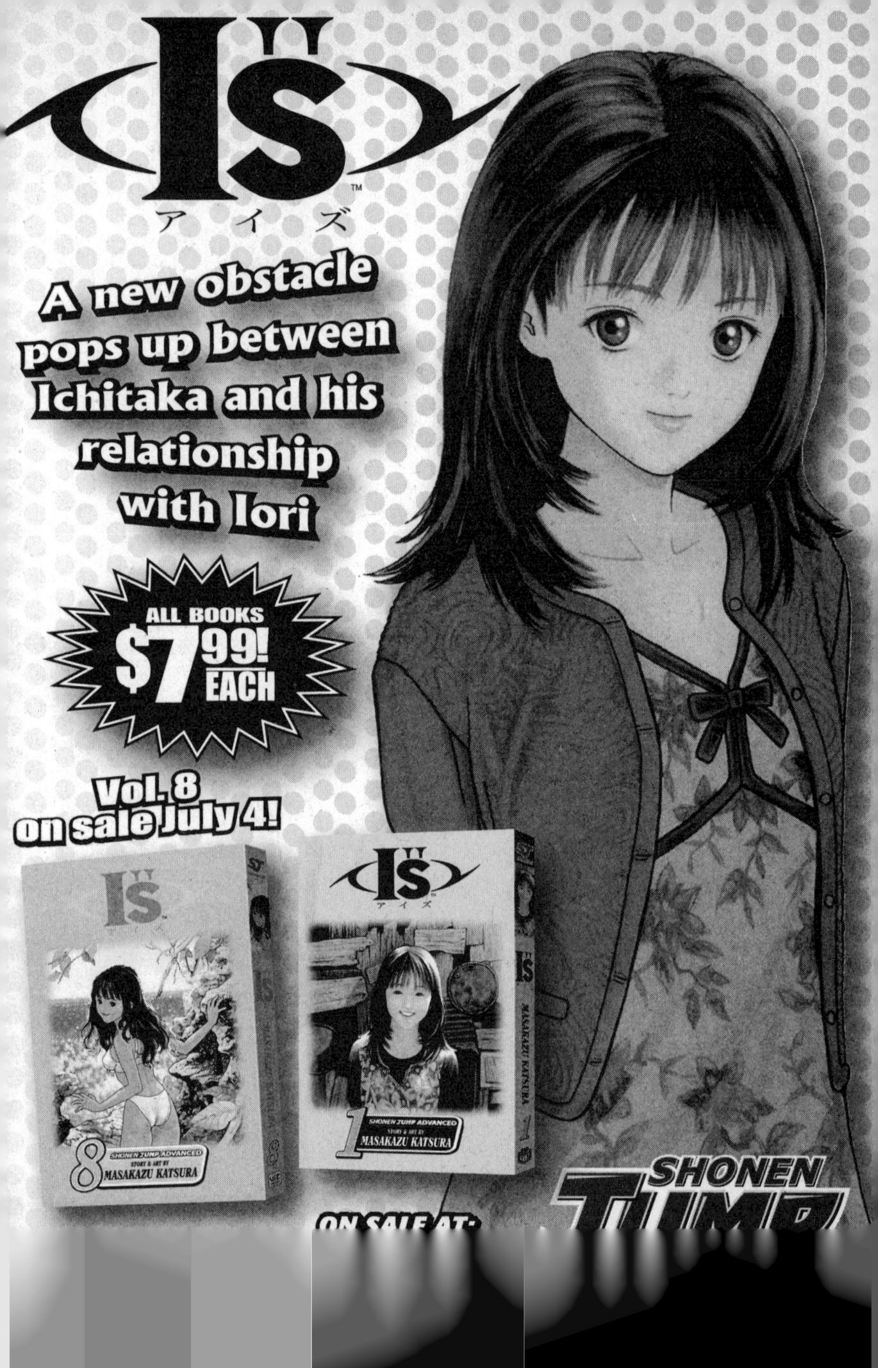
I"s
アイズ
A new obstacle pops up between Ichitaka and his relationship with Iori
ALL BOOKS
$7.99!
EACH
Vol. 8
on sale July 4!
SHONEN JUMP ADVANCED
STORY & ART BY
MASAKAZU KATSURA
ON SALE AT:
SHONEN

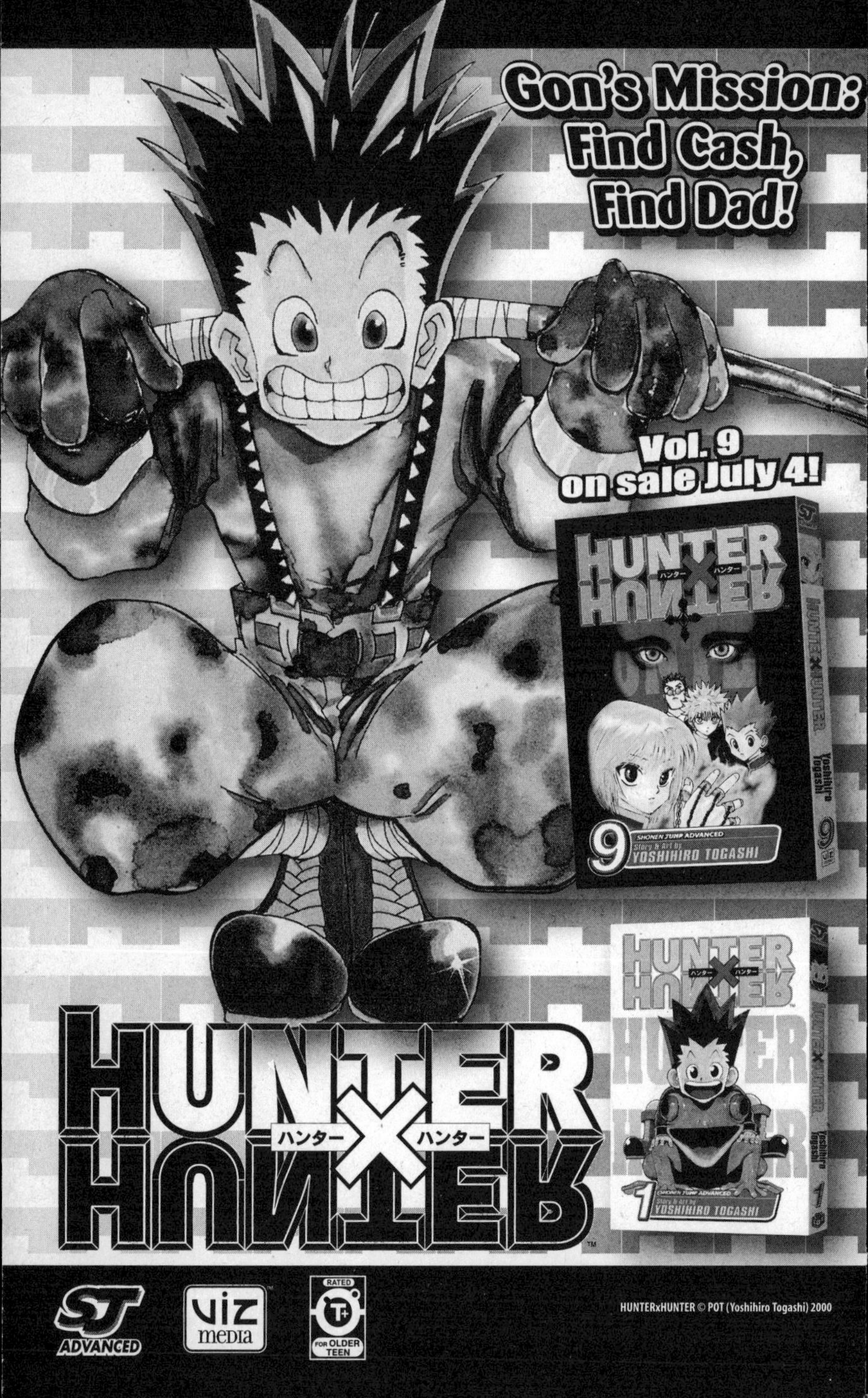
Gon's Mission: Find Cash, Find Dad!
Vol. 9 on sale July 4!
HUNTER × HUNTER
ハンター ハンター
9
SHONEN JUMP ADVANCED
Story & Art by YOSHIHIRO TOGASHI
HUNTER × HUNTER
1
SHONEN JUMP ADVANCED
Story & Art by YOSHIHIRO TOGASHI
HUNTER × HUNTER
ハンター ハンター
SJ ADVANCED
viz media
RATED T+ FOR OLDER TEEN
HUNTERxHUNTER © POT (Yoshihiro Togashi) 2000

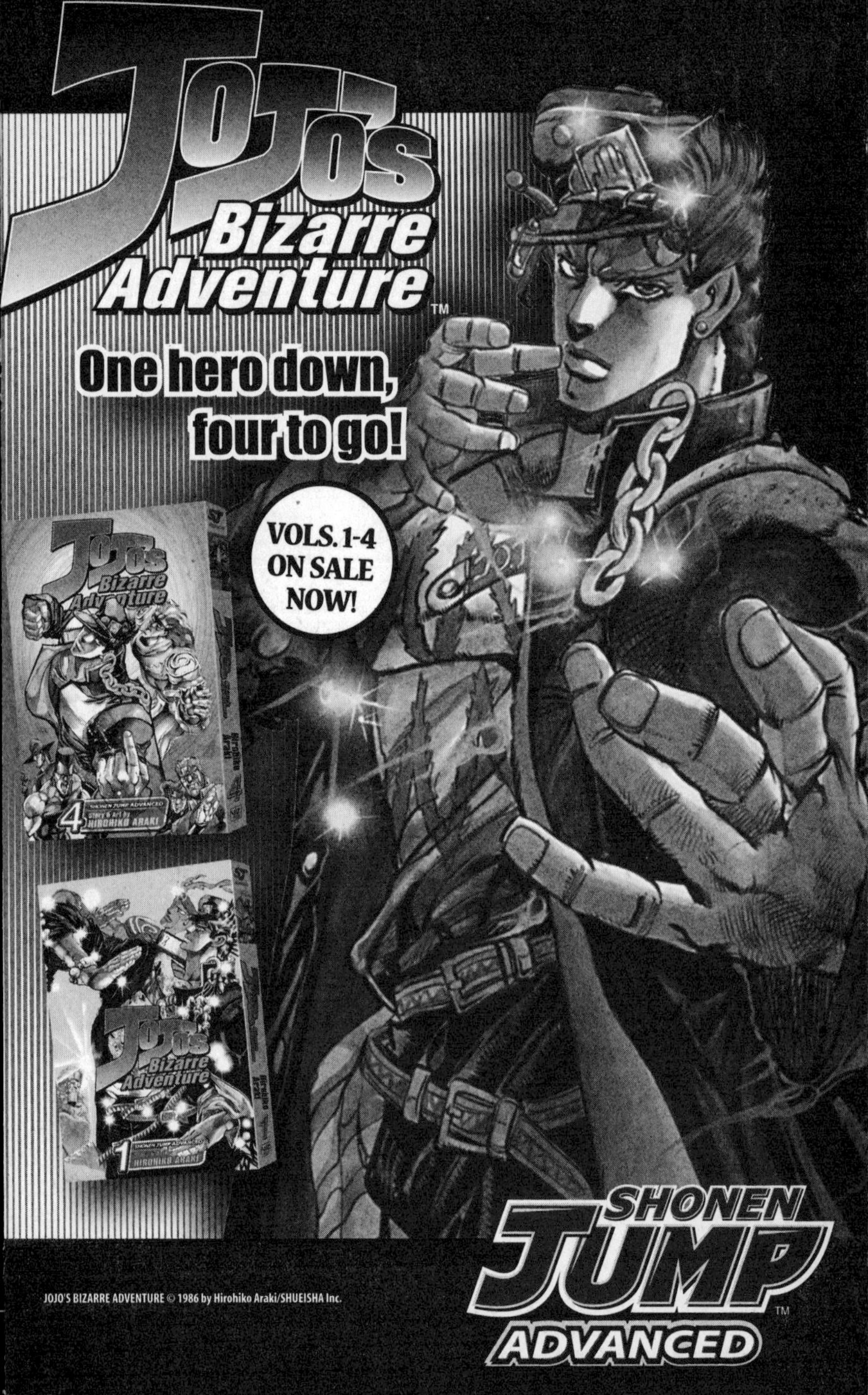
JoJo's Bizarre Adventure™
One hero down, four to go!
VOLS. 1-4 ON SALE NOW!
JOJO'S BIZARRE ADVENTURE © 1986 by Hirohiko Araki/SHUEISHA Inc.
SHONEN JUMP™ ADVANCED

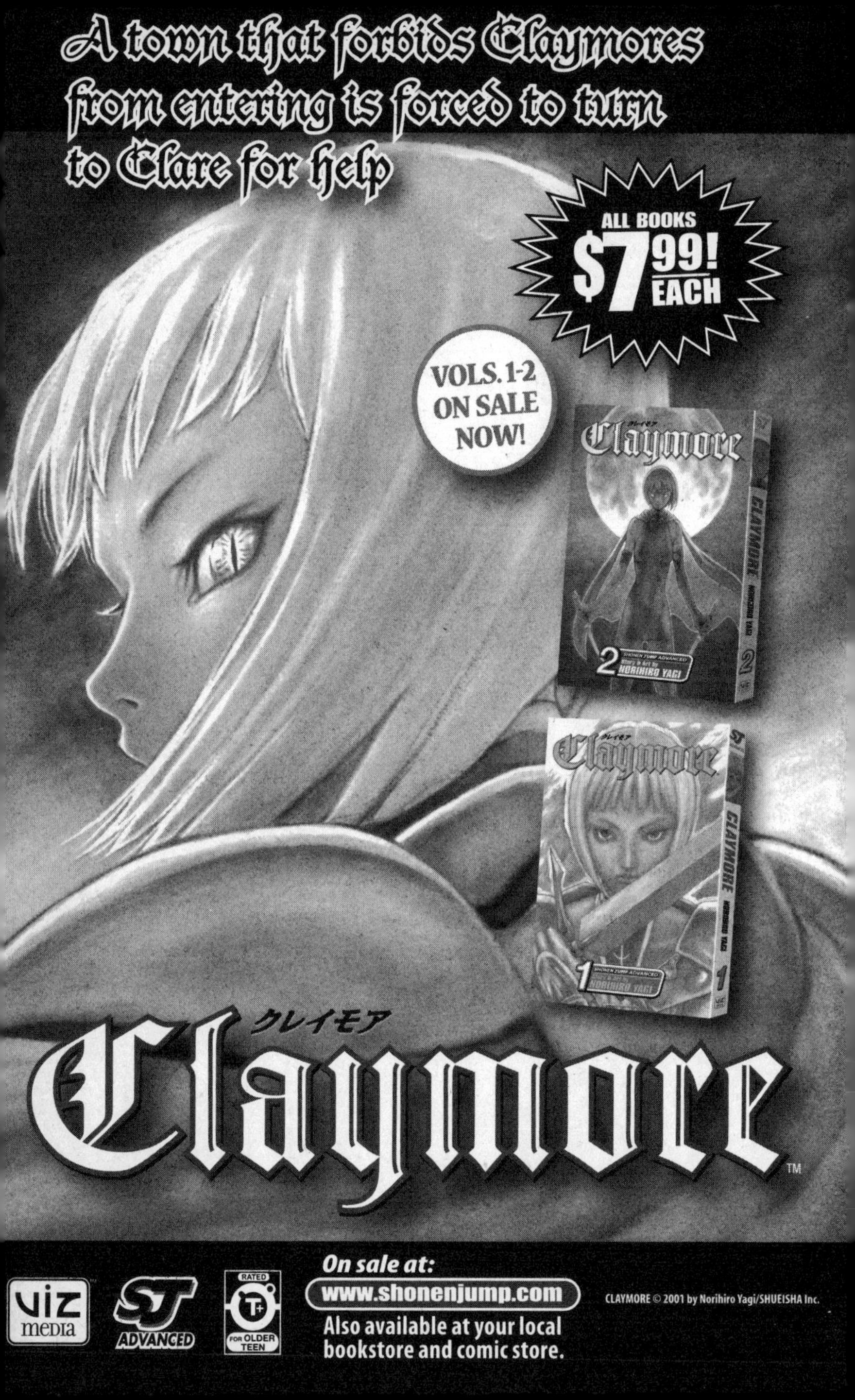
A town that forbids Claymores from entering is forced to turn to Clare for help
ALL BOOKS $7.99! EACH
VOLS. 1-2 ON SALE NOW!
クレイモア
Claymore™
On sale at:
www.shonenjump.com
Also available at your local bookstore and comic store.
viz media
SJ ADVANCED
RATED T+ FOR OLDER TEEN
CLAYMORE © 2001 by Norihiro Yagi/SHUEISHA Inc.

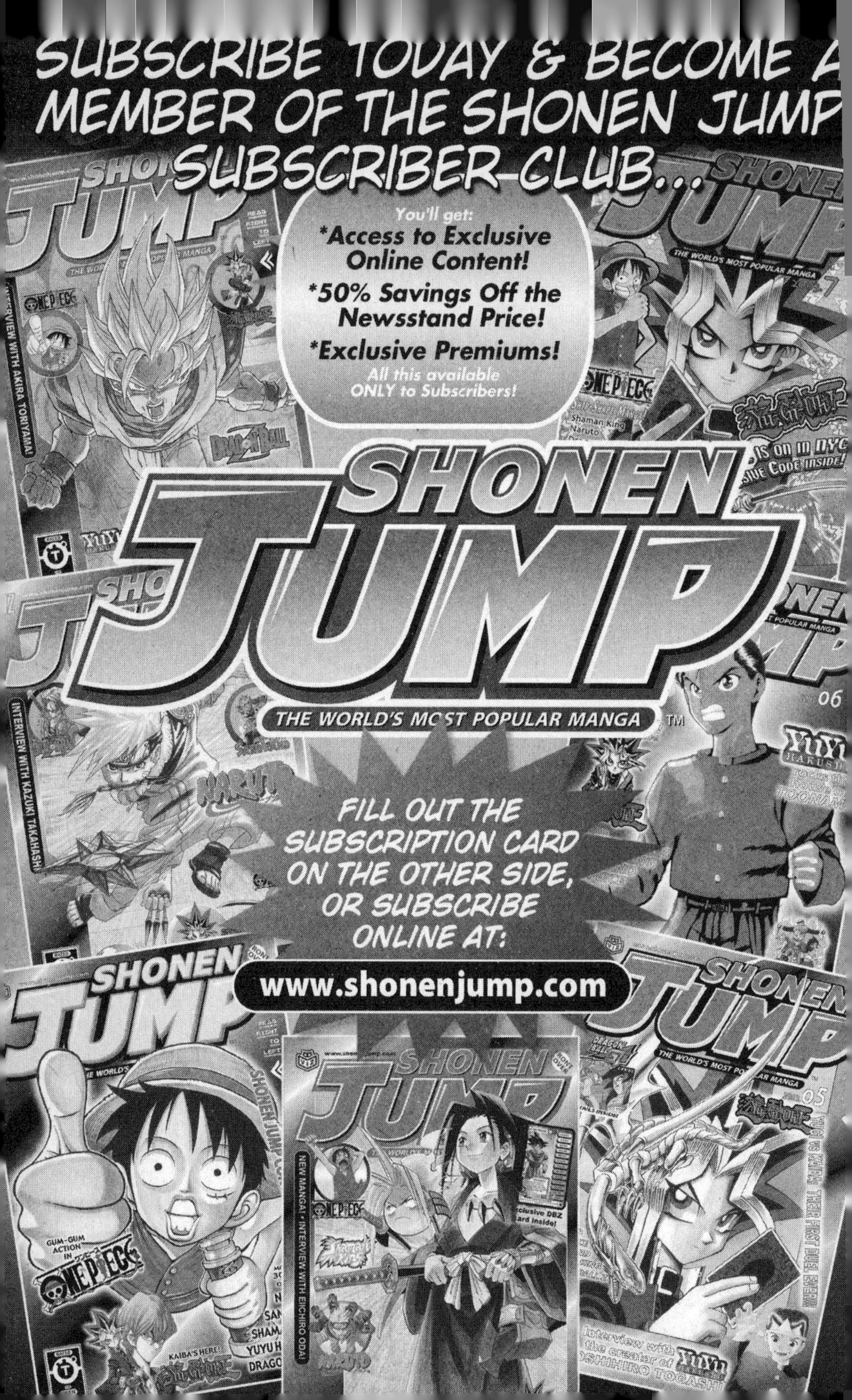
SUBSCRIBE TODAY & BECOME A MEMBER OF THE SHONEN JUMP SUBSCRIBER CLUB...
You'll get:
*Access to Exclusive Online Content!
*50% Savings Off the Newsstand Price!
*Exclusive Premiums!
All this available ONLY to Subscribers!
SHONEN JUMP
THE WORLD'S MOST POPULAR MANGA
FILL OUT THE SUBSCRIPTION CARD ON THE OTHER SIDE, OR SUBSCRIBE ONLINE AT:
www.shonenjump.com